# Funny Money

# Funny Money

Stephen Jory

JOHN BLAKE

Published by John Blake Publishing Ltd,
3 Bramber Court, 2 Bramber Road, London W14 9PB, England
First published in hardback in Great Britain 2002

ISBN 1 903402 57 3



British Library Cataloguing-in-Publication Data:
A catalogue record for this book is available from the British Library.

Typeset by Jon Davies

Printed in England by CPD, Wales

1 3 5 7 9 10 8 6 4 2



Papers used by John Blake Publishing Ltd are natural, recyclable products made from wood grown in sustainable forests. The manufacturing processes conform to the environmental regulations of the country of origin.

# CONTENTS

# AUTHOR'S NOTE

The format and content of this book
dictates that various persons cannot be identified.
For the most part, this problem has been overcome
by the use of sobriquets and, in some instances,
simply by forenames without surnames.
No doubt, those identified protagonists
will recognise themselves, as will their associates.

Enjoy the ride.

*SJ*

For the people who make sense of the madness,
and give me a reason.

Lubba Lubba and B double F.

# GLOSSARY

| | | |
|---|---|---|
| *AOS* | arsehole (as in slag) | **persons without scruples** |
| *Apples* | Apple core: Score | **£20 notes** |
| *Auntie Maud* | | **fraud** |
| *Bail* | | **to give credit on a deal** |
| *Bird* | | **time in prison** |
| *Bender* | | **a suspended prison sentence** |
| *Boat* | Boat race: face | **active villain** |
| *Bottle* | Bottle and glass: arse, arsehole | **bravery** |
| *Bristols* | Bristol City | **breasts** |
| *Brown bread* | | **dead** |
| *Bubble* | bubble and squeak | **Greek** |
| *Charlie* | | **cocaine** |
| *Cockles* | cock and hen: ten | **£10 notes** |
| *Cornered* | | **to be tricked out of money (dosh) or goods (a parcel); derives from waiting hopefully on a corner for someone to return with what's yours** |
| *DDS* | deep, deep shit | **great deal of trouble** |
| *Dig* | dig in the grave | **shave** |
| *Firm* | | **group of criminals, usually heavy boats, working together** |
| *Full SP* | starting price (racing term) | **all the details** |
| *FUs* | | **fuck-ups** |
| *Gregory* | Gregory Peck | **neck** |
| *Heavy Boat* | gangster | **heavy villain** |
| *Hoisters* | as in 'hoisting goods' | **shoplifters** |
| *Jeckylls* | Jeckyll and Hyde: snide | **fake** |
| *Line of Gear* | | **line of cocaine to be snorted** |
| *Long Firm* | | **company set up to go bankrupt after acquiring maximum debts and credit** |
| *Long 'un* | | **£100 cash** |
| *Mazuma* | | **amount of money** |
| *McGarrets* | from Steve McGarrett of *Hawaii 5-0*: 5-0 | **a £50 note** |
| *Old Bill* | | **the police (never *The Bill*)** |
| *To Roll Over* | | **become a grass due to police pressure** |
| *Rub-a-dub* | Rub-a-dub-dub, three men in a tub | **boat/yacht** |
| *The Run Out* | | **illegal auction run from empty premises selling deficient goods and empty boxes** |
| *Scouser* | | **Liverpudlian** |
| *Shovel* | shovel and pail | **jail** |
| | shovel and pick | **nick** |
| *Slag (also Low Life)* | | **man with no scruples** |
| *Slaughter* | probably from slaughterhouse | **house or place used to divide up illegal pickings** |
| *Spieler* | | **gaming club** |
| *Spondooliks* | | **ready cash** |
| *Steak* | steak and bubble | **trouble** |
| *Tank* | | **cash, capital** |
| *Tanner* | 6d (old money) | **general lack of cash** |
| *A trade* | | **an illegal transaction** |
| *The Ville* | | **Pentonville Prison** |
| *Wanno* | | **Wandsworth prison** |
| *Wedge* | | **cash in pocket** |
| *Wheel came off* | | **operation going wrong** |

# PROLOGUE

## It Might Be a Fake, But It Seems to Work OK

My first, tenuous, involvement in the printing of counterfeit money came about just prior to Easter 1985. At the time, I was on bail for the illegal manufacture of counterfeit perfume. In fact, perfume was the only connection I had with anything counterfeit. My partner (a printer whom I nicknamed Walter, after Walter Mitty, because of his penchant for telling blatant lies) was approached by an acquaintance who had in his possession a set of printing plates for £50 notes. In 1985, £50 notes were relatively new and, as such, were few and far between. The advantage in this situation was that the public at large wasn't particularly familiar with them and, consequently, wouldn't really be aware of what to look out for. Another advantage was that no counterfeit £50 notes had been produced before.

The guy with the plates needed a printer and, although it wasn't the kind of printing that Walter himself was capable of doing, it was generally known that he had numerous contacts in the printing industry. In fact, at the time of the approach, Walter's printing contacts stemmed from his involvement with me in the perfume business. We'd been partners for several years in the manufacture of counterfeit perfume, and we'd served a prison sentence together for related offences.

Walter told me about the approach and asked me if I thought any of the printers I used for the packaging side of the perfume business might be interested in doing the work. I had one in mind, whom I thought might well be interested, so Walter and I, together with another guy who worked with us, Ritchie, met the man with the plates, who was known as Bearsie.

As far as I was concerned, he was a loud-mouthed bully-boy whom I didn't particularly like although, in fairness, I didn't really know him. However, I knew plenty of people who did, and no one seemed to have a good word to say about him. From the very outset, it was clear that we wouldn't be able to do any business together. When I told Bearsie that I had a printer who would probably be interested in doing the work, his initial reaction, understandably, was one of pleasure. When I then informed him that he would have to give me the plates to show the printer, his attitude changed, and he told me that under no circumstances could the plates leave his possession and he would have to go with them to the printer. This, of course, was his prerogative as the plates belonged to him, but equally it was my prerogative to protect the identity of the printer.

The negotiations never really got off the ground, as the two of us were equally adamant about the only way we were prepared to do business. So that was that, as far as Walter and I were concerned. However, Ritchie saw a chance to make some money (quite literally), as he knew of a printer located somewhere near Southend, who he felt most definitely would be up for it.

From then on, it was Ritchie and Bearsie's piece of work, and nothing to do with Walter and me. Sure enough, they got the work done and looked set to make a killing. The original plan had been to flood the market with the fake £50 notes over the Easter weekend. This would have given the gang the late-night shopping period in the West End on Thursday, Good Friday, Saturday, Sunday and Bank Holiday Monday, and possibly, the following Tuesday, before the 'scream' went up.

The scheme appeared foolproof as none of the High Street banks would be open until the Tuesday and, therefore, until the shopkeepers paid in their Easter takings, nobody would be aware of the counterfeit fifties flooding the country. The job was completed the weekend before Easter, and the stage was set. The fake notes had turned out every bit as good as had been expected, and Bearsie, Ritchie and Co looked set to make a major financial killing.

Then something extraordinary occurred. So good were the fakes, that one of the gang couldn't resist the urge to try them out, so to speak, and on the Thursday afternoon took one into a betting shop. He placed a £1 bet and eagerly took his £49 change. Now, he and the gang knew that the fifties 'worked' and they looked forward to a highly profitable

Easter. But, of course, by using just one note before the banks had closed that afternoon, they ran the risk of alerting the authorities before the notes were presented *en masse*. And that's exactly what happened.

The betting office that had inadvertently taken the fake fifty paid in their daily takings to the bank before it closed on the Thursday. The bank, of course, recognised the counterfeit note for what it was and the Bank of England was alerted.

It would seem that the greatest cause for concern was the quality of the fake. The Bank of England security experts realised that the one note they had was clearly just the tiniest tip of what was potentially an extremely large iceberg. Just what the Bank of England's strategy was, though, isn't really clear. In all probability it was one of 'make the public aware, then sit tight and wait and see'.

The 'scream' went up on the Saturday afternoon or evening. I recall it quite clearly, as I was in a bar called the Pheasantry in the King's Road with a girlfriend, Lynda McQueen. Whilst there, I saw a friend, Frankie Shea, who was with his wife Barbara and a group of people whom I knew only vaguely. Frankie came over to me and started talking and during the conversation asked me if I'd heard the latest news. He then went on to tell me that he'd heard a broadcast on his car radio earlier warning shopkeepers to be particularly vigilant when accepting £50 notes, as there were a number of excellent forgeries circulating. Shortly after this, I went to the bar to buy a drink, and noticed a sign pinned up by the till that read: 'No £50 notes taken, not even genuine ones'. The whistle had well and truly been blown.

In spite of this, Bearsie, Ritchie and Co did very well out of their weekend's work and, shortly afterwards, Ritchie was seen driving around in a Rolls-Royce Silver Shadow. It was just a pity they couldn't have resisted the urge to satisfy their curiosity in the first place with the £50 note that was passed in the betting office.

Bearsie carried on with the fifties long after this initial venture, using various different printers along the way and paying very few of them. In fact, I heard through the grapevine that the original printer became something of a nervous wreck due to the bullying and greedy nature of Bearsie. Apparently, after doing several more runs and receiving very little financial reward, the printer decided he'd had enough. This in itself presented him with something of a dilemma, as Bearsie was threatening and bullying him into doing the work until finally he just upped and disappeared. Bearsie and Co turned up one morning at his premises to find it empty, with no forwarding address.

It wasn't long after this that the Bank of England introduced what it regarded as a virtually infallible security feature on to the £50 notes, an intermittent silver strip which was woven into the paper. But this was soon overcome by hot-foiling a silver 'dashed' strip on to the notes. Although it wasn't the same as the genuine process, it was nevertheless good enough to fool most people because once they saw the silver line they looked no further and accepted the note as genuine. So, initially, the silver line was a bit of an own goal.

It was at this time that Walter had one of the very few good ideas that he'd ever had in his life. We had in our possession £500,000 worth of the fake fifties and Walter suggested getting the silver lines applied to them with a couple of small, hand-foiling machines. The parcel hadn't cost us anything, as we were looking after them for somebody who had since been imprisoned for quite a long time and who'd sent a message out to us that we could do whatever we wanted with them. Since the silver line was a recent feature, we most definitely would have had a good earner.

However, for my part and for whatever reasons, I couldn't see anything other than aggravation as far as the funny money was concerned. Eventually, we ended up throwing the parcel of fake fifties away.

It was to be many years before I had anything to do with counterfeit money again and, with hindsight, I wish I'd stuck to my original assessment of the 'funny money' business.

# CHAPTER 1

## A Train Ride from Ford, Dodgy Dollars and Dodgy Paddies

Sitting on the train back to London in October 1991, I couldn't help reflecting on my life. I had been released from Ford Open Prison that morning, after serving eight months of a sixteen-month prison sentence for offences under the Trades Description Act. My crime involved the manufacture of fake perfume, primarily Chanel No. 5 and Opium by Yves Saint-Laurent. I had been involved in the manufacture of fake perfume since 1973 and I suppose the title 'Perfume Pirate' would have been an apt description. Over the years, I had made and lost several fortunes and, at one stage, had a factory in Acapulco exporting bogus Chanel No. 5 to the Middle East. One of my court cases had made headline news — £300 MILLION INTERNATIONAL PERFUME FRAUD — and a programme, centred around my exploits, had been screened on ITV.

I should have been an extremely rich man, but the reality of my situation as I sat on the train was that, at the age of 41, I had relatively little to show for my life as a perfume pirate. I had a nice house in Barnet where I lived with my wife Laraine and our two children, Stephanie, aged 14, and James who was nearly 6. The house had a big mortgage and, apart from a house in Chingford I'd bought for my mother in 1974 — and had since borrowed heavily against — I had precious little else.

Now I was heading back to the family home thinking about my past and contemplating the future. I had one more court case to face with regard to my perfume exploits but had no idea when that would be heard. The truth of the matter was, I was sick of the perfume business. But having been involved in it for so long, I was hard pressed to know what else I could do.

At the back of my mind, the seed of an idea was germinating, but one which would require a fair degree of finance. Whilst in HMP Ford, I had become friendly with a guy with the unlikely name of Bert Shakespeare who had been involved in the fake poster business. This, like my perfume business, was very much a pirate line as the operation involved the copying of popular posters and exporting them abroad, as well as selling them to market traders in this country without paying any copyright fees or VAT. It was strictly cash only and, according to my friend, it was big business.

The reason Bert thought I might be interested was because of the business. He knew that, obviously, there was a good deal of printing involved in the packaging and thought that I might be able to work something out with his partner who was still on the outside. He explained that they were always on the lookout for new printers because of the volume of work. But it had to be a very hush-hush operation. The printers they had been using were becoming too expensive, even though they paid them in cash.

I knew from experience that it would be pointless going to the printers I'd used for my perfume, as the volume of the poster work would monopolise the presses 24 hours a day, whilst mine could be fitted in between their legitimate work. Apart from which, with me as the middle-man, the cost to the 'poster man' would make the operation as expensive as before.

I thought about these different factors on the journey back to London and had come to the conclusion that the only practical solution was to start up my own printing business. This, of course, presented several different problems, not least of which was the question of finance. Furthermore, since I wasn't a printer myself, I would need to find a printer whom I could trust absolutely, one who was willing to work cash-in-hand and able to keep his mouth shut. This was something else I didn't have. Apart from these problems, I had the little matter of the impending perfume case hanging over my head. Until that was out of the way, with the very real possibility that I might be locked up again, I couldn't undertake anything as involved as setting up a printing business. Nevertheless, realising the potential in such an operation, I kept it very firmly in the back of my mind.

So for the time being at least, it seemed as though it was a case of back to the perfume pirating. My situation there was quite sound. Whilst

I had been in prison, I had arranged for a business associate to be set up to manufacture the fake Chanel No. 5 and Opium. My associate, Bernie Farrier, had his own workshop premises in High Wycombe and, whilst I had been away, he had plodded on at a steady pace. By the time of my release, he had about 50,000 bottles made up.

Initially, it seemed as though my release from prison was a classic example of good timing, inasmuch as it meant that I was out just in time to catch the Christmas rush. However, during my brief spell of incarceration, the counterfeit perfume world had undergone a seismic upheaval.

Now, far from being the undisputed king of the perfume pirates, I was just one of several, the others being little more than interlopers who had hijacked my previously profitable bandwagon. Although the rival brands, which for the most part came from 'up north', were of an infinitely inferior quality, they were, nevertheless, very popular simply because they were much cheaper.

The writing was very much on the wall when even my main punter, Hungry Jim, bought just a fraction of what would normally be expected during the run-up to Christmas.

Hungry Jim, who bore a marked resemblance to Oliver Hardy, was so called not only because of his legendary voracious appetite, but also because of his avaricious nature when it came to squeezing every last penny out of every single deal ever put to him. It was proverbial knowledge that he once bought a lorryload of stones and ended up with enough of the red stuff to start up his own blood bank. If Hungry Jim couldn't sell perfume, nobody could.

In the normal run of things, I would have expected to clear something like £200,000, but as it was it barely earned me £30,000, enough for a good Christmas but not much else. Feeling like a latter-day Theodosius the Great — the last true Roman emperor — I had to read the writing on the wall; the Goths and Vandals, to say nothing of one or two Scots, were at the gates and my fragrant empire was under siege and crumbling. Clearly, I had to think again if I wanted to raise the kind of money I needed to start the poster printing business.

After Christmas, I made a point of paying a visit to Bert Shakespeare's partner Ivan, who lived in a large detached house in Chigwell. Apart from the poster business, he also had a large portfolio of property in the Essex area, and several other business interests. Unlike me, Ivan had obviously invested the money that he had made from the posters over the years in a shrewd manner. He seemed to be impressed by my past exploits regarding the perfume business, and sympathised with the fact that I hadn't managed to keep my hands on more of the money I had made.

I explained that, in 1977 when I had over £100,000 in cash, I made the mistake of not diversifying into legitimate business and ended up losing everything, even when at one stage I was actually worth closer to £200,000. After that, even though I had made a great deal of money, I had always lost it when my factories had been raided and closed down by the police.

The work that Ivan described to me was certainly worthwhile. I calculated that if I could set up a relatively small printing business then it would be worth something like £10,000 per week. Unlike the perfume business, it wouldn't have been just a seasonal line and, further, it didn't require a large staff. He assured me that, if I could set the operation up, then he would most definitely guarantee me the work. But for the moment, it was no more than something for the future. Until I could raise the necessary finance, there was nothing I could do about it.

In my attempts to get the printing venture off the ground, I decided to sell off my perfume stock at less than cost price, in order to raise some capital. I started making a few enquiries, but still had no more than a lukewarm response. Hungry Jim wasn't interested at any price and the couple of people who expressed an interest merely said they would get back to me. But I wasn't too despondent, feeling that it was only a matter of time before I found a buyer.

Apart from the finance, I still had the problem of finding a suitable printer. For this, I approached my ex-partner Walter, who told me that he knew someone who might be interested. The man in question, Colin, had some kind of business that was constantly in debt so Walter said that he would make an approach to him. A week or so later, Walter told me that he had spoken to him and that, when I was in a position to buy a machine, he would definitely be interested in working full-time for me.

Another contact I needed was somebody with access to a scanner. This was the work that needed to be done to develop the film from the original posters to make the printing plates. Once again, Walter had a contact in that field, but as he didn't know how to get hold of him, we decided to visit various companies that Walter knew did business with the man. We left my mobile number at several different places with instructions that, if they came into contact with Walter's friend, they were to ask him to get in touch with Walter as he wanted to speak to him. Walter also gave the number to his friend Colin.

At this stage of the proceedings, there was no particular rush as, of course, there was nothing positive with regard to the finances for the operation.

On the home front, there was a major problem with Laraine's

mother, May, who was desperately ill with heart problems. A heavy smoker since the tragic death of her husband, who had been murdered 21 years earlier, May was looking and becoming increasingly frail. Laraine and I did as much as we could for her, by way of having her stay with us and taking her out, but for my part I felt that May didn't have much longer to live. Laraine and her sister Linda, who lived with May, tried to close their minds to what I think, deep down, they also knew. All in all, it was quite an upsetting time for the family.

When Walter had approached his friend Colin with a view to coming to work for me, he had also asked him to keep an eye out for any decent presses that might be on the market and, a few weeks later, he contacted Walter to tell him that he had come across a decent, rather old, machine for sale at £20,000. Even though the outstanding perfume case wasn't due to be heard for several months, I was more than interested. I had about 15,000 bottles of perfume in stock and set about finding a buyer, even if it had to be at a give-away price.

With this in mind, I went back to the potential buyers who had expressed some interest earlier. This time I asked them to make a bid, but the problem was finding anyone with the kind of cash I needed. A few people wanted to take the perfume and pay for half of them, and the other half 'as and when'. This was unacceptable. It had to be very strictly COD.

Eventually, I found a buyer prepared to take 15,000 bottles of Opium at £2.50 per bottle, 50p less per bottle than it cost to produce. I still had a further 10,000 bottles of Chanel, but my buyer wasn't interested in them. So at least I managed to raise £37,500, of which I owed Bernie £8,000 for making up the perfume while I was away. I now had enough to put the wheels of industry in motion. Walter went back to Colin and told him to go ahead with ordering the press. I gave Walter £5,000 to give to Colin to use as a holding deposit on the machine.

As soon as I had found a suitable workshop premises, I intended to give him the balance and arrange to have the machine shipped down from Birmingham where the sellers were situated. Through my experience in the perfume business, I was aware of the easiest and quickest ways to obtain a suitable premises without the hassle of signing a lease and providing accountants and bank references. To this end, I went to look at some vacant units on an industrial estate where the units were let on a monthly licence basis. That is to say, no more fuss than a month's deposit and a month's rent in advance. I soon came across a suitable unit and told the estate manager I'd get back to him. I decided not to rent the unit in person, but instead paid a friend of mine to act as the front man, an acquaintance I had met during my time in Ford, whom

I had nicknamed 'Hopalong Limpy', which became shortened to Hopalong. I called him this because he suffered from severe rheumatoid arthritis and he walked with a severe limp. I suppose it might sound like a rather cruel nickname, but it didn't seem to bother him at all.

Although his movement was considerably impaired, he was still able to drive and so, amongst other things, I employed him as a delivery and pick-up driver for the perfume business. Hopalong duly went into the estate manager's office and, after being shown around the site, plumped for the unit that I had told him to rent. After paying the necessary money, he came out to me in the car parked up outside the estate. I took the receipt and rental agreement together with the keys and we drove off.

Unbeknown to me, whilst I was making all these preparations, Colin was busily making up plates for $100 bills. Whether or not Walter knew anything about Colin's extra-curricular activity I don't know, but if *I* had, I might have saved myself £20,000.

After securing the workshop, I gave Walter the balance of the money to pay for the printing press. Sitting in a wine bar in Hatton Garden, shortly after handing over the money, Walter informed me that several people had been arrested in connection with the seizure of forged US dollars. I asked him what it was all about.

'Well, apparently,' Walter told me, 'it was some kind of a set-up and the fellas with the forgeries were trying to sell them to the Old Bill.'

'Common problem,' I said, unaware of what Walter was leading up to. 'Just goes to prove, you can only deal with people you know really well.'

'Yeah, you're right.'

'Was it anyone we know?' I asked.

'I know a couple of them. They come from around this way.'

'Really?'

'Yeah, and I think we might have a bit of a problem over it,' Walter said.

I looked at Walter, somewhat surprised at what he had just said. 'Why should it be a problem for us?' I asked.

'Well, I know for a fact that one of the blokes is a very close friend of Colin's. I know he used to do a lot of plates for him a year or two ago.'

I immediately realised the implication of what he had just said. 'You reckon he did the plates for the dollars then?' I asked.

Walter picked up his glass of wine and nodded his head as he sipped the drink. 'Mmm.'

'Fuck it. Have you been in touch with Colin to see if he's all right?' I said.

'Not yet.'

'Why don't you give him a call then?'

'Yeah. Good idea.'

Had I not prompted Walter to get in contact with his friend, then in all probability he would have left it and buried his head in the sand hoping that any potential problems would disappear. Walter called Colin from the wine bar and told him about the arrests, and then came back to the table with the predictable news that Colin had made the plates.

'What did you tell him to do?' I asked.

'What d'you mean? About what?' Walter asked.

'Well, didn't you tell him to clear out anything incriminating that he might have in case the Old Bill go round to him?'

'No, I didn't think of it.'

'Well, don't you think it might be an idea to tell him? That way, if they do go round to him, if he hasn't got anything there, y'know at home or at his workshop, all he's got to do is deny it. Go and phone him back.'

Walter finished off his glass of wine, and stood up. 'Yeah, I'll phone him back now.'

'And tell him to make sure he's got nothing relating to the printing press as well. Also tell him to get in touch with the firm in Birmingham to put off delivering the machine, just in case.'

'Just in case of what?'

'Just in case he gets pulled in, and he's not available when the machine arrives.'

'Oh yeah. Right, I'll tell him.'

Walter went back to the phone, and gave Colin his instructions, with the further advice that no matter what, if anyone had stuck his name up, then just deny it. With nothing incriminating around him, there was nothing the police could do.

This was on Thursday. Arrangements had been made to deliver and install the printing press on Saturday. On Friday, Colin was arrested at his home, where the police found various items such as film for producing plates to print the dollars. Amongst other things, there was paperwork relating to the printing press. Obviously, there hadn't been much point in Walter wasting his breath giving him advice about clearing out his home and workshop. When the police searched his workshop, they found several plates for the $100 bills. Colin made a full confession to everything and was held in custody.

Meanwhile, the printing press was delivered to the industrial unit on Saturday morning. With nobody there to meet him, the driver went to the estate office, and the manager unlocked the unit with a spare key.

The press was unloaded and placed in the empty unit.

The police contacted the company in Birmingham the following Monday, to be told that the printing press had already been delivered. The company gave them the delivery address and the police promptly made their way to the estate. Finding the premises locked up, they asked the estate manager who had rented the unit, to be told it was a Mr P Roberts who hadn't left a permanent address. The police kept an eye on the premises, waiting for Mr Roberts to turn up. But, of course, he never did.

Although the forged $100 bills had nothing to do with me, I didn't fancy answering questions from the police as to what I intended to use the press for. Apart from which, as the press had been bought in Colin's company name, I had no legal claim upon it. Not for the first time, I had lost a fair amount of money I could ill afford to lose, £20,000 well and truly down the drain.

This was not, however, an end to the matter. Some time later, I received a call on my mobile phone.

'Hello, Walter?' said the voice at the other end of the line.

'Walter? I think you've got the wrong number. There's no Walter here.'

I immediately recognised the voice as being that of Walter's friend, Colin. Obviously, when Walter had left my mobile number with him, he hadn't told him it was my phone.

'It's Colin.'

'Colin? Colin who?'

'Colin. You know, we did some business together.'

'Colin? Business? I'm sorry, I don't know what you're talking about, mate.' And with that I pressed the disconnect button and switched the phone off.

What made me particularly wary was the fact that I knew Colin was still in custody. So why would he be phoning Walter? Unless, of course, he was trying to implicate him in the forged dollars episode, in order to do himself a favour with the police. Fortunately, even though I had nothing to do with the dollars, Colin had never actually met me and, as far as I was aware, didn't know who I was, as I'd spoken just once to him on the phone.

It wasn't long after this that Laraine received a visit from the police. I had just dropped James off at school when the phone rang. It was Laraine. Her voice sounded as though she was in something of a panic. 'Steve?'

'Yeah. What's the matter?'

'The police are here.'

'What do they want?'

'I'm not sure.'

'What d'you mean? I thought you said they were there.'

'Well, they're actually sitting outside.'

'What are they doing out there then?'

'Well, I came back from doing some shopping about ten minutes ago, and they were sitting in their car, parked outside the house.'

'And?'

'They got out and asked if they could come in.'

'What for?'

'They said they wanted to ask me some questions about my phone.'

Immediately, I knew what was going on. The mobile phone I was using was registered in Laraine's name. Having got nowhere with Colin's phone call to me, they had obviously decided to follow it up with an enquiry about the registered owner.

'Did you let them in?'

'No. I told them I was busy. I told them to go away.' This meant they didn't have a warrant to enter the house, and I knew it wasn't a situation to be too concerned about.

'What did they say when you wouldn't let them in?'

'They weren't very pleased and now they're just sitting outside in their car.'

'Well go out to them and apologise for being so abrupt and ask them in.'

'No.'

'Please just do as I say. Any questions they ask you about your phone, just tell them your husband uses it.'

'No.'

'Please, Laraine. Just go out to them.'

'No.'

'Why not?'

'I don't want to.'

'If you don't go out to them now, they'll only come back some other time. Please go and get it sorted out now.'

'No.'

'Please.'

Laraine hesitated. 'All right, then, I'll go out to them.'

'Good, and be nice and polite to them. Call me back and let me know what happens.'

A couple of minutes later, the phone rang again.

'Well, what happened?' I asked.

'Nothing.'

'Nothing?'

'Yes, they drove off just as I opened the door to go out to them.'

I resisted the urge to comment that the sight of her marching towards them probably scared them off!

That evening at home, I explained to a concerned Laraine the situation with regard to the telephone. In spite of my reassurances, she continued to worry about the inevitable return of the policemen. Two days later, again just as I had dropped James off at school, the phone rang. Once again, it was Laraine.

'Those policemen are back. They're knocking on the door. What shall I do?'

'Just keep calm, and remember what I said. Invite them in, make them a cup of tea, and be nice and polite and you'll have nothing to worry about. Call me back and let me know what happens.'

Five minutes later, the phone rang again. By now I was on the M25 driving out to see Ivan the poster man.

'Steve, it's me, Laraine.'

'Yeah. Did you do what I said?'

'Yes.'

'And what happened?'

'They didn't want a cup of tea, and now they're searching the house.'

'What?'

'They're searching ...'

'Yeah, I heard you. Put them on the phone. I'll have a word with them.'

Laraine handed the phone to one of the detectives.

'Hello,' he said.

'Yeah, hello. This is Laraine's husband here, what's this all about?'

'Well, actually, it's not really her we want to speak to, it's you we're interested in.'

'Well, that's no problem, what are you searching the house for?'

'We're looking for counterfeit money.'

'Counterfeit money? What — £50 notes?'

'No, US dollars actually.'

'US dollars? Well, I can assure you there's nothing like that in the house, and even if there ever had been, you don't think, after your visit the other morning, they'd still be there, do you?'

'Mmm. I suppose not. Where are you now? Can't you come back and talk to us?'

'Not really, I'm a bit busy at the moment.'

'Well can you meet us at Barnet Police Station some time?'

'Sure. Not today though. When?'

'What about tomorrow morning, say 10 o'clock?'

'Sure, no problem. But do me a favour — don't drive her mad searching the place, there's fuck all there.'

To my surprise the detective agreed. 'OK, fair enough. We'll be off now. See you in the morning.'

They put Laraine back on the phone and, true to their word, left straight away.

The following morning, I turned up at Barnet Police Station accompanied by my solicitor, Ian Oxford. Although I didn't really feel that I needed his presence, he insisted upon coming along after I told him what had happened. I was at the station for about an hour, during which time I was asked numerous questions concerning counterfeit dollars, to which my reply was 'No comment'. After several minutes of this, the officers asked me if I was going to say 'No comment' to everything they asked me, to which I said, 'No comment,' and then, after laughing at my own little joke, said, 'Well, what did you expect? The fact of the matter is, I know nothing about any counterfeit dollars.'

'Well, supposing we throw a few names at you, will you tell us if they mean anything to you?'

'Try me.' I was curious to know what names they had.

After asking me if I knew four different names, I could honestly say none of them meant anything at all to me. That was more or less the end of the matter, but the police wanted me to attend an identity parade, to which I had no objection.

Shortly afterwards, I received notification that my presence was required at Kilburn Police Station to take part in the identity parade. I turned up on time and was locked up in a police cell for an hour, something which annoyed me no end, as my attendance at the station was completely voluntary and, had I so desired, I would have been within my rights to tell them what they could do with their identification parade. As it was, in spite of my repeated complaints, the officer in charge of the ID unit insisted I had to remain locked up in the cell. Those were the rules, he said.

I was still completely in the dark as to what the ID parade was all about, and whom it concerned. Obviously, it had something to do with the forged dollars, but what that had to do with me was a complete mystery. Ian Oxford, my solicitor, turned up shortly afterwards and even he couldn't get me out of the cell. Eventually, the unit was ready for the ID parade to take place.

The first problem was to find at least eight people to line up in the parade who had a similar appearance to me. This is normally done by a constable standing outside the station and asking passing members of the public if they would be prepared to take part in an ID parade for which they would be paid a small fee.

This being Kilburn High Road, the choice of willing volunteers seemed to consist entirely of drunken old Irishmen, eager to get their hands on a few quid to go and buy a few more cans of Guinness. One by one they traipsed through, unshaven for the most part, with barely a decent tooth between them. They really were a sad and sorry-looking parade of old dossers. Naturally enough, since he was there to safeguard my interests, Ian rejected every one of them as they came through. 'Can't you get a group together which at least doesn't look like a group of old tramps?' he asked the officer in charge.

'I am very sorry, sir, but at the moment this is all my constable on the pavement can get hold of. Unfortunately, that's the problem with being in the centre of Kilburn,' the officer replied.

'Well, in that case it's bloody stupid having a special ID unit in a station in an area like this,' said Ian.

The policeman made no reply and carried on parading the old tramps and dossers in front of us, hoping against hope that Ian would agree to any of them being in the line-up. It wasn't too long before I was beginning to tire of the endless parade. Looking down at my watch I realised that I had been at the station for over two hours, and was still no nearer to getting the ID parade finished and out of the way.

'Ian,' I said, my patience running thin, 'I don't really care what the people on the ID parade look like, because whatever this relates to has got nothing to do with me. As far as I'm concerned I could be standing alongside eight ginger-haired, one-legged midgets, and I still won't be picked out.'

'But, Stephen, I really think ...'

'Ian, the next eight that walk through the door are the eight I want on the ID parade. I don't care one little bit what they look like.'

The next eight volunteers were much the same as all the others, reeking of stale beer, unshaven and looking as though they had slept the night on the local park bench.

The officer in charge sat the magnificent eight down and told me I could choose a seat anywhere in the line-up. I sat in the middle with four either side. I nudged the Paddy sitting next to me.

' 'Ere. What you gonna do if you get picked out?' I said.

'Pardon?'

'I mean, if you get picked out, you might get done for murder or something.'

Paddy looked alarmed. I maintained a serious attitude. 'After all, you've only come in here for a couple of quid, and a cup of tea and biscuits,' I said.

'Dat's roight.'

'It won't be very nice if they keep you here for the next ten years, will it?'

Paddy looked even more alarmed and then a broad grin spread across his unshaven face and he flashed a set of teeth not dissimilar to a row of derelict houses. 'Ah, get away with yer,' he said, and started rocking backwards and forwards in his chair, slapping his knees as he laughed out loud.

The ID unit was a plain room with just a row of chairs in it. Behind each of the chairs was a number. Opposite the chairs, several feet away on the other side of the room was a long, glass panel, which was blacked out. From the other side of the panel the witnesses were able to see the suspects and volunteers, but we were unable to see the witnesses, apart from one or two vague shapes moving along. After we had been sitting down for a couple of minutes, the voice of the duty sergeant came over the intercom.

'Now then, gentlemen, if you'd kindly listen to my instructions, I'll tell you what I'd like you to do.'

He coughed, and then carried on. 'Just sit as you are and look straight ahead of you. Above the glass panel you will see a red light. When that comes on, please remain perfectly still until it goes off. Is that understood?' A couple of the parade grunted their acknowledgement and the duty sergeant seemed satisfied. 'Jolly good then, just keep an eye out for the red light.'

At this stage, I was ready for my *coup de théatre*, my revenge for being locked up in the cell for so long and so unnecessarily. Prior to attending the police station, I had bought a pair of glasses from a joke shop. They had a pair of bulging bloodshot eyes popping out of them, and underneath there was a false nose and a moustache. I swiftly put the disguise on and sat there.

At first there was no reaction, as nobody behind the panel realised what I had done. But then as the vague shapes moved along, I noticed the first one stop, and there seemed to be some kind of disturbance between the shapes. Seconds later, the red light went off and the intercom came back on. 'Yes, very funny, very funny,' the duty sergeant declared, sounding just a trifle annoyed. In the background, the sounds of female laughter could be heard. 'Please take that ridiculous mask off, and try to take this seriously.'

The Paddies became confused, and looked up and down the row. 'Ah, Jesus,' one of them declared, and immediately burst into fits of laughter. With that, all of them started falling about laughing and giggling uncontrollably. This, not surprisingly, aggravated the duty sergeant even further.

'Gentlemen, please show some respect. Just take that mask off and let's get on with it!'

'I've already taken it off. This is how I normally look,' I called out. My audience in the ID parade started giggling even more, and one actually fell on the floor, convulsed in fits of laughter.

'Gentlemen, please, gentlemen.' By now the duty sergeant sounded as though he was on the verge of hysteria — and not the laughing kind!

I put my disguise away, and eventually a semblance of order was restored.

The ID parade was concluded and, needless to say, nobody was picked out. I went into the office to see Ian who was talking to the officers in the case. The duty sergeant was there, still looking extremely agitated. Apparently the new ID unit was his pride and joy, and I suppose the idea of somebody like me not showing it the proper respect was too much for him. Seeing the grim expression on his face, I put the mask back on.

'Well, I was told you were looking for a man with bloodshot, staring eyes.'

He failed to see the humour, turned his back and walked out. The officers in the case smiled and were able to see the funny side.

'Well, Stephen,' Ian said, 'you'll be pleased to know that none of the witnesses identified you.'

'That's because whatever it's to do with, it's nothing to do with me,' I replied. 'And by the way, what is it to do with?'

'Apparently, somebody rented a workshop where a printing press was delivered. The officers here thought it might be you,' Ian told me.

Hearing this, I felt slightly annoyed, as Hopalong who had rented the workshop looked nothing like me at all. Apart from his chronic rheumatoid arthritis, his crippled hands and joints, he was totally bald. From that description, the officers in the case must have known it wasn't me, and that the identity parade would be a complete waste of everybody's time. Perhaps they were being paid overtime or something.

# CHAPTER 2

# The Lucky Briefcase

The outstanding perfume case was eventually heard in August at Luton Crown Court and, much to the dismay of the police officers involved, both Walter and I were acquitted.

After this, Laraine urged me to give up the perfume business but, having no other way to earn a living, I was unable to promise her that I would go straight. Apart from which, I was still determined, one way or another, to raise the money to start up the poster printing business. The fact that I couldn't make any promises to Laraine became a bone of contention between us. Over the years, we'd had many ups and downs, too many in fact, and had separated on a couple of occasions. Our marriage was under a particular strain, with Laraine wanting us to make a fresh start now that I had nothing hanging over my head. At this stage of her life, she felt, quite rightly, that I had taken enough risks with hers and the children's happiness and stability. However, as much as I could see her point of view, I still couldn't see what else I could do. With hindsight, the best thing I could have done — and should have done — was turn my back on anything criminal and make a fresh start in my life.

But far from giving up a life of crime, I became involved in a transaction that was far more criminal than anything I had ever been involved in before.

I was approached by Walter to do a job which required some fairly sophisticated printing work. The merchandise was a large quantity of official documentation, for which Walter had somehow come by the plates. The fact that there was a buyer eager to part with £750,000 in cash in just three instalments made it an opportunity too good to miss.

Through the perfume business, I had acquired a useful contact in the form of a small, but nevertheless hi-tech, printing business in the Midlands run by an inoffensive and extremely affable little man by the name of Ronald. Unfortunately for him, but fortunately for me, Ronald was on the verge of bankruptcy and so was susceptible to the promise of a good, but highly illegal, pay day. In this case, the pay day amounted to £50,000 for a weekend's work, more than enough to stave off the creditors.

Although Ronald wouldn't normally have considered doing this type of work — labels for perfume bottles were one thing, but these particular official documents were most certainly something else — the fact of the matter was, the wolf had to be kept away from his door.

That was all good news as far as I was concerned but Ronald, not unreasonably, was adamant that the £50,000 had to be paid up front in cash, which, of course, wasn't such good news. I set about trying to raise the money, but all to no avail. Without being told all the details, nobody was prepared to lend me that kind of *mazuma* and, bearing in mind that the majority of criminal enterprises founder as a result of police informants getting to know about them, I couldn't afford to take the risk.

Eventually, I gave up attempting to borrow the £50,000, and trying to come up with an alternative solution, it wasn't too long before inspiration raised its mischievous head.

I informed Ronald that I had managed to sort the money out and that I needed to meet him to discuss arrangements for the following weekend. I told him that, as I didn't want to be seen too much at the firm's premises, I would meet him outside a pub a couple of miles away. I then arranged for Hopalong to call me on my mobile phone at an agreed time. I met Ronald as arranged and got into the passenger seat of his car as he pulled up outside the pub. After talking and discussing various matters for a couple of minutes, my phone rang. I answered it, knowing, of course, who was on the other end of the line.

Hopalong said very little and, for about a minute, he and I had a pre-arranged conversation. With Hopalong not speaking, and Ronald sitting next to me in the car, I pretended to become very agitated as I spoke into the mobile handset.

'You're never gonna believe what happened over the car site the other day. Listen, I'll tell you.' I paused as though listening to something being said at the other end of the line, and then continued. 'Like I said, I'm sitting in the office, when that plonker Micky Fingers comes in — yeah, that's the one — anyhow, I know what he's come in for. I bought a couple of cars off him the other day. A BMW and a Jag. Anyhow, all told it comes to 21 grand I've got to give him. Well, I've got the dosh ready for him in a carrier bag. But then — and you're not gonna believe this, the mug only starts counting it out to check it. I've got a right good punter in the office with me, and that mug starts checking the money, even though I've told him it's all there. Anyhow, I've gone fucking mad. "What's the matter, don't you trust me?" I said, and he looks at me as if to say, "No." Well, I've gone fucking mad. I got hold of him round the neck and give him a right clump. Then I kicked him out and flung the 21 grand out after him. Can you believe it? Actually had the front to check the money. Then I've heard him mumble something as he walked away. Well, that was it. I've ended up chasing him down the road with a baseball bat, but the fucking mug got away. But anyhow, next time I see him I'm gonna break his fucking neck, the fucking mug. Nobody, and I mean nobody, mugs me off like that. Checking the fucking money! Fucking cheek.'

All the while, I could see Ronald out of the corner of my eye, sitting nervously staring straight ahead, hardly daring to look my way as I all but screamed into the mobile phone.

'Sorry about that, Ronald,' I said in a perfectly civil manner as I pressed the disconnect button on the phone. 'But you know how it is, don't you?'

Ronald nodded his head, too wary of uttering a word.

'Well, anyway, what was I saying?'

Ronald just about recovered his voice and for the next five minutes or so, we sat in the car discussing the arrangements for the following weekend. I left him, knowing he'd formed the required impression as to my character.

The next part of the plan involved a battered, old, brown briefcase that had belonged to Laraine's beloved Uncle Lennie. In fact, it wasn't really a briefcase, but rather the kind of miniature suitcase that doctors often used many years ago. I then made up five piles of paper, cut to the exact size of a £50 note, and the same height that £10,000 in new fifties would be. I then put a £50 note on the top and bottom of each pile and put a couple of rubber bands around each of them. The piles of money were then put into the briefcase, and so it looked as though I had a case containing £50,000. I turned up at the firm the following Saturday at midday as arranged in a small van containing the special paper required for the job. We offloaded it into the building and pulled the shutters down. I had with me the plates and, of course, the briefcase containing the '£50,000'.

I held the battered old case aloft, and gave it a gentle pat and smiled at Ronald. 'You know what's in here, don't you?'

'Er, erm, er, the er, the m-money?'

'That's right, Ronald. £50,000.'

Ronald paused and took a deep breath before speaking again. 'I erm, I, I er ...' Ronald stuttered nervously before managing to say, 'Do-do you think that m-maybe I could have a l-look at it?'

I stopped smiling and shot him a serious glance. 'Pardon, Ronald? What for?'

Ronald began to stutter even more as he said, 'It's j-just that I've n-never seen that much m-money before. I just w-wanted to s-see what it looks like.' He smiled nervously.

I changed my scowling expression to one of smiling geniality. ''Course you can, Ronald, let's go in the office.'

I placed the case on the desk and flipped open the two combination locks. I opened the lid to reveal five perfectly neat piles of what appeared to be £50 notes, each with a couple of rubber bands around it. 'It doesn't look very much, does it?' Ronald remarked.

'That's because they're all brand new, 200 notes in each pile, £50,000, Ronald,' I assured him. Ronald gingerly moved his hand forward as though to touch one of the piles. I quickly slammed the lid shut. 'Right!' I announced. 'Let's get to work, eh, Ronald?'

After swiftly retracting his hand, Ronald agreed it was time to get to work, and during the course of the next 30 hours, he operated the machine and I worked as his eager assistant. As the help that I was giving consisted mostly of making sure that the piles of paper were in place next to the machine, ready for Ronald to load it in, I had long intervals when I was doing nothing.

The main purpose of my presence was to act as moral support and to reassure Ronald that there was no risk of anything going wrong, police-wise. After all, if there was any real risk, I would hardly have been there myself. It was during one of the intervals that I told Ronald I was going to try and get some sleep in the office for an hour or so. Once in the office I stared at the old brown case on the table. And the old brown case stared seductively back at me. All manner of mean and wicked intentions infiltrated my somnolent thoughts but, dismissing them all, I closed my eyes and tried to get some shut-eye. But I couldn't sleep. The old brown case was an irresistible temptation.

Checking to make sure that Ronald was fully occupied, I opened the case and took the ten £50 notes from the five piles of blank paper.

I felt a bit mean taking even the paltry £500 but, such was my dire financial situation at this particular time, I felt I had no option. Anyhow, I intended giving Ronald the £50,000 as soon as Walter and I completed the first deal. I closed the lid of the case and turned the combination lock so that it couldn't be opened, and then got some sleep in the chair by the desk.

The work was completed by late Sunday afternoon, after which we loaded the newly-printed documents on to the van. We then spent the next hour cleaning up and going through the premises with a fine-tooth comb to make absolutely certain there was no evidence whatsoever of the weekend's clandestine activities.

'Right, I suppose you want your money now then?' I said to Ronald, who smiled broadly by way of reply. We went into the office, where I attempted to flip the two locks open. 'That's funny,' I said. 'It looks as though the combination has been moved. You haven't touched it have you, Ronald?'

'No. Not me,' he said.

'Mmm. I don't know what to do,' I said, as though deep in thought.

'Just break it open. It's only an old case,' Ronald suggested.

I looked at him aghast. 'Break it open? No way, no way.'

Ronald looked astonished. 'Why not?'

'This case,' I said, 'may look like just an old case. But in actual fact it belongs to a very dear friend of mine. I took it because it's what my friend calls his lucky briefcase. It's always brought him good luck. He even blessed it before I took it away.'

Ronald nodded his head knowingly. 'What we going to do then?'

I paused before answering. 'Tell you what, Ronald. If you promise me you'll take extra special care of it, I'll let you take it home with you, and tomorrow I'll find out what the combination is, OK?'

'Right, OK, then,' Ronald said.

'But, Ronald ...'

'Yes?'

I assumed an air of sanctity and said, 'Promise me absolutely faithfully that you won't let anything happen to this case.'

'I promise,' Ronald vowed solemnly.

'Apart from anything else, my friend is an old Italian, and he's kind of like a Godfather in the Mafia. If anything was to happen to that case, it would be curtains for the two for us. Understand?' I pulled my index finger across my throat.

'I understand.'

'Good man. Well, just remember I'm trusting you to take good care of the case. Don't let me down.'

'I won't. You can trust me.'

With that, we both departed in opposite directions, me with the weekend's work for which I would be collecting £250,000 the next day, and Ronald with his '£50,000' in the lucky briefcase.

The following day, things started to go wrong. Walter explained that his buyer, a man by the name of Laurie Jacobs, didn't actually have the money up front. In fact, after some lengthy and heated discussions, it soon became apparent that Walter had been somewhat economical with the truth. In other words, the whole episode amounted to little more than a dangerous charade. Whether this was Walter's fault or that of the people he was dealing with, I don't know. But it was a scenario that was all too familiar in my dealings with him.

With no ready buyer for the documents, I was now in something of a dilemma, inasmuch as I genuinely didn't want to let Ronald down. My original intention had been to meet him with his money and take the lucky briefcase back, leaving him none the wiser as to its real contents. Instead, I called him at his home and informed him that my elderly Italian friend had gone away to his homeland for a few days and that I had to wait for his return before I could get the combination.

In the meantime, I managed to secure one small deal on the documents and just about raised £5,000. I went to see Ronald, who, of course, was still hanging on to the briefcase, and succeeded in stalling him further by saying that my Italian friend was likely to be away for another two weeks. I did, however, give him £2,000 to tide him over — 'until we get the combination for the locks, Ronald'.

Ultimately, finding a buyer for the documents proved to be too much of an uphill struggle and, much to my very real regret, I was unable to pay Ronald the balance of his money.

I learned some time late that eventually Ronald's patience expired and he broke into the case. At that moment he realised he wouldn't, after all, be able to fend off his creditors. Shortly afterwards, he went bankrupt, and I heard that he emigrated to Canada where he joined the Royal Canadian Mounted Police.

# CHAPTER 3

## George the Actor, 'Little Caesar', a Gangster and a Grass

After the lucky briefcase episode, it was back to the perfume business. Christmas was fast approaching and, once again, although I was making a decent living, sales were nowhere near as good as they should have been. In the New Year of 1993, although certainly not rich by any stretch of the imagination, Laraine and I were reasonably well off and lived a fairly extravagant lifestyle. After Christmas we holidayed in Eilat and stayed at the best hotel there, The Princess, probably the most luxurious hotel I've ever stayed in.

We regularly dined out in the most expensive restaurants and spent a considerable amount of money improving the house. Consequently, although we lived well, I was never able to build up a substantial amount of capital. And then, during the summer, a piece of work came my way via Hopalong, which I honestly believed would change my life for ever. As well as providing me with the finances for the poster business, I looked like earning myself a couple of million pounds.

Hopalong told me that his friend, Laurie Jacobs, had been offered a quantity of documentation that was entirely genuine and had a face value of several million pounds. The problem was that the documentation needed various details printed on it to make it complete. The work involved was relatively simple but, of course, due to its highly 'sensitive' and illegal nature, it couldn't be hawked around all over the place. Knowing what a complete messer Walter was, Hopalong chose to approach me about it. However, at the mention of Jacobs's name, my immediate reaction was to tell Hopalong I wasn't at all interested. Apart from which, I found it hard to believe Jacobs actually had what he said he had.

The situation was one in which I had found myself on several occasions previously. Not for the first time, I was being told about a parcel of genuine documentation. Only a short while before, I had been messed about by an otherwise sensible person who honestly believed he had several pallet-loads of genuine banknote paper. It turned out that he'd paid out a ridiculous amount of money for sheets of plain paper that were available at any legitimate paper merchants.

In spite of this, Hopalong was adamant that Jacobs really did have something that was absolutely genuine. Eventually, I told him that if he showed me a sample I would be able to let him know if it really was what it was supposed to be. But, until then, I was completely dubious about what I was being told. I thought no more about it until some time later Hopalong called and said he had something to show me. I went over to his flat in Euston, where he answered the door with a boyish grin on his face.

'I've got it,' he said.

'Got what?' I replied.

'The sample sheet you wanted to see.'

Still sceptical I merely said, 'Oh yeah, I can't wait.'

I went through to the front room where Hopalong produced a cardboard tube from behind the couch. 'Take a look,' he said, passing the tube over to me.

I removed the plastic cap from one end and took out a rolled-up sheet from inside. I opened it up and spread it out on to the coffee table in front of me. At once, I realised the sheet was genuine. But in order to double-check I felt the texture of the paper and held it up to examine the watermark. I felt as though I had just discovered the Holy Grail.

'Fuck my old boots!' I declared in as profound a voice as I could muster. 'It *is* the real thing after all.'

Hopalong sat there with a smug, self-satisfied expression that was fully justified. 'I told you so,' he said.

'You certainly did,' I replied.

'Wouldn't believe me, would yer?'

'No. Quite right. But I believe you now, that's for sure.'

'Can you get the printing done then?' he asked.

I looked at the sheet. The work involved was simplicity itself. I knew a guy who'd done a bit of work for me in the past who I felt certain would do the job with very few questions asked.

'Sure I can get the work done, no problem. How many sheets are there?'

'About 19,000,' Hopalong replied.

Looking down at the sheet, it didn't take me more than a couple of seconds to realise that I was staring at a fair-sized fortune. The value of the single sheet was £1,000.

At last, the opportunity to make a real killing. I wasted no time in going to see my printer friend. The job, being so simple, was tailor made for him. Added to this was the fact that his was a one-man band business, so there were no worries about prying eyes within the firm. My friend, Eric, was more than agreeable and I made arrangements to get back to him, giving him a few days' advance warning.

I gave Hopalong the good news and agreed to meet Jacobs soon after at a hotel called The Brunswick in Holborn. To my surprise, he was accompanied by a mutual friend. It was explained to me that Laurie Jacobs and Jon-Jon Hardy were partners in the scam, with the pair of them pulling up an equal amount of cash to buy the high-security sheets from the people who had actually stolen them.

'So when can you let me have the sheets? I'll take them into my man straight away and he'll run them off over a weekend,' I told them.

Both Jacobs and Hardy, not surprisingly, were delighted at this news, and Jacobs asked me how much I wanted for doing the work.

'I want to be in the swindle,' I said.

'In what way?' Jacobs asked.

'I want some of the sheets for myself.'

'How many?'

'5,000 sheets.'

'No, we can't do that,' Hardy said. 'We've got another partner in the coup.'

'How many sheets, then?' I asked.

'Well, first of all, we just want to get 3,000 sheets done. Just in case.'

I knew what he meant by 'just in case'. It was a prudent decision to risk just a part of the total stock. That meant, should anything go wrong, then all would not be lost. After the first batch was done, then the rest would be covered financially.

After some discussion, during which Jacobs and Hardy informed me that the first 3,000 sheets were already sold, we agreed on the financial details. For the first 3,000 sheets I charged them just £8,000, a mere pittance in comparison to the value of the paper. Of this, I gave Eric the printer £3,000, and kept £5,000 for myself. As the work only took a day in total, Eric was more than satisfied.

The reason I was being so magnanimous was because I could see the 'prize' lay in getting the next 16,000 sheets printed. After some negotiation we agreed that I would keep 3,000 sheets and charge nothing for the work.

The first part of the deal was carried out without hitch and I eagerly awaited delivery of the next batch. After a couple of weeks I began to get restless, and couldn't understand what was holding things up. With the thought of earning £3 million, less £16,000 for the printer, and a good drink for Hopalong, I was more than eager to get cracking.

I got on to Hopalong to find out what was causing the delay. After speaking to Jacobs and telling him that I was in a hurry to get the job finished, Hopalong met up with me to put me in the picture.

He explained to me, in the strictest confidence, as I wasn't supposed to know, that it looked as though Jacobs and Hardy had been 'had over' for the parcel. Hopalong told me that the documents had been given to a couple of street traders, one of whom was known as George the Actor.

The two men had travelled abroad with their families with the intention of turning the documents into hard cash. Unfortunately, since neither Jacobs nor Hardy had any bottle whatsoever, they allowed George the Actor and friend to travel half-way across the world without them. Their reasoning was that, if anything should go wrong, their good selves being several thousand miles away, nothing would connect them to the documents.

Consequently, whilst Jacobs and Hardy were sitting back waiting for the money to come rolling in, George the Actor had other ideas. The last I heard at the time was that the wives returned and the lads stayed on in the sunshine.

That anyone could do such a ghastly and dishonest thing came as something of a shock to the two gutless wonders, not least because the third 'partner' in the scam was a genuine and well-known heavy brought on board precisely to prevent anything of such a nature happening.

The plan was that, by his very involvement, nobody would be so foolhardy as to pull any strokes. But of course, when someone's on the other side of the world, and he's got so much cash in his pockets, it doesn't take the brains of Einstein to see how he can change his priorities.

From my point of view, this shouldn't really have made too much difference. The obvious course of action now would have been to get the rest printed up as soon as possible — like the following weekend!

What I wasn't aware of at that time was just how mean-minded and penny-pinching a man Laurie Jacobs really was. This truly was a man who would run a mile in tight shoes to pick up a pound coin if he heard it fall from somebody's pocket. The loss of £20 on a deal would cause him to take to his bed in a fit of chronic depression.

The relevance of his parsimony was revealed to me soon afterwards. A normal person would have moved heaven and earth to pull up the money to buy the complete parcel, which was what I thought Jacobs and Hardy had in fact done. But, of course, Jacobs being such a tight-fisted little mongrel, he thought he could pull it off with the very minimum of financial outlay.

Having bought a part of the parcel, he put his name to the rest. He let the thieves know that he and Hardy were in partnership with his heavy friend, whom I'll refer to by his nickname, Jimmy Trunks. Once again, he reasoned that, knowing Jimmy Trunks was involved, people wouldn't dare think about selling the remainder to anybody else. Of course, once there was a hold-up after the first batch, the thieves became impatient to offload the rest. But such was Jacobs's supreme confidence, he felt he could keep the thieves on the hook indefinitely.

The sheer, near-sighted stupidity of Jacobs's attitude was compounded by the fact that he was a wealthy man in his own right and could in all probability have raised the money without too much of a problem. But, unfortunately, the thieves became tired of waiting and told Jacobs that, as the goods belonged to them, they would sell them to whoever they chose. And that's what they did. And far from making a fortune out of the deal, from then on, all I got was aggravation.

The thieves, not knowing anything about printing, entered into an agreement with a Pakistani who assured them he could get the necessary printing done. However, the work was 'botched' and as a result several people were arrested. All this I found out later.

Unknowingly, after being told about the delay with George the Actor and Co, I waited for a call telling me to collect the rest of the documents for printing.

It came one evening several weeks after the first batch of work had been done. It was Hardy asking me to meet him at a venue in which we had met several times before. I immediately drove to a spieler in Hackney called Corals, a dive frequented for the most part by elderly Jewish gamblers and hoisters trying to sell the various items they had stolen during the day.

When I arrived, Jacobs and Hardy were sitting at a small table huddled together in conversation. I sat down opposite them, and it wasn't long before I realised this wasn't a meeting to make arrangements regarding the rest of the work. As I smiled and said hello, neither man was able to look me straight in the eye and both seemed to be staring down at the table and moving about in their seats.

'How are you, Steve?' Hardy said.

'Yeah, I'm OK. So what's happening then, chaps?' I replied cheerfully.

'Well, erm, what we, er, wanted to see you about was that bit of work you did for us,' Hardy said.

'Oh yeah, what's up then?'

'Well, there's been a bit of a problem. A couple of people have been nicked.'

'Really? How did that come about then?' I replied.

I had heard from Hopalong that a couple of people had indeed been arrested abroad, but apart from the fact that it wasn't George the Actor's little firm, I didn't know the details.

Jacobs and Hardy then went on to relate how the problem was caused by the ink that my printer had used. They then came up with a complete cock-and-bull story that the pair of them had concocted involving red and green lights that showed that the ink was the wrong type. To which I replied, 'I think it's all a load of bollocks. Absolute rubbish.'

'I'm telling you, mate, it's not. The poor fellas are stuck in the shovel on the Continent and all down to your printer, mate,' Hardy said.

He had a particularly sycophantic way about him and, as I looked at him, I realised what the game was. 'Well, I don't care what you say, I know the job was done right. No two ways about it,' I told him.

'Mate, honest. I wouldn't lie to you. Maybe your printer just said he used the right ink. Maybe it wasn't your fault, mate. But I'm sorry, mate, we've got to have our money back, mate.'

I looked at the fat little toad in amazement. 'Pardon? Well, I'm sorry as well. But I'm afraid the man's done the work, and he's been paid, and that's all there is to it – *mate*!'

'In that case, you'll have to give us the name of your printer and we'll go and sort it out with him. After all, it's down to him that innocent people have been nicked,' Jacobs piped up.

'No way,' I declared. 'The printer's got my word that nothing will ever go back to him, and that's how it's got to be.'

Up until this point the discussion had been conducted in a fairly conciliatory fashion. Both Jacobs and Hardy seemed keen to maintain the illusion that they didn't think the 'problem' was really my fault and that they were trying to do me a favour by giving me the option of returning the £8,000 they had laid out.

Then Jacobs said, 'Well, anyway, Jimmy wants to speak to you about it. He'll be here soon. You can sort it out with him. He's not too happy about the situation.'

He looked at me and I suppose he was expecting me to fold up like a deckchair at the mention of the name. He appeared a little crestfallen when I merely replied, 'OK, then, we'll have to sort it out with him.'

Both Jacobs and Hardy were devout cowards and so my lack of reaction must have come as something of a disappointment to them, as Jimmy Trunks was a genuine, if somewhat elderly, heavy from a family who, in the past, had been associates of the Krays. However, as far as I was concerned, I'd kept to my side of the deal and there wasn't really too much to discuss.

We sat and waited and shortly afterwards Jimmy Trunks arrived and motioned to us to follow him upstairs. At once, Jacobs's whole persona changed dramatically, and he trotted up the stairs behind his mentor. Hardy and I followed.

Upstairs was a large, empty room, bare of all furnishings, save for a table and a few chairs.

*'This must be the VIP lounge,'* I thought to myself. Jimmy Trunks sat down and I took a seat opposite him. It was at this point of the proceedings that the full extent of the transformation of little Laurie Jacobs manifested itself. In something of a parody of Dr Jekyll and Mr Hyde, the pseudo midget-mobster became Little Caesar. He started bouncing up and down and growling at me, all the while jabbing his stubby finger at me in a menacing fashion. (I couldn't help noticing just how filthy his fingernails were. If there's one thing I can't abide, it's dirty fingernails.)

I was on the verge of bursting into laughter at such a ridiculous temper tantrum when Jimmy Trunks asserted his authority and instructed Jacobs to be quiet while he spoke. Predictably enough, Jacobs immediately desisted. He sat down and glared across at me, his little feet on the end of his little legs barely reaching the floorboards. Hardy, for his part, sat silently staring at the floor, an embarrassed expression on his face.

Rather like the chairman of the board, Jimmy Trunks proceeded to lay down the law, how it was all down to me and my printer that decent people had been nicked and liberties had been taken. I feel that I should mention that Jimmy Trunks was in a different position to Jacobs and Hardy in that, only knowing what he had been told by them, he genuinely believed that the fault lay with me and that I had ruined the scam.

I explained to him that the job had been done properly and that if anybody had been nicked, it wasn't down to me. But he was having none of it and, after some fairly heated discussion, and taking into account the circumstances — alone and unarmed with a 'heavy boat' and his two sidekicks (albeit a pair of cowardly arseholes), I decided that discretion would have to take precedence over valour.

'Listen,' I said, 'I'll tell you what I'll do. I'll check the situation out, with regard to the ink used and the circumstances of the two fellas who've been nicked and, if it turns out that it really is my fault then, of course, I'll have to return the money that's been paid for the job. Fair enough?'

Jimmy Trunks seemed to be placated by this suggestion and then I further suggested that Jacobs and Hardy get me the details and circumstances of the hapless villains who had been captured. Then it happened.

Laurie Jacobs went back into Little Caesar psychopath mode, jumping out of, or more accurately down from, his chair. He began screaming and shouting, swearing abuse and threats at me.

'You just get that fucking money back to us, you cunt!' he screamed. 'Seven days. That's all you've got, you fucking understand? Seven fucking days, that's all. Just fucking get it!'

As he jumped up and down in front of me gesticulating in his most threatening manner, I stared wide-eyed in amazement and wonder. And then, in spite of myself, I started to laugh. Not a hearty guffaw, but a restrained smile. Little Laurie Jacobs looked for all the world like a demented version of the little fat one out of Abbot and Costello.

This, of course, wasn't the wisest of reactions under the circumstances, but I just couldn't take this pathetic little scumbag seriously. Somewhat bemused by my reaction, Jimmy Trunks slammed his fist down on the table and boomed, 'He's laughing. He's fucking laughing!'

I tried to assure him that I wasn't, but he was having none of it. He stood up.

'I can't talk to this fella. He's laughing. He thinks it's a joke,' and then he stormed out of the meeting shaking his head.

Little Caesar Jacobs looked slightly confused by this. His head swivelled left and right, from me and then back to the departing form of Jimmy Trunks, and back to me, as though he was watching a high-speed tennis match.

'And, and ... er,' he spluttered, 'you get that, er, fucking money.' He then trotted after Jimmy Trunks who was disappearing down the staircase. 'Come on, you don't want to stay up here with this cunt,' he said to Hardy, who was rising from his chair.

Hardy looked at me and shrugged his shoulders in an apologetic fashion, and turned to go back down the stairs.

'Give me a call a bit later. I'll talk to you about it then,' I said.

He nodded his head and Jacobs's dulcet tones came floating up the stairs. 'C'mon. Down here, don't talk to the cunt!' Hardy quickly departed and left me staring at the austere décor of the 'boardroom'. I stood up, went downstairs and left Corals, not altogether sure what was going on but determined to find out.

The next day, my first port of call was Hopalong, who then told me about the Pakistani printer. Later on in the day, he found out the details of the two guys who'd been arrested on the Continent. Sure enough, it was down to the dodgy printing.

Now that I knew the full facts, it became obvious what Jacobs and Hardy were playing at. Having been had over by George the Actor, and having lost the right to buy the rest of the documents, they decided to try to recoup some of their losses.

Of course, what they didn't realise was that I knew all about George the Actor and now I also knew the full facts about the rest of the documents being printed up by the Pakistani. No doubt they regarded me as a soft touch who would roll over at the first hint of any kind of violent retribution. Not so.

Of course, I had no intention of paying back a penny for something that wasn't my fault. With regard to any repercussions, I took the view that I would cross that bridge when I came to it.

A couple of days later, Hopalong spoke to Jacobs, who asked him if he had seen me. Upon being told that he had, Jacobs told him about what happened, to which Hopalong replied that he had heard the details from me. No mention was made of the fact that he, and consequently I, knew the full facts regarding the dodgy printing and George the Actor. Jacobs asked Hopalong if I had said anything about the £8,000 being repaid. 'Yeah he did mention it,' Hopalong told him.

'And?'

'Well, he didn't seem too bothered about it,' Hopalong said.

Taking this to mean that £8,000 wasn't a great deal of money to me, Jacobs said, 'Ah, that's all right then. So he's gonna have the money for us, then?'

'No, I don't think so,' Hopalong enlightened him. 'He just didn't seem particularly worried about it. In fact, I think he'd more or less forgotten about it.'

Apparently, Jacobs seemed somewhat surprised and upset by this bit of bad news and left Hopalong in a rather confused frame of mind. The following day, Hardy rang me on my mobile phone. 'Hello, mate,' he said in his usual sycophantic tones. 'It's me.'

'Yeah, I know who it is,' I said. 'I thought I asked you to call me back the other night, so you and me could talk about this properly?'

'I'm sorry, mate, I couldn't. I was told not to get in touch with you.'

I thought about what Hardy had just said. The reason I had asked him to call me and discuss the situation without Jacobs was because I had known him for several years, as opposed to Jacobs, who was Hopalong's friend. And now here he was telling me that he had been warned off talking to me. I had always known he was a wimp to say the least, but this was ridiculous.

'So what d'you want now, then?' I said.

'I just thought I'd call and remind you that we've got an appointment for a couple of days' time. The money ... you got it all sorted out?'

'No, I don't think so,' I replied and then decided to put the ball well and truly in his court. 'Anyway, before we can do anything, like I said the other night, I need all the details of the fellas that got nicked. Y'know, their names, where they got nicked, how they got nicked, all that sort of thing. *Mate*.'

Hardy paused for a moment, and then said he'd get Jacobs to call me back.

'Yeah, you do that, mate,' I said, and he hung up.

At the time of the call, I was on my way to see my old friend, Lynda McQueen. Whilst I was drinking a glass of lager and sitting talking to her in her kitchen, my phone rang. It was Jacobs.

'I've just spoken to the other fella. He said you won't have the money, that right?'

'That's right. I told him I want all the details of the two geezers that got nicked. So I can check it all out,' I replied.

'You just get the money, I'll give you the names then.'

'Yeah, 'course ... tell you what, give me the names now. You must know who they are. That way I can check it out right away.'

'Listen, you just get the money. Don't try and get clever. I've told you, I'll give you the names then.'

'No way. Till you give me the names you can go fuck yourself, you little scumbag.' (As I'm sure Shakespeare once said.)

'Do what? You don't want us to come round your house, do you?' he said.

Upon hearing this clumsy threat to my family, I completely flipped.

'Come round my house, you dirty little slag?' I shouted down the phone. 'You come anywhere near my house, you'll get the biggest fucking shock of your life, you fucking stinking little scumbag!'

At this outburst, Jacobs's shock was apparent, even though he was at the other end of a telephone line. Nothing was said for a few seconds so I shouted again, 'D'you hear me, you little piece of shit?'

'I'll get back to you,' he replied and the line went dead. Still livid, I stared down at the phone in my hand, then heard Lynda say softly, 'You all right?'

'What? Oh yeah. Sorry about that,' I said, trying to calm down.

'I think you'd better sit down, you're all red in the face, look at you. I thought you were going to have a heart-attack or something. Who on earth was that you were talking to?'

'No one important.'

Minutes later, just as I'd managed to calm down, the phone rang again. This time it was Hardy.

'Hello, mate. It's me.'

'Yeah. What?'

'You just had a bit of a row with Laurie, he told me, that right?'

'Yeah, that's right.'

'Listen, mate, there's no need for all that, we just wanna get this sorted out. How long we known each other? Years now, right? You know me, d'you think I'm a cunt?'

'WHAT?' I replied, feeling my anger rising again. 'Listen, I don't even want to talk about it. Just get me the names of the two fellas; until then, there's nothing to talk about.'

'Listen, mate. You know me. I wouldn't put you wrong. Laurie'll have the details when you meet us, mate. You don't think I'm a cunt, d'you? This is me, do you think I'm a cunt?'

'Bollocks! Go fuck yourself, you fucking mug cunt,' I screamed, and hung up. As a normally easy-going type of person, I found all this excitement a bit too exhausting. It certainly wasn't a particularly civilised way to behave as far as I was concerned. Once again, I needed a bit of time to calm down as Lynda sat there shaking her head in a condescending fashion.

'You really should try not to get so worked up. I'm sure it can't be good for you,' she said.

I smiled at her. 'Yes, I know. You're quite right. I do need to calm down. I tell you what, since you're not going out, why don't we go upstairs to bed for a couple of hours?'

Lynda returned the smile and said, 'I don't think so, you've had more than enough excitement for one day. Besides, you've got a nice wife and two lovely children at home waiting for you.'

I took her point. Lynda was particularly fond of reminding me about my marital status. After another lager, I left her company and thought about Jacobs's threat to come round to my house. Of course, he didn't mean himself, but rather a couple of heavies. I decided I had to be prepared for any eventuality and I certainly wasn't disposed to be dragged away from my own doorstep and have my family subjected to such trauma.

After making a couple of phone calls, I met up with an associate the next day and collected something that would ensure that should any unfriendly faces turn up at my house I would have the advantage.

Although I'd taken what I regarded as a necessary precaution, I really didn't want the situation to degenerate to such a level. Serious implications could have ensued. With this in mind, I went to see Hungry Jim.

I explained the situation. My reason for involving him was due to the fact that, at that particular time, he was very friendly with another 'face' who was very much higher up the heavy scale of things than Jacobs's friend Jimmy Trunks. I knew that at the mention of this person's name, Laurie Jacobs would most certainly have second thoughts about the whole affair. The problem, of course, was that should I stick up this particular name without prior approval, I could well have been turning a relatively minor problem into a much bigger one.

Hungry Jim agreed to help out and spoke to the person in question and gained his assent. 'Any problems, send them round to me,' Hungry Jim was told. This having been sorted out, I told Hopalong to meet up with Jacobs.

A couple of days later, I spoke to Hopalong who had seen Jacobs. 'What happened? ' I asked.

'Well, I told him what you said. I told him that, if he wanted any money back, then he would have to go and see Terry **** about it,' he replied.

'And? What did he say?' I asked.

'He didn't really say anything.'

'What? He must have said something,' I said.

'No. The blood just seemed to drain out of his face and he looked like he was going to faint.'

We both had a good laugh about it, and that was the last I heard from Jacobs or Hardy.

Some time after this, Jacobs contracted lung cancer and died several months later, but only after finally conceding defeat in his attempts to work out a way to take his money with him. Amazingly, he told Hopalong, shortly before he finally kicked the bucket, that he had been kidding during our little dispute and that, when he had said, 'You don't want us to come round your house ...' it was intended as a friendly warning, an attempt to help me out. As I had long suspected, beneath that padlocked wallet there beat a heart of stone!

The last I heard of Hardy was that he took a liberty with the wrong people when he broke into somebody's house accompanied by another couple of chaps and tied up the woman of the house and took several thousand pounds' worth of valuables. Unfortunately for him, the house belonged to a big-time drugs dealer from South London and, although the gang was masked up, word soon got out that Hardy was involved. Rumour has it that one of the gang disappeared, never to be seen again. Hardy was tracked down and after breaking down in tears and begging for mercy, and swearing on everything that was dear to him that he wasn't involved in the actual tie-up, he was given the benefit of the doubt and allowed to live. After that, several years later, I was shown some official documentation detailing Hardy's activities over the years as a police informer, in what's called 'running with the foxes and hunting with the hounds'.

As for the documents that I really thought were going to change my life for the better, there was one final little postscript.

Somehow or other, Hungry Jim got hold of the balance. Apparently, after causing so many problems, and quite a few more people coming unstuck, the Pakistani lost the printing franchise. By this time, although what was left wasn't anywhere near as much as the millions that there had been originally, it was still a worthwhile little earner for me.

Some time later, Hungry Jim told me that he was in contact with the original thieves. The good news was that, in the not too distant future, they would be in a position to steal some more documents. This time it would be something in the region of £20 million, and this time it would all be done properly and we would cut the proceeds up between us. A nice few million each. Ultimately, the bad news was, it never came off. *C'est la vie.*

# CHAPTER 4

# Spineless Sid Sells Some Stamps

After the near-miss of the Laurie Jacobs episode, it was very much a case of being back to square one. The only good thing about it from my point of view was my willing and able printer, Eric. Although somewhat limited in the kind of work he could do, he was nevertheless a useful contact. And then, quite by chance, I had another approach for some printing. A friend I hadn't seen for a number of years had heard that I was able to get printing work done and told me he had a very big outlet for postage stamps.

As it sounded quite promising I told him I'd find out if it was feasible. The printing aspect didn't appear to be a problem as Eric was able to get the plates done and do the work on his press. The perforations, however, turned out to be something of a major problem. After making several enquiries, I discovered, much to my surprise, that circular perforating is a highly specialised job, done by only a handful of highly reputable companies.

I was about to abandon the scheme when my associate told me he had a guaranteed order coming to a few hundred thousand pounds. All that stood between me and more than enough cash to set up the poster printing business were a few silly little holes. There *had* to be a way to get it done.

I happened to mention the problem to Bernie in High Wycombe, still plodding along with the perfume business. He told me a friend of his worked in a security printing company named Harrisons, not far from his workshop. He knew that amongst other high-security items such as foreign currency banknotes, Harrisons also printed postage stamps for the Post Office. With this in mind, he told me he would find out just what was involved in perforating the sheets.

It wasn't long after our discussion that Bernie found out all the ins and outs of paper perforation. Not only that, he had managed to locate an ancient perforating machine, through a trade journal, advertised for sale at a price of £2,500.

If I was willing to buy the machine, he would be more than willing to do the work. This I agreed to, and wasted no time in getting the latest scam under way. Unfortunately, the genuine stamps proved to be more of a problem to counterfeit than I had anticipated.

Whilst the printing and the perforation caused no headaches, the hidden difficulty lay in the gummed paper, which had to be specially coated. It had the effect of giving the stamps a 'matt' finish. There was no gummed paper like it available from the normal channels in this country, so I had to compromise and bought the closest match I could find. This meant that the printed stamps came off the press with a very slight sheen to them.

My friend who wanted them felt that they would be OK and I went ahead with the work. By the time the first batch was done, I had £15,000 invested in the scheme. Apart from the plates and printing, I also had to lay out a few thousand for exact specification pins to be made by a firm of specialist precision engineers. These were done to exactly the same dimensions as the originals.

But then my friend reneged on the deal. In fairness, it wasn't really his fault. His main outlet, whom I found out afterwards was a businessman with some sort of mail-order business, decided they weren't up to standard. This was particularly annoying as he had already approved a couple of proof sheets I'd sent him.

'What's the problem?' I asked my friend. 'After all, so long as the letters arrive at their destination, what difference if they're not quite as matt finish as the originals?'

We knew there was no practical problem as we had already posted about a hundred letters to various people. They'd all arrived safe and sound.

'I don't know,' my friend replied. 'All I know is he doesn't want them.'

'Fucking hell, like I mean, what does the man expect? We are, after all, talking about a humble postage stamp. You're not meant to fall in love with it. It's not supposed to have sentimental value, after all. Nobody pays attention to the poxy little things. D'you know how many letters go through the system, get posted every day?'

'No. How many?'

'What? Er — lots. Take it from me, a few thousand each week won't even be noticed. And what if, by chance, some X-ray vision person spots one amongst millions. What they gonna do, try and track down the culprit who used a forged 21p stamp? I don't think they could afford too much of that, do you?'

'No. I agree with you absolutely. Unfortunately, I'm not the one with the wonga. And if he won't take them, what the fuck can I do about it?' my friend said.

The answer to his rhetorical question, as we both knew, was quite simply nothing. But, to his credit, he put himself out to move as many as he could. So, once again, I was in very much the same position as I had been with the lucky briefcase episode and the Laurie Jacobs saga.

My friend and I managed to sell a reasonable amount and then Walter told me that a friend of his, Spineless Sid, whom I had met a few times, had a punter for a large quantity, cash on delivery. Walter and I spoke to Spineless Sid about it and, after some negotiations, it was agreed that he would take a relatively small quantity at first, then a larger amount if everything was OK.

The first parcel came to £2,500 or thereabouts. He took the stamps and came back with the money. Walter took his share out of it and I pocketed the rest. Soon afterwards, Spineless Sid told Walter he wanted the remainder. The agreed price for these was £12,500. Although a bargain basement price, this meant that, with the stamps that I had already sold, I would make a small profit on my original outlay and all the stamps would be gone.

For Spineless Sid, this seemed to be a major transaction. So much so that he even asked me how to go about it and what he should say about the stamps.

'Say whatever you like,' I advised him.

'Yeah, but what if they ask whether they're genuine or not?'

'Tell them they're genuine if you think it'll make any difference. Say they're knocked off.'

As far as I was concerned, it was no big deal, a simple matter of giving Sid a couple of boxes and him paying Walter and me the money. However, I don't think Spineless Sid had ever seen 12 grand in one go in his life before.

At this stage, I had no idea who was buying the stamps from

Spineless Sid, and wasn't really interested. But then the day before the 'big deal', he let it drop that he was serving a couple of guys who were known to both Walter and me — Tofty and Sussy.

Tofty I had known for many years, although I had never had any dealings with him. The truth of the matter was I had never particularly liked him, mainly, I suppose, because of his repulsive appearance. He always reminded me of some kind of slug draped in a camel-hair overcoat. He had a manner and a way about him of slinking along, with his hands in his pockets and trying to give off the impression that he was a mini Al Capone.

He was always to be found on the fringes of underworld activity but never really had the bottle to be actively involved in anything more serious than illegal street-trading. Far from being a villain, he was more like a gangster's groupie.

Sussy, on the other hand, I had a lot of time for. Although I had only known him for a few years, I always found him to be straightforward. I'd had one or two deals with him involving the perfume and, above all else, he had done me a very big favour the previous year, by giving evidence at the last perfume trial, when Walter and I were acquitted.

It's my belief that the evidence he gave was crucial to our defence and played a significant part in the result. I hasten to add, by stating that he did me (and Walter) a big favour, this is not to suggest that he perjured himself in any way, but rather he did bother, at some inconvenience to himself, to come to court to give evidence for us.

By way of showing my thanks at Christmas 1992, I gave him a couple of thousand bottles of perfume to go to work with, even though he was adamant he neither expected nor wanted anything. In spite of his protests, I more or less forced them upon him. It was also my intention to give him a further 5,000 bottles of Opium before Christmas 1993. Walter, even though he, too, benefited by way of not losing his liberty, seemed indifferent when I mentioned to him the matter of giving Sussy a 'good drink'. Although he was in favour of the idea, it was a half-hearted agreement and, as far as I am aware, Walter never put his hand in his pocket.

When Walter told me that Spineless Sid was serving Sussy, I immediately suggested he should call him and we could serve him direct and give him some credit if he needed it. Later on, Walter told me he had phoned his home three times and left messages for Sussy to get back to him. As Sussy hadn't done so, and Spineless Sid was literally begging us to go ahead with the deal, presumably because he was desperate for his bit of profit, we made arrangements for him to carry on as planned. When Spineless Sid declared just who his customers were, he also said that Tofty knew they were forgeries. No problems as far as I could see.

The deal was done the following day and all went smoothly. As Sussy and Tofty had once again emphasised that the money had to be returned in the event of any problems, Walter and I held on to the cash for seven days, just in case. After speaking to Spineless Sid, and being told by him that there didn't seem to be any problems, we cut the money up. And that was that. Another day, another dollar, so to speak.

With the stamps out of the way, once again I was looking for whatever move was waiting around the next corner. Unfortunately, there wasn't too much happening and I was barely getting enough to pay the bills.

Five or six weeks after the trade with Spineless Sid, he contacted Walter with the news that Sussy and Tofty had been in touch demanding their money back. They didn't seem too happy and were making all kinds of growling noises.

As I no longer had the money to repay them, and bearing in mind the lengthy period of time that had lapsed since the sale, my initial response was to tell Spineless Sid that it was a bit late in the day for refunds. I suggested he tell Sussy and Tofty this, and that there was no way he could get back in touch with the people he had bought them from.

Spineless Sid tried this approach but, sadly for him, they were having none of it and demanded to be told the names of the suppliers. By the time Walter and I met up with him, he was a total wreck and looked to be on the verge of a nervous breakdown. (It was precisely because of this type of reaction that he was known as Spineless Sid.) I had a sneaking suspicion that Sussy and Tofty had called him all sorts of nasty names and, in all probability, had even poked their tongues out at him, or, heaven forbid, used bad language, possibly even the 'F' word.

After a few more meetings with Spineless Sid, when he gradually appeared more and more pathetic, I finally told him to tell them he had got them from Walter and me and that we would sort it out. By this stage, Sid's pathetic pleas for a way out of his dilemma had ceased to be funny. I told him that if Sussy came to see me, I would work it out with him and explain that I would return him his money but it would take a few weeks. This upset Spineless Sid even more and, close to tears, he said, 'I can't do that. If they know I got them from you, they'll know that I must have known they were a print-up. In fact, they asked beforehand if they were coming from you or Walter, and I told them "No". If I tell them now that I did get them from you, they'll go mad.'

'Well, what the fuck d'you expect us to do about it, then?' I said, beginning to feel a sense of exasperation about the whole affair.

'What if I say you've got a buyer for them?' he suggested.

'OK, do that if you want.'

'I'll get him to call you, OK?'

'Yeah, do that.'

'But don't forget, whatever you do, don't say that you sold them to me. Please don't let them know I got them from you, OK?' said Spineless Sid, a pleading tone in his voice.

'Yes, don't concern yourself about it,' I replied wearily.

Shortly after this, Sussy called me and I gave him my address and made arrangements to meet him at my home. This he did and, after some discussion, I told him I felt certain I could get them sold but that it would take a couple of weeks or so. He seemed satisfied with this but, as he was leaving, he asked me if they were anything to do with me and, not wishing to put Spineless Sid under any more pressure, I lied and said 'No'. But then Sussy adopted a more aggressive tone and said something along the lines of, ''Cos if I find out they're anything to do with you ...'

'What?' I replied, beginning to feel just a trifle annoyed with the whole affair. 'What you getting at? I said I'd get it sorted out, didn't I?'

Sussy then adopted a more conciliatory tone and said, 'Yeah. 'Course. OK, I'll leave it up to you, then.'

As far as I was concerned, this should have been an end to the matter and within a couple of weeks I would have got Sussy his money back. Walter had already given Sid the share that he had received and Spineless Sid, although he had spent his, managed to borrow his share, and so Sussy had received a reasonable refund of money already.

But then, not long after I had spoken to Sussy, Walter told me that Spineless Sid had been back on to him in a worse state than ever. Apparently, he had been threatened by the deadly duo, who were still demanding to know where he had got the stamps. So frightened was Spineless Sid that he had moved out of his house after being told that a certain 'leading underworld figure' wanted to see him about the matter. The threat was that he was going to be kidnapped and 'taken for a ride'.

I met up with Spineless Sid, who was in a spectacularly pathetic state. I knew for a fact that he actually knew the leading underworld figure and had once done him a small favour. This being the case, I couldn't understand why he didn't just go and see the man and explain the situation, that the money would be repaid in due course. But Spineless Sid was too petrified to do anything and could barely even speak.

I then helped him out again by contacting Hungry Jim, who was on good terms with the leading underworld figure.

In fact, Hungry Jim had, at one stage, become quite involved with the man and had actually gone through a brief metamorphosis when he adopted many of the mannerisms of a 'heavy boat' himself. For a while, he was Enfield's answer to Bugsy Malone.

I realised the remarkable transformation that had come over him when I went to see him about some property he had acquired. It was a house in Totteridge that had belonged to a well-known ticket tout by the name of Stan. Somehow or other, Stan the ticket man was heavily in debt to the leading underworld figure, or maybe to his brother, someone whom Hungry Jim was also close to. Hungry Jim had a charge on the house, which was connected to the debt. The reason Hungry Jim wanted to see me was to try and get me to buy it. He explained how he had come by it and, in the course of doing so, related a little incident that had occurred not long before.

Stan, as a result of the debt he couldn't pay, had been making himself scarce, to the extent of almost being invisible. All things considered, this wasn't really too surprising. Becoming increasingly annoyed and frustrated at his inability to nail Stan down (literally or otherwise), the leading underworld figure and friends, together with Hungry Jim, plotted up outside the house. After several hours, they tired of waiting for Stan to come out and knocked on his door. Eventually, his wife answered and told them her husband wasn't at home.

'In that case, I'm sure you won't mind us taking a look round,' they said, walking past her.

Stan was found in his underpants hiding in one of the cupboards. He was pulled out by his ankles in a most undignified fashion, squeaking and squealing. Not surprisingly, Stan was something of an incoherent wreck, pleading for mercy. He was warned in no uncertain terms that, if he didn't pay up, he would have to forfeit the house. And to emphasise just how strongly they felt about the issue, Stan's teenage son, Stan Junior, was seized.

'My baby, my baby. Please, not my baby,' Stan's wife implored them. Her 'baby', from what I've seen of him, is a rather overweight baby. In fact, he really is, or at least was then, very much a mini Stan — bulging great cheeks, and a big fat, waddling body.

Since the men in her house weren't exactly angels of mercy, her pleas fell on deaf ears. Amidst a great deal of panic and screaming and shouting, Baby Stan was held by a couple of heavies out of an upstairs window. By now, it seems, Stan Senior, still in his underpants, had got the message.

But Baby Stan most certainly hadn't. He just wouldn't keep still! Wriggling and writhing, and then it happened ... he slipped out of their grasp. They dropped the baby! Amazingly, Baby completely escaped injury and was last seen haring off down the garden as fast as his fat little legs would carry him.

So, at the time of our visit, Hungry Jim was a bit of a 'face' himself. I had earlier told him about Spineless Sid's traumatic dilemma and, after we went to see him, he called the leading underworld figure whilst we were there. He had already spoken to him, and this time put Spineless Sid on the phone to talk to him directly. Spineless Sid put the phone down greatly relieved to have heard the person tell him that it was nothing to do with him and was between Sid and Sussy (and not forgetting Tofty, of course).

Spineless Sid looked as though he had just had a reprieve from a death sentence and couldn't stop thanking both Hungry Jim and me. Yet again, I thought that was an end to the affair and, as I had a couple of little deals on the horizon, I knew I would have the cash to pay off Sussy within two or three weeks and life could carry on as normal. But I was mistaken.

A few days later, Spineless Sid was back, shaking like a leaf. Sussy and Tofty had been threatening him again and again demanding to know who he had got the stamps from. 'I can't take any more,' Spineless Sid blubbered, as I drove him and Walter past the Angel Tube Station. 'I'm going to have to tell them I got them from you.'

I looked at him in amazement. 'Do what?' I said. 'After all that shit when you begged me not to tell them, and now you're trying to tell me you're going to tell them anyway? You pathetic little shitbag.'

'I just can't take it any more. I've got to tell them,' he whined.

At this point, I lost my temper and felt like beating up the spineless old git myself. But I felt I couldn't degrade myself by hitting such a feeble excuse of a man. Instead I just said, 'Say whatever you like.'

Walter then piped up , 'Don't say I was involved.'

'Oh no, I won't,' Spineless Sid reassured him.

I looked at him in disgust and felt much the same about Walter. 'Get out of the car, I'm going,' I said, and drove away leaving the pair of them talking on the corner.

About a week or two after this, as I was leaving my house and about to get in my car, Tofty and Sussy pulled up alongside me. I turned to look around and saw Tofty leaning across from the driver's seat and calling out through the open passenger side window, 'Get in this car now!'

I looked down and noticed that Sussy was sitting in the back seat shouting out something as well. At the time, I was holding a set of printing plates in a folder for a little job somebody had asked me to get done.

'Go fuck yourself. Who d'you think you're talking to?' I replied.

I turned away and continued what I was doing, putting the plates on the back seat of my car. Suddenly, I felt a blow to the back of my head and, in the next few seconds, I had the pair of them kicking and punching me. I lurched forward but remained on my feet. It was lucky for me that neither one of them was able to punch his way out of a wet paper bag, otherwise I would most certainly have been in a bit of trouble.

As it was, I managed to push them off and the scuffle was reduced to a slanging match. At this stage, my main concern wasn't to carry on fighting the terrible two, but to get rid of them as I knew that one of the neighbours would certainly call the local police, probably thinking that I was being mugged or something.

With the plates on the back seat of my car, the police were the last people I wanted to see. Should they arrive and make themselves busy, and look in the two cars, I would have been in a great deal of trouble; a lot more than Sussy and Tofty presented. After much screaming and shouting, the pair of them drove off screaming that I had better have the money by 7.00pm 'or else'.

I went back into the house to find a concerned-looking Kay, the cleaning lady, standing in the hallway. She had witnessed the event, along with the builders who were doing some work in the house, from behind the curtains. I looked at her and smiled, 'Just a little scuffle. Very annoying though, first thing in the morning.'

She looked very confused as I went up the stairs to clean up. I looked in the bathroom mirror and saw that I had a slightly bruised eye. But to my horror and amazement, one side of my jaw had swollen up to the size of a balloon. I knew it wasn't broken as I could move my mouth and it didn't really hurt. I assumed one of the blows must have struck a nerve or something. It certainly looked much more serious than it was.

Just after I had washed up and changed my blood-stained clothes, the phone rang. It was Sussy once again screaming and shouting and telling me to have the money by 7.00pm, to which I once again told him to go fuck himself. Unfortunately, the answerphone was on, and the 'conversation' was recorded. I left the house and went about my business. When Laraine returned home during the day, Kay told her what had happened. After listening to the answerphone recording, she began to panic, as she had no idea what it was all about. Some time later, Sussy called the house again and, upon speaking to Laraine, gave her the message that he would be turning up at the house that evening to see me.

Realising the message was connected to the day's fun and games, she panicked, not knowing what time I would be home. Thinking that some big-time villain might be knocking at the door when she was alone with the children, she told him that if he came anywhere near the house she'd call the police. Apparently, this rather took him by surprise and he seemed at a loss for words. And that was the end of that conversation.

Later on in the day, I spoke to Laraine and, after her initial relief to hear that I was still alive and quite cheerful, she told me about the phone call. I told her she had nothing to worry about and that I would be home before 7.00pm anyway.

A couple of hours later, Tofty rang me on my mobile and, after making it clear that I didn't want him coming round to the house again, I agreed to meet him and Sussy the next day. At the meeting, it was obvious that the pair of them were wary of what my reaction to what had happened might be, as Tofty, the gangster's groupie, had some kind of weapon wrapped in a plastic bag shoved down the waistband of his trousers.

But the truth of the matter was, now that tempers had cooled, I really didn't want to quarrel with Sussy. Not because I was particularly concerned about him, and I certainly wasn't in the remotest way frightened by him, but simply because I remembered how much he had helped me out. I tried to explain this to him, but he had got into the habit of acting like a 'heavy boat' and kept on growling. I suppose he must have been a bit more concerned than I was because he warned me, 'If you're thinking about any comebacks, I'll kill you!' I tried not to laugh out loud, and reiterated that he was the last person I wanted to argue with but, no matter what, he refused to 'shake little fingers' and say, 'Make up, make up, never do it again ...'

I took the stamps off him and told him I would get his money back as soon as possible, which was what we had agreed before, anyway. I checked the stamps afterwards, and found they were short by several thousand.

I didn't say anything, but then Tofty called me to say they had left some in the boot of his car by mistake. No big deal. But then a day or two later, Tofty called me again to say that Sussy had been raided by the police, with regard to an unrelated matter, and had fled the house via the back door. Unfortunately the stamps had been in the boot of a car that had been parked on the drive of his house. The police had found them and taken them away. I listened to this bag of bollocks and said how sorry I was to hear such a sad story. Amazingly, after returning to his home, Sussy was never arrested. Surprise, surprise. Now that's the kind of Old Bill I dream about — after finding something illegal, they just wander off and don't return!

Eventually, over the next couple of months, I paid the money back in dribs and drabs, even though I had the total amount in my possession. At one stage of the protracted proceedings, Sussy became so irate that he felt we simply had to have another fight if I didn't immediately pay him the total balance owed. I agreed to meet him outside a wine bar in Hatton Garden. Knowing that he would be accompanied by the gangster's groupie, I turned up with a friend of mine, Tom.

The pair of them were waiting outside when we arrived. Immediately, Sussy started glowering at me, but I managed to persuade him to come inside the wine bar, where I bought myself and Tom a drink. I asked Sussy and Tofty what they wanted, but the offer was declined. When I then gave Sussy the news that I had no money for him, he insisted we go outside and have a fight. As much as I tried, he wouldn't be dissuaded, and eventually I went outside with him. Sussy immediately started walking away and I stood there, bemused.

'Where are you going?' I asked, whilst he was still within walking distance. He turned round and had a strange, faraway look on his face. Then he came back and we stood face to face, with Sussy bouncing up and down and mumbling incoherently. It was something of a bizarre showdown with no actual punches being thrown. Very much a case of handbags at 40 paces. Then suddenly, and inexplicably, Sussy jumped into his car, which was parked outside the wine bar, and started shouting, 'Forget about the money. I don't want it now. It's too late. It's *on yer*.' (In other words, I was being told I would soon be dead.)

I looked at him and shook my head. I felt embarrassed to be a party to such puerile behaviour, and walked back into the wine bar and finished my drink. Ultimately, I paid him back, but then Tofty called me to say that all I now owed was £4,000.

'I don't think so,' I told him.

'Why's that?' he asked.

'Because I've paid you back for all that you've returned,' I said.

'But what about the ones the Old Bill seized?'

'Like I said, I've paid you for what you've returned. If you've got any more to come back, I'll give you the money for them,' I repeated.

'So we're knocked then?' Tofty asked.

'No, I wouldn't say that. But if you think I'm paying you for stuff you haven't returned, you can think again.'

He hung up sounding rather disgruntled. Shortly afterwards, Sussy rang me, growling again.

'What's this about you're not gonna give us the 4 grand you owe?' he said.

'That's right. Because I don't owe you fuck all. You've been paid back and that's that,' I told him.

'Where are you now? I want to meet you,' he screamed down the phone, obviously once again very angry. I pictured him with steam coming out of his ears.

'I'm busy at the moment. I've got more important things to do than meet up with you. Give me a call in the morning and I'll meet you tomorrow, wherever you want, no problem at all. I'm free all day.'

I hung up the phone expecting to hear from Sussy the following morning, but that was the last time I spoke to him.

I found out afterwards that Spineless Sid, when he had told Sussy and Tofty that he had got the stamps from me, had emphasised that Walter wasn't involved in the deal at all, which I thought was a bit rich since he was Walter's friend in the first place, and I hardly knew him. I think Walter was as petrified as Spineless Sid. Sad, really.

It's a crying shame that the whole sorry business was over a mere £12,000. Had Sussy and Tofty handled it differently, I would have been more than willing to have given it to them in one lump sum within three weeks.

As well as this, I had intended giving Sussy the 5,000 bottles of fake Opium at Christmas, in itself worth something like £20,000, in return for the favour he did me — which I have never forgotten — but, of course, this was now abandoned. As it was, I sold the stamps that were returned without any problems. And at a better price than I had agreed with Sussy and Tofty.

I decided after this to give up on any more illegal printing work until I could get the poster business under way.

It's a bizarre irony that the stamps have since become collector's items and, apparently, are quite valuable and much sought-after.

# CHAPTER 5

## My Dad's a Printer

So all I had now to keep my head above water were one or two perfume deals which, on a regular basis, just about paid the bills and the stock of paperwork from the lucky briefcase affair.

This was all stored in a self-storage unit in South London which I used to visit whenever a trade was called on. I would take whatever was required and then make sure everything was in order and locked up. A fairly simple procedure, with no real risk of anything going wrong. But once again in my life, Murphy's Law very nearly tripped me up.

Walter called me one morning with a reasonable little deal that would earn us a few quid, no fortunes, about £1,000 each but a nice little pay-day all the same. As Walter was absolutely petrified at the thought of going anywhere near the self-storage unit where the documentation was kept, it was always up to me. On this particular occasion, the same routine as usual was carried out. I drove over to the unit in South London and parked my car in the road outside. I went into the warehouse building and made my way to my unit. Once there, I took what I needed and packed it into a small holdall. I double-checked that everything was in order, locked up and made my way back to the exit.

As I turned a corner at the end of the corridor where my unit was, I almost walked straight into a regional crime squad officer who had been involved in one of my perfume cases several years before.

He was standing at the reception counter with another detective, talking to the young receptionist who was looking at some photographs. As luck would have it, neither man noticed me as I stopped dead in my tracks and then proceeded to walk backwards to my unit. The moment I rounded the corner, I turned and made my way rather swiftly along the corridor. I quickly opened the door to my unit and hid the holdall in the corner behind some boxes. I remained in the unit for about five minutes, trying to decide my next move. I had to get past the detective without him seeing my face. There was no doubt in my mind that should he see and recognise me, he would want to know just what I was doing there with a storage unit. And more crucially, what I had in it.

I locked up and walked slowly back to the reception area. Very cautiously, I peered around the corner. To my horror, I saw not only the detective I wanted to avoid and his partner, but several others milling around. Two of the units in the reception area were open, with a couple of young detectives looking in a number of boxes. Another officer was studying some boxes of files that were on the floor in front of the reception counter. Whatever they were up to, it looked very important, and one or two of them seemed to be quite excited. But, for me, it could hardly have been more nerve-racking. I retreated back to my unit before I was noticed, and tried to work out a plan of action. I wasn't concerned that their presence was anything to do with me, clearly it was something else. In all probability something big.

What worried me more was the time, 5.55pm, and the building closed at 6.00pm. From what I saw of the police at the reception, they looked as though they had made camp. And then I heard the sound of one of the staff checking up to make sure there were no customers left in the place.

I was aware that the police were still there as I was able to hear the crackling noises of their walkie-talkies. Now I was beginning to panic and had to make a decision. Knowing that the young girl would soon be standing next to me telling me to lock up and leave, I took drastic action. My unit was packed out with large boxes containing the documentation, and there was barely room to move.

With a quick bit of shuffling about, I made a space in the corner. I then pulled the door to and hid myself behind the boxes. I was hoping the girl would just look along the corridor and assume it was empty and turn off the lights. My plan then was to wait for a couple of hours, creep out and, provided the building was empty, look for a means of escape. I knew there were several small windows that had no interior locks on them, and it would be simplicity itself to slip out. If I say so myself, a plan devilishly cunning and brilliant in its simplicity.

Hidden behind the boxes, I listened intently, and then held my breath as I heard the sound of footsteps coming along the corridor. And then, to add to my earlier horror, the footsteps stopped outside my unit. I heard a gentle tap on the door, followed by the sound of it being gently pulled open.

'He-llo? He-llo?'

It was the young girl checking the units. Statue-like, I stood, my whole body tense from the strain of remaining completely motionless and silent.

I heard a faint sound of air coming from the girl's mouth, a rather thoughtful exhalation, followed by the door being pushed to.

Click.

'Oh no, fuck it,' I thought to myself. I had inadvertently left the padlock hanging on the hasp, and being the type that just clicks shut, the girl had locked the door with it.

I couldn't call out to her to come back, and tell her that she had accidentally locked me in, as that would only draw attention to my presence. What to do, grasshopper? I cursed my carelessness in forgetting my tele-transporter. There would be no *'Beam me up, Scotty'* without it, that much I knew. I can't say I had a particularly comfortable night's sleep amongst the boxes and, apart from anything else, it was cold. I felt a certain empathy with these people, usually from India it seems, who stow away in the luggage holds of aircraft. I pictured my frozen body being discovered at a later date, but somehow I came through the ordeal alive.

Come the morning, I had to get out. Remaining in the unit certainly wasn't an option. The building opened for business at 8.00am, and I had devised a way of escape without too much fuss.

At 9.00am, there was a general sound of people milling about and going to their units, and I could tell the building was wide awake, which was more than could be said for me.

At 9.15am, I heard somebody walking along the corridor, and I decided that now was my opportunity. As the footsteps passed my unit, I called out, 'Hello. Hello.'

The footsteps stopped abruptly, and if it's possible for footsteps to sound surprised, I could have sworn that's exactly how they sounded.

'Hello? Is there somebody in there?'

Ooh, the embarrassment of it all as I called back, 'Er, yes, there is actually, I'm, er, sort of locked in.'

There was a pause and then the voice on the other side of the door said, 'How did that happen then?'

'It's a long story. D'you think, if I pass the keys under the door, you could open the padlock for me?'

The voice chuckled, 'Yeah, sure.'

Then I heard another voice call out, 'Who are you talking to, Howard?' and my anonymous saviour called back, 'There's someone locked in here, Sarge.'

The last word, as I was on my hands and knees passing the key under the door, froze me almost as surely as the stowaway that I had earlier imagined myself to be. My rescuer was obviously a policeman. And the way my luck was going, more than likely the policeman I had been trying to avoid. I heard him opening the padlock.

*I wonder if he'll think there's anything strange if I walk out with a cardboard box on my head?*

I made an involuntary little squeaking sound as the door was pulled open.

'There you are, mate.' The young, uniformed constable handed me my keys with a smile. I took them with a sigh of relief that it wasn't the face I had dreaded seeing. And feeling that for the sake of normality I owed him an explanation, I shook my head, and said to him, 'I can't believe some people. Some idiot's come along and locked me in while my back was turned. I suppose it's their idea of a joke!'

The constable started laughing. 'Yeah, it's funny, some people's sense of humour,' he remarked.

Eager to retain the relaxed atmosphere and allay any possible suspicious thoughts, I replied whilst locking the door, 'I bet it was you! Policemen like locking people up, don't they?'

He laughed and walked away. I took a deep breath and walked towards the reception area, and prayed that I wouldn't see anybody I knew. My luck was in, and I quickly walked out.

I left it for a week before returning to the storage unit. Everything appeared to be back to normal and, out of curiosity, I approached the girl at the reception counter.

'I've just come to pay my rent on unit 105 ... Mr James,' I said, then added as she looked for 'Mr James's' account sheet, 'So, what's been happening lately? Anything exciting?'

'Didn't you hear, Mr James?' she replied, holding my card in her hand.

'Hear what?'

'We've had the police here all week. They found a load of cocaine in one of our units and over a million pounds in cash in another. It was part of a big drug-smuggling gang from all over the world. We even had some FBI men in here.'

'Well, I never. How exciting. I always seem to miss the fun.'

I paid my monthly rent, and went to the unit and took the holdall out. This time I left with no mishaps. I had, in fact, read about the drugs case in the newspapers. It was a large international smuggling ring, with people being arrested simultaneously in South America, USA, Italy and London. In fact, the report stated that the police had raided a South London 'depository'. If only the report had stated 'South London Self-Storage Units', I'm sure I would have made the connection and been on my guard. Murphy's Law!

* * *

As the documents and perfume barely paid the weekly bills, I became involved in certain bits of ducking and diving, some legal, some not; some profitable, some not. And bearing in mind my undeniably amoral attitude in many respects, not surprisingly I didn't confine my activities to printing and perfume. But even allowing for the benefit of hindsight, I have to question the wisdom (or rather the lack of it) of some of the deals I participated in. I suppose it was some time in the autumn that I once again became involved in a little deal that caused me more grief than it was worth. Without going into detail, for obvious reasons, part of my involvement concerned a guy named Frankie Jonham, who came out of Hoxton in London. Frankie Jonham is a thinly-disguised corruption of his real name but, no doubt, he and his associates will recognise who I'm referring to.

I was acting as the middleman for an associate of mine, Big Nose Bob, and a little firm from South London, who assured me that their man, Frankie Jonham, was 100 per cent reliable and trustworthy. In reality, as I was to find out later from several people who knew him, Frankie Jonham was an out-and-out scumbag.

As a direct result of his own brain-dead stupidity and big mouth, the low-life managed to get himself nicked one afternoon and in the process lost a considerable amount of money belonging to the South London firm.

That evening, I received a call from my associates in South London, telling me that Jonham had been arrested. At first, I thought nothing of it as I had kept my part of the deal. All it meant was that I wouldn't earn anything out of it. It certainly wasn't the end of the world. This all happened on a Saturday, and on the following Monday morning Frankie Jonham appeared in court and to everyone's surprise was released on bail.

I was further contacted by the South London firm who wanted to see me about the weekend's events. I had no problem with this, even though they were suggesting that there were one or two 'problems' that were down to me. Big Nose Bob and I met the people in South London, and a fairly heated exchange of words took place, during which nothing much was resolved.

Not long after this, I was told that the 'Guv'nor' of the South London firm wanted to see me, and that he wasn't too pleased about the situation. The Guv'nor in question was a well-known 'face' in South London and was one of the older school of villains, being a very good friend of Freddie Foreman and an associate of the Krays when they were at large. Without naming him, I'll simply refer to him by his nickname, RO. I was told that RO wanted to see me by a friend of mine, Big John, who had originally introduced me to the South London firm.

I had no qualms or reservations about meeting RO, even though he was generally known as a 'heavy boat'. For my part, I had done nothing wrong or underhanded and had nothing to hide. For these reasons I didn't feel the need to meet RO and the firm accompanied by anybody. Big John came along, but he was very much the middleman, and not there to take sides. At the meeting, RO was there with just one of the firm, Kevin. RO immediately went on the offensive and started slagging off Big Nose Bob who wasn't there. I told him that as far as I was concerned he was wrong about my friend, whom I had known for 30 years, and that I just didn't believe that there had been any wrong-doing. (Although subsequent events later caused me to have grave doubts about his integrity.)

After a while, RO calmed down, and appeared to be satisfied that, as far as I was concerned at least, everything was above board. In fact, I pointed out to him, I had been led to believe that Frankie Jonham was someone they had known for many years and was completely trustworthy and reliable. In reality, they hadn't known him for that long at all and just regarded him as the mug that he was. Once again, nothing much was resolved, and that really should have been an end to the matter. Shortly afterwards, however, word got back to me that Frankie Jonham was putting it about that I had set him up to get arrested. Since being a 'grass' in the criminal fraternity is about as low as a man can get — in fact, it is more or less on the same social level as a paedophile — I wasn't too happy at what I was hearing.

(The irony of this kind of situation is, although known grasses are despised, the uncomfortable truth is that the vast majority of criminals given the right circumstances will grass their own mothers to avoid going to prison. It's just a question of whether or not they think they'll be found out. As the late Frank Norman once wrote, 'The underworld is knee-deep in grass.')

At this point, I took two courses of action. First, I contacted Kevin from the South London firm, and told him about the latest developments. As far as I was concerned, since Jonham was their man it was up to them to deal with the problem and make sure he kept his mouth shut. As we were planning to do some further business together, Kevin agreed to this.

Second, I contacted a bent copper who was useful when it came to providing various snippets of information about situations such as this. What he told me didn't really come as too much of a surprise. Basically, the reason that Jonham had got bail so easily was that he had given the police as much help as he could. This also ensured him a relatively light sentence when the case eventually came to court; five to seven years plus a fine or twelve months on top would have been par for the course. He got just three years.

Further, the reason the police had raided the warehouse where he'd been caught — which, incidentally, I didn't know the whereabouts of — was because they had been watching him for a week previously and listening to him on his mobile phone. In a nutshell, he had got himself arrested down to his own big mouth, and had accused me of setting him up in order to deflect from his own activities which he had engaged in for the purpose of getting bail immediately.

At the time, the story that Jonham had spread about me stopped, and I assumed that the people from South London had said something to him, and I thought little more about the matter, although a year or two later the malicious lies started to circulate again, but as nobody ever said anything to my face, I paid no attention to it. I had more important things to worry about.

Fortunately, the people who knew me well and had known me for many years and done business with me without the slightest problems knew what a load of rubbish it all was. Having never grassed anybody up in my life, I was hardly likely to start now, for no logical reason whatsoever, particularly for a low-life slag like Frankie Jonham from Hoxton.

As so often seems to happen, there was a little addendum to the sorry saga when Kevin contacted me saying that he had something of interest for me. I agreed to meet him on the condition that if we did any business together, it had to be strictly between ourselves and nobody else. By now, I'd had quite enough of being introduced to so called 'proper people' such as the low-life Frankie Jonham.

As usual, I met Kevin at a venue in the Old Kent Road. In the boot of his car, he had a few golf clubs in an old case and, at the bottom of the case, he had a cardboard tube. Away from prying eyes, he took a sheet of paper from the tube. Immediately, I recognised it as being a part of the batch of documents that had originally been shown to me by Laurie Jacobs. Of course, without being told, I knew what was required.

'Any problems?' Kevin asked.

'No. None at all,' I replied.

'Good. Now what I've got here is just the start. The value of this lot is about 30 grand, but the people just want to see how we get on with this lot first and then go from there. If it's all sweet, then the next lot should be a right big parcel. Maybe a few million.'

I shook my head dubiously, and gave him just the briefest of outlines of what had happened with Jacobs and Hardy. I knew that what Kevin had in his possession was more than likely just the remainder of a few dribs and drabs that hadn't been done at the time.

'I've got to tell you, Kevin, but I doubt very much whether there will be any more to follow,' I said.

At this, Kevin seemed to think that I wouldn't be interested in getting such a small piece of work done, and assured me that he was confident there was a nice big parcel to follow.

'Well, if there is, all well and good. But I won't hold my breath,' I said.

'So what about this lot, then?' Kevin asked.

'Like I said, no problems. I'll have it done by the weekend for you. And as there's no real money in it, I'll just charge you the printer's fee. Fair enough?'

'Fair enough. But don't worry, I'm certain I'll get my hands on the rest,' Kevin assured me.

A couple of days later, I met up with Kevin and handed over the completed job and charged him just £700, the exact money I had paid Eric. And, of course, the 'big parcel' never followed, which didn't surprise me. But even though I didn't earn anything, I was quite happy to have helped out.

It was about this time that I met Clare. Although our relationship was relatively brief — up until the point when she found out that I was married — it would ultimately have a far greater bearing upon both our lives than either one of us could ever possibly have foreseen.

Shortly after meeting Clare, she told me in conversation that her father had a printing business, something which was of particular interest to me. Ever since the episode with Ronald and the lucky briefcase, I had been looking for a decent printer to do some of the work for the perfume business. She introduced me to her father, Ken, who was quite willing to do the work I required, and was particularly eager as it was cash in hand.

I got to know her father quite well, and when he told me he was hoping to sell his business and become semi-retired, I began to think he might be interested in going into business with me on the poster printing project. I gave him a basic outline of the idea and, of course, I emphasised the fact that it would all be cash and no VAT or tax.

What attracted me to the idea of going into business with Ken was the fact that he lived in a spacious house set in a couple of acres and next to the house was a large workshop which was ideal for what I had in mind. I asked him how much he thought we could get a decent 4-colour litho press for. He replied that he thought we would have to pay about £50,000. After discussing the various possibilities at length, Ken became more than interested in starting up this new venture.

I asked Ken to keep me updated as to how the sale of his business was going, and we both decided that, for the moment, there was nothing to be done, but that we both wanted to get it off the ground some time in the not-too-distant future.

Christmas 1993 came and went, as did my relationship with Clare, although we still remained good friends, and met occasionally for lunch. The perfume business was still ticking over, but doing no more than that. At least it paid the bills, and now that I had a potential printer for the poster business, I set about in earnest trying to raise the money for a decent 4-colour press.

# CHAPTER 6

# Walter in Wonderland and a Faceless Enemy

Immediately after Christmas, I tried to put together a couple of deals involving the documents that Walter and I still had from the lucky briefcase episode. I explained to him that I was desperate to raise as much money as possible, as quickly as possible, for a particular business venture I was going into.

Walter said he would put a few feelers out to see if anything could be done and, a couple of days later, the situation looked promising as Walter told me he was on the verge of sorting out a deal to shift the complete load of documents.

Although it was at a considerably lower price than we had hoped for, it would provide me with all the finance I needed. Added to this, it meant getting some highly illegal paperwork off our hands.

I met up with Walter in order for him to give me a progress report. This wasn't exactly necessary, but he had developed an annoying habit of phoning up and saying that he had something of great importance to talk about. Invariably, the important conversation entailed talking about some blatantly imaginary deal that he'd concocted involving millions of pounds to be earned. He did this not only with me but several other people, all of whom eventually tired of being called out on the proverbial fool's errand. It wasn't long before the 'boats' around Hatton Garden, which was where he used to hang out, realised just why I called him Walter Mitty.

I was hard pressed to think of a logical reason why Walter had started behaving like this, and finally came to the conclusion that, since we were no longer partners (apart from the lucky briefcase documentation), and that I had 'carried' him for all the years we worked together, then he found himself with no real 'moves'. And so, in order to perpetuate the myth that he had all kinds of deals going on, he simply made them up. Either this or he was quite simply not playing with a full deck. Although I have to admit that he always had a bizarre penchant for telling lies.

A supreme example of this came about when he was first involved with his current wife. For some reason known only to himself, he chose to tell her that he had an ex-girlfriend in the USA, who had three children by him, but with whom he had lost contact. When I asked him why he had told such a meaningless lie, he was at a loss to explain, and merely said, 'I don't know really.' Knowing all this, I suppose I should have been able to anticipate the probable consequences of Walter's deal regarding the lucky briefcase documents. But being eager, if not exactly desperate, to get the poster business under way, I went along for the ride, so to speak.

During the 'progress report', Walter informed me that the buyer for the documents was a very 'heavy' underworld figure. At this stage of the proceedings I should have called a halt, as I felt certain that the documents wouldn't really have been this person's line of work. But there again, if there's a pound note to be earned, all things are negotiable.

Walter went on to say that we needed to get the documents sorted into some kind of order. This in itself was a sizeable operation, due to the bulk of the documents. He told me that he had arranged for this to be done and wanted me to meet him the following day with the goods and he would get the necessary sorting work carried out.

Since I was somewhat wary about the validity of the deal, I told him that I would deliver just a selection of the documents to him. If all went well, we could then do the rest. This suggestion seemed to irritate Walter for some reason or other, but I didn't attach any significance to it. That was how it was going to be done and that was all there was to it. After a few days, and many more phone calls and meetings with Walter, he told me there had been a slight hitch, and the deal with the leading underworld figure had fallen through. No real surprises there. But then he told me that he had arranged another deal with a mutual friend named Herbie. Once again, I had my doubts, but I thought that if this situation was a genuine proposition, then something beneficial might happen.

After this latest development, Walter told me at yet another meeting that another mutual friend of ours, Tall Mick, had a cash buyer for the documents, but it had to be done by the following Tuesday. All at once, it seemed as though there was a mad rush of punters for the documents.

'And?' I remarked.

'And what?' Walter replied.

'What's happening?' I asked.

'I told Mick that we weren't interested.'

I looked at him in amazement. He had already told me the price that Tall Mick was offering and it was more than we had discussed up until then.

'You said what? What the fuck did you do that for?'

'I reckon we can get more money out of him. Besides, we've still got the deal with Herbie going through,' he declared.

I couldn't believe what I was hearing. 'Well, for fuck's sake, get back to Mick and tell him we'll do the deal. Provided he's got the cash, we can get it all sorted out for Tuesday. I'll get the rest of the parcel sorted out straight away.'

I left Walter and collected the rest of the documents from the South London slaughter and took them over to the empty house in Chingford, where I began sorting through them and putting them into some kind of order.

A few hours later, Walter rang me on my mobile phone. 'Good news,' he said.

'Yeah? What's happening then?' I asked.

'The deal with Mick's back on for Tuesday. So we've got to make sure everything's been sorted through by Monday. How you getting on?'

'Yeah, I'm getting stuck in now. What are you doing about the parcel you've got?'

'It's all in hand,' he said.

The following day, having made good progress sorting through the goods, I decided to give Tall Mick a call. 'Mick, it's Steve here.'

'Hello, how's it going?' Mick replied.

'Yeah, fine. That's what I called you up for, to let you know we're on schedule for Tuesday as planned.'

'Sorry? What are you talking about?'

'The paperwork. Your big punter that Walter spoke to you about.'

'That's all off, Steve. I told Walter. But I've got a little order that I could do with today if you can manage it.'

I paused for thought then said, 'Yeah, OK, Mick. What time?'

'An hour's time,' Mick replied.

'OK. I'll meet you outside Walthamstow Dog Stadium.'

An hour later, I was sitting in the passenger seat of Tall Mick's car, discussing Walter Mitty. Mick told me he did indeed have a cash customer lined up for the documents but the man was going abroad and the deal had to be done by Tuesday. But Walter had turned the offer down, saying the price was too low. This much I knew, but surely Walter had got back to him to tell him the deal was now on?

'Yeah. He did. Yesterday, but I told him it was too late. The man has already left. There's nothing to be done.'

I shook my head in utter disbelief. Just what was going on in Walter's head?

'But anyway,' Mick continued, ' he said Herbie wanted them so it didn't make any difference. He said he was going to make arrangements for next week with him.'

By now I didn't know what to believe. 'Have you got Herbie's number?' I asked.

Mick looked through his address book and found the number. I gave Herbie a call and asked him if he had made any arrangements with Walter for next week. He seemed baffled by my question.

'Next week? No, not me, Steve.'

'Did you tell him you were interested in the paperwork?' I asked.

He chuckled, 'No, 'course not. I'll tell you what happened. Walter gave me a call a little while ago and asked me if I was interested in making a bid on the parcel. I told him straight it wasn't really my line of business. I wouldn't have a clue where to go with them. But I did say if I happened to hear of anybody, I'd let him know.'

I thanked him and, after pressing the disconnect button, sat there barely able to believe what was going on. Both Tall Mick and I were at a loss to make any sense of the situation. In fact, I had the impression that Mick wasn't sure whether or not I was telling the truth. Maybe I was just trying to convince him that Walter was a bit of a dope or something? Then, by chance, Tall Mick's mobile phone rang. He answered it and, after saying hello, he mouthed silently to me that it was Walter. He held the phone away from his ear and the pair of us listened in on Walter speaking. He was calling to see if there was any chance at all of the document deal being given the kiss of life, to which Tall Mick replied that it was as dead as a dodo. Finito. End of story.

'Oh, OK, then,' Walter said. 'Whereabouts are you now, Mick?'

'I'm right out in the country, why?' he replied.

'I've got to see you, urgently. It's really important. Could be a lot of money involved. Can you meet me in about an hour?'

'No, I'm sorry, mate. I'm miles away, unless you can come out to me, if it's that important.'

'No, I haven't got any wheels, otherwise I would do. Can't you get down the Garden?' Walter implored him.

'No, I'm sorry, mate, it'll have to wait till tomorrow I'm afraid.'

'All right, I'll give you a call tomorrow then. 'Bye.'

Tall Mick and I looked at each other. But before either of us could speak, my mobile phone rang. It was Walter. Now it was my turn to hold the phone away, so that Tall Mick could hear what was being said.

Incredibly, Walter said, 'I just called to let you know that the deal with Mick is definitely on for next Tuesday, so it's double important to make sure the paperwork's sorted out properly.'

Not really sure what to say, I responded by reiterating what I had just heard. 'So you're telling me it's all definitely still on for Tuesday?' I glanced at Tall Mick as I spoke, who looked just as astonished as me.

'That's right. 101 per cent. Whereabouts are you now?'

'I'm a bit busy, why?'

'I need to see you right away. Urgent.'

'Where are you? What's it about?' I replied, knowing what the answer would be.

'I don't care what you're doing, I've got to see you. I'm down Hatton Garden. How soon can you get down here? Something's come up, could be a lot of money involved,' he said.

'No, I'm sorry, mate, I'm too busy. I'll have to meet up with you tomorrow some time.'

Walter sounded disappointed, and said, 'All right, then, it'll have to wait. Catch you later. 'Bye.'

Again, I looked at Tall Mick. 'I told you, didn't I? As far as Walter's concerned there might be a light on upstairs, but there's definitely nobody at home.'

I now knew for certain that Walter wasn't really on the same planet as the rest of us mere humans, and my brief optimistic expectation was no more than an episode in Walter's make-believe fantasy world.

After this, I told Walter I knew all about his 'silly boy lies' and that I had been with Tall Mick when he'd called him. He seemed embarrassed by this unexpected revelation but, far from trying to explain the inexplicable, he merely excused himself by saying that he was 'just trying to keep the deal alive' — a totally incomprehensible piece of logic as there was no deal to keep alive. I couldn't be bothered to tell him what I knew about the non-existent deal with Herbie. All I knew was that such crass stupidity was exceptionally dangerous. I knew I had to get away from Walter Mitty and have nothing more to do with him. And that's exactly what I did.

Not long into the New Year, I thought I had come across yet another opportunity to raise the cash to fund the poster business. It was a foreign venture which initially seemed to be going well and all concerned were highly delighted with the impressive returns. With the wheels of industry turning smoothly, I decided to get away for a few days, and so Laraine and I drove over to Paris with the children and had a short break shopping and seeing the sights. As a special treat for James, we stayed a couple of days at Euro Disney. Not really my idea of a good time, but he enjoyed himself. Stephanie at the age of 15 wasn't too impressed with Disney's best efforts, but had at least enjoyed herself in Paris.

It was now March 1994 and, upon my return from France, very bad news awaited me. One of my business associates abroad called to say that he had been trying to contact me for the previous couple of days. Disaster had struck.

The foreign venture had come to grief and various people had been arrested. This was particularly bad news for a number of reasons. First, it meant I'd lost most of my immediate capital and, second and more importantly, there was a possibility with the arrests that the trail might lead back to me. This was only a vague possibility but, nevertheless, a possibility. Whether or not it would have been a matter to concern the British police, I wasn't too sure, but I didn't really fancy taking any chances.

Working on the foolproof philosophy that absence is invariably the best defence, I decided to keep out of the way for a while. I went to stay at a town house in Maida Vale where a friend, Dave Hawkins, lived. Fortunately, there was just one spare bedroom left, as Barry, a friend of his — whose most memorable feature was his height, 6ft 9in — was also staying there. He was keeping out of the way due to the fact that there was a warrant out for his arrest with regard to a number of mortgage frauds. So the town house became the *fugitives' retreat*.

With the collapse of the foreign venture and the loss of the capital I had managed to build up, I was very much back to square one. And then the situation became considerably worse and I was plunged into one of the worst and most dangerous periods of my life. With hindsight, it would be more accurate to say that, rather than being plunged, maybe I dived.

It was while I was driving to meet one of the people involved in the failed foreign venture that my mobile phone rang. A voice I didn't recognise asked for Steve and asked when I would have his 175 grand. After asking him what he was talking about, he informed me that he had £175,000 invested in the foreign venture and he wanted it back. I informed him that since everything had been lost and people had been arrested, obviously there was no money to be returned. This wasn't, after all, a business deal commensurate with an investment in ICI or the like. There were no shareholders' meetings and reimbursements of X amount of pence in the pound. The cash was lost and that, sadly, was all there was to it. I told the stranger that he wasn't the only one to lose money and that, under the circumstances, I owed him nothing, let alone 175 grand. After some pointless conversation regarding the money, the voice at the other end of the line said, 'So you're not going to pay up then?' to which I, of course, replied that I wasn't. The mystery caller told me he would be back in touch. Over the course of the next few days, I received several more calls from different people, none of whom I knew, but all connected to the first caller. Each call became more threatening than the previous one and, in spite of my attempts to make some arrangements to meet them, they remained anonymous.

I managed to find out through some other associates in the failed enterprise that the people involved were a firm of Scousers. As far as I could make out, they had dealt with somebody that I had met briefly. The problem arose because this person hadn't been entirely truthful with the Scouse firm or with me. Consequently, when the venture collapsed and their money was lost, they genuinely believed that somebody was trying to have them over.

This came about because what they had been told didn't tally with the known facts of the operation that had come on top. The tortuous trail then led from the person who had told the lies in the first place, but who didn't know how to contact me or who I was, to another contact, and then to the person who had introduced me to these different groups of people originally.

Initially, I wasn't too concerned about the situation, as I knew that I hadn't stolen anybody's cash. The fact that the operation had failed, and that several different groups of people had lost their investment, certainly wasn't my fault, and all concerned accepted the situation as part of the game. All except the Scouse firm and they weren't at all happy.

Since they wouldn't agree to meet me and be told the full facts of the situation, there was little that I could do. Although I wasn't too happy at this latest turn of events, I tried not to let it worry me too much. I always made it policy to give only my mobile phone number to people I didn't know too well and, as that was registered to a fictitious name and address, I felt that Laraine and the children were quite safe at home.

With the little matter of losing virtually all my capital and the possibility of the police looking for me, I had more than enough on my mind, or so I thought.

During the course of yet another heavy-duty phone call and after yet more futile attempts to persuade the person on the other end to meet me, a bombshell dropped into my lap.

'Well, I'll tell you something, pal, if you're not gonna pay up, you'd better get your wife and kids out of the house and emigrate or something.' And then, before I could reply, the anonymous stranger said, 'We know where you live, pal, believe me.'

'What?' I exclaimed.

'Beaconsfield Road. That right, pal?'

I held the phone, stunned and in a state of near shock. I felt an ice-cold shiver creep down my spine. I tried desperately to think of what to say in response, but then the line went dead. I was totally unable to take in the enormity of what I had just been told. The people I loved more than life itself were in danger from an invisible enemy. I felt completely and utterly helpless. I didn't dare mention the problem to Laraine as she was totally unaware of what was going on. Furthermore, I knew there was absolutely no possibility of her moving out, and even if there was, where could we all go? If I moved back home, there was the possibility that the police might arrive on the doorstep with a warrant for my arrest. Whatever course of action I took, the possible consequences didn't bear thinking about. If only I could get to meet these people, whoever they were, I could sort the problem out. And if couldn't, then at least it would only be me who would be facing the wrath of this anonymous firm.

I received another call the following day, when I again tried to arrange a meeting, instead of which I was given an ultimatum — 'Pay up in five days or face the consequences.' By now I was starting to feel like a nervous wreck, barely eating and hardly sleeping, even though I had been prescribed some anti-depressants and sleeping tablets by my GP after I explained to him that I had some serious business problems, and needed something to help me until they were resolved.

At least I knew that Laraine and the children would be safe for the time being. I decided that if, in five days' time, I still couldn't meet up with these people, then I would have to go back home and face whatever consequences fate had in store for me.

After a couple of days and nights of worrying and not sleeping, I knew I was no closer to any kind of solution. Despite all my efforts, I was totally unable to find out exactly who the Scouse firm were or how to contact them. The more I thought about it, the more depressed I became. On about the third or fourth day after the ultimatum, I can recall going to bed at about midnight. I had intentionally drunk a considerable amount of lager and spirits in an attempt to numb my senses. I thought the excessive amount of alcohol might help me sleep. Before getting into bed, I took some anti-depressants and twice the amount of sleeping tablets. I was desperate to get a full night's sleep and believed that twice the prescribed amount of sleeping tablets wouldn't be dangerous.

Sure enough, in my drunken and drugged state I crashed out as soon as my head hit the pillow. But after just three-and-a-half hours I was awake again. The very split-second my eyes opened, all the worries and problems came rushing into my mind. It was as though a floodgate of panic and depression had been opened up.

I knew I hadn't been asleep for long and, as I turned over and then strained my eyes in the darkness to look at my watch, an overwhelming rage hit me when I saw that it was just 3.30am. Without thinking properly, I got out of bed and went into the bathroom. For some bizarre reason, I was so angry and annoyed at being awake, that I grabbed the bottle of sleeping pills and poured them down with a glass of water and then did the same with the anti-depressants.

The last thing I can remember is saying to myself in some kind of frustrated rage, 'Let's see if I can fucking get some sleep now!' I also have some vague recollection of thinking, just before I got back into bed, *'If I can just sleep solidly for a couple of days, when I wake up, I'll have no problems.'* My very last memory is of pulling the covers up to my chin and thinking how cosy and warm it felt. Secure and trouble-free.

I opened my eyes briefly and became aware of an array of tubes and bottles just inches away from my face. But opening my eyes was about the only action I was capable of. That was all I had enough strength for. I immediately closed them again, seduced by the warmth and security that sleep offered. Darkness. Oblivion.

When I finally woke up several hours later, the tubes and monitoring paraphernalia were still there. I lay, barely awake, with absolutely no idea where I was or how I had got there. I was in a bed somewhere. I had various tubes attached to my body. But where was I? I remained still for some time, trying hard to make sense of the jumbled maze of confusion that was running around in my head. Just one question concerned me — where on earth was I?

I knew that if I could work that out, then it followed that I would know how I had got to this place. And from there I would understand just what was going on.

*I'm in a clean, crisp bed somewhere. There's a collection of tubes and equipment. Hospital, yes, that's it. I'm in hospital. But why? I must have had some kind of accident. Yes, I can vaguely recall drinking too much. That's it, I must have got drunk and driven my car. A car? But, no, I don't feel as though I'm injured. I can move my legs, my arms. Pills. Sleep. I can remember being in a bathroom, desperate to get some sleep. All I want to do is sleep. Yes, now I can remember. Oh, Jesus, no, this can't be happening.*

I felt a sudden compulsion to leave the warm, enticing, comfort of the bed I was in. This was no answer. I had to get out of the hospital and try to do something about the problems that were dragging me down.

I pulled myself up and put my feet on the floor. Everything was still very much a confused blur, but I remember having one or two tubes attached to my body and to my head. Whether they were some kind of drips or breathing aids or just leads connected to some kind of monitoring equipment I don't know, but whatever they were I disconnected them from my body.

My clothes must have been on a chair or something beside the bed, because I got dressed very quickly. I recall looking around the ward and seeing a nurse some distance away. I believe she was a fairly large black woman, sitting at a desk doing some writing. She glanced up at me but, surprisingly, took no notice and carried on with whatever she was doing. As soon as I had dressed, I made my way on unsteady legs towards the exit. Again, the nurse at the desk looked up and again she paid me no attention and carried on with her work. I made my way to the main entrance and out into the street.

I looked up and down the busy road, still not sure where I was. But I knew I was in London. My head was spinning and my thoughts fuzzy. I could see two of everything, and the people and cars appeared to be moving along at high speed, with trails of light behind them. I had to hold on to a set of railings to steady myself. After a few seconds, I proceeded to walk along the pavement, not really certain of which direction to take, but painfully aware that I was lurching along like a drunken sailor. A number of times I very nearly toppled over, face forward on to the pavement, which seemed to be drawing me downward like a magnet.

Somehow or other I managed to reach Goodge Street Underground station. Then I realised I must have been in University College Hospital, or possibly the Middlesex. Still struggling to think straight, and realising I must have looked like an escapee from the funny farm, I made a reverse-charge call to Dave and Barry at the house in Maida Vale.

The next thing I can recall is sitting in the front room, talking to the pair of them. They both seemed amazed to be speaking to me, although for the most part I kept fading away and closing my eyes as though on the verge of falling asleep.

They explained to me that, a couple of days earlier, they were both about to go out for the day and got no response from me to their farewells. They looked in on me, seemingly sound asleep. Knowing that I hadn't been sleeping properly, Dave thought it would be best if they let me remain in the land of nod and not disturb me.

Barry told me that, as they were about to depart, something about my state of sleep disturbed him. Somehow it seemed abnormally deep. He tried to rouse me and soon realised that there was something amiss. After trying and failing to wake me, it was clear that I wasn't just having a lie-in. They shook me, and tried everything they could think of to bring me round, but only managed to elicit a dull moaning sound from me. Dave made some strong coffee and they tried to force it down my throat. All to no avail. They decided I had to be taken to a hospital as quickly as possible. Fortunately, one of them had the foresight to check if any of the sleeping pills were missing from the bathroom.

When we arrived at the hospital, Barry carried me into the emergency admissions, over his shoulder. After giving all the details he told the medical staff my name was Stephen Brown. When asked my next of kin, he merely said that he didn't know. After telling them what I had taken, and approximately how much (a great deal), I was immediately given a stomach pump. After that, he was informed it was a case of praying for the best. At an opportune moment, he crept out, and I remained unconscious for something like 30 hours.

As they sat talking to me, they found it impossible to believe I had tried to commit suicide.

'I mean, you didn't even leave a note or anything,' Barry remarked.

I tried to explain, as best I could in my still drowsy state, that I hadn't tried or intended to kill myself, I merely wanted to get a proper night's sleep. Obviously, with the effect of the drink and the sleeping pills I had taken before going to bed, I wasn't truly aware of the enormity of what I was doing. They seemed even more baffled and confused when I said that, in my disorientated and unbalanced frame of mind, I'd had this bizarre notion that, if I could just sleep solidly for a couple of days, then all would be well when I woke up.

When I think about how close I had been to sleeping for a lot, lot longer than a couple of days, it sends a shiver down my spine. Before this dramatic event in my life, I had often been dubious when I had read about people taking overdoses without meaning to. I found it hard to believe that an overdose could be accidental. Now I know from first-hand experience how it can be done.

After shaking hands with the Grim Reaper, I still had the problems of the Scouse firm hanging over my head and, although I was grateful to be alive, albeit in an extremely depressed frame of mind, I really didn't know which way to turn, or what to do for the best. I'm ashamed to admit that there were times when I wondered if I wouldn't have been better off if I hadn't been saved.

After another two or three days, I decided I had to go back home.

At least that way, if it came to it, I would be there to protect my family. I just prayed that the police wouldn't come knocking on the door for me. Then I received another phone call from the firm demanding the money they believed was owed to them. I told them there was no way I would be paying them anything, even if I could. If they weren't prepared to meet me there wasn't anything more I could do.

A short while later, I received another call, and a guy with a Scouse accent said he would meet me at King's Cross railway station. I agreed to be in a burger bar situated in the station itself, and further agreed to be alone. At the time of the meeting, Dave dropped me off a short distance from the station. He then parked the car around the corner and he and Barry kept an eye out for me at an inconspicuous distance.

I waited in the burger bar reading a newspaper, and it wasn't too long before a dark-haired stranger with a moustache came up to me and made himself known. When I had originally agreed to this meeting, I had no way of knowing what would happen. In order to be prepared for all eventualities I had something with me that would ensure that if I was stabbed or shot, then my attackers wouldn't get away unscathed. Fortunately, I found myself talking to a reasonable type of guy who explained that he was an arbitrator trying to find out on behalf of others just what had gone on, and who was telling the truth.

It wasn't long, after asking me various questions and letting me know what his people had been told, before he started to form an accurate picture of the truth of the matter. After a short bit of discussion, he finally said, 'I know you're telling the truth. We'll have to get back to that other lying scumbag,' a reference to the man who had originally told lies in an attempt to wriggle out of the mess he had got himself into. 'Now I know what's gone on, you won't hear any more from us.' We shook hands and he left. To this day, I don't know who he was, and wouldn't recognise him now if he was standing next to me in a telephone box.

The only slight mystery about the whole affair was just how people I didn't know, and had never even spoken to before, had obtained my home phone number and from that my home address. Like most mysteries of such a nature, it was just a matter of elimination. The only person who could have given out my number was a 'friend' in England, who had introduced me to various other contacts. Although I couldn't remember giving this person my number, as he wasn't a particularly close friend, there seems to be no other explanation. Unless of course, Mystic Meg gave it to them.

Finally, the police never came to arrest me and I never heard any more about the matter. The arrests abroad came to nothing.

# CHAPTER 7

## 'Wedding Bells', a Loan Shark and a Printing Press

During the early part of 1994, I managed to secure a couple of deals on the perfume, but I was still a long way off my financial target of £75,000. I had estimated that, apart from the printing press, the cost of various incidentals, such as plate-making equipment and a guillotine, would probably add another £25,000 or so. I decided to sell the house in Chingford and, by the time the mortgage and second mortgage were paid up, I expected to raise something in the region of £20,000 to £25,000.

I had a ready buyer in Barry who was dealing in property, and was interested in buying the house in order to rent it out. He was able to arrange his own finance through the various contacts that he had in the property business.

It was at this time that Ken told me that he had found a buyer for his business and was hopeful for a relatively quick sale. Upon hearing this, I asked him if he would be interested in putting up half the capital required to get the business off the ground, and coming into the business on a full partnership basis. After giving the matter careful consideration, and being assured by me that the orders for the work were guaranteed, Ken decided it sounded like a worthwhile venture and accepted my proposition. Confident that I would be able to raise several more thousand pounds from the perfume, I told Ken to look out for a suitable press, as soon as possible. The wheels were set in motion and I really felt as though my plans were beginning to take shape.

I contacted Ivan, the poster man, and told him the progress I was making, and that there was a good chance that I would be set up by the summer. I wanted to make absolutely certain that he could still guarantee me the work. He assured me the situation was still the same as when we had last spoken and, as soon as I was ready, he could immediately give me orders worth £15,000 per week. I came away from our meeting feeling more confident and optimistic than ever.

A week or so later, Ken called me with the news that he had located a press that seemed like a good deal, even though it was for sale at £60,000 plus VAT. However, as Ken knew the owners personally, they were prepared to do a part cash, part invoice deal, which would save us a considerable amount of VAT. With the £20,000 or so that I would clear from the sale of the house, plus £10,000 in cash that I had, together with Ken's share from the sale of his business, I felt confident in telling Ken to sort out the fine details. I gave him £5,000 to use as a holding deposit on the press. The final agreement was that the company would invoice the sale at £20,000 plus VAT coming to a total of £23,500 to be paid by cheque, and the balance of £40,000 to be paid in cash.

The sale of the house was on course for completion some time at the beginning of August. However, Ken was unable to guarantee that the sale of his business would be finalised by then, and would probably carry on over till September or possibly even later. By now, I had become fired with enthusiasm for the fledgling enterprise and was determined to make sure that we didn't lose the press (or my £5,000 deposit). We had already promised the company that the funds would all be in place by August, and so it was imperative that I raised the balance one way or another, as there was another interested customer waiting in the wings.

I spent the next couple of weeks trying to borrow the money from various friends on the promise of a good return on their money. My first port of call was Lynda McQueen who, not surprisingly, turned me down flat. In spite of all my pleading and cajoling, she was adamant, her savings were staying where they were — in the bank. Apart from which she only had about £20,000, she said, although that would have been half the problem solved.

I tried a few other friends, but all to no avail. But then fate stepped in, when one of my punters on the perfume, a man called Pat, told me that he could put me in touch with a money-lender, or rather a loan-shark to be more accurate. I was a bit wary at first as, obviously, such loans don't come cheap and are usually secured, not by property, but rather by the borrower's limbs and, in the case of a £40–£50,000 loan, by his life.

My first reaction was to turn down the offer, but after a while I thought, perhaps, that it might be worth the risk. I asked Pat to find out what the monthly repayments would be, and then I would be in a position to decide whether or not it would be worthwhile.

A day or two later, I was told that on a loan of £50,000 the repayments would be £3,000 per month and that only represented the interest. After giving the matter some thought, I reasoned that I would only need the loan for a couple of months or so, and the profits from the poster printing would more than cover the loan cost, and with the sale of Ken's business, we would be in a position to repay the loan within three or four months at the most. Although the interest would amount to something like £12,000, I calculated that, with the profits from the printing, it would still be more than worthwhile.

I got back to Pat and he arranged a meeting in a restaurant in Battersea. Walking across to the table where his contact was devouring a huge bowl of pasta, I felt as though I was looking at a ghost. 'Wedding Bells,' I declared.

The man looked up from his food, strands of spaghetti dangling from his closed mouth being sucked up like a collection of worms. He nearly choked. Hurriedly attempting to swallow the mouthful of food, he managed to splutter my name, 'Steve, I don't believe it!' He wiped his mouth with the napkin and then reached across and shook my hand vigorously.

'So you two know each other then?' Pat said.

'Yeah, Fucking 'ell. 'Course we do. Why didn't you say it was Steve Jory?'

'You didn't ask,' Pat replied and we sat down opposite the large man with a face like a battered lump of rock.

'Fuck me, Tony,' I said, 'I haven't seen you since when?'

'1981. Wanno. D Wing. I'd just come out of the block and you were doing a long sentence for perfume,' Wedding Bells replied.

'That's right. I can't believe it's you. So what you been up to?' I said.

'I was out in Australia for seven years. Soon as I got out of the shovel, '82, I had a bit of trouble with a couple of faces out of Canning Town and I thought bollocks to it, and pissed off to Aussie.'

'What were you doing out there?' I asked.

'I met up with a few of the chaps grafting there, doing the run out. Got into that, earned a fortune. Really cracked it,' he replied.

'And now you're in the money game? You must be holding plenty to be sharking. So I suppose you're going to do a special rate now you know it's me?'

Wedding Bells laughed. 'It's not me, you silly sausage, I 'aven't got a tanner. You know what I'm like, every penny I get hold of goes to the bookmakers' benevolent fund. Naw, I'm just the mug on the firm. Y'know, a bit of heavy work, a bit of muscle if people don't keep up their repayments.'

'Oh, right. So who is it that's actually lending out the dough, then?' I asked.

'It's a Jewish businessman. Name's Jack. Nice fella. Everybody calls him Jewboy Jack. You'll be all right, Steve. But anyway, how come you need to lend this kind of dosh? I heard you was cracking away when you got out. I heard you was a multi-squillionaire, yeah?'

Bearing in mind his grim appearance, I always found his turn of phrase somewhat anomalous. 'Silly sausage' and 'squillionaire' just didn't sound right coming from his well-worn features.

'Well, you're half right. I was cracking away. Got right back on my feet, had a factory out in Acapulco, getting hold of a fortune. Then it all went pear-shaped. Lost the lot. Got nicked again. The Old Bill called it the biggest international fraud of all time. A couple of newspapers said it was a £300 million swindle,' I told him.

Wedding Bells's eyes lit up. 'I remember now. It was even in the papers out in Aussie land. Just before Christmas 1983, right?'

'Yes. That's the one.'

Wedding Bells slowly shook his head. 'Y'know, I wondered if that was anything to do with you. Well I never. Dear me, dear me ...'

The three of us stayed in the restaurant drinking and eating for the next couple of hours, during which Wedding Bells and I talked in more detail about what we had both been up to since Wandsworth Prison in 1981. Before Pat and I left, I made arrangements with Tony 'Wedding Bells' to meet the money lender, Jewboy Jack, at noon the next day in a small back-street pub in South London.

On our way home from Battersea, Pat said, 'Tell me something, Steve, why does everyone call Tony "Wedding Bells"?'

I laughed at the thought. 'Well, when I first knew him, years ago, he had a reputation for always playing practical jokes. I remember one day he got hold of some rope and tied it to the wheels of a fruit and veg stall that was close to a bus stop. His pal kept the fella that ran the stall busy talking and then, as soon as a bus pulled up, he got on it and hooked the end of the rope around the pole on the platform where you got on at the back of the bus. Then, as the bus pulled away and dragged the fruit stall along the main road, Wedding Bells was standing on the platform laughing his head off. Mad as a hatter, I'm telling you.'

Pat laughed and said, 'So why do they call him Wedding Bells, then?'

'Well, if ever he happened to pass a church where there was a wedding going on, he couldn't resist slipping in and sitting right at the back. He'd wait until the vicar got to the part where he asks if anyone knows of any reason why they shouldn't be married. Y'know — "Speak now or forever hold your peace." And then he'd jump up screaming and shouting out that the bride was already married to him. He'd make a right old row, and go rushing down the aisle. When he got to the bride, he'd pull her veil up, and then say, "Oh, I'm very sorry. Wrong one. Carry on!" And then he'd run out laughing his head off.'

Pat laughed again, but said, 'I wouldn't like it if he did that to my daughter or sister. Would you?'

'No. I wouldn't. I think it's a wicked thing to do. But everyone was too scared to tell him he shouldn't do it. He doesn't give a fuck for anyone. I remember he threatened to give Lenny McLean a slap a few years ago when McLean dug out some kid in a pub. McLean didn't want to know. Bottled it in front of everyone. Backed right down. Mind you, he came unstuck one day. As he was running out of the church, he tripped up. All the men in the church, top hats and tails, they steamed into him. Gave him a right kicking. Put him in hospital for two weeks. Still, serves him right, I suppose. Didn't stop him, though!'

The following day, Wedding Bells and I arrived promptly at midday as arranged. The pub was almost deserted with just two people standing at the bar.

'This way,' Wedding Bells said, and walked behind the bar and into a back room, where, sitting on a sofa, was a small, dark-haired man about 45 years of age. He was immaculately dressed in a navy blue suit and seemed to be studying a set of accounts laid out on a coffee table in front of him.

'Jack?' Wedding Bells said as we entered.

The man looked up, as though taken by surprise. 'Tony. You shouldn't creep up on people like that!' he said.

He stood up and shook Wedding Bells's hand, who turned to me and said, 'This is my friend, Steve, that I mentioned to you, Jack.'

'Good to meet you, Steve. Sit down, make yourself at home.'

Wedding Bells and I sat down in the armchairs opposite Jewboy Jack, who asked what I was drinking.

'Wait there, gentlemen, I'll just go and ask the girl to bring them into us. A lager for you, Steve, and a vodka and orange for you, Tony, right?' he said, rising from the couch.

Seconds later, he was back in the room and clearing the bookwork off the coffee table. After the barmaid had brought the drinks into us and left, closing the door behind her, Jewboy Jack leaned back and assumed a relaxed position with his arm on the back of the couch. 'Now then, Steve, Tony tells me you're after borrowing some money, that right?' he asked.

'That's right,' I replied.

'How much was you looking for?'

'£50,000.'

I had decided to borrow more than I needed, to cover various incidentals and, since the difference in monthly repayments between £40,000 and £50,000 was just £600, it didn't seem to make much difference.

Jewboy Jack nodded his head slowly and, after a few seconds' pause, spoke. 'You know the terms, Steve?'

'Yeah. Tony told me,' I replied.

'That's quite a bit of money, Steve. 50 grand comes to 3 grand a month. You sure you don't mind paying that much?'

'Yeah, I understand. It's OK, I can afford it.'

'And I don't know whether Tony remembered to mention, but the agreement's for 12 months. Should you want to settle up before that, it's a big penalty.'

'No, Tony forgot to mention that. How much is the penalty?'

'Six months' interest.' Jewboy Jack's face remained expressionless as he noticed me gulp. 'You change your mind?'

I thought about it for a moment, then pictured the 4-colour printing press. 'No. That's OK. I still want to go ahead,' I confirmed.

'I just want us both to be sure about this, Steve. After all, I wouldn't want any misunderstandings later on, you know what I mean?'

I understood what he meant, and told him I was perfectly clear about the arrangements.

'Tony tells me you need the money for a printing press, that right?' Jewboy Jack asked.

'Yeah. A 4-colour press,' I told him.

'What you intending to print on it, or shouldn't I ask?'

'No, that's OK,' I replied, and went on to explain to him the basic outline of my poster enterprise.

Jewboy Jack seemed suitably impressed, and nodded his approval. 'Sounds like a good idea, Steve. I'm sure you'll do well. There's no problem with the cash. When did you want it?'

'Soon as possible,' I replied.

'Well, what's the date today? Yeah, 15 July. Well, your best bet,

Steve, would be to wait till 1 August, otherwise you'll be liable for a month's interest on the first, if you take it now. You see, all payments are made on the first of the month, and we charge the same for part of a month as for a whole month, see what I mean?'

'Yeah, I know what you mean. OK then, I'll wait till 1 August,' I told him.

'You know, Steve, we don't lend this kind of money to just any old Tom, Dick or Harry.' Jewboy Jack paused and peered over his glasses at me. 'It's only because Tony recommended you that we're even talking about it. That right, Tony?'

'Yeah, that's right,' Wedding Bells agreed. 'But like I said, Jack, Steve's OK. I know there'll be no problem.'

Jewboy Jack turned to me and smiled. 'Tony's a good friend, Steve, you remember that. I've known Tony a long time, and if he says you're OK, that's fine by me. Just don't let him down now, will you?'

'No, I won't,' I assured him.

After that, the deal was agreed and confirmed for 1 August, with Jewboy Jack taking down all my personal details such as my address and phone number and, perhaps more significantly, the personal details of my children, such as their ages and where they went to school. I left the meeting feeling confident about the future and working out in my mind how much Ken and I would be making over the next few months. I estimated that we should be clearing something like £8,000 per week between us and, quite possibly, more if the poster business went as I'd been led to believe it would.

I went to see Ken to give him the good news about the finance, and told him to arrange delivery for 10 August, as the sale of the house was due for completion on the eighth. We worked out the various other pieces of equipment we would need, such as a guillotine, a plate-maker and a few other sundry items. All told, apart from the £58,500 balance owed on the press, we needed about £12,000, so with the loan money and the £22,000 from the sale of the house, we were well covered.

On 1 August, I once again met Jewboy Jack at the South London pub, where he handed me £50,000 in £50 notes, which I put into the briefcase I had with me.

'Now then, Steve, don't forget, we've got a deal here. On 1 September we'll meet again, and you'll have £3,000 for me, right?' he said.

'Right,' I replied.

'And Steve, the first means the first, not the second, or the third, but the first — we clear on that?' he said emphatically.

'Yeah. Perfectly.'

'Good man.'

With that he wished me luck, and told me he looked forward to seeing me again in a month's time. The cheque from the sale of the house came through on time, and the press was duly delivered on 10 August, as arranged. Over the next week, the rest of the equipment arrived and within a few days the whole operation was set up and ready to run. But then disaster struck. Ken's buyer pulled out. I sat in his front room listening in a state of near panic as he explained and apologised.

'I'm sorry, mate, I can't believe it myself,' he said.

'So what we gonna do about the poster business then?' I asked. 'You'll still be able to work at that, won't you?'

'Not really. You see I'm down the firm six days a week as it is,' Ken replied. 'There's no way I'll be able to find the time to get away to do anything worthwhile.'

The enormity of my predicament rose like a spectre before me. Without the poster business up and running, I had no way of keeping up the interest repayments. Although I had enough money to keep them up for a couple of months, obviously that would be no solution, and would only be putting off the inevitable. Ken wasn't aware of my dilemma but, of course, even if he had been, there would have been little he could have done about it. The fact of the buyers pulling out wasn't his fault and I couldn't expect him just to walk out on his regular business.

Ken came up with a suggestion which at first seemed like a good idea. He told me that he would make a few enquiries with regard to finding a printer who would work cash-in-hand. This gave me some hope. I implored Ken to do his best, but reminded him that, if he did come across someone, then it had to be a person who could keep his mouth shut, as strictly speaking the business wasn't very legal. If the relevant authorities came across it, then we'd be slapped with a considerable VAT bill, plus a legal action for various breaches of copyright. Ken explored every avenue, and made as many enquiries as possible, but unfortunately he made no headway, and I was back to square one.

The 1 September deadline was fast approaching and I was beginning to worry. Although I had enough to make the first payment, what concerned me were the subsequent ones. I went to see Wedding Bells and explained the situation. As he listened, his expression became more and more concerned. When I'd finished talking, he sat there without uttering a sound and, at length, exhaled long and hard. 'I think you're in a bit of a pickle, Steve,' he said, then added, 'In fact, I'd say you're in a fucking lot of pickle!'

'Yeah, I know that, Tony, but what the fuck can I do about it?' I said.

'To be honest, at the moment I can't think of anything. Can't you sell the press or something?' he suggested.

'I could do, but it'll take time. First of all, we'd have to find a buyer. Who knows how long that would take?' I told him.

'Well, I'll tell you something, Steve, you're going to have to go and see Jack and explain the situation. You can't just bury your head in the sand. This puts me in a blooming terrible position. It really does.'

'Yeah, I know.'

Wedding Bells gave me a knowing look. 'You want me to give him a call now and fix up a meet?'

'Yeah, I suppose you'd better, then,' I said, somewhat apprehensively. 'Might as well get it over and done with.'

The following day, Wedding Bells and I went again to the pub in South London.

Jewboy Jack listened without saying a word as I explained the situation, and then at length said, 'Well, to be honest, Steve, I don't really see what this has to do with me.'

I looked at him, not really knowing what to say. He looked directly at me and, after a slightly embarrassed pause, I said, 'Well, I just didn't want you to think I was mucking you about or anything.'

Jewboy Jack's expression remained blank. 'Steve, you've got to understand a couple of things here. What I think or don't think doesn't come into it. This is business. We've got a deal, right?'

'Right.'

'Well, that's all there is to it, then. As we agreed, on the first of every month, you will pay me £3,000. Any time you want to stop paying, the solution's relatively simple — you pay back the 50 grand plus the penalty. OK?' Jewboy Jack's tone was uncompromising, and I realised there could be no other options. It was a black and white situation.

I felt an overwhelming sense of despair, and stared at the half-empty glass of lager on the coffee table before me. 'So, then, that seems to be it. Anything else, Steve? Tony?' Jewboy Jack's words interrupted my thoughts and I looked up at him. I knew my expression conveyed my feelings of deep dismay, and I muttered an almost inaudible, 'Yeah, OK, then.'

'Well, I'll see you on the first, then, Steve.' Jewboy Jack stood up and extended his hand, which I shook half-heartedly as I rose from the chair. I nodded my agreement, and turned to leave. Wedding Bells got up at the same time, and went to follow me out. 'Can you hang on for a minute, Tony?' Jewboy Jack said. 'I just want to have a quick word with you.'

'Yeah, sure,' Wedding Bells replied. 'I'll see you in the bar, Steve.'

I went out to the deserted pub and ordered a large vodka and ice, which I gulped down. I leant against the bar, a million thoughts racing around my head, trying to figure a way out of my situation. After five minutes or so, Wedding Bells came out and we both left the pub. I sat in the passenger seat of his car in silence.

'You OK?' Wedding Bells asked.

'Yeah. I suppose so,' I replied. 'What did Jack want to see you about, anything interesting?'

Wedding Bells made no reply, and concentrated on the traffic.

'Tony?'

'Er, yeah. I heard you, Steve.' Once again Wedding Bells remained silent, then said, 'Well, actually, he wanted me to make sure that you completely understood the situation.'

'And?'

'You remember Danny Goodman?' he asked.

'I remember him, but I didn't really know him. Got shot, didn't he?' I replied.

'That's the one. Well d'you know what that was about?'

'Not really.'

'Well, he owed these people some money.'

'How much?'

'About 35 grand. Well, anyway, he fucked them about. He was a compulsive gambler, y'know. When he couldn't pay them back, he tried to fuck off out of it. Well, anyway, as you know, he ended up dead. Understand what I'm saying?'

I thought about his words before speaking. 'Yeah, 'course I understand. If I mess these people about, I'll end up dead. Just like Danny Goodman.'

'I just don't want to see anything happen to you, Steve. Know what I mean? Like, you've got to get this thing sorted out one way or another. If you can't give them their money back, you've got to keep up the payments. And don't whatever you do, miss any. Just one late payment and you put me in an embarrassing situation. Y'know what I mean?'

'Yeah.'

# CHAPTER 8

## Bernie and the Scan-Man

Obviously, I now found myself in a very precarious situation and, as much as I hated the idea, I decided the only possibility was to try to sell the press and, in the meantime, keep up the repayments. I approached Ken and asked him to make some enquiries concerning the possibility of selling the press through the trade. He told me the quickest means of selling it would be to a dealer but, of course, the problem would be how much they would be prepared to pay for it, in all probability nowhere near as much as we had paid. Ken showed me a trade journal and pointed out the lists of machines for sale. With the general state of the printing industry in decline, and businesses going broke every day, the machines on offer seemed endless.

Ken, however, did what he could and made several calls to some of the dealers in the journal. The majority weren't even interested, as they had a surplus of stock, and the few that expressed any interest at all offered ridiculously low sums in the region of £30,000. Over the next few days, I tried desperately to find a solution to my predicament. Ken had placed an advertisement in the trade journal for a private sale, which attracted no response whatsoever. Whichever way I looked, I could see no way out. Then Wedding Bells came up with a suggestion, 'Why don't you do some hooky-work on the press?'

'Such as what?' I replied.

'Well, I'll tell you something now, if you could get any Scottish money done, y'know, £20 notes, I could do as many as you can print. Provided they're good, of course.'

'Well, for a start, you need the right plates. And, second, I haven't got anyone to run the press.'

'Well, what about the old geezer you was gonna get to do the posters? Won't he do it for yer?' he said, trying his very best to be helpful.

'He works down his firm, that's the problem. And, anyway, I don't think he'd do anything that serious,' I answered him.

'Well, for a start he's only got to work a few weekends. I know people what's done the Jeckyll notes at weekends. And surely he'll help out if he knows what a big problem you've got?'

I thought about his suggestion. 'I don't know, I suppose he might do. Mind you, I haven't got the plates, so I can't do them anyway.'

Wedding Bells shrugged his shoulders. 'I wouldn't have thought it would be too hard to get the plates done somehow. Like, I mean, Steve, you gotta get somefin' sorted out a bit lively. Know what I mean?'

'Yes. I do, Tony. I'll give it some thought.'

After speaking to Wedding Bells, and thinking about his suggestion, the more it seemed like a solution to the problem. But where could I get someone to do the plates? I asked a few close friends, but had no luck. And then I remembered Bernie, and his contact who gave him the low-down on the postage stamps.

As I had anticipated, Bernie was quite willing to make a few enquiries on my behalf and, within a few days, came back with the good news that he had found someone who would do the work. Bernie, who now lived on the Isle of Wight, had travelled to High Wycombe to see his friend who had advised him on the postage stamps. His friend had given him the name of somebody who had the right equipment to do the job and, after Bernie explained what was required, he agreed — at a price.

Bernie's contact had told him that what we needed was a set of 4-colour film. This was obtained from a computerised scanner. And that was what he had.

'So what you're telling me, Bernie,' I said, 'is that he's a scan-man?'

'Yes, I suppose you could call him that.' Bernie went on to explain that, once we had the set of film, we could make as many plates as we needed from it. Basically, from what Bernie told me, when it comes to reproducing something as complicated as currency — and, in particular, English currency — a good scan-man, with access to a state-of-the-art scanner, is an absolutely essential requirement. Although the Scottish currency isn't as complicated as English bank notes, the problems are still basically the same.

In simple terms, a scanner is a high-tech machine involving the very latest computer-aided processes to do what is termed 'colour separation'. Imagine a crisp new £20 note being fed into one end of the machine, a few appropriate buttons and dials being pushed and twiddled, and then through the wonders of modern day science, at the other end, a set of black-and-white film is delivered with several different images of a £20 note on it. That's a rough approximation of what happens.

Of course, the whole process is considerably more complicated than that, and is very much dependent upon the sophistication of the scanner, and the skill and expertise of the man operating it, the scan-man. What, hopefully, is then produced are several sheets, rather like photographic negatives, from which a full set of printing plates can be produced.

Producing the actual plates is a relatively simple process, involving the individual sheets of film being placed on a special aluminium printing plate and then exposed under an infra-red light which leaves an image on the plate. As litho plates tend to wear out after a while, it is a good idea to have an exposure unit available in case one of the plates should start to wear or become damaged during the course of a print run. That way, the plate can be removed and a replacement made within half-an-hour or so. It's always important to keep the wheels turning if one is to be awarded the Queen's Award for Industry. An unlikely accolade under the circumstances I must admit, but nevertheless one doesn't like to let one's standards drop, now, does one?

After all this technical detail, Bernie gave me the price — £20,000. After explaining my dire financial straits, Bernie got his scan-man to agree to take £10,000 on delivery of the film, and £12,000 as soon as I was in production and drawing some money in.

Just days afterwards, Bernie had a set of film, together with a chromalin. This is effectively a copy of how the end product will turn out using the original film to create it. I looked at the chromalin, which showed an absolutely perfect copy of a Scottish £20 note. Absolutely perfect.

I had no hesitation in giving Bernie what was very nearly my last £10,000. All I had left was £5,000. But here in my hands, in the shape of a perfect copy of a Scottish £20 note, was the answer to all my financial problems.

Now all I had to do was convince Ken to do the work over a

couple of weekends. But even after explaining my problems, and how desperate I was, Ken just couldn't bring himself to agree to it. As much as he wanted to help me, he just didn't have the nerve. I could see I would never be able to persuade him.

Having the film in my possession, however, and knowing how much the Scottish £20 notes would increase my life expectancy, I wasn't about to give up that easily. I put another proposition to Ken. If I could find a printer to operate the press, could we rent the workshop? Ken thought about it and, knowing how serious my problem was and, I suspect, feeling a trifle guilty at not having the nerve to help me out, he finally agreed.

'But I don't know what's going on in there. As far as I'm concerned, it's soft pornography,' he said.

'I thought you just said you don't know what's going on in there?' I replied with a grin. But Ken just seemed puzzled by my remark.

'Pardon?' he asked.

'It's OK, Ken. I'm off to find a printer to do some soft porn.'

I already had a possible candidate in mind. Eric, the printer who had done the stamps for me. I wasn't sure whether or not he could operate a 4-colour press, but I certainly prayed that he could on my journey over to see him.

It was all good news and, as he wasn't very busy, and wasn't working at his own little firm at the weekends, he was more than happy to help me out. And, yes, he could operate a 4-colour press.

# CHAPTER 9

## A Heavy Boat and a Raft for a Drowning Man

Shortly afterwards, I received a call from Wedding Bells telling me that Jewboy Jack wanted a meet. I knew it couldn't be anything to do with the first payment, as I still had a couple of day's grace, but nevertheless I decided to take the £3,000 with me. Paying a day or two in advance made no difference to me in financial terms.

Upon our arrival at the pub, Jewboy Jack was waiting with another, younger man aged about 35. He had short, black hair and a tanned complexion, which gave him a Mediterranean appearance, but his voice belied his looks. Although well spoken, his accent was unmistakably that of a Londoner. I knew full well who he was, as I'm sure Jewboy Jack realised, when he said, 'Steve, this is Eugene.'

Eugene extended his hand, and stared hard at me in a penetrating manner. As I shook his hand, he said, 'How are you, Steve? I've heard a lot about you.'

Feeling apprehensive, I smiled, and wondered just what he meant. Although I didn't know Eugene personally, I knew of him, a man whose reputation as one of the most feared heavies in London, preceded him.

'Nice to meet you, too, Eugene, I've heard a lot about you as well.'

Eugene's stare remained locked and he allowed himself just the vaguest hint of a smile. 'Nothing bad I hope, my friend,' he said.

Aware how thin the ice could easily become, I resisted the urge to make any kind of ambiguous reply and played safe by showing him the respect I knew he felt was due. 'No, nothing bad. Nothing bad at all,' I assured him.

Eugene's tentative smile widened. 'I'm pleased to hear it. Let's go through to the back.'

Jewboy Jack told the barmaid to bring a tray of drinks through to us, and we made our way into the office. Once in the back room, it soon became clear that this was more than just a social gathering, but then, of course, I'd been aware of that when Wedding Bells had originally told me about the meet.

After the barmaid had brought the drinks in and closed the door behind her as she left, Jewboy Jack came to the point of the meeting. 'I've been telling Eugene about your little problem with the printing press,' he said.

'Oh yeah, right,' I replied.

'Yes, Steve,' Eugene said. 'Seems like you've had a bit of bad luck there, my friend.'

'I suppose you could say that,' I said.

Eugene paused before speaking again. And, again, he fixed me with a penetrating gaze, as though he was trying to induce some kind of reaction on my part. I maintained eye contact as a means of concealing the apprehension I felt.

'So what's the situation with regard to the payments, then? Have you got it sorted out?' he asked.

Knowing I had the first payment in my pocket, and feeling I had the problem solved with the forged Scottish money, I was able to say confidently, 'Yeah. I've got it all sorted out. As a matter of fact, I've got the first payment on me now.'

Both Eugene and Jack seemed slightly taken aback by this.

'Really?' Eugene said.

I reached into the inside pocket in my jacket and pulled out an envelope containing £3,000 in crisp new £20 notes. I had taken the precaution of changing up some of the fifties that Jewboy Jack had given me into twenties. I didn't want them suspecting that I was merely paying them back with their own money, which of course I was.

'3 grand,' I declared as I reached across and placed the package on the table before them. 'It's all there, I checked it myself. And then again.'

Eugene appeared satisfied. 'So you're going to be OK with the repayments, then?'

'Yes. I should think so,' I replied. But my words were ill chosen, as I soon realised.

There was a brief silence and, after a suitable pause, during which

Eugene again studied my features intently, he said, 'Don't tell me you "should think so", Steve. That makes me think that maybe you're not too sure. Understand me?'

I knew what Eugene was doing. Having pre-empted him by making the first payment a couple of days in advance, he clearly still felt the need to stamp his authority on the situation. After all, that was what he was there for.

'I didn't mean it like that,' I hastily replied.

'Well, that's what it sounded like,' Eugene said. His tone of voice sounded just a shade more aggressive than before.

'Well, believe me, I *didn't* mean it like that. Really, there's no problem,' I assured him.

'I know there's no problem. No fucking problem at all.' Eugene's tone was now downright hostile, and I knew that whatever I said, whatever words I chose, he would seize upon them to make sure I was in no doubt whatsoever about how earnest he was. Even though he must have known such a display of 'heavy manners' was completely superfluous, such was his persona that he persisted in driving home to me the gravity of the situation.

Pointing his finger at me, he said, 'If there's ever any more problems ...' — I resisted the urge to remind him that he had just said there was 'no fucking problem at all' — 'then believe me you are in serious trouble. Serious fucking trouble, my friend. Understand?'

'Yes.'

'I don't ever want to hear from Jack that you might not be able to make a payment. This is strictly fucking business. No excuses, no fucking nothing!'

Eugene stopped and once again the penetrating stare of a man on the brink of losing it seemed to pin me to the back of the chair.

'Is that fucking English to you, is it?'

By now the implied threats were coming out several decibels louder than when Eugene had first spoken to me.

'Yes. Believe me, I understand, Eugene.'

Another pause. I was aware of the lack of sound coming from either Wedding Bells or Jewboy Jack. Eugene, still staring, still inert, looked as though he was waiting for the rage within him to subside.

'Just make sure you do, my friend,' he said at length. I dared not risk incurring any further outbursts by opening my mouth, and so merely nodded in agreement. It did occur to me that if the fact of my making the payment a couple of days in advance evoked this kind of reaction, what would have happened if I'd been late? There's no pleasing some people!

Then the pendulum that so patently governed his temperament

swung back and Eugene was all smiles and actually patting me on the back and wishing me the best of luck.

It wasn't long afterwards that Wedding Bells and I left the pub. We walked silently to his car and he drove me back to North London.

'Why the fuck didn't you tell me it was *him* behind it?' I said.

'I couldn't. That's why I emphasised to you in the first place that it was a right heavy firm. You can't say I didn't tell you, Steve. Besides, I didn't think there would be any problems. And, anyway, would it have made any difference if you'd known about Eugene being involved?'

I recalled how confident I had been about the poster business, and how eager I was to get my hands on the money. 'No. I suppose not,' I conceded wearily.

'Anyway, once you get the Scottish money done, there won't be no problems. Right?' he said, trying to instil some positive thinking into me.

'Right,' I said.

'Well in that case, izzy-wizzy, let's get busy.'

I smiled at Wedding Bells's unlikely words of encouragement. We continued the rest of the journey in silence and I thought about the predicament I was in. In debt, big time, to one of the most dangerous men in London. A genuine, bona fide gangster. A man who had most definitely buried several people to my certain knowledge. I then consoled myself with the knowledge that the Scottish money coup should solve the problem. That was all there was to it. The Scottish money had to come off. It had to.

That day, I contacted Eric, and told him I needed to check out the Scottish money film as soon as possible. He was quite agreeable to starting as soon as I wanted, and the next day, Saturday, we were over at Ken's workshop making the plates. This took Eric about an hour or so, and then we were ready to try them out.

Positioning the printing plates turned out to be more complicated than Eric had anticipated, as each one had to be 99.9 per cent accurate, due to the nature of the finished product. With a regular, straightforward, 4-colour process job, such as the posters, such pin-point accuracy isn't necessary. All that occurs is a slight difference in the tones of the various different colours if one of the plates is a fraction out of position; barely noticeable on a printed poster. But, of course, on a £20 note, be it Scottish or English, it really doesn't do if Robbie Burns and the Queen look as though they've just returned from a two-week holiday on the Costa del Sol.

On a modern, state-of-the-art computerised machine such as the one Ronald had during the lucky briefcase affair, this wouldn't have been such a problem. But on our press all the positioning had to be done by hand, and it was very much a case of trial and error.

Eventually, after a dozen or so false starts involving re-positioning and then a short run, and then a tiny adjustment to the left, and then another run, and then a further fractional movement, the plates were positioned as accurately as was humanly possible. By now it was early Sunday morning. We had been working solidly through the night.

'That's as near as I can possibly get it,' Eric commented, a weary, drained tone to his voice. We both looked down at the last sheet that had come off the press. It would be no exaggeration to say that I felt like crying.

'But what about this poxy chromalin?' I asked.

Eric shrugged his shoulders in a resigned gesture of despair. 'That's the problems with chromalins. They always look better than the actual print. That's because they are produced by a different process. Everybody in the business is always complaining about them.'

I listened in a state of tired shock, my eyes glued to the printed sheets I held in my hands. 'Well, it shouldn't be allowed. It ought to be a criminal offence,' I said, but nevertheless the hard, brutal, kick-in-the-bollocks truth of the matter was — a blind man could have seen it was a forgery.

'Isn't there anything at all that we can do? Like, you know, maybe all it needs is a bit of fine-tuning on the film or something?' I spoke as much in desperation as anything else.

Eric paused and stared down at the Scottish forgeries. He shook his head and, as I looked at him, hoping to spot just the tiniest glimmer of hope emanating from his tired being, I could tell he had the kind of dejected look of total despondency that a man who knows his business assumes when he also knows he's flogging a dead horse. But I was willing him on to give me even a straw to clutch at. Anything.

'If you want, I'll show the proofs to a chap I know. I'll see if there's anything he can do or suggest to improve the film. It's up to you,' Eric said.

'If you know him well enough and can trust him, then by all means. Anything's worth a try,' I replied.

We cleaned up the press and tidied up the workshop, and at 7.00am on Sunday morning we locked up and left. I was tired and exhausted and just a tiny bit worried. I had barely four weeks left before the next payment was due. If the film couldn't be improved, what would our hero's next trick be? Learn to play the harp, I suppose.

On Monday, I spoke to Eric who had been to see his friend first thing that morning. He pointed out several different things and wrote out a small list of possible improvements. But as he gave me back the film,

Eric said, 'Don't hold your breath, old chum. My friend didn't think they could be improved using the same equipment they were produced on. But like you said, anything's worth a try.'

I agreed, took the film and paid him £500 for the weekend's work, which seemed to please him. I called Bernie and informed him I was returning with the film.

A few days later, the new, improved film was ready. The following weekend, I had a sense of déjà vu, as Eric tried again with the latest set of film. But, in spite of my prayers and promises to The Almighty that I would always be a good boy, the poxy plates were no better than the first set.

The only noticeable difference was that a blind man might not have known the notes were forgeries. But to the vast majority of the population, the sighted ones, they would have stood out as blatantly bad forgeries. We finally had to admit defeat and late on Saturday afternoon we cleaned up. I gave Eric another £250 and apologised for all the messing about.

On the Sunday morning, I travelled down to Bernie to return the set of film, together with the sheets that Eric had tried unsuccessfully to print, approximately 500 in total. After looking at them, Bernie agreed they were pretty appalling.

'So you'll have to tell the scan-man I've got to have my 10 grand back, Bernie,' I said.

I sat on his couch with my head in my hands knowing that the return of 10 grand would do little more than keep up the repayments for a short while. But at least it would give me a breathing space, and time to think.

Bernie coughed nervously. 'Erm, that's what I was going to, er, speak to you about, Steve.'

*'Oh no. Please don't say what I think you're going to say,'* I thought to myself. I looked up at Bernie, and clearly he could see by the look on my face that I was in some distress. I smiled a silly disbelieving smile and shook my head. I remained silent and waited for him to continue.

Another nervous cough. One or two 'er-errums' and then Bernie started actually speaking.

'My, er, mate, well, it seems that his business is in a bit of trouble,' — more smiles and coughs on Bernie's part — 'Well, er, actually, it's a bit more than that — his firm is well and truly in the shit. On the verge of bankruptcy actually.'

I continued shaking my head, and tried to speak. 'So what ...' — my first attempt at understandable communication came out in the form of a high-pitched squeal, not dissimilar to the uncontrollable vocal strains of a young boy in the throes of puberty; now it was my turn to clear my throat — '... so what are you trying to tell me, Bernie?' I said.

Deep breath from Bernie. 'He's used the 10 grand to pay off the firm's creditors.'

Bernie stepped back and dropped the sheets of paper he was holding as I let forth a loud, howling kind of noise, reminiscent of some poor wounded and demented creature about to be devoured after a long and debilitating attempt to escape his tormentors.

'No, Bernie, tell me you're having a little game with me. Please, Bernie, this just can't be happening, tell me it's not so.' As I pleaded with him, I thought about the constant flow of prayers, all the promises, and found myself looking up at the ceiling. Bernie seemed slightly taken aback and tilted his head to see just what it was I was looking at.

In the overwhelming trauma of the moment, I was once again overcome with religious outpourings. 'Oh Lord Almighty,' I cried, 'where art thou in my moment of need?' I started wringing my hands and making all the movements that I seemed to recall Charlton Heston making in the *Ten Commandments*.

No doubt thinking that I had completely flipped my lid, Bernie took another step further back. 'Pardon? You all right, Steve?'

At the sound of his voice, I was at once back in more secular surroundings. 'What? Oh, er, yeah, sure. I was just wondering what the fuck I'm gonna do now.' I began chewing furiously on my thumb nail. 'How d'you know the bastard spent it all? He might just be saying that.'

Bernie shook his head. 'That's what I thought. So I told him that the people involved were really heavy gangsters. Like the Kray twins.'

'And?'

'He showed me the cheques he'd written out. He also showed me the repossession order that's been taken out on his house and his machinery. He shit himself when I said the people would kill him if the film isn't any good and the money isn't returned.'

Looking at Bernie, I knew it was a hopeless situation. Since there was little doubt that the man had spent the money, there was certainly no point in making a bad situation worse by paying him a visit and threatening him. And as I certainly wasn't anything remotely akin to a latter-day Kray twin, I wouldn't have derived any satisfaction whatsoever in beating him up just for the sake of it. It looked as though I might have to start learning to play the harp sooner than I'd expected.

Bernie's sincere and sympathetic apologies rang hollow as I got into my car. 'If anything crops up, Steve, if there's anything at all that I can do to help, let me know. Anything, Steve, anything.'

At the time, I was unaware that the type of scanner necessary to produce the quality of colour separation essential for our purposes was a state-of-the-art, computerised piece of equipment that involved something called an optical disc. Without it, the film produced would never be up to the required standard.

'Thanks, Bernie,' I said half-heartedly and waved goodbye. I left Bernie's place feeling more dejected and despondent than ever.

Now I've often heard it said that the Lord moves in mysterious ways. How true this is, I couldn't really say. I mean, what's the point? Why move in mysterious ways? Why not just come straight out with it and fire a thunderbolt from the sky with a note attached to it saying something like, 'Oh, all right then. You're not really a bad sort of chap. Turn left at the end of the road and you'll find a holdall full of cash in an empty telephone box.' I suppose that's probably what happened to the lucky person who found £150,000 in cash in a holdall in a remote telephone box at the time of the Great Train Robbery. But then, the person handed it all in to the authorities. Now that really *is* moving in mysterious ways as far as I can fathom. Absolutely unbelievable. What can it all mean? I ask myself. Perhaps that's why The Almighty doesn't bother with anything like that any more. No point in pointing people in the right direction if they're going to behave in such an ungrateful fashion, I suppose.

But, in my case at least, it would seem that he hadn't completely given up. Five minutes after leaving Bernie, my mobile phone rang. It was Gersh, an old friend of mine. He knew about my predicament and that I was hoping to sort it out by means of the Scottish notes. In fact, he had said he had one or two moves for them himself.

At first, it seemed to me that it was just the notes he was calling about as he said, 'How are you getting on with the highland games?'

'Don't ask,' I replied. 'Complete fucking disaster. No good whatsoever.'

'Really? Well, as it happens, I've got something you might be interested in then. Whereabouts are you now?' he said.

'Quite a long way away. Where are you, indoors?' I replied.

'Yeah. Come round as soon as you can. I'll be in all day.'

A couple of hours later I was knocking on his door. After seeing me in to the front room and pouring me a beer, he produced a folder. 'Have a look at that,' he said.

I pulled out some sheets of film. I looked down at them and saw several distinct images of £20 notes. My heart started pounding, and for a moment I could have sworn that the Queen had a wry smile on her face and was winking mischievously at me. I screwed my eyes shut and then opened them again. I wasn't dreaming. This was real. Really real.

'Where d'you get these?' I asked.

'Off a pal of mine. As it happens, you know him. He's desperate to get them printed. He's got all the paper and everything, but he hasn't got a printer. What d'you reckon?'

Bearing in mind what a disaster the Scottish money had turned out to be, I wasn't getting too excited. I knew from painful experience it was virtually impossible to tell how good the film was before it was actually printed.

I told Gersh about the weekend's heroic failure and he told me that his pal had assured him that this particular set of film was absolutely, definitely, as good as it could possibly be without being the genuine article. Apparently, it had been done in Germany by a corrupt employee who operated the most technically advanced scanner in the world for one of the biggest graphic companies in the world. Fritz the Scan-Man was an expert operator who had been doing the same kind of legitimate work for the previous 20 years or so. On the point of retirement, he had decided to boost his pension with a few extra Deutschmarks by doing a bit of unauthorised overtime.

After listening to Gersh and looking down at Herr Scan-Man's film, I found myself looking up at the ceiling for the second time that day. 'Why can't you just be a bit more straightforward, eh? What is it with you? You like playing games or something? Is that it?'

'Steve? You all right?'

'Er, what? Oh yeah. Sure.'

Gersh looked at me with a dubious expression on his face. 'Want another beer?' he asked.

'No thanks. I'm going to shoot off. I'll take these straight over to my man right now,' I replied.

'OK, when can you let me know, then?'

'I'll give you a call tomorrow, and we'll go from there.'

With those words I left and immediately made my way over to Eric's home. Being fully aware of the extremely dire straits I was in, he agreed to check the film out the following day. I drove home feeling just a bit more optimistic about my future prospects than I had been just a few hours before.

By lunchtime the next day, Eric and I could see that Fritz's film was everything that Gersh's pal had claimed it was. It really was the best forged note I had ever seen. Without extremely close scrutiny, it was virtually indistinguishable from the genuine article. All that was missing at this stage was the intermittent silver line, the serial numbers and the watermark, none of which would present any real problems.

I rang Gersh, and arranged to meet him at a local pub. I took with me half-a-dozen samples of the counterfeit twenties which I showed to an appreciative Gersh shortly after my arrival at the pub.

'Pity they haven't got any numbers or silver lines on them. We could have had a cheap drink for the next couple of hours,' he commented.

We stayed in the pub all afternoon celebrating, and ended up rolling out of there slightly drunk, to say the least. I got a cab home and told Gersh I'd wait for him to get back to me in the very near future. As drunk as I was, I remembered to emphasise to him the urgency of the situation, and he was equally adamant that he would put the wheels in motion as soon as was humanly possible.

The very next day I was making the journey back over to Gersh's house. He had been in touch with his pal and told him about the samples I had given him, and how good they were. Up to this point, it was very much a case of so far, so good. And then we came to an impasse. Gersh explained that his pal wanted to pay me a set rate for doing the work. However, what he wanted to pay and what I was prepared to accept were two very different figures.

The only possible solution would be for me to meet his pal. Since Gersh assured me that I knew the man, and wouldn't have any objection to working with him, I agreed. Gersh called the person in question, and he was equally agreeable to meeting me. At this stage, Gersh suggested that, as I would be dealing direct with our mutual friend, he would bow out of the operation and just take a 'drink' out of it as a form of an introduction fee.

Gersh told me the name of our friend and I immediately remembered him as somebody I had known not very well quite a few years before. I had never actually done any business with him, although he had been involved to some degree with the theft of a million pounds' worth of Persian rugs in 1979, an episode that resulted in an acquittal for me and one or two others at the Old Bailey. The last I had heard of him, he was something to do with the management of the late Lenny McLean who, years later, wrote a best-selling autobiography entitled *The Guv'nor* shortly before his death at the age of 49 from cancer.

I met up with our friend, whom I'll refer to simply as Dan, that evening. I explained to him that I had the perfect set-up for carrying out the work, but not under the terms that he expected. He wasn't too happy at first, and I soon found out that he was the type of person who was prone to silly temper tantrums if he couldn't get his own way. But in spite of this, little Dan, or Dinky Dan as I called him, eventually came round and we worked out an acceptable financial arrangement. The wheels of industry were set to start rolling.

# CHAPTER 10

## Dinky Dan, the KO Man; Eric Waits for a Licence

Dinky Dan explained to me that he had a large quantity of security paper he wanted to use for the notes. Whilst not exactly the same as genuine banknote paper, it nevertheless had the distinct advantage over more readily available paper of being resistant to ultra-violet light. This meant that the counterfeit notes wouldn't light up like a Christmas tree when subjected to the standard security test that most shops and bars employed by means of a small box housing an ultra-violet tube. This, combined with the superb quality of the printing, would certainly make any other counterfeits on the market seem to be no more than ... counterfeits, so to speak.

Although Dinky Dan knew that I could sort out the printing without any real problem, he was rather concerned about the silver line on the notes. This, he knew, was a completely different process to conventional 4-colour litho printing.

I got the impression, without him saying as much, that he had got a batch printed some time earlier, and that the silver line had proved something of a major problem. I knew that a little firm had done some twenties at the beginning of the year, round about Easter 1994, and had employed a few women to apply the silver lines using hand-operated hot-foiling machines.

This had presented several problems, not least of which was the security aspect. Having a group of women travelling to a workshop in the East End of London and carrying out that kind of serious work is most certainly a cause for concern. Apart from this, with the women being inexperienced in this type of work, there were all kinds of production problems involving the heat control on the machines. Consequently, the quality control wasn't all that it should have been and an unacceptable number of the notes were badly singed. All things considered, it was a wonder the workshop didn't catch light.

It was clear from the outset that Dinky Dan wanted to impress upon me that this was very much his operation and that he was in charge. He tried to do this in a particular way that manifested itself in the style of his speech. Not surprisingly, we had a great many mutual friends and acquaintances and it wasn't long before the name of Bearsie cropped up, who was well known, amongst other less savoury things, for his involvement in the funny money business.

After telling me that he had worked with Bearsie a great deal over the years, I expressed the view that I would never have anything to do with him.

'From what I know of him, he's no good,' I said. 'I wouldn't trust him as far as I could throw him. Apart from which, I can't stand loud-mouth bully-boys.' I went on to say that, as far as I was concerned, he was typical of all bully-boys, inasmuch as he picked his victims very carefully. 'Mind you,' I said, 'the last I heard of him was a few years ago. Apparently, he dug out a young kid in a club in Stratford. Started mouthing off to his girlfriend. Unfortunately for him, the kid left the club and then returned with a couple of friends plus baseball bats. As I heard it, they gave him a real good bashing.'

Dinky Dan laughed and remarked that he recalled the incident and then said, 'As it happens, I knocked him out once.'

'Oh really?'

'Yeah. We had a row about something and I steamed into him. Knocked him spark out.'

From this impressive statement, I gathered that I was supposed to be in awe of the tiny terrier, as he continued to pepper his conversation with accounts of how he had knocked out this person and then that person. Dinky Dan, the KO man!

In the course of our initial conversation, during which Dinky Dan had knocked out half the East End of London, I happened to mention the name of a pub I frequented. Immediately, he told me he knew the landlord, a friend named Derek, with the inevitable comment, 'Yeah, I had a row with him. Now I really *did* knock him out.'

I got the impression from the manner in which he made this

statement that perhaps he had been just a touch over-enthusiastic in describing his other KO victims. Apart from which, Derek was the least likely person in the world to be rolling about in a fight, being a dumpy little chap with an inoffensive personality.

Another mutual acquaintance he mentioned was a petty crook known as Mother Greens, so called because of his absolute inability to keep his mouth shut. Although he was known to have little deals in various things such as counterfeit twenties, I personally wouldn't have anything to do with him, as it would have been tantamount to placing a full-page advertisement in the *News of the World*.

Once again, Dinky Dan had a tale to tell, regarding an occasion when, together with Mother Greens and several others, he had been pulled in for some kind of fraud. He told me how, being placed in a cell next to Mother Greens, 'I heard him having a little cry to himself.'

'What did you do, call out, "There, there, little Mick"?' I said with a smile. Dinky laughed and then I said, 'Did you knock him out?'

The hint of sarcasm in my words went over his head as he merely replied, 'No. No need for that, but I had to have a few sharp words with him.'

During the course of our business relationship, I got used to this style of conversation, to the extent that I took it all with a pinch of salt and smiled sweetly when Dinky Dan went off on one of his flights of fancy and reeled off the seemingly never-ending list of KO victims.

He was pleasantly surprised when I told him that applying the silver strips would be no problem. I had Bernie in mind for the work. I knew that his plastics moulding business wasn't doing too well and, of course, he was morally obliged to do whatever he could to help me out.

My final agreement with Dinky Dan was that he would provide the paper as well as all the necessary film and artwork for the various different serial numbers we would be using. I would get the printing and silver line work done; he would arrange the sales. From the start, he assured me that he had more orders than we could handle. Cash on. And we would split the profits.

During the week, I collected the paper for the first run of 100,000 and delivered it to the workshop ready to start production at the weekend.

My next port-of-call was Bernie, on the Isle of Wight. I phoned him first and arranged to meet him, when I would give him the details of a 'little job' he might be interested in, cash-in-hand. Without knowing what it was, his immediate reaction was to say, 'I don't care what it is, I'll do it.'

The following day, once again sitting in his front room, I explained exactly what the little job entailed. 'Y'know those useless fucking Scottish twenties that I gave your idiot friend 10 grand for?'

Bernie looked embarrassed and nodded, saying 'Yes?'

'Well, I've got them done properly — at least I will have in a couple of weeks. Only they're not Scottish, they're English. I'll have something in the region of 100,000 pieces. But they won't have any silver lines on them. That's where you come in.'

'How much does it pay?'

'By rights, I shouldn't pay you fuck all until I've got my 10 grand back.' I paused and Bernie started to squirm and move about in his seat. 'Actually, I'll pay you 10p per note. And don't you dare say it's not enough!'

Bernie's eyes lit up, as he immediately worked out that the total sum was £10,000. 'Yes, mate. No problem. I'll do that for you.'

I told him I would supply him with a couple of hand presses required to apply the silver line to each note, and that I would get back to him as soon as I had the machines sorted out for him. I knew that Bernie would be able to manage the job OK, and that he would have no problem sorting out a couple of reliable, trustworthy people to work with him.

Having sorted out all the initial problems, I was looking forward to starting work at the weekend. Eric and I arrived at the workshop early on Saturday morning. My job for the most part was to help Eric as he cut down the sheets of paper to the correct size. Effectively, I was the labourer, moving the stacks of paper into position, and various other jobs that left Eric free to get on with the main work. Another role I fulfilled was that of security guard. That's to say, I spent a great deal of time peering out of the window at the long drive leading up to Ken's house and the workshop. As soon as a visitor came into sight, I would let Eric know that there was a car coming along the drive and he would switch off the machine. (Later on, we installed an advance warning security system, making me virtually redundant.)

Generally speaking, there weren't too many unexpected guests, and the only cars that came along on a regular basis were those of Ken's wife or his daughters, Clare and Julie. These presented no problem as Cherie, his wife, and the girls just went straight into the house and didn't concern themselves with what was going on in the workshop.

That first weekend, we managed to get all the watermarks completed and the sheets were left to dry. Seeing the stacks of sheets piled ready for the next stage, I couldn't help feeling an amoral sense of achievement, coupled with excited anticipation at the thought of all the cash that would soon be rolling in.

The following Thursday, after managing to sort out the affairs of his business so that he could leave it vacant for a couple of days, Eric and I started on the main printing work. As with the Scottish notes, a fair amount of time was spent just setting up the press and making sure the printing plates were perfectly aligned and in exactly the correct positions. But at least this time we were guaranteed that the finished product would make it all worthwhile.

By Sunday, the main body of printing work was complete, and all that remained now was for the serial numbers to be added. For this, several plates were made up, with different numbers on each, 21 in all, and the job of printing them, though time-consuming, was relatively straightforward.

After completion, I detected just the merest hint of apprehension on Eric's part as the unequivocal criminality of our joint enterprise must have dawned on him. Slowly shaking his head, he remarked, 'Fuck me old boots. If a bloomin' Bobby was to walk in here now, me old mate ...'

'No problem,' I said. 'We'll just say we're waiting for the licence.'

'Do what?'

'Well, you've heard about having a licence to print money, yeah? We'll say we sent our application form off to the Bank of England and we just thought we'd run a few notes off while we're waiting.'

Although we both laughed, the idea of the police coming across our newly established cottage industry was certainly a sobering thought. But as I assured Eric, just like Bill and Ben at the end of the garden, so long as nobody knew we were there, then there was simply no way that the gardener, in the shape of the counterfeit currency squad, would come knocking on the workshop door.

That same day, I rushed the notes down to Bernie who, in the meantime, had been practising on a couple of hundred samples that Eric had printed when we had first proofed Dinky Dan's film. By the time I had delivered the 100,000 notes, he had perfected the technique and, with a couple of trusted family friends to help him, he estimated that he would have the lot completed in ten days. This was good news, as I had anticipated several unforeseen problems with the silver foilings, particularly with the exact position of the line.

But my fears proved to be unfounded as Bernie had mastered the technique of using the hand-operated machines without any major problems. I informed Dinky Dan that the first batch would be ready within a few days but that I needed some money to pay the printer and the silver line man. He told me there was a slight hold-up and that the money was a problem. In short, his cash-up-front punter wasn't immediately available.

This created something of a problem not only for me, from the point of view that both Bernie and Eric were impatient to be paid, but also for Dinky. He seemed to be in something of a panic as, presumably, he owed a considerable amount of money. Without really knowing the facts, I got the impression that he might have borrowed some cash to pay for the film and paper.

As the need for quick cash was mutual, I offered to sell the first batch the moment they were ready. I had a couple of reliable people in mind whom I knew would be eager to buy the new super twenties. Dinky was more than agreeable to this proposal, and then even suggested that I could pay him some money out of the first batch to be sold, as he had debts that he was being pressed for. He had pulled up a few thousand pounds for various expenses such as the hot-foiling machines and so I agreed, but I wasn't too happy about the situation.

Although this veered away from our original agreement, it suited me, as I needed to start getting some cash in as soon as possible. Apart from the need to keep Eric and Bernie happy and having a considerable amount of bills to pay indoors, the spectre of Jewboy Jack and Eugene was looming on the horizon. I had less than two weeks till the next payment.

As soon as Bernie had 10,000 notes ready, I made my way down to the Isle of Wight and, without bothering to stop for a cup of tea, headed back to London with a box of goodies on board. Wasting no time, I called my punter, a little leprechaun named Don, from the ferry. 'You're fruit order's ready,' I told him and a couple of hours later, I was in the lobby of a hotel in the West End talking to my little Irish friend. After a couple of drinks and general small-talk, we left the hotel and Don drove off with the box of twenties on the understanding that he would give me a call in a couple of days and pay for the parcel. Don was a trustworthy character so I had no qualms about giving him a bit of bail on the goods.

The next day, I went to see Dinky Dan and, after sitting in his kitchen discussing the overall situation, which as far as I was concerned was extremely promising, I sensed that the KO Kid was on edge. The tone of his voice seemed to be building up to something. After a short while, he asked me if I had any money for him.

'Money?' I asked, surprised by his question. 'What money?'

'I need some money. You've had a nice few quid off me. What you done with that 10,000 a couple of days ago?'

'Yesterday, actually.'

'Whatever. So how much you got for me?'

'I haven't got anything. I haven't been paid yet. And, anyhow, most of that's already accounted ...' but before I could finish, the blood rushed to Dinky's face in an almighty surge of red and in a split-second he screamed 'WH-AA-T?' and slammed the table across the room. (This wasn't quite as impressive as it sounds, as it was a very lightweight piece of furniture.) As various pieces of crockery that were on the table, including a cup of tea that I had just put down, went flying in the same general direction as the table, Dinky Dan leapt up from his chair, which went hurtling backwards, and propelled his body towards me. I, too, jumped up in a simultaneous movement, and prepared myself for a fight in his kitchen. This all happened in the blink of an eyelid, and I pulled my right fist back ready to smash it into his face, expecting him to start throwing punches from all directions. But, somehow, at the very last minute, he stopped with the top of his head just a couple of inches away from my chin. His face was an amazing psychedelia of reds and he puffed himself up to his maximum height and stuck out his chest.

It was more luck than judgement that I didn't lash out at him in a reflex action, but the sight of him huffing and puffing, but not actually doing anything other than screaming and shouting, almost made me burst out laughing. I had this bizarre image of him standing before me with steam coming out of his ears and nostrils, rather like some cartoon character out of *Tom and Jerry*. As if this wasn't enough, Dinky suddenly turned away and proceeded to smash up his kitchen. Suppressing the urge to laugh, I said, 'What are you doing, Dan? You're smashing up your home, try and calm down, eh?'

He continued kicking the cupboards and a bin that was in the corner (it was just as well he didn't have a cat) and slamming a few cups and saucers on to the floor. This ludicrously infantile display of temper lasted for about ten, maybe twenty seconds, during which time I tried to shout some sense into him.

All the while, however, I kept my fist clenched ready to give him a dig, should his attention be diverted away from the perfectly innocent household goods, back to me.

Rather surprisingly, he quickly calmed down, and marched over to the kitchen sink under the window that looked out on to the garden. By now his temper tantrum had subsided into a weird-sounding collection of grunting and wheezing noises. I think that probably the shock of seeing me standing up ready to have a row with him, as opposed to cowering in some form of submission, took him completely by surprise. But, if he had thought that by regaling me with all his fanciful *Rambo*-style tales I was in any way frightened of him, he surely found out he was mistaken. It took him a couple of minutes to compose himself and start talking in a reasonably coherent fashion.

'You finished now?' I asked him.

'Er. Yeah,' Dinky mumbled.

'Well, d'you mind making me another cup of tea, then? I seem to have spilt the last one.'

At this he managed a slight smile, not dissimilar to a small child who's just broken his own toys out of temper.

'D'you often behave like that ?' I asked.

'Yeah. I can't help it. Everyone says I've got a bad temper.'

I wasn't impressed by this limp excuse and told him so. 'Well, you might as well know right now, Dan, if anything like this happens again, you can find yourself another printer. I haven't got time for this kind of silly behaviour. You ever thought about seeing a doctor, or perhaps a psychiatrist? Perhaps they could give you some pills or something.'

Dinky Dan made no response, opting to sulk for a while, and eventually made a grudging apology. I reassured him that everything was in hand, production-wise, and that the money would soon come rolling in. The little sulker saw reason.

Soon afterwards, his wife came home. She was a charming and attractive woman quite a few years younger than him. As she walked into the kitchen and surveyed the scene, she looked at Dinky and asked what had been going on. Her wary gaze turned to me, whereupon I smiled and said, 'Nothing much, Dan just had a little accident.'

Noting the lack of surprise on her face, I concluded that this might not have been the first time that Dinky Dan had vented his rage on the fixtures and fittings. No doubt, given enough time, in Dinky Dan's mind he would come to believe that I was another of his KO victims.

It seemed that my warning about having to find another printer had had a sobering effect and, after that, business proceeded without mishap. I managed to make Jewboy Jack's payment in good time and the money started to come in at a steady pace and the wheels of industry were turning smoothly.

The first 100,000 notes were sold in no time at all. The initial reaction when they first hit the streets was very nearly one of panic. The daily tabloids were full of reports warning the general public and businesses — in particular pubs and clubs — to be extra vigilant. The fact that the notes were not detectable under the ultra-violet security light really caught everyone unawares. I remember being told by one of my punters that, after the weekend of their début appearance, one unfortunate publican in Hackney Road, in the East End, went to bank his takings and to his dismay was told that nearly £1,000 of it was counterfeit twenties.

There were even reports in the newspapers of banks themselves handing out the counterfeits; over the counter and via cashpoint machines. One report I found rather amusing was of a police force withdrawing £2,000 in twenties from the bank in sealed packets. Back at the station, after dividing the money up for whatever reason, Mr Plod discovered that £700 of it was counterfeit. All good fun and games!

There was, however, one little fly in the ointment. When Eric had run the first batch, although we had the 4-colour set of film, and film to print 21 different serial numbers, we decided to produce the film and plates for the watermark ourselves. The reason for this was that the image, being invisible unless held up to the light, was impossible to scan. It was a print that needed to be done from original artwork. This wasn't too difficult as all that was required was a basic shape of the Queen's head and various bits of shading to denote the royal features. Being something of an artist, I quickly knocked up a decent copy using an ordinary soft lead pencil. From this, Eric produced the film and, from the film, the plates. At first, the printing of the watermark proved to be a bit tricky because, of course, although printed, it had to be invisible to the naked eye.

By a process of experimentation through the press, any colour difference is constantly noticeable and easily corrected. But, although this is fine with a straightforward printed image, with an imitation watermark that has been printed to be undetectable unless held up to the light, any such variation isn't visible to the naked eye.

Consequently, some 50,000 or so of the first 100,000 gave the Queen a heavy five-o'clock shadow. This was also accentuated, in part, by the fact that the special inks being used changed slightly during the drying process.

Amid all the publicity surrounding the invasion of the 'bad apples', it wasn't too long before the tabloids seized upon this fact. One or two of the punters started to panic and, shortly afterwards, Hungry Jim called me, sounding like a worried man. I met him at our regular rendezvous, a small café next to a garden centre. I walked through the door and immediately noticed the worried expression spread across his fat face. I sat down opposite him and he immediately started bleating about the problems caused by the watermark.

'Have you seen this?' he said, passing me a copy of the previous day's *Sun*. It was opened at an article which described how the watermarks on the forgeries flooding the market depicted HRH in dire need of a shave. It labelled the twenties 'The Bearded Lady Forgeries'. I found myself laughing out loud as I read the comments of an investigating police officer, who stated, 'Her Majesty the Queen looks more like an armed blagger about to go out on a bit of heavy work.' Unfortunately, Hungry Jim wasn't able to see the humour in the situation and declared, 'I've got quite a few punters who want to back out. They reckon everybody knows about them now.'

Since I had realised beforehand what Hungry wanted to see me about, I was able to anticipate his desire to return the Bearded Lady notes. But to be forewarned is to be forearmed, as Shakespeare once said. Knowing Hungry as I did, I had the perfect riposte.

'No problem, Jim,' I said. 'Let me know how many you've got to come back and I'll get your money sorted out straight away.'

'Er, well, if you want, I'll just swop them over for some without beards. That'll be better for you, won't it?' he said.

'I'd love to, Jim, but I haven't got any more left.'

'What? Well, when will there be more ready, then?'

There was a concerned note in his dulcet tones, quickly followed by a look of alarm as I replied, 'There might not be any more. I can't get the paper. So when shall I pick up the returns then?'

Hungry's eyes scanned the café and he ran his tongue around his lips and over his Oliver Hardy moustache. The inner workings of his avaricious brain seemed to be contorting his features, like a cash till on overload.

'Er. Erm, I think I might hang on to them, then, just in case I can do anything with them,' he said.

'Sure? It's no problem, Jim. I'll pick them up this afternoon if you want,' I continued.

Hungry shook his head vigorously. 'No, no. That's all right. I'll leave it as it is, I think.' Not for nothing was he known as Hungry Jim.

I spun a similar yarn to the handful of punters who, like Hungry Jim, initially wanted to return the Bearded Ladies. Suffice it to say, none of them were ever actually returned.

The printing of the delicate and finely-tuned job such as Her Majesty the Queen's currency was very much a learning process. And it wasn't too long before Eric became something of a virtuoso in his newly acquired skill as counterfeiter *nonpareil*. And, of course, by now HRH was clean shaven. In fact, Wedding Bells thought the five-o'clock shadow batch was a deliberate ruse on my part.

'Just when everybody thinks they can spot the Jeckylls by looking out for a bearded lady, old Queenie goes and has a dig. They won't know whether they're coming or going. What a giggle!'

He smiled to himself and put the box of twenties into the boot of his car. As he slammed it shut and shook my hand, he slowly nodded his head in a gesture of unbridled admiration. He turned and opened his car door, and walking away I heard him mumbling, 'Genius. Sheer fucking genius.'

Although the business was running as smooth as a baby's bum, Dinky Dan invariably found something to get worked up about, and every now and then I had to endure the boredom of one of his silly outbursts. However, there was never anything as extreme as the kitchen fiasco. It normally took the form of Dinky moaning about delivery times and then declaring that he had found another printer and wanted his film back, together with the paper that I was holding in stock.

I would then reply, 'Fair enough, sort out a suitable van for me and I'll drop it all off in the morning.' Generally speaking, it wasn't too long before Dinky changed his mind, and it was back to business as usual. After a while, I got used to his childish behaviour and regarded it all as some kind of little game that he felt the need to play in order to satisfy his autocratic phobias. This was all water off a duck's back as far as I was concerned, but there were one or two other aspects about the business that I wasn't too happy about.

Little Dinky Dan told me that on every other batch of 100,000, the profit had to go three ways, as he had included the man who had the scanning contract in Germany. In fairness to him, he had brought this up during our initial negotiations, but upon reflection I had my doubts. After doing business for a short while, he didn't strike me as the type of person to give away a third of the profits on a regular basis to a man whose role was over and done. Once maybe, possibly twice, but not ad infinitum.

Secondly, the payments on his sales were taking longer to come through, even though we had originally agreed they would be on a cash-up-front basis. And finally, he wasn't moving anywhere near as many as he had said he had taken orders for in the first place. This meant that I was selling more and more to make up the figures to a worthwhile amount. I was on the point of making my feelings known, and sorting out a new deal, when an incredible opportunity presented itself. One of those genuine, once-in-a-lifetime opportunities.

# CHAPTER 11

## Vindiloo and the Crime of the Century

One of my regular punters was an old friend by the name of Tony Van Derlee or, Vindiloo as I nicknamed him. Like most of my friends, he lived by his wits, ducking and diving. With regard to the twenties, he took regular orders of a couple of thousand pieces. This was very nice, but he kept on about a contact he had abroad who would definitely be placing a mega order, cash up front. He explained that this man had access to a Swiss deposit account that contained untold millions belonging to a South American drugs cartel. Apparently, the cash was stored in vaults which the contact had access to without suspicion. His plan was to exchange possibly $50 million for the counterfeit twenties.

Of course, I had my reservations about the deal. Uppermost in my mind was the possibility that it might be a set-up of some sort. Either it might be police involvement or it might be a firm at the corner — in other words, somebody trying to get their hands on a large quantity of the twenties without paying for them. And there again, of course, it could be genuine. All things are possible.

Vindiloo was adamant that he had dealt with his contact many times before on several big deals, and there had never been any problems. He went on to tell me the man was a multi-millionaire, and certainly wouldn't be involved in anything underhanded. As far as

Vindiloo was concerned, he was a man of integrity. I doubt very much if the drugs cartel in South America would have agreed with Vindiloo's assessment of his character, but I took his point. After some time, it seemed as though something might be happening when Vindiloo told me his contact had ironed out the problems, and he wanted me to make preparation for two million notes to be ready over the course of the next few months.

The plan was to deliver the notes in batches of 100,000 over a period of four weeks. My share of the profits was an agreed amount of £7 million, payable at the rate of £350,000 after each delivery.

As excited as I was at this prospect, I was still very wary. It all seemed too good to be true. And experience has taught me that, if something seems too good to be true, it's usually because it is. For this reason, I delayed mentioning the deal to Dinky Dan and coming to an agreement on his share of the profits until I was absolutely certain it would come to fruition.

In an effort to allay my fears, Vindiloo offered to introduce me to his contact. This I was vehemently opposed to. If the deal was on the level, I most certainly didn't want to get too close. It took a much braver man than me to pull a stroke on those charming chaps from South America. Then again, perhaps braver isn't the most accurate word — others that spring to mind are greedier and crazier. Or just downright insane.

In fact, I felt uneasy just knowing the bare outline of the scheme. Too much information can be a very dangerous privilege. As far as I was concerned, I was merely supplying a large quantity of counterfeit £20 notes. Their ultimate use was not my concern.

'Listen,' Vindiloo said as we discussed the situation in a pub near to where he lived, 'I've got to go and see the man tomorrow. I'm flying to Spain. Why don't you come with me?'

'No. Like I said, I don't want to meet him. You go, I'll stay here,' I replied.

But Vindiloo was persistent, and eventually I agreed to go along for the ride if only because a couple of days in the sun appealed to me. Vindiloo told me he was being picked up by the man's driver in the morning and flying over there in his private jet.

As tempted as I was by the sheer opulence of the situation, I refused the offer of a free lift, and opted for a standard BA flight to Malaga Airport on my own, the ticket paid for in cash by me. I had agreed to go to Spain on the condition that I didn't meet the man and that he didn't know I was there. But there was method in my madness. I decided this after Vindiloo explained to me that his contact had a yacht.

'I'm telling you, it's the biggest fucking boat you've ever seen in your life. Your eyes will be on stalks when you see it.'

'In that case, then,' I said, 'I'll meet you over there. Where's his yacht floating? Puerto Banus?'

'Yeah.'

'All right, I'll find out the flight details, and we'll sort out a time to meet at the bar on the corner of the port as you go through the car entrance. The one next to that bar Sinatra's. Know where I mean?'

'Yeah, I know it.'

'Good. I'll be sitting outside, no doubt pouring an ice-cold lager down my Gregory. And, please, whatever you do, don't bring anyone with you on the meet.'

'OK. Promise.'

The point of my travelling to Marbella was ostensibly to see the kind of league that Vindiloo's man played in. I would be able to see for myself the pair of them sitting on the deck of the yacht talking and eating, and then come to a decision as to whether or not I felt the man was genuine. Apart from this, I really fancied the break.

I got out of the cab at the entrance leading into the port. I glanced down at my watch and noted the time, 3.00pm, made my way to the meeting place and sat down at a table. I ordered a beer and looked around at the sun-drenched luxury surrounding me, in particular the boats and yachts berthed in the port. By the time my beer arrived, my eyes had focused on one particular craft, a yacht so *everything* it caused me to raise my sunglasses. No doubt about it — my eyes were most certainly on stalks. *'If that's the man's rub-a-dub, then you weren't exaggerating, Tony,'* I thought to myself. *'I am impressed.'*

Five minutes later, half-way through my second beer, I saw Vindiloo making his way towards me. Grinning broadly, he sat down and signalled to the waiter. 'How are you, me son?' he said.

'Fine,' I replied, ordering another couple of beers from the waiter standing by our table.

'What do you think about the old boat, then?' he said and motioned with his outspread arm towards the yacht.

'The big one, that's it?' I said.

Vindiloo looked as though nothing less than major surgery could remove the Cheshire cat grin from his face. 'What did I tell you?'

'You told me, Tony. You told me.'

'Why don't you come and meet my man?' Vindiloo suggested. There was no denying I was sorely tempted, particularly when he added, 'We can stay on his yacht for a few days, won't cost a penny. Yeah?'

I was on the verge of succumbing to this invitation into a world of sheer unadulterated luxury, but somehow managed to refuse. Some time in the future maybe, but not just yet. At length, Vindiloo tired of trying to entice me and, after making arrangements to meet up that evening, made his way back to the floating palace. I finished my drink and paid the bill. I then took a stroll along the harbour in the direction of the boat. As we had agreed, Vindiloo was sitting on the deck talking to his friend. They were in the company of someone I immediately recognised as an international playboy who regularly graced the pages of *Hello!* magazine and the Nigel Dempster column.

Vindiloo's friend was a short, stocky man with thinning black hair and a swarthy appearance. Aged about 60 or so, there was something vaguely familiar about him, but I was unable to pinpoint just what. There was a small group of holidaymakers standing on the quayside admiring this marvellous craft, and a man taking a photograph of his wife posing with the yacht in the background. I wasn't sure whether Vindiloo noticed me strolling past, but I certainly saw him. He was still grinning. I was now convinced.

I stayed in Puerto Banus for three days, just long enough to sample a few of the local delicacies and down a few bottles of wine. Vindiloo remained for another few days. As he was quick to point out to me, it didn't cost him a penny.

Upon his return to London, he told me the deal was being sorted out but, in the meantime, his Marbella contact needed a small order of just 10,000 pieces. This I gave him immediately, and he delivered it to his friend's courier at the Inn on the Park in Mayfair.

I put Eric on full alert, and managed to convince him to start taking a few days off from his business during the week. In this way, and by working flat out, we would be able to get the work done within the time schedule required. Another influencing factor was that I promised Eric £750,000 if it all went smoothly and the full two million pieces were printed and paid for.

That weekend Eric started on the preparatory work, by running off several sets of plates, and then on Sunday, making a start on the printed (clean-shaven) watermarks. By now, the adrenalin was flowing, and I really began to believe the deal would come off. At long last, Mrs Jory's little boy had cracked it. Big time.

And then on Monday, Vindiloo phoned to say he needed to speak to me. The deal was off. I found it impossible to disguise my disappointment when Vindiloo explained that the notes weren't acceptable, as they didn't have consecutive serial numbers. In his enthusiasm, he had forgotten to mention this little detail to his friend. He asked me what would be involved in printing the notes with consecutive numbers as opposed to the 21 numbers that we used. I explained that this would require several custom-made numbering boxes, in itself a major problem. Apart from the time and expense such an order would present, there was the problem of the unique and instantly recognisable design of the typeface used on the £20 notes.

Without doubt, any legitimate engineering company that manufactured numbering boxes for the printing trade, of which there are only a handful in Europe, would most certainly ring the alarm bell upon being asked to undertake such a task.

In short, it just wasn't a viable proposition. Before talking to me, Vindiloo had assumed that it would just be a matter of additional expense to arrange the consecutive numbering system, something he had mentioned to his friend. The Marbella Sailor had agreed in principle to fund any outlay required, and naturally enough Vindiloo didn't think it would be that much of a problem. Upon hearing the bad news, he sounded crestfallen.

I suppose, given enough time, it could have been done. But it entailed finding an engineer with not only the specialist skill to manufacture such a complicated tool as an automatic numbering box, but also the necessary specialist machinery and equipment. In spite of the riches to be had, it just couldn't be done at this stage of the game. Heartbreaking. Truly heartbreaking. Vindiloo's contact nevertheless paid me £20,000 for the 10,000 that he had taken, and gave them to him to sell and return him his money as and when. This at least proved to me that Vindiloo's contact was a man to be trusted, and at least I had a reasonable little deal out of it. But this wasn't the end of the story.

After telling Eric that the big deal was off and just to carry on at a regular pace, I consoled myself with the knowledge that the twenties were going well and at least I was earning plenty of money, and living well. I reasoned that within a year or so, I would be able to get out of the funny money business, Ken would probably have managed to sell his printing company, and we would revert to my original plan — the poster printing. And the icing on the cake? I would have a rather large wedge of dosh tucked away.

So, now, my situation was just hunky-dory. Apart from the occasional outburst from Dinky Dan, the KO man, which really didn't concern me at all, I was living a carefree and extravagant life. Although there was one extremely sad event when Laraine's mother, May, died after spending several months in and out of hospital with severe heart problems, and in some respects her death was a merciful end to her suffering.

Laraine and I regularly dined at the best restaurants in town, I had bought her a white Mercedes Sports, a car she had long dreamed about, I spent a considerable amount in cash on the house and the payments to Eugene and Jewboy Jack were always there on time. In less than a year's time, I would be able to repay the loan as per our agreement, and so far as the eye could see there wasn't a cloud on the horizon.

In fact, very soon after the failed Vindiloo deal, the future suddenly looked brighter than I ever could have imagined in my wildest dreams. Just as I was getting back into the routine of day to day counterfeiting, Vindiloo came back into the picture as a major player. Once again, his jetsetting contact played a pivotal role.

Vindiloo called me from Amsterdam, a city he visited regularly for some reason or other. It was immediately apparent from the sound of his voice that he was in a state of extreme excitement. Barely able to speak in a coherent fashion, he was virtually begging me to fly over right away.

My initial reaction was to say I was too busy, but then something told me that, once again, he just might be on to something big. After allowing myself to be persuaded, I agreed to make the trip across to see him. Rather than fly, I drove to Amsterdam via the ferry. My car at the time was a Renault Bacharat, a large, rather sumptuous saloon with the kind of leather upholstery that you could feel yourself sinking into. So, driving the couple of hundred miles or so was no real hardship.

I met him in the bar of the Hilton Hotel, an easily located landmark. Once there, instead of buying me a drink, Vindiloo left the one he had in his hand on the bar, and hastily ushered me back out and into the street. As before, he couldn't stop grinning, and it was all he could do to stop the excitement within from exploding.

'Where we going?' I asked as we hurried along the street.

'Not far. I've got a little apartment just around the corner, I've got something to show you,' he replied.

'What's that then?'

'You'll see.'

A few minutes later, we were climbing the stairs in a small apartment block in a narrow side street. On the third floor, he opened the door to a one-bedroom apartment in need of some terminal housework.

'Sit down there,' Vindiloo said, indicating a small sofa strewn with newspapers and clothes. I cleared a space and waited for him to come out of the kitchen.

'Can of beer?' he called out.

'Yeah, so long as it's nice and cold.'

I heard the fizzing sound of a ring-pull being opened. Vindiloo walked through, pouring the beer into a glass. He put the drink on to a small table at the end of the sofa and hurried into the bedroom. Moments later, he came back in carrying an artist's portfolio case. He sat down on a chair opposite me and, placing the large case on the floor between us, he unzipped and spread it open to reveal the contents.

I looked down at the pile of about a dozen large sheets of paper. 'Take a look at them,' Vindiloo instructed me.

I reached down and took the top sheet from the pile. I knew, immediately, this was no ordinary sheet of paper. Just the feel of it told me it was something very special. After rubbing the sheet between my index finger and thumb, and then running my hands over it, I held it up to the light.

There were a number of unfamiliar watermarks placed equidistant from each other. A quick check revealed there were 20 in total. I then licked my thumb and rubbed the paper vigorously, in a vain attempt to wear a hole in it. It's a little-known fact that all genuine banknote paper is, more accurately, a linen fabric. Consequently, although it can be torn, it can't be worn. (Try it.) There was no doubt about it — this was a sheet of genuine banknote paper. Certainly not anything from the UK, but nevertheless, some foreign country's currency paper all the same.

'Well?' Vindiloo said. 'What d'you reckon?'

'Very interesting. Where's it from?'

He handed me a brown envelope. I opened it and took out several notes from a third-world nation.

'How much are these worth?' I asked.

'About 35 quid each. That's their most valuable note,' he replied.

'So what's the move, then?'

'My man's just had a deal with some people and bought in a warehouse full of that stuff. And it's all absolutely genuine.' Vindiloo kept shuffling and moving about in his seat and, of course, the grin never left his face.

'Sounds like a lot. How much is it worth, then?' I raised the glass of beer to my lips. Vindiloo said nothing. He just stared at me with an inane grin on his face. Before taking my first sip of beer, I said, 'Well?'

He spoke in slow motion — 'Five ... billion ... pounds.'

A reflex action caused me to eject the beer from my mouth. The sheet I was holding with my left hand was showered.

'Do fucking what?'

Vindiloo's grin spread even wider across his face, if that was possible. All Cheshire cats take note. In spite of the breathtaking information I had just been given, it didn't take me too long to recover.

'You serious?' I said.

''Course. He don't fuck about.'

I wiped my mouth with the back of my hand and shook the excess beer off the sheet I had showered. 'So what's the deal? What's in it for us?'

'He wants me to get it printed for him.'

'I gathered that much. But what's the deal?'

'He's prepared to pay us 3 per cent of the face value.'

I tried to work out the figures mentally, but an overflow of noughts kept crowding the picture.

'Three per cent?' I said.

'Yeah. And according to my calculator, that comes to £150m,' Vindiloo said.

I shook my head slowly and couldn't stop myself repeating the figure. 'A hundred-and-fifty-fucking-grand. No, not grand, a hundred-and-fifty-fucking-million. *Million*, for fuck's sake. Jesus.'

'Unbelievable, eh?'

I had to agree with him. Truly unbelievable. After all, this wasn't the once-in-a-lifetime opportunity we all dream of, but rather *once in ten lifetimes*!

Vindiloo explained the full SP to me over the next couple of beers. Obviously he didn't know the exact details of how his contact had come by the paper, but he was under the impression that the Russian Mafia might have been involved somehow. I didn't ask what made him think this, for the truth of the matter was, I really didn't want to know. After telling me the relevant details, he said almost as an afterthought, 'Oh, and another thing. There's a time limit. It's got to be done within six months. At the very latest.'

The one thing I was very much aware of was, if I proceeded with this deal, there really couldn't be any FUs whatsoever. The whole operation had to be planned and worked out to the finest detail; the finished product, delivery times, the absolute minimum of waste sheets, and those that were would have to be kept and returned with the actual printed notes. But all this was just a matter of paying attention to detail. Vindiloo went on to tell me that the notes had to be consecutively numbered, something that, not surprisingly, he was very concerned about. The smile returned to his face when I told him this presented no real problems. I pointed out that the numbers on the genuine notes didn't have a particularly recognisable typeface, unlike the serial numbers on English currency which has an unusual trumpet shape, whereby they expand in size, from left to right. Further, the numbers are printed in three different colours, technically a very complicated process, which, of course, is the point of the exercise.

Since the typeface we would require was similar to many standard typefaces, it wouldn't be a problem ordering the custom-made numbering boxes from one of the handful of manufacturers in Europe. This could be done under the guise of a legitimate job.

There were one or two minor details that would need to be sorted out if the job was to be done as perfectly, or as near-perfectly, as possible. After all, with the genuine banknote paper, it would be nothing short of criminal not to ensure that the finished job was indistinguishable from the real, officially printed notes (as opposed to the real, unofficially printed notes).

I told Vindiloo I wanted to return to England immediately, in order to get the show on the road as soon as possible. I told him I wanted to take a few of the sheets with me and, as I rose from my seat, he asked me about the scanning situation.

'Have you got a man sorted out for the plates?' he asked.

I sat down again, and Vindiloo couldn't help but be aware of the concerned expression on my face.

'Problem?' he asked.

'Could be,' I replied, then added hastily, 'but most definitely not insurmountable.'

Although I had no real starting point as to how I could locate a first-class scan-man willing to do the colour separation work and provide the film necessary to produce the plates, at the very back of my mind I felt there was always Dinky Dan's contact. But, for the moment, he would have to be filed under the heading 'VLR' — Very Last Resort.

'You got anyone in mind?' he asked.

'One or two possibles,' I lied. 'But don't worry, one way or another I'll get it sorted out. You know the old saying, "Where there's a will there's a way".'

Vindiloo paused for a moment then said, 'D'you want me to have a word with my man? After all, he's got a mile of contacts. You never know.'

I was completely opposed to this suggestion for two reasons. First, I didn't want him to form the impression that our printing set-up wasn't quite as sophisticated as he no doubt imagined. Second, we didn't dare run the risk of him putting out feelers and, in the process, coming across another printer. After all, scanning work and printing are two industries that go hand in hand.

I explained this to Vindiloo and, reassuring him that I would get it done, said, 'Just give him the good news. Emphasise the good points like why the consecutive numbering won't be a problem. Make sure he's in no doubt that we can definitely do the work. No problem at all.'

# CHAPTER 12

# The Wheels of Industry

I left Vindiloo the same day and lost no time at all in making the initial enquiries and preparations. Of course, my first port of call was Eric. Like me, he was overwhelmed by the sheer size and audacity of the job. However, unlike me, he could see no end of problems. These all concerned the immense size of the task. Incredibly, his first reaction was that he couldn't take any time away from his business. 'I mean to say, it'll take for ever working at weekends. And when could we do the twenties?' he said.

The problem was soon dispensed with when I told him how much his share would be. 'Are you being serious?' he asked, an incredulous smile on his face.

'Yes. Not all at once of course. But we'll be paid proportionately for each batch as we do them. Your share will come to £10 million once we've finished the job.'

I could see Eric's eyes glazing over and he seemed to go into a trance. He drifted back to planet earth when I asked him what he thought.

'Well, er, I suppose I could sort something out down at my place,' he said. 'How many do they want first of all?'

'As many as possible, I should think.'

Eric got out his calculator and started tapping out a few numbers and writing down some figures. 'Making maximum use of the sheet size, working all the hours under the sun, we might be able to turn out about 1.4 million per week.'

I made a quick calculation, and worked out this would come to just under £50 million. A staggering amount, but even so, for the complete amount to be printed at that rate would take two years. But even that was totally impractical as it would require non-stop work without any mishaps. Undoubtedly, the time factor was a huge problem, a seemingly insurmountable obstacle. I couldn't commit myself to the work by printing the first consignment and then botching up the rest of the job. I had a sneaking suspicion that the kind of business company that the Marbella Sailor kept weren't the type of people who took too kindly to being messed about. As I had no intention of letting this opportunity slip away, I knew that, somehow or other, I had to overcome the problem.

Very often, when confronted by a major obstacle in an operation, the solution can be staring you in the face. But because of the logistics and size of the figures all around, both Eric and I were unable to see the wood for the trees. And then it came to me. It was so obvious, I felt silly saying it. 'Why don't we get a bigger, faster press?'

Eric thought about it, but didn't seem too impressed. 'The kind of machine we'd need would come to about a million quid.'

'So?' I replied.

'So? So have you got a million quid in your back pocket, then?' he asked.

'No. But I can get it just a couple of days after we finish the first batch.'

Eric looked at me and said, 'If you think you can definitely get hold of that kind of cash, then that's the way forward.'

'So how many could we turn out then?' I asked. 'Each week I mean.'

Once again, Eric started writing down a few figures and tapping out a few numbers on his calculator. After about five minutes writing and tapping he finally said, 'About £500 million worth I should think. If we kept on at it, I suppose we'd get the whole lot done in about 12 weeks or so. Let's say about four months to be on the safe side.'

'That's more like it,' I said.

'Of course, we'll have to find someone to do the guillotining,' Eric said.

The cutting down of the printed sheets into banknotes was a time factor I hadn't taken into account. But as he spoke, I realised immediately what he meant. From my experience as his assistant in the printing of the twenties, I was aware of what a time-consuming job it was.

'Yes, of course,' I replied, 'don't you know anyone?'

Eric thought for a moment and then came up with the name of a friend of his who was semi-retired, but who still did some trade work. As always, I asked, 'Is he someone you can trust?'

'Oh yes. I should say so. He was always up to different things years ago. Football tickets were his favourite. Never any good, mind you. In fact, I don't recall him ever doing any without fucking them up, one way or the other.'

'You sure he won't fuck up this work, then?' I said.

Eric laughed. 'Oh no. It was just the actual printing he used to get wrong. Guillotining though, that's no problem.'

After being told he lived locally, I suggested that we should go and talk to him immediately. I knew that if Eric's friend was willing to do the work, then inevitably I would have to meet him. And so I had no qualms about meeting him at the very beginning. It was now early Friday evening, and Eric knew that his semi-retired friend would be in the pub next door to his workshop. We got into my car and drove the couple of miles to the pub.

'There he is,' Eric said as we walked into the saloon bar. His friend was aiming for double top on the dartboard. We waited until he had thrown the winning dart before making our presence known.

Eric shook his hand and then, turning to me, he said, 'Dermot, meet Steve. Steve, meet Dermot.'

Dermot and I exchanged greetings, and Eric explained that we had come to put some cash his way. Dermot, a spindly little Irishman with a large red nose riddled with purple veins, smiled a toothless grin.

'Ah, well now, isn't that a very welcome thing to hear. And how much of the old spondooliks might we be talking about?'

The bar was quite busy, and both Eric and I were reluctant to talk for fear of being overheard. At Dermot's suggestion, we went next door to his workshop. Still carrying his pint of Guinness, he led the way. He had left the premises unlocked with a handwritten sign on the door: 'In the pub next door'.

The lights were still on as we walked into the back, where there stood a large, state-of-the-art, computerised guillotine. Ideal for the job. I couldn't help wondering just what a semi-retired little Irish printer was doing with such a sophisticated piece of machinery. It turned out that some friends of his in Southern Ireland had somehow managed to steal it from a large printing company that was going into liquidation. Although it far exceeded his needs, Dermot could see a bargain at the knock-down price the thieves wanted for it. And so he bought it and, to my surprise, knew how to work it perfectly. Apart from the guillotine, I noticed another machine in the far corner. It was a Heidelberg platen.

'Can you operate the platen?' I asked.

Dermot almost spat out his Guinness. 'Can I work the platen? Yer asking me?' he said indignantly. 'Tell him, Eric, me old pal. Tell this cheeky young pup who he's talking to. Go on, Eric, tell him.'

'He already knows. I've told him,' Eric said with a smile.

Dermot turned to me, a look of pride on his face. 'So yer know then? The finest ticket forger this side of the Emerald Isle. Oh yes, me boy, that's who you are talking to all right.'

'So Eric's told me,' I said, by now smiling as much as Eric. 'What I've got in mind, apart from the guillotining, is a bit of specialised work on the platen. It'll pay good money.'

Dermot's toothless mouth broadened into a grin from ear to ear. 'Well, I don't care how specialised it is, I'm yer man. Dermot Flint, the man for yer print!'

Now that we could see how enthusiastic he was, we gave him the details of the guillotining work. And I then explained what the specialised platen work entailed. At the top of the notes, the printing that detailed the name of the third-world country's national bank was very slightly raised. So slight, in fact, that it wasn't noticeable to the naked eye, but was apparent when an enquiring finger or thumb was run over the section in question. This effect is pretty much universal on all paper currency. On English banknotes for example, the script that reads 'Bank of England' at the top of the note is raised together with one or two other, smaller details lower down. This is achieved by a printing process called *intaglio*. For our purpose, it wasn't really necessary for the counterfeit twenties to have this feature as the notes were invariably scrunched up and treated in various ways to make them look old and tatty by the punters who worked them at street level.

But, of course, this third-world currency was a whole new ball game. Since it involved the use of genuine banknote paper, every detail had to be attended to. In short, the finished note had to be as near-perfect as possible. If a job's worth doing, it's worth doing right and, undoubtedly, this was a job worth doing.

The *intaglio* printing process was too involved and complicated to undertake, although had there been no other way, I would have done whatever had to be done. Fortunately, for our purposes, there was an alternative. I had already discussed the problem with Eric and had arranged that he would do the work on his two platens, but as it was a comparitively slow process, the input of another machine would ensure that completion of the job wasn't significantly delayed.

This was where Dermot — the 'Little Printer', as he liked to be called — had a pivotal role to play. I explained to him what I had in mind and his enthusiasm knew no bounds. It was a somewhat innovative method that involved having an engraved copper plate made to the exact specification of the wording that would need to be raised. With the plate positioned accurately, the printed sheets would then be run with the sheets being forced against the plate in such a way that the engraved wording would hit the compatible area with sufficient pressure to force the paper through, giving the raised effect. This was only possible because of the miniscule degree of raising required. Any more, and it wouldn't have been achieved without a complementary plate with raised print etched on to it. In engineering terms, the engraved plate is referred to as the 'female' and the raised plate the 'male'. This process is called embossing, but was not appropriate for my purposes as the impression of the wording is sunk into the paper on the reverse side to that which is raised.

As it was, even the minimum degree of raising could only be achieved by using an excessive amount of pressure. As this is not what the press is designed to do, over time, a great deal of damage is inflicted upon the machine. But before the damage makes the press unworkable and in need of repair, a great many sheets will have been run through. The possibility of any damage to the Little Printer's Heidelberg platen was more than offset by the financial rewards involved. An added bonus was the fact that his general engraving work was done by a personal friend whom he could trust to do the plates with no questions asked.

After going over every last detail, we left him to get back to his darts and told him I would be back as soon as I had some sample sheets on which he could start his work. 'Oh, by the way, Dermot,' I said, 'remember, not a word to anyone, OK?'

Again, Dermot was most indignant. 'Eric, me boy, will yer tell this young toe-rag. You don't teach yer granny to suck eggs. Goodnight!' And with that he closed the pub door behind him.

In the car, driving Eric back to his place, he said to me, 'I know this might sound like a silly question, but have you got the colour separation work sorted out? You know, the film? The plates? I know it's only a minor detail, but have you?'

I shook my head. 'But you know what they say ...'

'What's that?'

'Where there's a million pounds, there's a way!'

Even though the most important obstacle had yet to be overcome, I really felt that, in the few hours since I had spoken to Vindiloo, I had got the show on the road. Nothing would stop me.

That evening, I went through the brochures I had from the leading numbering box manufacturers in Europe. It wasn't too long before I was able to identify a box that matched the typeface almost exactly. The actual size of the numbers was just a fraction larger than those on the notes. The size difference was so slight as to be of no significance. Short of actually measuring them, it was impossible to detect. But what was noticeably different was the figure four. In the brochure, it showed as '4', but on the notes it showed as '4'. I didn't feel that this presented too much of a problem and, the following morning, I paid a visit to a small engineering company that had done several jobs for me in the past.

By way of business, I had come to know the owner of the company personally, an elderly man who always welcomed the chance to do some work for cash. I showed him the brochure with its many illustrations of different numbering boxes and explained just what I wanted done — I needed to know the feasibility of modifying the number 4 to my specific requirements. In the manner of a great many men who work at a skilled job involving a high degree of expertise and knowledge, he took in a lungful of air and shook his head slowly as though deep in thought.

'Bloody awkward, Steve, I don't mind telling you. Bloody awkward.'

'Bloody awkward's one thing. Impossible's another. Well?'

'Oh yes. It can be done. All things are possible, but it won't be an easy job. In fact, it'll be a bugger of a job.'

This was his 'subtle' way of saying it wouldn't be cheap. But then I hadn't expected it to be.

'Good. That's all I need to know. If I get the boxes to you, could you start on them straight away?'

'Cash job?'

''Course.'

'You bring the boxes in and I'll get started right away.'

'I'll be back as soon as I get them. I'll give you a call on Monday and let you know how long. Work out a price for me, could you?'

'No problem,' my engineer friend replied, and I left him with a smile on his face. On Monday morning, I called the numbering box manufacturers and placed an order for ten of the required boxes. Fortunately, they had them in stock and I was told they could dispatch them to me by courier service upon receipt of the cash. I gave them the name of a fictitious company registered at an accommodation address I regularly used in the City and took their details. I said I would arrange a transfer of money into the company's account and then nearly fell off my chair when I was told the invoice total. Including various taxes, it was the local currency equivalent of over £5,000. After quickly regaining my composure, I told the female sales rep I would do the necessary within the hour, and she told me the boxes would be in London by Wednesday at the latest. I returned home, and delved into the stash of cash I had hidden away. I arranged the transfer and then went to a pub for a quick drink and a sandwich.

I sat down with a cold Budweiser and went through my notes and went over what had been sorted out and what needed to be done. The starting point, of course, and the key to the enormous safe full of money, metaphorically speaking, was the paper, and that was safely tucked away in a warehouse somewhere. The printing of the sheets had been discussed with Eric and, as involved as it was, we both felt it was in hand.

The guillotine work — arranged.

The raised print details — arranged.

The consecutive numbering — arranged.

What else? Ah yes, of course, the scanning work and plates.

As pleased as I was with myself about the progress I had made in just a couple of days, the fact remained, none of it counted for anything without a set of film. So here I was, sitting in a pub, a series of ticks followed by a big cross! I went through my address book and picked out several names, different contacts with links to printing, no matter how tenuous, who might, just might, have access to a scan-man.

I made a number of calls from the pub payphone. As expected, few of them held out any hope, but then it seemed as though I may have struck lucky when a couple of my calls resulted in the promise of a 'possible'.

That afternoon, I paid a visit to one of the 'possibles' and took with me, not the actual notes that I required to be scanned, but instead a red herring in the shape of a couple of bank notes from a central African republic. I reasoned that the degree of work involved in scanning these was comparable to the notes I really needed to be done. If the 'possible' was able to provide the necessary high standard of film for the red herring, the actual work required shouldn't be a problem. I explained my situation to my contact, and that if his scan-man was up to the task, then there was a good earner in it for them. With this in mind, he went to work immediately. He had my mobile phone number, and I knew he would get back to me ASAP.

I then went to see my second 'possible' and, once again, explained the situation. And once again, after giving him a couple of the African notes, I waited for him to get back to me. With a couple of different irons in the fire, I felt cautiously optimistic about the prospects of finding a good scan-man. As I had anticipated, both contacts came back to me that evening. The first man was extremely enthusiastic. 'Good news. Stan the man can do the scan,' he sang down the phone.

'You sure?' I replied.

'My man's absolutely confident. Absolutely.'

With the memory of the Scottish notes fiasco still fresh in my mind, I simply said, 'Good.'

'Yeah. And, what's more, it gets better. I'll be able to pick up a set of film tomorrow. Just a single image, back and front. He's going to work through the night when he's alone.'

This really was good news. 'I'll meet you tomorrow morning then,' I told him, and we made arrangements for ten o'clock the following morning.

No sooner had I finished speaking to my first contact, than the second man called me. He, too, told me he had good news and wanted to meet me the next day. Suddenly, it seemed, the operation was gaining momentum. A great deal of momentum.

At 10.00am the following morning, I was at my first contact's business premises as arranged. He gave me a brown A4-sized envelope containing the set of film. I took them out and examined the four sheets, each one with two impressions of the African note on it, the front and reverse. To my inexperienced eye they looked perfect. But then again, so had the film for the Bank of Scotland notes. It was very much a case of the proof of the pudding being in the eating.

Before taking the film to Eric, I met my second contact. As he had informed me on the phone, his scan-man felt confident that he could do the job. However, unlike my first contact, he needed some cash up front.

'How much? I asked.

'5 grand,' he replied.

Once again, I recalled the Scottish note fiasco and wasn't really inclined to risk making the same expensive mistake again. I declined the offer with the explanation that I needed to see what I was buying before I parted with any cash. I left him looking slightly disappointed, but as I told him, if his contact was well known to him, then there had to be an element of trust all round.

I made a call to Eric and informed him about the film and he agreed to meet me at the workshop as soon as possible. First, he would make the plates and then, after that, he would set the press up and we would know shortly afterwards how good the film was. Five o'clock that evening found me standing next to Eric whilst he made the four plates we required. This didn't take too long, and then he set about putting them on the press. As with the plates procedure, I was standing at his elbow trying to look useful, the eager 'young apprentice'.

'So, what d'you reckon?' I asked. A futile question, but the kind of thing that most people in my position would ask.

'Well, the film looks quite good. But until we actually run it off we won't know one way or another. We'll just have to wait and see.' Which, of course, was exactly what I expected him to say.

We stopped for a cup of tea. Like an excited child, I quickly finished the drink and hurried Eric along. Ten minutes later, we were both back at the press, Eric working, me watching.

At last, it seemed as though the plates were in position. The inks were put in the ducts. A couple of turns. The sound of the motor whirring as the press started was music to my ears. A couple of minutes later, the first few sheets came through. Eric studied them closely. I said nothing as he looked down and mumbled a few words to himself. 'Fraction to the left.' There was a movement of his hand over the sheet. More thought.

Seconds later, he moved to the side of the press. A touch on a small spanner. Once again, he looked down at the sheet next to him, then moved to another section of the machine where one of the other plates was positioned. Another delicate turn of the spanner.

'Let's see what that does,' he remarked, moving to the far end of the press. Once again, the rollers started turning as the machine was started up. And then, once again, the sheets of paper started to run through. Eric stood watching them with one hand still on the operating panel. Seconds later, he pressed the 'stop' button and walked to the end of the press and took out the last sheet to come through.

I stood beside him whilst he studied the sheet in his hands. I could see the image of the note clearly enough, but the colours were all wrong and parts of the image were blurred. He put the sheet of paper down on the light box — a glass-top contraption with a light inside which shone through. He switched it on and examined the illuminated image through an eyeglass. Carefully he switched his attention from one part of the image to another and then another. Again, he went through the same procedure as before, making tiny adjustments to the positioning within the press. And again he ran a number of sheets of paper through. This procedure was repeated several times, and on more than one occasion it looked as though we were very nearly there. But as we both knew, nearly, or even very nearly, wasn't good enough.

After a couple of hours, Eric had to bow to the inevitable. The film just wasn't up to standard. 'Perhaps if I show my man the proof, he can make some fine adjustments?' I said.

'Maybe,' Eric replied. But I could tell from the tone of his voice that he wasn't too optimistic. 'The problem seems to be that he hasn't used a fine enough screen.' He then went on to tell me about the quality of the 'pixels' and the number of dots per square inch and various other technical specifications and details. None of this really meant anything to me, but I was fully aware of one thing — the film was no good. Nothing too technical about that.

The following day, the automatic numbering boxes arrived at the office address. I took them to my engineer friend and left them with him. 'I'll have them done by this time next week,' he assured me. It was now Wednesday, just five days since I had first been told about the Crime of the Century.

When I thought about how much had been achieved in those five days, I felt I had done well. Very well, but all the same, not yet well enough. Without a first-class scan-man, it all meant nothing and as much as the prospect of involving Dinky Dan was something of an anathema to me, I was beginning to feel that perhaps I'd have no choice.

I decided to give myself another ten days and, if I made no further progress, Dinky Dan, the KO Man would have to be pulled in.

During the next week, I tried every contact I knew and, unfortunately, the man who supplied the set of film was unable to improve upon the first effort. I managed to persuade the second contact to provide a set of film on trust after showing him the poor quality of the African notes that Eric had printed. But once again, the standard wasn't good enough. All in all, I acquired five different sets of film. And in each case the finished product was no good.

After running off the different sets of proofs, with all the problems and work that involved, Eric looked as though he could do with a long holiday. Of course, had one of them come up trumps, I'm sure he wouldn't have looked so tired. But as it was, he had been working hard to no avail. An air of despondency hung about us. It seemed as though I would have to involve Dinky Dan. But even then there was no guarantee that he would want to know. Knowing his nature, I felt there was a possibility that he wouldn't be interested, in spite of the money to be earned. For the moment, he was more than happy with the way the twenties were going.

But time was passing, and it was now nearly two weeks since I had seen Vindiloo, although I had spoken to him several times on the telephone. Two weeks isn't very long in the scale of things, but I was still no closer to making contact with a proper, state-of-the-art scan-man. It was obvious that I would have to make a decision very soon.

I decided that I would go to see Dinky Dan at the weekend. I knew there was virtually no chance of the situation changing during the couple of days before then, as I had exhausted all my contacts. But then, as I was on the verge of phoning Dinky Dan, Vindiloo called me. I detected a familiar strain of excited urgency in his voice.

'I need to see you. Right away. Very important.'

'Are you back in London?' I asked.

'No. I'm still in the 'Dam. But you've got to get over here. Right away.'

'OK,' I told him. 'I'll be over in a few hours. What's it about? Not bad news, is it?'

'No, no. Just the opposite. And bring one of those little magnifying glasses jewellers squeeze into their eye to examine diamonds,' he said.

'No problem. What for, though?'

'I'll tell you when you get here. What time do you reckon?'

'I'll be there this evening. Any time after seven.'

'Fine, I'll meet you in the hotel bar. 'Bye.'

# CHAPTER 13

## Caroline, Fritz and a Blue Pot

I made my way to Amsterdam immediately, stopping off at the workshop en route to borrow the small eyeglass that Eric used to examine fine printed detail. That evening, once again Vindiloo was sitting in the bar of the Hilton Hotel waiting for me. This time, he bought me a drink and, although excited, was more composed than when I had met him nearly two weeks previously.

'I think we've cracked it,' he declared triumphantly.

'What do you mean?' I asked.

The bar was deserted apart from the two of us, but still Vindiloo nodded in the direction of a table situated at the far side of the lounge. Carrying our drinks, we moved away from the bar and the bartender drying glasses. After sitting down, he asked me if I had that 'little magnifying glass thing' with me. Making a quick visual check that the lounge was still empty, he took out a couple of £20 notes from his pocket. He passed them across the table to me. I saw immediately that one was counterfeit. They were placed reverse side upwards and, on the left-hand side, each had a small circle drawn on it in biro.

'Take a look at those two with the magnifying glass. Where the circles are.' He leaned back in his chair and watched while I did as instructed.

'What am I supposed to be looking for?' I asked.

'See them little pots on that little table?' he said. I saw the section of the design he was referring to.

'Yeah?' I said.

'Well, see anything funny?'

'Not really. What are you talking about?

'One of those little pots on the real note is blue. But if you look carefully, you'll see that on the moody note the little pot's clear.'

I looked again at the genuine note then down again at the counterfeit note. He was right. One was blue, one wasn't. (In fact it was, more accurately, the lower half of a bowl.) An imperceptible difference, not noticeable to the naked eye, unless of course it was brought to your attention, just as Vindiloo had done. Even then, very good eyesight was essential. Undoubtedly, this was a difference that had been deliberately incorporated into the final film produced from the scanning. This was no accident, that much was obvious. What wasn't so obvious was why it was there. More importantly, what was its relevance? And why was Vindiloo so excited by this discovery? And how did he know about it? So many questions. So few answers. What could it all possibly mean? This certainly felt like a case for Sherlock Holmes — *The Mystery of the Blue Pot*.

'Well, what d'you reckon?' he said.

Still slightly perplexed, I replied, 'Er, yeah, sure. It's definitely different. Yeah, no doubt about it. I think we can definitely say that the tiny pot on the genuine note is blue and on the Jeckyll it's clear. And?'

'Well, I can get hold of the man who made the plates for the twenties.' He grinned across at me.

My mouth dropped open. Completely stunned by this bombshell, I was unable to respond and simply waited for him to continue. He then went on to explain just what had occurred since I had last seen him. It involved one of life's amazing little coincidences, one of those situations that makes you wonder if everything isn't somehow pre-ordained like some master plan, the whole of our lives being played out according to a script in a monstrous great tome entitled *Fate*.

In part, Vindiloo's reason for being in Amsterdam was to supply a couple of punters with the twenties. One of these punters was a young prostitute by the name of Caroline. A couple of days earlier, he had delivered a batch of the twenties to Caroline who, by way of a joke, said, 'I bet you don't know how to tell the difference between these and the real money like I do!'

'How's that, then?' he asked.

It was then that she pointed out the blue pot to him, although without his glasses or, better still, a spyglass, he couldn't really see properly what she was referring to.

But, nevertheless, he took her word for it and asked, 'So how d'you know that, then?'

Unfortunately, all Caroline knew was that somebody had told her, but she couldn't remember who. Vindiloo found this little snippet of information interesting, but didn't attach any significance to it and it was soon forgotten.

Then, moments later, as he was walking away from her apartment, Caroline's voice called out after him, 'I remember now, it was Herman.'

More out of curiosity than real interest, he turned and called back, 'Do what? Who's Herman? What are you on about?'

Unable to hear her response properly, he strolled back.

'What are you talking about?' he asked, looking up at her leaning out of her first-floor apartment window.

'You wanted to know who told me about the blue pot. Well, now I remember, it was Herman.'

'Who's Herman then?'

'He's a very good friend of mine. You understand?'

At this point, Vindiloo looked down at his watch and realised he was running late. He had to be somewhere else, somewhere more important than standing in a side street talking about a blue pot with a Dutch prostitute. Feeling somewhat annoyed with himself, he said dismissively, 'Oh, right, very interesting,' and waved goodbye.

He turned to walk away again when Caroline called out, 'Yes, Herman's uncle made the pot not blue. Funny, yes?'

Vindiloo stopped dead in his tracks and turned to see Caroline closing her window. He ran to the front door and buzzed the intercom like one of her most enthusiastic clients on heat. Back inside her apartment, he pressed her for more information about Herman. She told him that, a week or so earlier, one of her regular clients, a young German soldier by the name of Herman, had stayed the night. The pair of them had got drunk on bottles of Schnapps and in their inebriated state the subject of counterfeit money had come up in conversation. Not surprisingly, Caroline had told her young German soldier friend that she had some dud English £20 notes. Upon hearing this, Herman asked to see one and said he would show her something that nobody else knew about. Of course, Caroline, being the obliging girl that she was, showed him one of her twenties. He attempted to point out the blue pot to her, but since both of them were drunk, Caroline just nodded in agreement, not really able to see such a tiny detail even if she had been stone cold sober. Instead, she asked him, 'So how can you be so clever as to know that the little pot isn't blue?'

In a drunken boast, Herman declared, 'Because my uncle is the man who makes it possible for the English criminals to make the money. And just like Van Gogh, he leaves his signature on his work of art!'

Caroline stared at Herman, eyes wide with incredulity. 'You mean, he puts his *name* on the money? But surely he will get into trouble. Yes?'

'No, no. You don't understand. Please, you must listen to me. He does not sign the money with his name ...'

'But you said ...'

'No. When I said he leaves his signature, I mean he makes a tiny little mark that only he knows about. The blue pot. You understand?'

By this time, not only was Caroline drunk, but also thoroughly confused. But at least she understood enough to know that the little blue pot was different and Herman's uncle was responsible.

Vindiloo told her he needed to speak to Herman as soon as possible. Fortunately, with Herman being a regular client, she felt certain that it wouldn't be too long before he called her to book another session. Sure enough, the next day Caroline contacted Vindiloo to say that the young German soldier would be with her that evening.

Apparently, their relationship was more than just that of prostitute and client. It was more of a love affair. At least that was how Herman regarded it. In fact, Herman was madly in love with her and, on more than one occasion, had asked her to marry him, with the proviso that she gave up her profession. The prospect, however, of marrying a young German soldier, and living on a young German soldier's wage, didn't have the same appeal to Caroline. But still Herman loved her.

This being the situation, and knowing that she would no doubt make some money out of introducing Vindiloo to Herman, she arranged to go to a local restaurant late in the evening. Vindiloo would be there and introduce himself as a family friend from England. Caroline, in turn, assured Vindiloo that she would see to it that Herman was in a good mood. The restaurant table was booked for 10.00pm and, as Herman was due to arrive at her apartment at 5.00pm, there was ample time for her to work her charms on him.

That evening in the restaurant, Herman was in an exceedingly good mood and, to help him along, Caroline had made sure he drank plenty of wine with the meal. By the time Vindiloo happened to wander by, Herman was everybody's friend, and Vindiloo was welcomed to the table with open arms. It wasn't too long before Vindiloo got to the point. Herman's initial reaction, in spite of the drink and sex earlier on, was to adopt a wary and suspicious attitude, but with the right words of encouragement from Caroline, he soon opened up about his uncle, whilst prudently not revealing any personal details about him.

Since Herman was extremely drunk by now, Vindiloo made arrangements to talk to him in detail the next morning. He gave Caroline a farewell peck on the cheek and whispered the instructions to make sure that Herman was extremely happy when he called round at 11.00am the following morning. But Caroline was a shrewd granny who didn't need to be taught how to suck eggs, or anything else for that matter. Vindiloo left the young lovers with a smile on his face, as well as theirs.

The following morning at Caroline's apartment all went to plan. A happy Herman confirmed that his uncle was indeed a scan-man and that he had provided the film for the twenties. Although this was what Vindiloo wanted to hear, he pointed out that it was quite possible that his uncle might have provided the film for another counterfeit £20 note. An inferior one.

Once again, Herman referred to the blue pot. And this time, with all concerned sober, the counterfeit note was examined in conjunction with a genuine note. As he pointed out, how could he possibly know about the blue pot unless he had been told about it? And who was the most likely person to tell him? Answers on a post card please.

As there was no apparent reason why the German should be lying, Vindiloo decided he must be on the level. He showed him the notes we required, and asked him to speak to his uncle about doing the colour separation work and providing the necessary high-quality film. He gave Herman the German his mobile phone number, along with two of the third-world currency notes. Having been promised a good pay day, Herman assured him he would get back to him within 24 hours.

That was in the morning, and here we were in the evening, sitting in the Hilton Hotel. I was still gobsmacked when Vindiloo finished telling me the amazing set of coincidences that led him to Herman the German.

'Well, what d'you think? D'you reckon it's the same man?' he asked.

I nodded my head. Like Vindiloo, I couldn't see how the kind uncle could be anything other than the real McCoy. 'Yeah, I reckon we've struck gold here, Tony. I reckon he's definitely *the* scan-man.'

I examined the two twenties again with the spyglass. As I looked at the imperceptible difference between the two pots, I thought about Herman's comment, that it was his uncle's 'signature' — *Fritz the Scan-Man was 'ere*!

It wasn't long after this that Vindiloo's phone rang. It was Caroline. Herman would be back tomorrow morning, and could we be there to meet him? As Vindiloo told her, 'Yes, no problem,' he gave me the thumbs up.

That evening the pair of us went out on the town to celebrate. The next morning, before he left the apartment, I told Vindiloo to try and negotiate a price, assuming that Herman didn't want to see him in order to say his uncle wouldn't do the work.

'Try to keep it under 25 grand,' I said. 'Any more, and it could be a problem. Give him the impression that it's only a small job and there's no fortunes in it for anybody.'

'Don't worry,' he assured me. 'I'll get my violin out. By the time I've finished, he'll probably agree to do it for nothing.'

'Good.' I smiled at the thought and added, 'I doubt that somehow. But do your best.'

By midday, Vindiloo was back with the good news that the kind uncle had agreed to do the work, no problem. In fact, he had said that, compared to the £20 note, it was a piece of 'black forest gâteau'. With regard to the fee, Herman's uncle had already given him a figure, £20,000, non-negotiable. In actual fact, the price was in Deutschmarks and, at the rate of exchange at that time, it worked out at £19,700. Vindiloo, of course, agreed there and then and, as an added inducement, promised Herman a further £2,000 for a speedy delivery time. Plus free sex from Caroline for the next month. In response to her protests that he wasn't anything to do with her pussy, he charged Caroline just a pound each for the twenties she bought from him. For all intents and purposes, the deal was signed and sealed if not quite delivered.

Herman had to be back in Germany by 4.00pm as he had already extended his leave or whatever by 24 hours. Before saying '*Auf Wiedersehen*, Pet', he gave Vindiloo his word that the film would be ready for collection any time after the weekend, provided that we faxed all the precise planning and layout details to him. Apart from this, all he needed to know was that £22,000 or so would be waiting for him. For some reason or other, he was most insistent payment be made in Deutschmarks and not £20 notes!

All at once, the wheels of private enterprise were beginning to turn at a furious pace. Vindiloo contacted his man to inform him of the speed of developments and arrangements were made for the first consignment of paper to be made available in London within the next few days. I, in turn, concentrated my thoughts on making sure the £22,000 would be in place. Both Vindiloo and I agreed that it wouldn't be a particularly good idea to ask his contact for the money, as we were anxious not to create the impression that we were a two-bit operation. Apart from which, he was, of course, providing us, on trust, with a consignment of paper, which in itself would be worth a fortune on the black market. Fortunately, I had about £40,000 tucked away in the house and so the finance wasn't a problem.

As soon as I arrived back in London, I paid Eric a visit and we sat down to discuss the various pros and cons. I told him I expected to have the film and paper by the following Tuesday, a matter of just a few days. This meant that he had to make arrangements to take a couple of weeks off work. Fortunately, he was in the middle of a couple of long print runs, which meant that he could arrange for a friend to run his little business without too many problems. So, once again, I started ticking off my list of requirements.

Numbering boxes: at the engineers on schedule for Tuesday — *tick*.

Guillotining and raised effect on the top of the note: engraved plates in hand and due for collection by Dermot, my little printer friend on Monday — *tick*.

The film for the plates: ready for collection any time after the weekend, according to Herman — *tick*.

Money to pay for the film — *tick*.

This time there were no crosses. This time next week, Eric and I would be starting work on what undoubtedly would be the Crime of the Century. Feeling satisfied that nothing could go wrong, I started thinking about laying the ground work for the future success of the operation. I made a call to a long-term associate based in New York. The purpose of this call was to arrange the financing of the purchase of the type of press I would need to acquire in just a few weeks' time. Making a million pounds in cash 'clean' would be no problem. Just as soon as I had the money in my hand, my New York contact could arrange for a finance company cheque to cover payment for the press. My friend would fly to London and deposit the cash in an account at the finance company's London branch. Locating a press was no problem, as there were several that Eric knew of which were readily available for £750,000 and one for £800,000.

All we could do now was wait for a call from Vindiloo to say that Herman was on his way with the film. True to his word, Herman contacted Vindiloo on Sunday afternoon to say that he would be at Caroline's apartment at 10.00am the following Monday morning.

On Sunday evening, I was back in Amsterdam and, perhaps predictably, Vindiloo and I spent the night on another celebratory spree. The following morning, as before, Vindiloo left the apartment to pay Caroline a visit. As he picked up the case containing the Deutschmarks, I reiterated to him the importance of making sure that Caroline didn't let the young soldier leave before I had given the film the once-over.

Just 45 minutes later, Vindiloo was back, minus the money and carrying a sealed folder. I opened it and pulled out the sheets of film. There were eight main sheets with ten impressions of the notes on them and eight smaller sheets with just two impressions on them. I held the smaller sheets up to the light and examined them as best I could, remembering the salient points that Eric had told me to look out for. This really involved me just trying to ascertain whether the very fine detail looked as very fine and very detailed as it should. With my limited knowledge of colour separation and scanning, I was doing little more than guessing at what I thought I could see. But I took the view that, providing this film that I held in my hands had been done by the same person who had produced the film for the twenties, then there shouldn't be any problem. As far as I was concerned, I felt certain that we were dealing with the same man, and consequently I satisfied myself that the film was the real McCoy.

Significantly, Vindiloo informed me that Herman had mentioned something about an optical disc that his uncle would keep in case there should be any fine-tuning required, unless I wanted to take the disc myself. I was convinced.

I told Vindiloo to call Caroline with the good news that everything appeared to be in order. This he did, and we heard Herman calling out from the background, that should there be any modifications required, his uncle would carry them out immediately.

Well, you can't say fairer than that, I thought to myself. Very efficient, these Huns. *Vorsprung durch Technik,* as Herr Villie Shakespeare used to say. Before putting the film back into the folder, I spread the sheets out on the floor and admired the handiwork of Fritz the Scan-Man.

It had been just over two weeks since I had first laid eyes upon the sheets of banknote paper. I was barely able to believe how much had been achieved in such a short time. Never in my wildest dreams could I have foreseen being this far advanced this quickly. But even I had to admit that it wasn't just determination and know-how that had got me so far, so soon. *Lady Luck* had most definitely been on my side, lending an extremely benevolent helping hand.

At length, I picked the sheets of film up and carefully packed half away in the folder, which Vindiloo then hid safely in the apartment. This was a precautionary measure as only four out of the eight sheets of 10-up film were required to print the notes. The other four were a spare set, and similarly with the eight sheets of 2-up film. (The 10-up and 2-up specifications referred to the number of notes which could be printed from one piece of film.) The set of film I intended to take back with me was slid into the lining of a suitcase I had previously adapted. Once re-sealed, the modification was completely undetectable. With a selection of clothes in the case, I made my way back, confident that, should I be the subject of a routine check, there would be nothing suspicious to attract the attention of Her Majesty's Custom and Excise officers.

I left Vindiloo to catch the first available flight the following day, whilst I drove. Although I never concerned myself as to just what it was that he got up to on his frequent trips to Amsterdam, I felt there would be less risk of being stopped without him in the car. I journeyed without mishap. Safely back in the UK a few hours later, my first port of call was the workshop. I had already made arrangements to meet Eric there, and consequently I wasn't surprised to see the curtains at the windows of the workshop being discreetly pulled to one side as the tyres on my car crunched against the stones of the driveway. By the time I pulled up outside, I could see Eric standing at the open door smiling.

'Everything OK?' he asked.

'Yeah. Fine.' I opened the car boot and took the suitcase out and went into the workshop. Within minutes, I had removed the film from its hiding place and Eric was examining it on top of his light box. Without realising it, I was holding my breath whilst I looked on, trying to discern some kind of reaction from Eric's intense expression. I felt a flurry of panic as he lifted his head, a grim look on his face.

'What's the matter?' I asked.

He paused before speaking. 'I'm not sure.' He leaned his head forward and once again looked down at one of the sheets of film through his eyeglass. With the illumination from the light underneath, he was able to see every minute detail. And he didn't look too happy. I wanted to ask him what it was that was concerning him, but instead just watched him switching his attention from one sheet of film to another, and then to the other two. All the while I was aware that I had my fingers crossed. Running through my mind were the figures of how much I had laid out, not only for the film, but also the numbering boxes, and the cash I was committed to paying my engineer friend. 'Please be OK,' I was saying under my breath. 'Please.'

After what seemed like a very long time — in fact, no more than a couple of minutes — Eric surfaced from the top of the light box. Straightening up, he still wore a grim expression.

'Well?' I asked.

'I'm a bit concerned, to be honest with you,' he remarked. And then after another pause for a few seconds continued, 'They're nowhere near as good as the twenties. Nowhere near.'

My heart sank. 'Really?'

And then, offering me a straw to cling to, Eric said, 'Well, I can't be absolutely certain until we actually run them, I suppose. But, personally, I don't hold out a great deal of hope. In fact, from what I can see, they don't look any better than the other film we had. Y'know, them African notes.'

I had come to know Eric as a very innovative and perceptive man and, as such, I was painfully aware that he never made statements regarding work lightly or without a considerable amount of thought. But even so, as he himself said, we wouldn't know for certain until we had actually printed some.

'Can we get cracking now, then?' I said.

''Course. Let's just suck it and see, as the actress said to the bishop!'

I tried to smile at his little quip, but it was with a heavy heart that I followed him into the adjoining room. As soon as the plates were made, he set the printing press up. The plates were positioned to what he judged would be the nearest point for the first proof. He took a stack of ordinary white paper and loaded it into the front of the machine. He put the black, red, yellow and blue inks into their respective ducts. The press was switched on and the rollers turned for the initial layers of ink to spread over them. We both knew the first sheets through wouldn't be any good, as that was just a process to be gone through to allow him to make the necessary adjustments to reach the most accurate positioning. But even so I had to look at them.

Taking a printed sheet from the handful that had been run through, he once again went through the procedure of moving the edge of his hand over the sheet and mumbling to himself about 'points to the left' and 'up a fraction' and so on. And once again he made various minor adjustments to the press with his spanner. Although I was of no assistance from a practical point of view, I was nevertheless doing as much as I could. I was praying.

Another few sheets were run through the press. And another series of adjustments were made. And then the procedure was repeated, again and again. After an hour of this, I began to feel a sense of déjà vu. But then Eric said, 'It looks like we're nearly there.' But 'nearly' wasn't good enough, as we both knew. All the same, I thought I detected the tiniest hint of optimism in his voice.

'Oh, please God,' I said out aloud. I could feel my heart pounding as Eric pressed the start button.

'Keep 'em crossed,' he remarked before his voice was drowned out by the noise of the press. A minute later, he switched it off and scurried round to the end of the machine. I watched as he pulled out the last printed sheet to come through. Looking down, his blank expression displayed no emotion. 'Fuck my old boots,' he remarked.

'Is that "Fuck my old boots" good, or "Fuck my old boots" bad?' I asked.

He looked up from the sheet, and passed it to me. I extended my hand and took the sheet. I closed my eyes briefly before looking apprehensively down.

'Well, fuck my old boots!' I declared, and both Eric and I started laughing out loud. The images on the sheet were just about as near-perfect as they could possibly be.

'Well, I'll tell you something, mate, I really didn't think we were going to get there,' he gasped, 'I really didn't. Just goes to show what a funny old game this scanning business is. I would have staked my life that that set of film was no better than the other ones we tried out. I really didn't think it was any good. Just goes to show.' He pulled out another printed sheet and looked down, shaking his head and grinning. 'Just goes to show.'

After running off another 100 sheets or so, and satisfying himself the positioning was as accurate as it could possibly be, he cleaned up the press and left the plates on, ready for action just as soon as I delivered the numbering boxes and the banknote paper.

Soon after I left Eric, Vindiloo called me. He was back in London. From what he had to say, my precautionary measure in travelling back alone proved to be well founded. He had been stopped and searched as he came through Customs.

'It always happens to me when I come back,' he said, a tone of resigned acceptance in his voice, which cheered up instantly when I gave him the good news about the film. Naturally, he was delighted, and then told me he was waiting to hear from his man about collecting the paper. I told him to call me as soon as he heard and, in the meantime, I would hire a van in readiness to meet him immediately the paper was available.

Next morning, I hired the van and drove to the engineering company, having heard from my friend that the numbering boxes were ready for collection. His first reaction upon seeing me pull up was to remark that a car would have been sufficient to take the boxes away in. I laughed at his little joke, and was even laughing when I paid him his money. I had the numbering boxes. Everything in the world was just about as good as it could be. Even the birds in the trees sounded sweeter. All I had to do now was collect the paper.

I felt as though I didn't have a care in the world when the phone rang. I was just pulling out of the industrial estate where my friend had his engineering factory. It was Vindiloo.

'Tony, my old mate,' I greeted him. 'What's happening, my main man?'

Vindiloo's response wasn't quite as enthusiastic as I had expected. 'Er, not a lot at the moment, I'm afraid.'

I didn't like the dour tone of his voice, and sensed he might be the bearer of bad tidings. 'What's the matter?' I asked.

'I've got some bad news.'

'Don't say what I think you're going to say. Please don't.'

'Well, there's a bit of a problem. It looks like the paper's not ready yet.'

'What? You're fucking joking.'

'No, I'm not. Can you pop round to my place, I'll tell you all about it,' he said.

In one fell swoop my spirits had plummeted from way up there somewhere to rock bottom. I made my way to Vindiloo as fast as the van could get me there.

Sitting in the kitchen of his town house in the East End of London, I listened gloomily as he explained the situation. His jet-set contact with the warehouse full of banknote paper told him there had been some kind of hold-up. I found this hard to understand as we had been led to believe that the man already had the paper in his possession. Vindiloo was unable to enlighten me to any significant degree, other than to tell me that it might not happen. In fact, it almost certainly wouldn't happen.

'I knew it was too good to be true,' I said. 'I should have got hold of the paper before I laid out a tanner. I just can't believe I've been so stupid.'

'I'm sorry, mate. I'm really sorry,' Vindiloo said.

'How did you leave it, then?' I asked, hoping against hope that all might not be lost.

'He's going to call me back some time today,' Vindiloo replied.

'OK. Well, I've got a few things to do. Better try and sort out a few deals on the twenties.' I got up to leave and then remembered something I had in my pocket. I took out half-a-dozen of the printed notes that I had brought along to show him. 'I thought you might like to see these. Not that it makes much difference now.' I tossed them on to the table-top and left.

# CHAPTER 14

# Boris and Karloff

I took the van back to the hire company and then drove home. I couldn't bring myself to tell Eric just yet. Once home, I sat down and poured myself a glass of wine. Within a couple of hours, I was pretty well drunk and feeling rather sorry for myself. The house was empty and, with no one to interrupt me, I managed to convince myself I was the unluckiest, most hard-done-by little soldier in the whole wide world.

Then the poor little soldier's mobile rang. It was Vindiloo. He needed to see me urgently. Although the last thing I felt like doing in my drunken state was venturing out into the big wide world, I nevertheless agreed to meet him at a pub close to where I lived.

This would give me a bit of time to take a shower and try to sober up. An hour later, I felt quite normal. For some reason or other, the effects of drinking white wine never seem to be particularly long-lasting as far as I'm concerned, and I never suffer with a headache.

I met up with Vindiloo feeling totally refreshed and in control of my faculties. He explained that shortly after I had left, his man had called, and he had met up with him at his penthouse suite in one of London's leading hotels. His jet-set friend was in the company of several other men who, it turned out, were involved with him in the banknote paper deal. It was explained that the problem centred around the release of the paper without the consortium knowing its destination. Vindiloo explained my policy about refusing to let anybody know the printer's identity or whereabouts. He went on to emphasise how long he had known me and that he trusted me implicitly.

Whilst this was good enough for his contact, the others weren't convinced. What made it worse was the fact that even Vindiloo didn't know where the paper would be going. With the impasse remaining unresolved, the situation looked grim. And then, Vindiloo produced his piéce de resistance. He showed them the notes I had left with him. Although they had no numbers and I had cut them out of the sheet using a scalpel blade, the quality of the printing was there for all to see. And, as we all know, a picture can say more than a thousand words, or even *five billion* words.

Upon sight of the proofs, it became apparent to all concerned just how close they were to pulling off the Crime of the Century, a crime that would dwarf the Great Train Robbery, the Brinks Mat Gold Robbery and all the other major robberies and swindles of the previous 50 years combined.

It wasn't long before a deal was agreed. Unbeknown to Vindiloo and me, their original intention had been to make available to us enough paper to print £500 million worth, far more than we required to start the ball rolling. They now agreed with Vindiloo to give him enough to print approximately £200 million. He, in turn, had to guarantee to keep half of this in his possession whilst I was busy printing up the first £100 million. Of course, this was completely acceptable to me, and was no less than the kind of amounts and figures I had in mind anyway.

Vindiloo went on to tell me that arrangements had been made for the morning. I was to be at his house at 9.00am with the van I had returned just a couple of hours previously. The show was back on the road.

The next morning, I was knocking on Vindiloo's door. The time was 8.45am. Without concerning ourselves with such niceties as a cup of tea, we left in the van immediately, and Vindiloo directed me to a self-storage centre in South London. As we pulled into the loading area, Vindiloo jumped out and directed me back and up to the loading bay. He banged the side of the van as the back was flush with the loading ramp.

'Give the horn a couple of toots,' he said, and I did as I was told. I got out of the van and strolled to the back. Walking towards the loading ramp, I saw the awesome shape of a gigantic man pulling a pallet along piled high with packets of paper. The moment he came into view, another, slightly smaller giant followed him from around the corner in the warehouse building. He, too, was pulling a large pallet full of paper. Both men had short black hair, although one was naturally thin on top with just a touch of hair on the sides. Vindiloo nodded to them in acknowledgement. They grunted and nodded back to him. 'Not a lot of witty repartee here,' I thought to myself.

'I've often wondered what Godzilla and King Kong would look like in black suits,' I whispered to Vindiloo and smiled sweetly at the two 'porters'. They declined to return the gesture. Vindiloo chuckled.

'It's OK. They can't understand you. They don't speak a word of English. Russian.'

'Russian? Are they, you know ... Russian Mafia?' I said.

'Yeah, I should imagine so. Mean-looking bastards, eh? I wouldn't fancy fucking about with them, eh?'

'Not unless I had a machine-gun,' I replied.

'Even then I'd be a bit dubious. The bullets might bounce off them. Just make 'em angry. Know what I mean?' Vindiloo laughed at his own little humorous comment, but was quick to indicate to the two Russian heavy-heavies that he was their friend.

'ME — TONY,' he said in slow, laboured tones. Their grim, battle-scarred faces remained inscrutable as they stared at him. I was reminded of the blank expressions that gorillas at the zoo have whilst the massed hordes of the viewing public jump up and down in front of their cages. Vindiloo tried again. Pointing to me, he went to say my name before I stopped him.

'Call me Wilf,' I said.

He stopped and quickly glanced at me. 'Wilf?' He shook his head and then, turning back to the two Russians, loudly enunciated my alias — 'WILF'. He pointed to me as he spoke and then to himself — 'TONY.' One of the gorillas nodded, without smiling. Slowly he grunted the sounds, 'TONY ... WILF.'

There was no reciprocal exchange of names, and so I nicknamed them Boris and Karloff. Now the formalities were completed, and I felt as though we were old friends, I moved towards the first pallet of paper. I couldn't resist running my hands gently over the packets. I closed my eyes and savoured a non-existent smell. The smell of unborn money. Enough, surely, to make an innocent little counterfeiter like me positively swoon.

'Are we gonna get this lot on the van, then?' Vindiloo asked, and we set about loading it like men possessed. The physical work itself didn't tire me out too much, but I have to admit, the sight of the two giants picking up several packets at a time to my two, left me feeling thoroughly exhausted. (Vindiloo cried off from the physical side of the proceedings, claiming to have a bad back.) It wasn't too long before the van was fully loaded, and I pulled the shutter down. Vindiloo explained that he would be leaving in a van parked up on the other side of the yard. The van was already loaded with the other half of the first consignment. Vindiloo was under strict instructions to put it down in a safe storage place until the first batch had been printed and delivered.

'Right then, Tony. That's it, then. I'll get cracking on this lot straight away, and I'll give you a call to let you know how we're progressing. When you learn Russian, give my love and kisses to Godzilla and King Kong here,' I said, and made to jump down from the loading ramp. I felt a great weight as one of the Russians put his hand on my shoulder. I froze as I heard him say, 'Just one minute, Wilf.'

I looked across at Vindiloo who appeared to be as shocked as me.

'Jesus Christ,' I said under my breath.

Slowly, I turned round to face the Russian. I wondered if the feeling of all the blood in my body making its way down to my feet was physically apparent. The Russian wasn't smiling as he pinned me to the back of the van with his ice-cold gaze.

'I just need to know that we are all absolutely clear about the situation here.' He paused and I nodded obediently. He continued, 'We are trusting you with this paper. If anything should go wrong, if you should not do everything as your friend has promised you will do, you will be killed. You understand this?'

I coughed to clear my throat. 'I understand. Completely.'

He extended the huge mass of flesh and bone that made up his fingers, thumb and knuckles. He had a firm but surprisingly civilised grip as we shook hands. Thankfully, he wasn't the kind of macho man who takes great delight in squeezing the recipient's hand in a childish display of misconceived superiority.

'Good. As we shake hands, both ... Godzilla and myself,' another pause, accompanied by his ice-cold stare and expressionless features, 'are men of honour. We shake hands, we keep our word.' Another pause. 'In every respect. Farewell.'

He released his grip and I retrieved my hand. He turned and said something in Russian to the other man, who allowed just the faintest of smiles to crease his fearsome features. I got the impression that he, at least, genuinely didn't speak any English. After some more Russian, he suddenly laughed out loud and raised his massive hand in a farewell gesture. 'VILF!' I heard him say, in between great belly laughs.

'Good luck,' Boris said, and I quickly jumped down and got into the van. I started the engine, and called out to Vindiloo through the open window, 'I'll give you a bell tomorrow mate. Olli-Bierchi!'

Driving along at a steady speed, conscientiously within the limit, I couldn't help thinking about the first payment of 3 per cent of face value — £3 million. And then I thought about it again. And again. And again.

*'When you're hot, you're hot, and when you're not, you're not.'*

And right now, Mrs Jory's little boy felt like the surface of the sun!

# CHAPTER 15

## Hard Work and a Close Shave

I interrupted my journey to the workshop and called Eric from a roadside phone box.

'The eagle has landed,' I said and, in an equally excited tone of voice, he assured me that he would be at the workshop before me. Driving along, I took several detours through a myriad of back turnings, in order to satisfy myself that nobody was following me. It wasn't only the possibility that the police might be on my tail that was uppermost in my thoughts, but on this particular trip it wouldn't have come as any great surprise had Boris and Karloff, the Russian giants, tried to find out my destination. But all was clear in the wing mirrors of the van. As an added precaution, and a procedure I never failed to observe when paying the workshop a visit, I travelled up and down several long and winding, very narrow country lanes in the vicinity of Ken's house. It seemed to be all quiet on the Western Front.

Just over an hour after leaving the Russians and Vindiloo, Eric and I were enthusiastically unloading the packets of paper into the storage area of the workshop. After the load was neatly stacked in several large piles, Eric eagerly tore the outside wrapping off one of the packets. I watched him take the top sheet and hold it up to the light. I was unable to resist doing likewise.

The feel of the sheets, the image of the watermarks, it's impossible to describe accurately the feeling of holding and looking at these sheets and then at the stacks surrounding us. Just knowing there was the equivalent of £100 million within spitting distance. The knowledge that, in just a couple of weeks we would be set for life, gave me a sense of subdued euphoria. A comforting, cosy glow warming me inside.

Eric took the sheet into the print room and switched on the light box. He placed the paper on to the illuminated surface and then took one of the sheets of film out of a drawer and positioned it on top of the banknote paper. Gently, he manoeuvred it about with his fingertips.

'Bee-yoo-diful,' he remarked. 'Just perfect.'

What he was referring to was the position of the ten images on the film, something which was unalterable without sending it back to Herman the German. As the position of the watermark on the finished note was the same on each one, it was crucial that the film was compatible with the paper. Although we had made the necessary checks against the sample sheets in our possession, there was still the possibility that the positioning on the main batch might vary. Equally, each sheet of film in the set of four had to be exactly compatible with each of the other three. The tiniest fraction of inaccuracy and the film would have to be re-planned. This much we had already established, but now we were approaching the last hurdle with the watermarked sheets of banknote paper.

Although Herman had been furnished with all the dimensions and relevant details for his uncle, it wouldn't have been the first time that a mistake had been made in the planning of a job requiring absolute accuracy. But now, here we were looking at Fritz the Scan-Man's handiwork and, as Eric had been moved to remark, 'Bee-yoo-diful.'

It was now just after midday and Eric and I got to work immediately. The first job to be done was to guillotine the sheets in half, as the press wasn't large enough to accommodate the full sheet size. This in itself was no problem but, even so, it was a time-consuming job. Eric programmed the guillotine to the position required and left me to do the cutting whilst he set the numbering boxes up on the press. By the time that Eric had set them up in their correct positions and was almost ready to start the run, I was still only a small way into the huge mountain of paper that had to be cut down. But even so, there was sufficient ready to start the ball rolling.

As the actual banknote paper was so precious, the first few hundred sheets to be run through were plain cartridge paper. Last minute adjustments and checks were made. The numbering boxes were moved marginally one-way, and then another. And then the stage was set. Call for the star of the show!

I wheeled in a stack of sheets about 5ft high. Eric loaded about a third of them into the press and, after a quick visual check and mental appraisal of the state of play, pressed the start button. The sheets started to feed one by one through the machine, slowly at first and then gradually gaining momentum. Eric walked over to the end of the press where the printed sheets were being delivered. He whipped one out and we stared at it, both in awe of what he was holding.

'Bee-yoo-diful, eh, mate?' I said, grinning from ear to ear. I'm not normally an emotional man, but I think it's fair to say that both Eric and I were feeling lumps in our throats.

'Our first-born, darling, isn't she beautiful. I'm so glad I'm present at her birth,' I said almost kissing it.

Eric laughed out loud and walked back to the front of the press. 'This is going to be one hell of a multiple birth!' he called out and turned the handle to speed up the machine.

I took the sheet back into the guillotine room and placed it by my side as I carried on cutting. It was as well that the guillotine was equipped with a fail-safe mechanism that prevented the blade from engaging if the operator's hands or fingers were in danger of being chopped off. The sheet of printed banknotes was very much a visual magnet and I found it hard to take my eyes off it. So much so, that after a while I had to tuck it away, out of view. Several hours later, half the paper had been cut down to size, and Eric was counterfeiting like a printer possessed. We worked through to 10.00pm, by which time he was ready to collapse.

I helped him to clean up the press and leave it ready for operation the next day. Although we had barely made a dent in the colossal paper mountain, we nevertheless had a vast amount of money printed up and stacked in piles about 5ft high. At this stage, it wasn't at the 'real money' point, as only one side of the sheets had been printed and, of course, the individual notes hadn't been cut down to size. The plan was to print the reverse sides of the sheets the next day. But even so, just looking at the various partially-printed stacks was nothing less than inspiring.

The next morning, I arrived at the workshop ready for another industrious day. Eric was like-minded, having fully recovered after a good night's sleep. I took up my position at the guillotine and Eric started making the press ready. As the film and plates were planned to work and turn, there was no need to take the plates off the press and replace them with plates to print the reverse side. This was because the ten images on each of the plates were divided equally into images of the front of the note and the reverse of the note. Consequently, when the sheets were printed, the left hand row of five images showed the front and the right hand side row the reverse. The sheets were then turned and fed back through the press with the blank side being printed. In this way the reverse side image is printed on the back of the printed front side image and vice versa. Hence the term, 'work and turn'. This is a further example of the necessity for absolute accuracy in the original planning work. As our work schedule involved printing as many sheets as possible on one side on day one, and then the blank sides on day two, being able to carry on without replacing and re-positioning the plates each morning saved an enormous amount of time.

At the end of the second day, all the sheets that had previously been printed on one side were completed, and I had cut all the paper down to size. As before, I helped Eric clean up the press and then we wrapped the printed paper into packets, each containing 1,000 sheets. We loaded these on to the van, and as the time was only 8.00pm, I drove them to the Little Printer, whom I had arranged to be on standby.

Once there, the procedure was very much the same as with Eric. The packets were loaded into the workshop and, once they were stacked by the platen, he tore open the top packet. He gave out a long, low whistle as he gazed at the sheet. He nodded his head appreciatively.

'Noice bit of printing,' he said. 'Noice bit of paper as well. So now then, where did you say you got it?'

'I didn't. I'm just organising the work for some good friends of mine,' I replied.

'Mmmm. It feels just like proper banknote paper. Good stuff. If I didn't know better, I'd say it was the real thing,' he said, rubbing the sheet between his thumb and forefinger.

I scoffed at the idea, and the Little Printer responded, 'Yeah. I suppose so. Still, it's good stuff, bloody good stuff to be sure. Roight, no time to stand about admiring the material. Work to be done, Stevie me boy.'

I agreed with him and stood watching while he positioned the engraved plate on the machine. I realised that there would be a considerable amount of trial and error before the exact position was arrived at, and also realised this would involve a considerable amount of waste sheets.

Just as he was about to stack a pile of sheets into the platen, I put my hand on his arm. 'Erm, I tell you what. I think we'll leave it till the morning, and I'll bring some other sheets in. Different paper, just plain white cartridge paper. I mean, we don't want to waste any of this stuff, do we?'

'It's up to you, Stevie boy. You're the boss. What time in the morning, then? Noice and early?'

'It's up to you.'

'Seven o'clock.'

'OK, seven o'clock in the morning then.'

I said my goodbyes and, as I was going out of the door, he said, 'You *sure* this stuff's not genuine banknote paper?'

I smiled and shook my head. 'See you in the morning, mate.'

That night I slept well and the next morning I was at the workshop before Eric. I loaded the plain white cartridge sheets that had been printed for positioning purposes into the car and immediately made my way to Dermot's premises. Once there it didn't take too long for the Little Printer to position the engraved plate to correspond to the relevant printed areas on the sheets. That was the easy part. After that the pressure had to be increased sufficiently to create the desired raised effect at the top of the notes. The more the force of the impact was increased, the louder the noise the platen made. And the more concerned the expression on the Little Printer's face. I could see he was becoming increasingly worried, to the extent that I had to promise him that I would pay for any repair work should the platen collapse or explode there and then.

Even though the pressure was increased to its highest degree, there was no noticeable raised effect on the sheets. I was beginning to become more than just a trifle concerned. I had felt confident my improvised mock-*intaglio* would work, but so far all I had looked like achieving was a hefty bill to pay for any subsequent repairs to the machine.

But then a very rare event occurred. I had something of a minor brainwave. I suggested a makeshift method of padding out the platen to increase the pressure to more than its maximum limit. The Little Printer looked aghast. In his opinion, this course of action would most certainly cause the machine a great deal of damage. But necessity is the mother of invention, as I've often heard and, after giving the matter some thought, we came up with a possible solution. I used all my persuasive powers on the Little Printer and, at length, he agreed to pad out the platen with a material that is used in a process called 'cutting and creasing'. This material has a certain amount of give to it, and after some experimentation he managed to apply it in such a way that the printed area was just about pushed through to give the raised effect.

I breathed a sigh of relief as the machine began running the sheets, albeit extremely noisily. All the while, the Little Printer continued to wear a worried frown and constantly shook his head, despite my earnest promises to pay for any damage caused. After a couple of hours, there was sufficient to start the guillotining work.

Unlike the guillotining of the sheets at the workshop, the cutting down of the printed notes was a far more complicated exercise. Bearing in mind the value of the material to be guillotined, it certainly wasn't a job that could be entrusted to me. Fortunately, the platen, once it was running, required no more attention than someone to watch it and restart it each time it stopped, which it tended to do at frequent intervals. And so the Little Printer started guillotining whilst I stood there watching.

It wasn't too long before there were stacks of newly printed, crisp, banknotes all around the immediate area. Although they weren't English notes, it was an incredible sensation knowing they were more than mere counterfeits. They were, for all intents and purposes, genuine money. I took a handful from the top of one of the piles and, holding one edge tightly, flicked them in my hands. I also had some in my pocket from the original samples Vindiloo had given me nearly three weeks before. The official genuine notes were absolutely indistinguishable from the unofficial 'genuine' notes.

The stacks of fresh crisp money began to accumulate, and it seemed that, wherever I looked in the room, my eyes fell upon nothing but cash. I felt as though I was in a scene from a film where the star is locked in a bank vault piled high with money. But this was no film; this was *for real,* baby! And this river of cash I was splashing around in was just a stream, a small tributary leading to an ocean. An ocean of cash.

We worked late into the night, managing to complete the job, and packed the notes up into boxes, which we tucked away in a corner. During the day, I had called Eric who was making good progress and managing perfectly well without me. I also called Vindiloo to let him know that the wheels of industry were turning in the most profitable manner. For the moment at least, it was relatively plain sailing I assured him.

The following morning, I called into the Little Printer's workshop and collected the boxes of cash. I could tell that he was still concerned about the possible damage to his platen, and so I gave him £2,000 to be getting on with. This had the desired effect, and his enthusiasm immediately returned.

'So when will you be down with another lot, then?' he asked.

'Tonight,' I replied, and the toothless grin spread across his face.

I took the boxes to self-storage premises in Hackney, where I had a unit in the name of Paul Kay. It was ideal for my purposes, as it was discreetly tucked away in a back street off the beaten track and the staff never made themselves too busy. I had maintained a unit there for a couple of years and was a familiar face whose comings and goings aroused no curiosity or interest. After storing the boxes of cash, I made my way over to the workshop to see if there was anything I could do to assist. There wasn't much for me to do but, just by stacking the sheets

18p

Viscount Althorp

# Police smash £300m fake Chanel racket

By ANDREW SIMPSON

POLICE probing a worldwide racket in fake perfume arrested nine people yesterday.

They swooped on warehouses in East London and found counterfeiting equipment and imitation Chanel No. 5 and 19.

Seven men and two women—including an Italian and a Spaniard—were arrested and are being questioned at West Ham and High Wycombe stations. Further arrests are expected today.

The operation involved 60 officers from Thames Valley

UP!

s job back —

p left) An earlier taste of international infamy in 1984. And although Christmas 1 wasn't as profitable as I had anticipated, I still had enough left over to treat aine to a holiday in Barbados for her 40th birthday in January 1992 – as well as a sh party and a new car.

The units in South London where I got locked in overnight, down to an internationa drug smuggling cartel. See page 48.

next to the press as Eric required them and moving the printed sheets into the storage room, I helped to lighten the load, and the operation was speeded up considerably. A prime example of 'every little helps'.

That evening I was back at the Little Printer's premises, and we spent a couple of hours gaining a head start on the following day's work. The next day was the same as before. The platen continued to make a severe breaking-down type of noise each time a sheet was impressed into the engraved plate, and Dermot continued to groan along with it. The platen carried on working without collapsing, as did my little printer friend. Again, we worked late into the night and completed the job.

The following morning, I collected the boxes of cash and took them to the storage unit in Hackney, and then I went over to Eric and assisted him in whatever way I could. This routine continued to run quite smoothly until about half-way through, when I was driving from the Little Printer's workshop to the storage premises in Hackney. The route took me through an area called Hackney Wick. Ever careful to maintain a steady speed, and keeping a constant check in my rear-view mirrors to make sure I wasn't being followed, I came over the brow of a slight incline and drove into my worst nightmare — a police roadblock!

Although the time was just 10.30 in the morning, a perfectly respectable time to be driving about in a van, the police were pulling all commercial vehicles, apart from articulated lorries, into a layby at the side of the road. I did my very best to maintain a degree of composure, knowing full well the worst thing for me would be to show any outward signs of nervousness. I joined the queue of vans making its way into the layby, and watched in horror as the uniformed police officers searched the backs of each vehicle. I was virtually panic-stricken as I heard the sound of a police siren and then a squad car drive past me. The squad car stopped beside a van and I saw the miserable-looking driver, handcuffed, being placed in the back seat and driven off. Several black bin-liners, filled with something fairly bulky, were put back into the van, which was then locked up with another police officer standing guard by it. Without being able to see inside the bags, my guess was that they contained 'puff' — cannabis.

I toyed with the idea of jumping out of the van and making a run for it. But from the amount of Old Bill about, in cars, on foot and a couple on motorbikes, I knew it would be absolutely futile. If only I had my water pistol on me, I could blast my way out! Only this was no joking matter, I could well be in the shit here, in fact, well and truly in DDS — *deep, deep shit*!

I noticed a police officer walking along the queue of vans and having a word with the drivers. I could see he was checking their licences and documentation. Fortunately, I had all mine with me, driving licence and the van-hire form. At least I wouldn't be done for driving without a licence — what a result. The officer came to my window and I proffered my paperwork, which I already had prepared. Luckily, my hand wasn't shaking as I gave it to him. He gave me a perfunctory smile and said, 'Thank you, sir,' before walking to the van behind me. By now, my heart was pounding almost out of control as I edged closer to the front of the queue. I noticed that in a couple of instances the Old Bill merely glanced in the backs of the vans without even opening the door. I prayed this would happen to me, but knew this was most unlikely. After all, what's the point in carrying out a roadside search without opening up the easily visible boxes inside. In all probability, the vans that weren't searched were empty inside.

Very often at times of great stress, I find myself thinking about my late father, Freddie, and I invariably implore him to give the black sheep of the family a break. And most certainly this was a time of great stress. *Oh yes, Stevie boy, no two ways about it, you're in a lot of trouble here. A lot of trouble. Just one van ahead of me now. Oh please, Freddie, look down on your little boy. I could certainly do with a bit of help!*

I did a quick mental check, and ran through all my pockets in order to make sure I had no pieces of paper with anybody's names on them. I put my small address book down the front of my underpants, even though it had no incriminating names or numbers in it. And then, as the van in front of me was being searched, one of the officers standing fairly close to my van received a call on his radio. I watched as he spoke into it and, although I couldn't hear properly what was being said, he seemed very happy at what he had been told.

'They've got the bastards,' he said to the two policemen looking in the back of the van. 'Over in Lea Bridge Road.'

All the police seemed quite pleased by this piece of news, and then one of them said, 'Does that mean we can pack up here then?'

'Yeah. I suppose so,' another one replied. And with that, a couple of police officers started walking to their cars. The officer closest to me told me I would be able to go any second.

I couldn't believe my luck. My silent prayers had been answered. Just how close had I been! 'Thank you, Freddie!'

The collection of Old Bill now seemed to be keen to move the queue of vans on as soon as possible, and I had my foot on the clutch and the van in first gear ready to pull away as soon as I was given the go ahead. 'Oh, thank you, Freddie, thank you so much!' I began to edge forward as the van in front of me drove off. Then I saw a superior-looking Old Bill appear from nowhere. He was obviously a commanding officer, in all probability a superintendent, and I sat looking ahead in sheer, stunned disbelief as I heard him say to the others, 'Might as well just do these last few while we're here. You never know, might turn up something interesting.'

*No, this cannot be happening. Here I am, literally just on the point of driving off into the sunset, and this fucking lunatic wants to see if his men can turn up something interesting.*

I felt like crying real tears at the complete injustice of it all. I stopped a few yards ahead and, feeling like the condemned man making his final trip to the gallows, I got out of the van and trudged to the back. With just one of the officers looking on, I opened the back doors. It was plain that, slightly peeved by their superior's pedantic attitude, they wanted to get finished as soon as possible. The other officer was already looking into the back of the van behind. The policeman and I looked into the back of the van at the boxes inside. All told they contained about £8 million in forged foreign money. The young constable leaned forward to study the boxes at closer quarters.

'What's in the boxes, sir?' he asked.

'Paper,' I replied. By now, it was a wonder he couldn't hear my heart pounding against my chest.

'D'you mind if I take a look inside them, sir?'

The question was purely rhetorical. I resisted the urge to say, 'Do I have a choice?' and merely answered, 'Of course not.'

In total, there were 22 boxes in the back. I reached in and pulled one out towards the back. Before I pulled the brown tape off the top, I momentarily hesitated as I double-checked the tiny ink mark in the corner. I tore back the tape and opened the flaps. There inside were two piles of plain white paper.

The officer peered at them and then reached inside and flipped through the piles, so that he could tell, more or less, that all the sheets were the same. He gave a casual glance at the other boxes in the back, and for a moment his gaze seemed to be transfixed on one particular box. Why this should be I have no idea, as all the boxes were identical, apart from six which had an imperceptible ink spot on the top, denoting to me that they contained plain white paper. But I knew for certain that the box he was looking at wasn't one of these dummy boxes.

It was reminiscent of the kind of scene in an old war film where the hero is trying to escape across enemy lines hidden under a cart filled with hay. I imagined the policeman next to me as the Nazi soldier who prods the hay with his bayonet and misses the escaping POW by inches.

But then his thoughts were interrupted by the van behind pulling away. He glanced over his shoulder to see his colleague starting to look in the back of the next van. There was just one more after that. He turned back to the van and then said to me, 'Sorry to have delayed you, sir. Drive carefully,' and walked towards the last van in the queue. I closed the back doors and walked to the front of the van and got into the driver's seat. I could feel my hands shaking as I gripped the steering wheel. I pulled away cautiously and continued my journey to the self-storage unit.

Apart from this near-disaster, the wheels of industry turned completely smoothly until the first half of the first consignment of paper was printed. All £100 million worth. And I had just over 1,000 waste sheets, which I had wrapped up and marked 'Returns'.

After making the last delivery of boxes of cash to the self-storage premises, I stood outside my unit with the door open, and stared at the vast fortune in boxes piled high before me. And this represented just 2 per cent of the final total of £5 billion.

I stepped back, and leaned against the door of the unit directly opposite mine in the narrow corridor. I closed my eyes and stood there, head back, thinking about the mind-boggling figures involved in the enterprise, the kind of figures that can cause a calculator to overheat. I was aware of a strange floating sensation, in part I suppose, a physical reaction to working flat-out for two weeks and a sense of achievement at having completed the first batch without mishap.

'Working hard?' I very nearly jumped out of my skin at the sound of the young man's voice. It was one of the workers who operated the forklift truck and kept a general eye on things. I was momentarily caught unawares in the middle of my little dream.

'What, er?' I mumbled.

'I didn't mean to make you jump. I just thought you looked knackered, Mr Kay.'

I recovered my wits and replied, 'Yeah, I have been working quite hard.'

He glanced at the boxes as he walked past and remarked, 'Well, I just hope you're getting well paid for it, then.'

I affected an attitude of discontent. 'Well, you know how it is. Still, I suppose it pays the rent!'

He gave me a knowing chuckle. 'Yeah, tell me about it. By the time the old tax and everything's taken out of it, I sometimes wonder if it's worth it.'

'Yeah, me, too. I think I'll jack it in and live off the social.'

He carried on walking, still chuckling and nodding his head in agreement.

# CHAPTER 16

## An Extreme Case of Murphy's Law

I went to see Vindiloo at home and gave him the good news. He had maintained contact with the Marbella Sailor during the previous couple of weeks, and our first payment of £3 million would be available in two or three days.

Vindiloo's people had already been given a couple of hundred completed notes and could see for themselves the quality of the finished product. Needless to say, they were eager to take delivery of the first batch as soon as possible. Vindiloo had arranged to collect a van that afternoon from Boris and Karloff, which I would load up with the boxes of cash I had put down in the storage unit in Hackney. Once on board, he was to call the Russians, who would tell him where to deliver the van. Although we wouldn't be paid for a couple of days, I was completely happy with the arrangement, as Vindiloo still had the other half of the paper consignment. If anything should go wrong with the delivery, and we didn't receive our money, we were covered by a potential £100 million worth of genuine banknote paper.

That afternoon, Vindiloo and I drove over in his car to the self-storage unit premises in South London where we had met the Russians two weeks previously. As before, they were there waiting for us. The English-speaking colossus greeted me.

'Vilf. How are you?'

As I opened my mouth to speak, I could hear his bald-headed comrade chuckling and repeating the name 'Vilf!' I smiled, not quite as nervously as the last time we had met, and shook hands with the two of them. They shook hands with Vindiloo as well, and Boris said, 'So you do not have any problems, yes?'

'Yes. That's correct. No problems,' I replied.

'Yeah, sweet as a nut,' Vindiloo said.

'Sweets as nuts?' Boris looked slightly bemused.

Vindiloo smiled, and I said, 'Yes, that's just an expression. It means everything has gone to plan. No problems.'

Although not actually smiling to any noticeable degree, the Russian seemed to be amused. Their van was by the loading bay and, without wasting any time on pidgin-English small-talk, I left Vindiloo with Boris and Karloff and drove to collect the boxes of cash.

An hour or so later, Vindiloo called me for confirmation that the freight was on board. The sweat was pouring off me as I loaded the last few boxes into the back of the van.

'I've nearly finished loading,' I told him.

'You sound out of breath. Hard work is it?' he said, sounding rather amused. I could hear the sound of laughter and talking in the background. He was obviously in a bar or a pub.

'Something like that,' I replied

'You should have said. I'm sure Boris and Karloff wouldn't have minded helping out.'

'Don't worry about it. I'll manage. Any news on the meet?'

'Yeah. I'm in a place called the Kennedy Hotel. You remember it? I've met you here a couple of times before.'

'By the side of Euston Station, right?'

'That's the one. I'll be waiting in the bar.'

A few minutes later, I had completed loading the van and was headed in the general direction of Euston Station. As was the norm when freighted up, I drove in an observant and diligent fashion. Upon my arrival at the hotel, I parked up at a meter directly outside. As luck would have it, there was 30 minutes left. *'That's a pound saved!'* I thought to myself.

Vindiloo was waiting for me at the bar nursing a large vodka. I noticed the two Russians were drinking fresh orange juice and, predictably, Vindiloo was wearing an ear-to-ear grin on his face, which seemed to light up upon catching sight of me walking through the hotel lobby.

Again, the Russians shook my hand, and took the van keys as Vindiloo ordered a drink for me. Glancing down at his watch, Boris indicated that he and his comrade would leave immediately. 'Just as final confirmation,' he said, 'so all of the nuts are on the van?'

I smiled and replied, 'Yes. No problems.'

'Good, then we shall leave you now. My friend and I thank you.'

They both walked away, and I said, 'I will see you again soon, I suppose.'

'Yes. Sweets as nuts,' said Boris.

I didn't need a lot of persuading to remain in the bar drinking with Vindiloo, and it wasn't too long before I was beginning to feel the effects of the alcohol. The minimal amount of sleep combined with the maximum amount of work during the previous couple of weeks or so, to say nothing of the nervous energy I'd burned up, proved to be an extremely heady cocktail. My normal sturdy resilience to the debilitating effects of the demon drink had deserted me and I quickly became extremely drunk. Then Vindiloo, for reasons known only to himself, said, 'So why don't we go and pick up the rest of the paper?'

'What, now?' I asked.

'Yeah, why not?'

I thought about it and then suddenly it seemed like a good idea.

'OK, then. Let's go,' I said.

We downed our drinks and made our way out to the street, swaying as we crossed the road to where the car was parked. He struggled to locate the keys, then fumbled in his efforts to open the door. Somehow or other we managed to get into the car, and somehow or other Vindiloo proceeded to drive it away. Even in my drunken state, I was painfully aware that he was driving in a rather erratic fashion and the car was swerving from side to side. But, with the reckless indifference that an excess of alcohol invariably confers upon the recipient, the pair of us carried on regardless. In fact, it wasn't too long before I was fast asleep.

I was awoken by the sound of Vindiloo's voice telling me that we had arrived. How long we had been driving I had no idea, but for some reason or other I had the feeling that I had been in the car for quite some time. How on earth we had arrived in one piece without being stopped by the police, or worse still, having an accident, is nothing short of a miracle. We were parked up outside a lock-up garage, one of several in a small compound. I moved laboriously to get out of the car, and watched as Vindiloo made hard work of removing the padlock. Eventually, he got the door open and stepped inside. The packets of paper were stacked on pallets and took up about half the floor space.

'Well?' Vindiloo remarked.

'Well what?' I replied.

For a moment, the pair of us stood looking at each other trying to fathom just why we had gone there in the first place. And then Vindiloo arrived at the startling conclusion that we needed a large van to take the paper anywhere. Thank God, we didn't have one. It was bad enough that we had come this far driving a car in such a drunken state. The thought of attempting to load and drive away a van beggars belief. Although extremely drunk, I still couldn't believe what a stupid thing the two of us had done.

'Tell you what, Tony, why don't we leave your car here and get a cab home?' I suggested.

Vindiloo thought for a moment then concurred. 'Yeah, I think you're right. What the fuck are we doing here, anyway?'

He pushed the garage doors to, and we staggered away. But after walking around in circles trying to find a minicab office, Vindiloo decided he was fit enough to drive back. Unwisely, I agreed with him and we returned to his car. This was the last comprehensible memory I have of our mad journey.

The next thing I knew, I was waking up in bed to the sound of my mobile phone. Bleary-eyed, I looked at the bedside clock. 6.00am. This in itself brought me to my senses. I very rarely received such early-morning calls without prior notice. I made a hungover grunting sound, and immediately recognised Vindiloo's voice.

'Yeah. What's up, mate?' I asked.

'I just called to make sure you were OK, after yesterday,' he said.

'Yeah. You're up early.'

'I've got to get back over to the lock-up. You'll never believe what the fuck I've done. I left the fucking doors unlocked.'

I almost fell out of the bed. 'What?'

'Yeah. I can't believe it. I left the padlock on the ground with all my keys in it. That's why I'm up so early.'

I felt a rush of panic at the possible consequences of our stupid, drunken behaviour. If anything happened to the paper, then Vindiloo and I would be in a great deal of trouble. Suddenly, Boris and Karloff loomed even larger than ever before in my thoughts. And what if the police had chanced upon the open lock-up? How on earth could we have been so stupid with so much at stake?

'Jesus. D'you want a lift over there?' I asked.

'No. I'm leaving right now.'

'OK. Give us a call as soon as you get there, right?'

'Yeah. I've gotta go. Speak to you in about an hour.'

I put the phone down on the floor and lay back on the pillow. Sleep was impossible and I stared up at the ceiling.

'Everything all right?' I had woken Laraine, who had obviously sensed the urgency in my voice.

'Yeah. 'Course. Go back to sleep, it's still early.'

Laraine looked at the clock. 'No chance of that. Still, I've got to get up soon.'

'I'll make you a cup of tea, then,' I said and got out of bed and spent the next 50 minutes in a state of constant worry.

At 7.00am I woke Stephanie and James. I made the children's breakfasts and told Laraine she could have a lie-in, as I would take them to school.

7.10am, and I still hadn't heard from Vindiloo. I tried calling him, but his mobile was switched off. Another ten minutes, still no word.

7.30am, and I got into the shower, making sure the phone was within easy reach.

8.00am, and I was hurrying the children to get ready as we had to leave soon. Still no word from Vindiloo. His phone was still switched off. On the drive to Stephanie and James's schools, all I could think about was Vindiloo and, by the time I dropped Stephanie off after James, I was beginning to panic. It was now gone 9.00am, three hours after I had spoken to him. *Something's happened, I know it. Something's definitely gone wrong.*

9.30am, I tried Vindiloo's mobile again — nothing. I called his home — no reply.

10.00am, by now I was a nervous wreck. I couldn't believe it, after doing everything so well, so correctly. And now something so stupid looked like blowing up in my face.

10.30am, by now I had written the whole thing off. Without any doubt something had gone drastically wrong. The only thing I could think of was that the police had stumbled across the paper and Vindiloo had been nicked. What crass, absolute stupidity. The phone rang.

'Yes?'

'Steve?'

I felt as though my whole being was in a state of collapse at the sound of Vindiloo's voice.

'Tony? Where the fuck have you been. I've been in a right state. What's happening?' I blurted out.

'What? Oh yeah. Sweet. No problem. The lock was still on the floor with the keys in it.'

'Why didn't you call me? Y'know, just to let me know,' I said.

'Sorry, mate. I was in such a rush this morning, and what with a terrible hangover and all, I completely forgot to take your mobile number with me. And I just couldn't think what it was. Sorry, Steve, but it's all sorted out now.'

I breathed a weary sigh of relief, and declined Vindiloo's offer to supply a van if I wanted to pick the paper up that day. I was still suffering the effects of the previous day's drinking and, as the paper was in a secure place, I reasoned it would be pointless to move it until I needed it in a couple of days' time. Meanwhile, I intended to do nothing for the time being, apart from relax until Eric and I started work again.

'That's OK, Tony. Leave it till I need it. I'll just wait till I hear from you. D'you know when we're supposed to be picking up the dosh?' I said.

'Tomorrow.'

'Really?' I exclaimed. 'What time?'

'I've got to meet my man at the airport. He's flying in with it. Good, eh?'

'Yeah. What shall I do, give you a call?'

'You can't. I lost my poxy phone yesterday. I've just called my man and made all the arrangements. I'm meeting him tomorrow afternoon. I'll give you a call as soon as I've collected.'

'OK, Tony, I'll leave it up to you then. And whatever you do, don't forget to call me, right?'

'Yeah. 'Course. I promise you faithfully. If you don't hear from me, it means I'm brown bread,' he joked.

I laughed and said, 'OK, then. I'll speak to you tomorrow afternoon. 'Bye.' At long last I felt calm and relaxed. I called Eric to let him know that everything was on schedule. I would be over to see him either tomorrow evening or the following morning. In the meantime, 'Take it easy.'

I spent most of the day browsing through an assortment of auto magazines, just to get an idea of how much a decent Bentley would cost me. I decided £50,000 would be ample to buy a decent set of wheels for the time being. When the brand-new one that I would order to my own specifications came through, I would probably give it to Laraine. Or whatever.

That evening, I took Laraine out for a meal to my favourite local restaurant, Al Fresco, and made short work of a couple of bottles of wine. That night, I slept a deep sleep of blissful contentment.

The next morning I was up bright and early and drove the children to school. I had a couple of friends to visit such as Don the Jockey and Hungry Jim, who both had some money for me to collect for the twenties. Generally speaking, it was a relaxed and laid-back kind of day.

At lunchtime, I visited a couple of friends in a pub and had a couple of glasses of wine and a light meal. At 2.30pm or thereabouts, I was eagerly awaiting Vindiloo's call. In anticipation of a drive to meet him, I was now drinking Perrier water, whilst my friends were pouring vodkas and gins down their necks in their usual fashion. I had one or two enquiries about the twenties, which I fended off and promised to attend to in the near future.

It was now 3.30pm, and I couldn't help looking at my watch every ten minutes or so. It was a source of annoyance that Vindiloo had lost his mobile and again I cursed our joint stupidity a couple of days previously.

By 6.00pm I still hadn't heard from Vindiloo and tried to put the matter of the imminent phone call to the back of my mind, and made my way home.

At 7.30pm I was home eating my evening meal, with still no news from Vindiloo.

By 8.00pm I was feeling somewhat concerned. I would have expected him to contact me by now, even if only to say there had been some kind of hold-up. Although I knew it would be a futile attempt, I rang his mobile number, just in case he might have since found it. No luck, it was switched off.

By 9.00pm I couldn't stand the tension any longer, and called his home, something I rarely did and then only as a last resort to contact him. His son Bradley answered.

'Bradley, how are you, mate? Is your dad there?'

'He's dead.'

His words, said in such a matter-of-fact way, had the effect of a punch to the jaw from Mike Tyson. But I was still conscious. I paused and struggled with my monosyllabic response, 'Dead?'

My first, split-second reaction was perhaps something had gone disastrously wrong and poor old Vindiloo had been 'ironed out', but before I could say 'How, what, when ...' Bradley continued.

'This morning I went up to him. I knew he had something important to do today, but he was in a bad way. He was lying in bed having a heart-attack. Real bad. Me mum called the ambulance and I gave him the kiss of life, but it was no good.' At this stage his voice seemed more emotional, as he then said, 'They rushed him to hospital but there was nothing they could do. The old man's dead.'

'I don't suppose he said ...' and then I bit my lip to stop myself continuing.

'Sorry?' Bradley enquired.

Of course, now was not the time to ask whether his father had mentioned anything about me before he died, and I said, 'Oh nothing, Bradley, I'm really sorry, I really am. It just seems so incredible to think that it was only the day before yesterday that I was with him. He was right as ninepence then. A bit drunk, but OK. Y'know?'

'Yeah, I know what you mean. I can't believe it myself,' Bradley replied.

'Listen, I'll, er, give you a call back tomorrow. Give my

condolences to your mum, and if there's anything I can do, just let me know. You've got my number? Yeah?'

'Yeah. I'll tell me mum. Thanks for calling.'

I left the phone box I had been using and drove the short distance back home. Instead of watching TV with Laraine, I sat in the study and tried to get my thoughts together.

So what was going to happen now? What would be the next move? There was no way that the Marbella Sailor could contact me, he didn't even have my correct Christian name. How on earth would they set about locating Wilf from London? Well, if the worst came to the worst, I still had the other half of the paper, £100 million worth, in itself a fortune. If it proved impossible to make contact with the consortium, I would have to print it all up and set about changing it up myself. No big problem. But still I decided I would wait several months before changing it up, just in case Boris and Karloff appeared on the scene — out of the blue, so to speak. Provided I had it all printed and safely stored at my unit in Hackney, everybody would be happy and we could carry on where we had left off, with myself dealing directly with the consortium. So either way, the deal would be 'Sweets as nuts'.

I decided to hire a van in the morning and collect the paper. And then reality set in. Where the fuck was the lock-up garage containing the paper? I realised I had no idea. I was asleep for most of the journey there, and too drunk to remember anything of the journey back. I sat and racked my brains for a solid hour in a desperate but vain attempt to try and remember where the garage was. But my mind was blank. All I could recall about the garage was that it had green-painted doors. As for the area, I managed a vague recollection of some boarded-up shops. As hard as I tried, and as long as I sat and thought, I just couldn't get any closer to working out where the garage was.

But surely the Marbella Sailor would make contact sooner or later? If Vindiloo hadn't lost his mobile phone, there would be no problem, as undoubtedly his contact would have called him on that number. But as it was, he had told them about its loss and they wouldn't even be trying to call it, anyway. It then occurred to me that maybe Bradley knew where the lock-up garage was. This seemed to be my only hope of locating its whereabouts, and so the next day I paid him a visit. Under the circumstances, a certain amount of discretion was called for.

Vindiloo's wife, Colleen, being a very religious woman, faced up to the unexpected and premature loss of her husband with an admirable degree of stoicism. Bradley adopted a philosophical attitude and certainly wasn't too upset to tell me that yes, his dad did have a lock-up garage and he had the key to the lock. I couldn't help feeling a sense of guilt at the joy I was experiencing upon being told this. But the undeniable fact of the matter was, Vindiloo was dead and life had to go on. Bradley got into my car and directed me to the garage just a couple of turnings away. My heart leapt as I noticed a couple of boarded-up shops, for although such a sight wasn't uncommon in this part of London, I somehow thought they looked vaguely familiar.

A moment later, Bradley pointed to some garages along a dirt track behind the shops. This time my heart sank. I knew immediately this wasn't the garage we had visited in our drunken stupor. Even so, I went through the motions of waiting outside, whilst Bradley opened the doors. Inside was an old car that obviously hadn't been moved for several months.

'Sorry to have dragged you out, Bradley,' I said. 'I don't suppose you know if your dad had any other lock-ups?'

'Might have done,' he replied. 'But this is the only one I know about.'

During the short drive back to his house, I quizzed him about the possibility of the Marbella Sailor or Boris and Karloff ever visiting his home, or calling his dad on the land line. But Bradley confirmed what I already knew. He had never heard of them, and his dad had never mentioned them. As he got out of the car outside his house, I asked him to give me a call if he came across any documentation such as invoice receipts or maybe a rent book relating to the garage. He promised me he would let me know if anything turned up. But I knew by now that I was clutching at straws.

There was just one other possibility that I could think of, and that was to visit every local minicab office to see if they had any record of picking up a man from Vindiloo's address at about 6.00am a couple of days earlier and taking him wherever. Once again, I drew a blank. I just couldn't believe it when I had to give up simply because I just couldn't come up with any ideas as to how I could locate the garage. I even managed to get a list of just about every rented lock-up garage in London that wasn't attached to a private house or located underground. I enlisted the help of a couple of friends who were keen motorcyclists and in need of a few extra pound notes, and gave them the list of garage addresses and as much of a description as I could manage. With the promise of a worthwhile bonus to the one who found it, I had no doubts they would try their very utmost to locate the £100 million of buried treasure, although, of course, they weren't aware of exactly what was in the lock-up.

Whilst my two motorbike chums were scouring the streets of London, I made discreet enquiries at the storage premises in South London, only to be met with looks of amused bemusement as I described Boris and Karloff.

'No, sir,' the young receptionist said. 'I'm sure I would have noticed two men like you've described. We don't really get too many giants this time of year.'

I hadn't really expected anything different, but nevertheless I paid a young friend of mine to sit outside there in a parked car for a few weeks with strict instructions to call me immediately should anyone remotely resembling the two Russians show up. All to no avail.

As for the motorbike boys, although on more than one occasion I thought they had struck gold, and I rushed to different lock-ups in areas as far afield as Streatham and Loughton, each proved to be a false alarm, and ultimately I had no joy in my efforts to find the garage. The only possibility now was that, somehow or another, the consortium would find out about Vindiloo's absolute demise and make contact with his family, and then contact me.

But in the meantime, as the Marbella Sailor was now my only remaining clue, I set about trying to establish his identity. My first port of call, quite literally, was Puerto Banus.

I had one or two contacts in the Marbella area, and one in particular who was very knowledgeable with regard to boats. And so, within a couple of days I was back in the port giving my nautical friend the sparse details of the Marbella Sailor's yacht, which amounted to no more than the description and the bay in which it was moored, together with the date it was there.

But even though he soon obtained the name of the craft and its skipper, courtesy of a friend in the harbour master's office, that effectively was the beginning and end of the trail. In spite of his very best endeavours, and the fact of his very extensive worldwide contacts, it proved to be an insurmountable obstacle to track down the boat or its captain and identify the Marbella Sailor.

So now I was left with just one very tenuous connection to his identity — the international playboy I had seen sitting on the deck of the luxury yacht. My best hope in this respect lay with my ex-girlfriend, Lynda McQueen.

As an ex-croupier at the London Playboy Club, and former 'Bunny of the Year', she had an extensive list of 'high society' contacts and it came as no surprise to learn that she actually knew the man. But once again all enquiries proved to be fruitless.

All of his social circle had seen neither hide nor hair of him for several months — to the extent that a couple of female friends were convinced that he had been killed in a skiing accident — and my brief glimpse of the undoubtedly animate playboy was about as singular as a sighting of Lord Lucan going for a gallop on Shergar.

So now, having done everything I could possibly think of to find the lock-up garage, and knowing of no way that I could get in touch with the Marbella Sailor, wherever he may be, I had to resign myself to the situation.

Far from being the Crime of the Century that would change my life for ever and elevate me into the premier league of the super-rich, I was now considerably worse off in financial terms. All in all, the whole affair cost me over £50,000.

To this day, I can't believe that I was so close and that the prize to end all prizes was snatched away in such an unlikely manner. After all, what must the chances be of losing out in just about the only way that I could have lost out — Vindiloo kicking the bucket on that very morning. At least if he had held on for just a few days even, there would have been plenty of cash, not just for me, but for his family as well.

If Vindiloo's up there somewhere looking down, all I can say is, bad timing, mate, very bad timing!

Soon after the death of Vindiloo, I heard from a well-placed contact that the police were investigating a rumour that there was a plot in the pipeline to print a large number of African banknotes, the ones that I had proofed for the dummy run. A prime example of how the police always seem to hear about virtually everything that's going on — red herrings included!

# CHAPTER 17

## Barry in Prison, Colonel Blimp and Gersh in Paris

After flying so high for the previous month, I felt a bit like Icarus, the Greek mythological character who flew too close to the sun and melted the glue that kept the feathers attached to his makeshift wings. But, unlike Icarus, the impact of my fall to earth didn't kill me, and so it was a case of, 'Pick yourself up, dust yourself down and ...'

I felt terrible breaking the news to Eric, as he, too, didn't think for one moment that anything could go so completely wrong at this stage of the proceedings. And, Vindiloo dying at this particular time really was just about the only thing that could have caused such a disaster (although, of course, it was much more of a disaster for Vindiloo himself).

So now in financial terms, I was back yet again to square one. No cash, and still with Jewboy Jack and Eugene to be paid every month. Fortunately, the twenties were still selling well, and I knew that it wouldn't be too long before I was able to get some money behind me again. So it was a case of making myself busy and drumming up as much in the way of sales as possible. Dinky Dan was selling large amounts but, even so, still had to throw the occasional temper tantrum. With the collapse of the £5 billion coup, it looked as though I was stuck with the Dinky one for ever. But this wasn't too much to endure, as we were both making plenty of money, and the business was running relatively smoothly.

There was, however, one minor problem, and that involved the amount of waste that was accumulating at the workshop, in the form of printed sheets that were slightly out of position and consequently couldn't be used. Obviously, these couldn't be dumped in a rubbish tip, and the only solution was to burn them, in itself a sizeable operation. We weren't really able to do this as we were concerned about the possibility of the unwarranted attention it might attract. Apart from this, all of Eric's spare time was spent printing the twenties.

I mentioned this to Bernie and asked him if there was any way he could destroy them. Once again, Bernie was more than agreeable after I told him I would pay him £500 for the job.

Along with the next consignment of notes, I took along about half of the printed waste-sheets in several large parcels. When I later asked him about the burning, he told me it had been no problem, and described how big the bonfire had been. Good old Bernie had got rid of a minor problem for me and I told him I would deliver the rest of the waste in the near future. So now everything was running smoothly and, generally speaking, I was in a relaxed frame of mind and beginning to put the past misfortunes behind me.

I was taking as many precautions as I deemed necessary, such as having three different cars at my disposal. One was for everyday domestic use and parked outside my house, whilst one of the others was parked several streets away and the other in a local lock-up garage. The reason behind this was that if ever the police were to become aware of my activities and started to follow me or even bugged my car, then I would be able to change vehicles at a convenient moment when the police were not close at hand, and go about my business in a car unknown to them. In fact, I followed this procedure even before the police eventually started to follow me. Added to this, I had two mobile phones, one for 'straight' friends and family to contact me on, and another in a fictitious name for my business associates. I also had a pager so that, when I was at the workplace, I could switch off both phones and so eliminate the possibility of the signal being traced to Ken's address. Should anybody need to contact me, the pager was there for any messages to be left.

I also made a point of never phoning Eric or any of my business associates on the mobile phone, and always used call boxes, thus leaving no documentary record of any of the calls that I made. In spite of all these precautions, in October I very nearly came unstuck in a big way, over something totally unconnected with the funny money. Laraine and I were entertaining some friends at home when the phone rang. It was Madeline, Barry's girlfriend.

'Steve,' she said, sounding very concerned and upset, 'I've got some bad news.'

'What's that?' I asked.

'It's Barry. He's been arrested.'

'What for? When?'

'Mortgage fraud. It's to do with the house at Chingford. He asked me to give you a call. He wants you to clear the house out.'

I thought for a moment, then said, 'When did he get nicked?'

'Earlier today when he went into the building society office to see the manager.'

'How d'you know?'

'I was waiting outside in the car. He called me a little while ago. He said you'd know what to do.'

'Has he got a brief?'

'No, I don't think so.'

'Leave it with me. I'll come round to you first thing in the morning. Try not to worry. See you tomorrow. 'Bye.'

I put the phone down and went into the front room and told Laraine and our guests that something important had cropped up, and that I had to go out for an hour or so. It was 9.00pm and the last thing I felt like doing, after having drunk quite a few glasses of wine, was driving about and clearing out empty houses.

Laraine, after her initial surprise, quickly realised it had to be something very important, and didn't say too much, other than a concerned, 'Be careful.'

Luckily, I still had a set of keys to the house, and quickly departed. My main worry was not really Barry's stuff in the house, but something much more incriminating. I had my share of the lucky briefcase documents stashed away there. As I drove over to Chingford, careful not to exceed any speed limits, I tried to assess the situation, but the fact of the matter was, I had no way whatsoever of knowing whether the police had already been there and searched the house.

Under the circumstances, this was a very real possibility. My heart was very much in my mouth, knowing that, regardless of the possible repercussions, I had no option other than to take the chance of finding out the hard way. If the documents were found by the police, it would put Barry in a very awkward situation.

Bearing in mind the fact that I owed him my life, I couldn't allow him to carry a very big can for something that was nothing to do with him. If it came to it, I would have to own up. Would this be my last few hours of freedom for a very long time?

I pulled up just along from the house, my heart pounding. By now it was dark. I took a deep breath and got out of the car. I tried to contain my apprehension as I made my way along the pavement back to the house, and momentarily paused before pushing open the garden gate. I walked slowly along the path to the front door, which was at the side of the house. It was deadly silent and pitch-black. Then I jumped, startled by a light suddenly coming on.

I somehow managed to make no sound as I realised it was an automatic security light above the door. Swallowing hard, I put the mortise key into the lock and gently turned it. So far, so good. Then I turned the yale lock and cautiously opened the door. By now my heart was pounding even more and I flipped the light switch. To my overwhelming relief, a quick visual check revealed that nothing had been touched, clearly no one had been inside. I closed the door and went into the cloakroom under the stairs. Working as fast as possible, I removed the heavy boxes of documents and stood them by the front door.

I then hurriedly carried them out. As I hadn't been able to park immediately outside, I felt even more conspicuously suspicious carrying the boxes the distance to the car. Although only about ten yards, it felt like a hundred. Loading up boxes from an empty house at ten o'clock at night is most certainly a thin-ice action.

All it needed was a cruising police car to come along, and I would have had a great deal of unexplainable explaining to do. But I couldn't take the chance of waiting till the following morning; all I could do was keep my fingers crossed and hope and pray. It took me about five minutes to get them loaded into the boot of the car. Five very long minutes, after which I was literally soaked in sweat and gasping for breath, but nevertheless extremely grateful that there had been no mishaps.

I took out a couple of boxes containing Barry's stuff and put them on the back seat of the car. I locked up the house and drove home very carefully. That night, in spite of being well over the legal limit, I must have been the most conscientious and safest driver on the road.

Early the following morning, I stored the documents in the unit at Hackney and made my way over to the flat Madeline shared with Barry. I listened as she related to me the details regarding Barry's predicament. She told me that he had received a call on his mobile phone from the manager of the Woolwich Building Society branch office in Acton, asking him to call in to sign some outstanding forms appertaining to a newly-granted mortgage.

Barry immediately smelled a rat. The problem with regard to the mortgage he had obtained on the Chingford property stemmed from the fact that he had used an alias, William Atkins. This was one of several identities that he had acquired over the years, complete with bank accounts and various other identification details.

At the time of obtaining the mortgage, there was a warrant out for Barry's arrest concerning a number of offences mainly relating to obtaining mortgages and credit cards in bogus names. It was because of this that he was suspicious about the phone call asking him to call in at the Acton branch.

Without informing me beforehand, he decided to front it out and went to see the manager at the arranged time of 2.00pm. He did, however, have the foresight to travel in the car with Madeline, whom he left outside with the key.

She informed me that, after waiting outside for about 15 minutes, she looked up to see her beloved being escorted out by two burly men. After noting the handcuffs and the unhappy expression on Barry's face, she came to the conclusion that the poor boy was under arrest.

Following Barry's instructions in the event of such an emergency, she drove home and waited patiently by the phone. Unfortunately, she had been unable to let me know what had happened earlier, as she didn't have my telephone number. A small, but very nearly disastrous oversight on Barry's part. As good luck would have it, he was allowed to make a telephone call just a few hours after his arrest. It was even greater good luck that the police were in no hurry to search the house.

After being given all the details, I made arrangements for Ian Oxford, my solicitor, to go to the station to see Barry. The following day he was remanded in custody to Bullingdon Prison near Reading.

Madeline and I went to visit him at the first opportunity to find out just what had happened. Barry told us that, as bad luck would have it, one of the office staff at the Woolwich who had the job of processing the recent new mortgage forms, had just been transferred from another branch. The branch she had left was one where Barry had used a different name to obtain a mortgage previously. What immediately attracted her attention were the descriptive details on the form. 'William Atkins' was 6ft 9in tall, the same height as 'Peter Bottomley', the man who had obtained a mortgage at her previous branch. Unfortunately, one of the Woolwich's mortgage requirements is a passport-style photograph for their records. Comparisons of William Atkins and Peter Bottomley's ugly faces confirmed all suspicions. Clearly, being 6ft 9in and so conspicuous in a crowd is something of a handicap in the Auntie Maud business.

Barry remained in custody for several weeks before finally getting bail.

Apart from this little hiccup, the wheels of industry turned relatively smoothly. On impulse, I decided to treat Laraine to another little shopping expedition to Paris, travelling first-class on the Eurotunnel train service from Waterloo and staying in the executive suite at The George V. We paid the cab driver, and the hotel doorman beckoned to one of the hotel porters to carry our cases in. I felt good as the entrance door was held open for us and we entered the plush lobby, our feet sinking into the sumptuous pile of the carpet. '*This is the life*,' I thought to myself, looking around at the sheer splendour of our surroundings. We checked in at reception and deposited our passports. Upon being told that our room was being prepared and would be ready soon, we decided to have a drink or two at the bar.

Still soaking up the opulence that seemed to permeate the air, we strolled casually up the steps that led to the bar. And then I saw them. A white haired, red-faced man sitting next to a rotund little man with a highly-polished bald head. Both sat there grinning like two ageing, naughty schoolboys.

'What are they doing here?' Laraine exclaimed.

I looked at her, a sheepish expression on my face, and before I could reply, a voice floated across to us. 'Where you been? We've been waiting here for ages. Must be two hours!'

'Sorry about that,' I said sarcastically.

It was two friends of mine, Gersh and Colonel Blimp.

'What are you two doing here?' Laraine asked.

The pair of them grinned as though privy to an enormously funny secret. 'We've been sitting here for ages,' Gersh repeated.

'Why didn't you have a drink in the bar?' I asked.

'Couldn't,' the Colonel said.

'What? What d'you mean?' I asked.

'No money,' Gersh replied.

'That's why we've been waiting for you,' Colonel Blimp added.

The pair of them were in Paris on a credit-card excursion. Using newly-stolen credit cards was Colonel Blimp's speciality and his main source of income. France seemed to be a particular favourite of his, as checks on purchases under £100 were non-existent. Gersh, as far as I could make out, was along for the ride.

Although they were laden with goods, they had soon run out of hard cash. Knowing that Laraine and I would be arriving soon, they held on for another day and decided to ambush us in The George V Hotel. They had reasoned that since we were in Paris to do some shopping, then I would have plenty of cash. And, being the proverbial soft touch, they reasoned that I would loan them sufficient to keep them going for another few days. Within an hour of arriving in Paris, I had been relieved of £1,000.

In return for my generosity, Gersh and the Colonel helped Laraine and me polish off the couple of bottles of champagne that awaited us in our room. That evening the pair of them 'paid' for a sumptuous meal in a memorable fish restaurant, courtesy of someone else's credit card. I wasn't really too comfortable with the idea of a stolen credit card being handed over to the waiter. I had visions of being carted away by *les gendarmes* and, instead of basking in the luxury of The George V, languishing in the notoriously primitive conditions of the latter-day version of the Bastille. In order to make sure no such mishap befell us, Laraine and I left before the Colonel paid the bill, and met them in the adjacent bar afterwards. The following day, Colonel Blimp bought me a silk tie and a trinket for Laraine. After that, I left the pair of them to go about their business, whilst Laraine and I set about enjoying 'the loveliness that is Paris', as the song goes.

Apart from the beauty of Paris itself, and the exquisite shops, probably my most abiding memory is of Montmartre. The market square in which so many talented artists set up stall is a place to be visited again and again. It is a very rare pleasure, on a sunny day, to be sitting outside one of the bars or small restaurants watching the artists at work.

Another memory of that trip is a comical occurrence back at the hotel quite late one evening. Although it was after midnight and I had drunk a considerable amount of wine with our meal earlier, I felt as though I was just beginning to get the flavour. The piano bar was still open and we decided to have a quick nightcap.

The George V is undoubtedly one of the world's finest, and most prestigious, hotels and so, not surprisingly, a rather sedate establishment; opulence and sophistication personified. It's precisely for those reasons that the night's entertainment was so funny. When we walked into the bar, it was quite busy, bearing in mind the time. In the normal way of things, the resident pianist would have retired for the night, and the bar would have been catering for just a handful of nocturnal drinkers. On this occasion, however, a young London chap who was sitting down with his wife had persuaded the pianist to remain just a little longer. I believe he told him that he was in Paris on his honeymoon or something similar.

The atmosphere seemed quite lively, with a general air of bonhomie prevailing. We sat down, made ourselves comfortable and soon settled into the jolly sing-song-type ambience. The pianist appeared to be enjoying himself and was inviting his audience to request their favourite songs.

After a few drinks, the joint was rocking, albeit in a most civilised manner. In no time at all, the guests in the bar were all joining in with a hearty sing-song, and all the while the chap from London, whom Laraine and I were speaking to but whose name I'm unable to recall, kept the ball rolling and the spirit alive. He was rather like an informal master of ceremonies. As the drinks began to flow, so, of course, the inhibitions began to get lost somewhere along the way. As well as the sing-song, one or two of the guests gave impromptu solo performances.

By now I was pouring glasses of Pernod down my neck with relish and couldn't resist standing up and singing — I use the term loosely — my party piece, which goes as follows:

*'Last night I laid in my bed and pulled my plonker,*
*It did me good, I knew that it would,*
*First I tried the short stroke,*
*Up and down, up and down,*
*Then I tried the long stroke,*
*Up and down, round and round,*
*I tickled the crown,*
*I-I-I-I- smashed it, thrashed it,*
*Bashed it on the wall,*
*Eased it, squeezed it,*
*Couldn't come at all,*
*There are those that say that intercourse is very grand!*
*Speaking for myself, I'd rather hold it in my hand!'*

The song, I might add, is sung to the well-known operatic piece from *Don Giovanni*, in a mock operatic voice. How much of the lyrics the mainly French and German clientéle understood, I've no idea, but they seemed to find it riotously funny. I even managed to entice some of them into joining in with a repeat performance. The memory of a very aristocratic-looking elderly woman singing out loud in a heavily accented voice, '... Eased it, squeezed it, couldn't come at all ...' is certainly one to tell my grandchildren. And then again, maybe not.

After a few hours, the battle-fatigued pianist finally conceded defeat and the staff told us they really had to close the bar. Our new-found friend from London went round 'with the hat' to the drunken assembly all of whom gladly donated quite generously to a most worthy cause. All, that is, except a large, tight-fisted German who resolutely refused to contribute anything towards the pianist's benevolent fund.

Even the hoots of derision from the other customers couldn't shame him into parting with any of his Deutschmarks. And so, at 4.30 in the morning, a drunken, merry group of hotel guests made their way back to their rooms.

Soon after the Paris trip, Colonel Blimp made a return journey to France, courtesy of someone else's credit cards. This time he was accompanied by his girlfriend, Vicky. And this time, the trip wasn't so successful. In fact, it was more of a spectacular failure.

Both he and Vicky were arrested, and held in custody. At first, there seemed to be little chance of bail, but then after a few days, Gersh received a call from him. Somehow, his lawyer had managed to get the court to agree to bail, but there was one slight problem — £12,000, or rather the equivalent in French francs, had to be lodged with the court to ensure their attendance when the case was ultimately heard.

In fact, this was more than a slight problem. In the Colonel's case, it was a virtual impossibility. Vicky was in a different predicament in as much as she was able to raise her share of the money, £4,000, but the transference of the funds to France presented an altogether different kind of problem.

Vicky was married, and her husband, Simon, had no idea she was gallivanting *sur le continent* with the credit-card Colonel. She had no way of getting the money across without hubby finding out.

Gersh contacted me and explained Colonel Blimp's dilemma. He then asked me if I would send out the cash to liberate Essex's answer to Bonny and Clyde. Although Blimp was really Gersh's friend, Gersh said he didn't have the money to lend him, otherwise he would have done so. In all probability, he did have the cash, but didn't fancy risking it.

The truth of the matter is, although there was no compelling reason why I should help out someone who wasn't that close a friend, I felt a degree of sympathy for him. I decided literally to bail him out and sent £12,000 to his French lawyer. I did this because, as far as I could tell, he seemed like a nice enough person and I knew he had no other way of getting out. Apart from this, the accounts I had heard from friends who have been incarcerated in France sounded pretty horrendous.

Unfortunately my judgement of Colonel Blimp was sorely misplaced, as future events subsequently proved. But at this particular time, knowing nothing to the contrary, I was willing to do what I could for a friend. My only condition was that Vicky had to repay me upon her return. Vicky kept to her side of the agreement and repaid me immediately. As for The Colonel, I let him know there was no immediate urgency, but that I would appreciate the money being returned as soon as he was in a position to do so.

After his return, Colonel Blimp had to restrict his credit card activities to the UK as France was the only foreign country he ever worked. Consequently, he supplemented this regular employment with a few minor deals on the twenties, which I did more as a favour to him as much as anything. But overall, he was struggling to maintain the lifestyle to which he had become so accustomed.

Knowing this, a friend of mine, Paul Sabbato, who, together with another friend, Big John, was busy setting up an invoice-factoring scam, asked me my opinion as to The Colonel's reliability. I told him that, as far as I could tell, he seemed to be a sound enough guy, but I certainly couldn't guarantee him in any respect as I hadn't known him that long. Ultimately, the decision rested with Paul, who after some thought decided to take a reasonably calculated risk and recruited Colonel Blimp as a front man for the invoice-factoring fraud.

It's fair to say that at this point in time, Colonel Blimp was eternally grateful to me, and pledged his undying and everlasting friendship and loyalty. But as Shakespeare's accountant once said, 'Talk's cheap, money buys houses.'

# CHAPTER 18

## A Garage Full of Bad Apples

I now began to feel as though I was gradually getting back on my feet. My regular punters were all ticking over, including Hungry Jim, who called me shortly after my return from Paris. Apart from an order for some more funny money, he said that he needed to see me about something else.

When I walked into the front room of his bungalow, he was sitting in his dressing gown with an extremely worried look on his face. His voice was very subdued when he told me to take a seat. I knew instantly there was something seriously wrong when I noticed a large plate of food on the table that had only been half-eaten. Not only this, but beside it was a tray of cakes and biscuits that hadn't even been started on, and a cold cup of tea, virtually full. The whole table had the atmosphere of a gastronomic ghost town about it. Clearly out of sorts, and not his jolly fat self, I asked what was up. Quietly, Hungry began to relate the tragic details.

'I've got a bit of a problem. I owe the other firm some money.' I knew who he meant by the 'other firm', his leading underworld friends.

'How much?' I asked.

'264 grand.'

'I knew it had to be something important when I saw you hadn't eaten your dinner,' I said. 150 grand and I would have expected him still to be able to clear the plate, (though maybe not his afters!) But when I saw how much food had gone uneaten, instinctively I felt there had to be a much larger amount of money involved. And now I knew. At this rate, if there was an extortionate amount of interest to be paid as well, I was concerned that Hungry Jim could end up as Anorexic Jim!

Hungry Jim gave a woeful shake of his head, but couldn't resist looking at the food from the corner of his eye. And then he casually picked up a cake and opened his hippopotamus-sized jaws and dropped it in. *'That's my boy,'* I thought.

'So how did this come about?' I asked. Hungry explained that he had introduced a good friend to the leading underworld figures and, because he had vouched for the man, they allowed him to have some credit on a deal. As tends to happen in such situations, things didn't altogether go to plan. And now Hungry was being pursued for the money owed, on the grounds that he had guaranteed the deal.

'But I didn't guarantee the deal. I guaranteed the man,' Hungry said. I couldn't really see the difference under the circumstances, but voiced no opinion upon the matter, and let Hungry Jim continue. 'What I was wondering was, could you lend me 75 grand?' He paused to gauge my reaction and then hastily added, 'I just don't want to lose face.'

He was trying to impress upon me that he didn't fear the heavy boats, but didn't want them to think that he didn't have the money. If it hadn't been for the loss I had suffered over the Vindiloo affair, I probably would have loaned the money to him, but as it was, I was in no position to lend out anything at all.

'I'm sorry, Jim, but I just can't help you out at this particular time. I'm afraid I've just had a bit of a body-blow myself,' I told him.

Hungry Jim tried not to look too disappointed, and then started to quiver in a strange kind of motion I wouldn't have thought possible had I not seen it with my own eyes. It was rather like a large jelly on a plate being attached to an electrical current, vibrating at a speed far in excess of any safety limit. Hungry even put back the cake that was en route to his mouth. This was serious.

'You OK, Jim?' I asked.

'What? Oh, er, yeah. Is it cold in here, or is it me?' he said.

'Cold,' I lied, and averted my eyes as Hungry eventually shuddered to a halt. Not a pretty sight. But at least he was now back to normal, and stationary.

We carried on discussing the gravity of Hungry's predicament, during which he bemoaned the fact that he always believed that he had a special relationship with the leading underworld figures.

'Rather like Margaret Thatcher and Ronald Reagan?' I quipped.

But Hungry took no notice, and further told me that their attitude was that friendship and business always had to be kept separate, and this was most certainly business. After a while I decided to go, having no practical advice to offer, but said, 'Well, looking on the bright side, Jim, I shouldn't think they'll dangle you out of the window!'

It was at the beginning of December 1994 that I became aware, one morning, that I was being followed. I wasn't doing anything in particular, only driving into town to meet some friends for a lunchtime drink. At first, I thought perhaps I was being paranoid when I noticed a four-door Ford with two men inside behind me that I seemed to recall seeing some time earlier. But then, as the car turned off, another one took its place, once again with two men in the front. It didn't take me long to realise that, without any doubt, somebody was taking an interest in me and, of course, that somebody could only be the police. At first, I paid them little attention but then, after a few days, when I had quite a bit of running about to do in respect of the business, I decided I had to lose them.

This I did fairly easily and then, after a day or two, it soon became apparent that they had decided to stop following me. Fearing that maybe they had placed some kind of tracking device on my car, I made a point of using one of the two spare cars I'd parked up. Every morning, after leaving the house, I would drive about for half-an-hour or so and, after satisfying myself that there was nobody following me, I'd drive to one of the spare cars and switch over. I then quickly drove out of the area, feeling safe that I was able to go about my business with nobody any the wiser, but still never failing to maintain a painstaking observation routine in my rear-view mirror.

In this way, things ran smoothly virtually up until Christmas. But then, on 18 December, I had to hire a van to take a consignment of paper over to the workshop. Whilst doing that, I also took away a large consignment of waste that had accumulated. I called Bernie and asked if he would be able to come up to London to pick up the paper for burning. Unfortunately, he wasn't able to get away, and I wasn't able to get down to the Isle of Wight. The van had to be back to the hire company that evening, so I was stuck with the waste that I had on board. I decided to store it overnight in the lock-up garage where I had one of the cars parked. This done, I took the van back and drove home in my car.

The following morning, I was up and out of the house by about 8.00am. I had decided to take the waste down to Bernie and then meet up with some friends for a Christmas drink.

I followed my normal routine of driving around for a while to satisfy myself that there was nobody following me. I then drove to the lock-up and parked my car in a side street. From there, I walked via a footpath to the collection of lock-up garages around the corner. As was to be expected at that time of the morning, there was no activity around the complex, and I opened up the garage doors.

As I walked round to the driver's side of the car, I suddenly heard the squeal of rubber on the gravel outside. I was immediately alarmed, as I knew that nobody drives a car in that fashion on those small private roadways. I closed my eyes briefly and said a quick prayer, 'Please God, no!' Just as I opened them again, I heard a car braking outside the opened doors of the garage. I turned round to see a green Vauxhall car with three men rushing out and coming towards me.

The largest one of the three produced a warrant card, and said, 'Stephen Jory, you're under arrest on suspicion of possessing counterfeit currency.'

My heart sank and, once again, I closed my eyes, unable to believe what was happening. But what was happening was very real. The police officer introduced himself as DS Paul Wright, and one of the others started searching the garage. Obviously, it only took him a couple of minutes to open the packets and find the printed waste sheets of £20 notes. After that, I was taken back to the house where a search was made. Not for the first time in our lives, I had to try to console a tearful and incredulous Laraine.

Fortunately, James had stayed at a friend's house the previous evening, but Stephanie was there, and as I held her close to me she just looked stunned and saddened. No tears came from her eyes, and she just seemed to stare in a state of disbelief as I tried to reassure her that everything would be all right. But, of course, both she and Laraine knew that it wouldn't. The prospect of being locked up for Christmas filled me with despair and the guilt I felt at what I was putting my family through was almost more than I could stand. After finding nothing in the house, the police took me to Barnet Police Station, where I was placed in a holding cell.

An hour or so later, I was taken to an interview room. DS Wright was there together with one of the other officers.

'Well, Stephen, obviously you know what this is all about, don't you?' he asked.

I replied that I was aware what was going on, and they

proceeded to ask me what I knew about the counterfeit currency. I told them that my only knowledge was that I had been paid by a couple of chaps whom I knew only as Mick and Dave to burn some waste paper.

Both officers smiled when I told them I had no idea where these men came from or where they lived, and that I used to meet them in a car park in Tottenham. When I was arrested, I had £1,200 on me and I told them that £500 of it was payment for burning the waste. Why I didn't say the £1,200 was payment, I don't know. Either way I wasn't believed.

'£500, eh, Steve?' Paul Wright remarked. 'How much is that hire car you've got in the garage, £100 per week? And the lock-up garage, a few quid a week? Come off it, Steve, your wife's driving around in a Mercedes Sports, by the time you've paid all your expenses, £500 won't go very far, will it? In fact, I'd say you're probably out of pocket. You're not a very good businessman are you, Steve?'

I made no comment, and just stared at the two officers, shrugging my shoulders.

'Why don't you tell us the truth? You know what we want. If you tell us where the printer is, you can walk out of here today, fancy that? No charges, even.'

'I'm sorry. I can't help you,' I said. 'If I knew where the printer was, I'd tell you, believe me, but I don't.'

Then they attempted to persuade me to 'roll over' on the grounds that I had been grassed up by not one, but several, so-called friends. Although they naturally didn't name them, there was no doubt in my mind that someone had obviously stuck my name up, and what they were telling me was probably true. But this made no difference to my own code of conduct and, after a while, the police seemed to resign themselves to the fact that I probably didn't know the printer or, if I did, I wasn't telling them. Fortunately for me, DS Wright adopted a pragmatic approach when it came to bail and formed the opinion that, if I was going to help them, the only way I could find out who the printer was, would be by being on the street. This, combined with the fact that it was nearly Christmas and I had a young son and daughter at home, persuaded him to do what he could to see that I got bail.

The following morning, I appeared at West Hendon Magistrates' Court, where I was granted bail, albeit on a substantial surety of £150,000, provided by Laraine's sister Linda, and her best friend Sandy. The feeling of relief at getting out for Christmas was unbelievable, as I had resigned myself to being locked up for quite some time.

At home, James was none the wiser and Stephanie, although still upset, was happy that I was home for Christmas. For the time being at least, I was able to put my problems to the back of my mind and enjoy a relatively happy family Yuletide.

# CHAPTER 19

# Cockles and Cab Drivers

After Christmas and New Year, I went to see Dinky Dan, who understandably was somewhat apprehensive and concerned about the possibility that I might have been followed to his house. I assured him that I had taken every precaution to ensure that no one had been on my tail. The fact that the workshop premises hadn't been located, the one address the police wanted more than anything else, testified to the fact that I was more than capable of visiting my business associates without bringing the police along for the ride.

Dinky soon relaxed and asked me just what had happened. I proceeded to give him the details and told him that the police had swamped the area surrounding my house and must have seen me walking into the garage complex a few days before I was arrested.

(I was told several years later that the discovery of the garage was as a result of some fairly incisive detective work. Knowing that I was using a procedure involving switching cars, the police managed to locate my Renault parked in a side street a couple of miles away from my house. They scoured the immediate area and became curious about the complex of garages. Leaving no stone unturned, they contacted the landlords and, under the guise of being anti-terrorist squad officers searching for bombs, they acquired a list of tenants. One name stood out, Stephen James — yours truly.)

They had been watching the garage for a few days since seeing me going in, but had only decided to pounce when they had seen a few, very narrow strips of plain white paper outside the garage, and from that they deduced that there must be something of consequence inside. The barely noticeable pieces of paper must have fallen out of the back of the van when I had unloaded the waste. At any other time, all they would have found in the garage was the hire car.

I have to say, when things are going well for me, no matter how many precautions I take, no matter how careful I am, I invariably trip up over a matchstick and fall under a bus. The plain fact is, there is absolutely no room for any element of bad luck to encroach upon the proceedings of skulduggery. I can't think of any other business in which the principle of Murphy's Law applies so potently as it does in the business of crime.

Dinky Dan sympathised with my bad luck, and we both agreed that it would be as well to stop production for the time being. Not only this, but Eric was due to go away on holiday shortly.

As much as anything, I got the impression that Dinky was worried that perhaps my 'bottle' might have gone and I wouldn't want to carry on with the business. However, far from pulling the shutters down, I was now in the position whereby I needed to get as much money as possible together before my inevitable incarceration some time in the not too distant future.

Added to this, I've no doubt he wanted to assess my general demeanour and judge for himself whether or not I had 'gone over' in any way. But I think he soon realised he was quite safe. So much so that he told me that he thought it would be a good idea to switch over to printing £10 notes, now that I had been arrested for the twenties. I agreed with this plan of action and made arrangements to collect the new film a couple of days later. Although we wouldn't actually be working before Eric returned at the end of January, with the film we could check the £10 notes out for quality and any possible modifications that might be required.

Upon leaving Dinky Dan's house, I went to see Eric. I told him about the tens and he was quite agreeable to running off a couple of hundred sheets the following weekend, just before he left to go on holiday with his wife.

As my arrest hadn't affected Eric in any way, and I knew there was no way that the workshop would be discovered, I decided not to mention the matter to him. There had been no mention of it in the national newspapers or on the media and so he was blissfully unaware of the situation. What he didn't know couldn't harm him.

A couple of days later, as arranged, I went to Dinky Dan's house to pick up the film for the £10 notes. The time was about 9.00am, and his wife showed me through to the kitchen where Dinky was drinking a cup of tea. Without saying hello, he growled, 'I had a spin this morning. About 7 o'clock.' He stared at me, as though it must have had something to do with me. My first reaction, with the new film in mind, was to say, 'Did they find anything?'

'I wouldn't be sitting here if they had done,' he replied, a fairly logical assertion.

'No. 'Course not,' I said. 'Thank fuck you didn't have the film here.'

'Yeah. I had it put down somewhere else. I'd never keep anything here overnight.'

He went on to explain that the search of his house had been a most genteel and civilised affair. Unlike a usual police search, no drawers were removed and turned out, and Dinky got the impression that they were doing no more than going through the motions, as though they didn't expect to find anything. They informed him that they were looking for counterfeit money, and that if they found any then he would be arrested and taken to the police station for questioning. If nothing was found, then he would have no problems.

This in itself is most unusual, as the police normally arrest a householder after a search even if nothing is found. It's fairly standard procedure to take the suspect to the police station, question him, and then if there is no evidence against him, release him without charge. Dinky said that he got the impression it was a way of letting him know that they were on to him.

'A covert warning,' I said.

Dinky looked nonplussed then said, 'Yeah that's it, a covered warning.'

After some more conversation, Dinky told me he had the film tucked away ready for me to take. I was apprehensive about this, as the thought occurred to me that the police might be watching his house. Unlikely, but all the same, possible. The last thing I needed, in my situation, was to be pulled coming out of his house carrying a set of film for £10 notes.

As a precautionary measure, I decided to leave with just a large, empty envelope held conspicuously in my hand. After getting in the car and driving slowly off, I had a quick check to see if there were any suspect motor vehicles parked up with suspicious-looking characters sitting keeping observation. There was nothing untoward, and nobody tried to follow me. After cruising the adjoining streets for ten minutes or so, I went back to Dinky Dan's house and relieved him of the film, which I delivered to Eric.

By the weekend, we knew that the new line would be a bestseller. The film for the £10 notes was every bit as good as the twenties, if not better. Eric left to go on holiday, happy and content that he would return to a full order book.

As well as the change in production from 'apples' to 'cockles', I took the decision, for security reasons, to remove Bernie from the operation, and whilst Eric was away on holiday, I arranged for the silver foiling to be carried out by a company that had done some work on my perfume cartons in the past. It was a different, more efficient and cost-effective method that involved the work being done ostensibly as a legitimate job, on the plain white sheets of paper before they were printed up. Added to this, I bought a commercial shredder. This enabled me to dispose of the shredded and unrecognisable waste at an industrial incineration plant at Edmonton.

The affair of the half-hearted search at Dinky Dan's house puzzled me and I was hard pressed to make any sense of it. One or two other people had been turned over by the police, some of whom, like Hopalong, I had done some business with, and others, generally around the Hoxton area of London, I wouldn't have touched with a barge pole for a variety of reasons.

I decided to ask a contact that I had via a friend of mine, if any light could be shed upon the Old Bill's game plan. The contact was fairly close to the squad investigating the counterfeit twenties and was quite willing to find out whatever he could.

Within a couple of days, my friend who actually had the contact gave me a few little snippets, of which only a couple were of any consequence. Firstly, anyone who was even remotely suspected of being involved in the funny money business was being kept under observation, and in some cases their houses searched. The purpose of this appeared to be to evoke some kind of reaction as much as a real expectation of finding anything worthwhile.

This much I had more or less worked out for myself, but then my friend told me that the squad had a particular interest in somebody who used a name that meant nothing to me. For the sake of illustration, I'll refer to the name as Purdy. Dinky Dan had obviously been just one of several when the police had decided to give him a spin, but, nevertheless, I felt that he was entitled to know what I had learned, irrelevant as it seemed to me.

Surprise, surprise. When I mentioned the name Purdy to him, the huff and puff of his personality seemed to take hold. Immediately, he began to rant and rave at me as though somehow it was my fault that the name Purdy had arisen. The reason for his paranoid outburst stemmed from the fact that Purdy was a name he had used in the past.

After listening to his pathetic tirade on the phone for a minute or so, I tired of his silly antics and said, 'Look, all I know is what I've told you, I'm only telling you because I thought it might mean something to you, because the name Purdy means fuck all to me. But if you prefer, I won't fucking tell you anything in the future!'

Dinky Dan realised that I was just the bearer of what he regarded as bad news and, of course, not the instigator. But such was his mentality that, in any situation which didn't please him, his initial and instinctive reaction was always to start ranting and raving, regardless. It wasn't hard to picture him in an empty room, screaming at the four walls surrounding him. Anyhow, something must have clicked in his brain, because he told me that one of the very few people who knew him as Purdy was his old sparring partner, and ex-partner in crime, bully-boy Bearsie.

'It must be that slag Bearsie. He's the one who's grassed me up,' he said.

'Whatever,' I responded, not particularly interested in his personal vendettas. I was beginning to regret mentioning the matter to him in the first place and said, 'I've got to go now. I'll speak to you later.'

'No, hang on. Where are you now? I need to meet up with you and talk about this,' he said.

'Talk about what? I've told you all there is to know.'

'Yeah, but this is important. I need to meet you,' he persisted.

'I'm sorry, Dan, I'm a bit busy at the moment. You do whatever you've got to do. I'll speak to you tomorrow some time.'

I put the phone down and went straight into the pub next to the phone box, which was what I normally did after talking to Dinky Dan for more than ten seconds.

At the end of January, I received a call from DS Paul Wright to say that he wanted to see me. I met him at Whetstone Police Station just a couple of miles away from where I lived.

'Well, Steve, I just thought we might have a little chat about what's happening, if anything,' he said.

'Not a lot really,' I replied.

'I thought maybe you would have had some more thought about the little matter of the printer.'

'Well, I haven't really been able to find out anything.'

'You know you're in a lot of trouble here, Steve,' his younger colleague said. 'You're looking at a long prison sentence. A long time away.'

I was aware of the truth of his words, but knew there was little I could do about it.

'Yes, I do realise that,' I said.

'Well, why don't you do yourself a favour, and give us some help?' Paul Wright said. 'After all, you know how long Tommy Campbell got, don't you?'

Tommy Campbell. I thought about what my little Irish punter Don had told me about the day that Tommy Campbell had got nicked. Already on bail at the time for a disastrous deal involving counterfeit US dollars, he got involved in a trade involving dodgy tenners. The arrangements were made over the telephone and Tommy agreed to meet his punters, who were travelling down from his home town of Glasgow, in a pub in Islington owned by his sister. He sat waiting patiently in the bar, unaware that half of the customers in the pub were plain-clothes police officers. And what they were unaware of, was that Tommy's punters had been delayed and, consequently, every hour or so, a new shift had to be drafted in to allay any suspicion as, obviously, the police couldn't carry on drinking regardless. Tommy, of course, had no such problem, and so from 11.00am until 10.00pm he became more and more inebriated.

When his punters finally arrived, there was a ridiculously large contingent of Old Bill waiting for them, and Tommy Campbell was completely paralytic. Even though he was in the process of being arrested, he was totally oblivious as to what was going on and insisted upon buying drinks for everybody. By the time he was taken to the station, he was declared unfit for questioning and left to sleep it off in a cell for 24 hours.

I must have been smiling to myself, as Paul Wright's words interrupted my thoughts.

'Steve? Something funny?'

'What? Oh, er, no, I was just thinking about something. Sorry, what were you saying?' I responded.

'Tommy Campbell. Seven years. And that was just for 2,000 pieces. Dodgy dollars,' he said.

'Yes, I know. Diabolical sentence for a silly little trade like that,' I said.

'That's what I'm trying to tell you. That's the kind of bird they're handing out these days for the old funny money. You don't fancy a nine stretch, do you? 'Cos that's what you're looking at. So how's about a bit of help?'

I knew I was looking at a long sentence, but nevertheless said,

'There's nothing really I can tell you.'

I sat and looked at the two policemen, and then decided to take a chance on another possibility. Turning to Paul Wright I said, 'Could I have a word with you on your own?' I asked.

He nodded to the younger officer, who promptly got up saying, 'I'll go and get some coffees, then,' and left the room.

'So what is it, then, Steve?'

I hesitated before speaking, then said, 'I was wondering if maybe there wasn't some other way round this.'

Paul Wright looked quizzical. 'What exactly d'you mean?'

Once again I hesitated. 'I, er, was wondering if maybe we could come to some kind of financial arrangement.'

He gave me a wry smile. ''Fraid not, Steve. All I'm interested in is bits of work and bodies. Any information you've got, about anything at all, that's the only way we can do business.'

'You didn't mind me asking, did you?'

'No, not at all. Mind you, don't ask again, though, I might have to nick you, fair enough?'

'Fair enough.'

I left the station feeling completely dejected, their words ringing in my ears. I was in a lot of trouble, and there seemed no way out for me.

I was feeling extremely depressed and concerned at the prospect of spending the next few years in prison, and it was something I was having a hard time coming to terms with. But it looked as though there was nothing I could do about it. And, as depressed as I was, the easy option offered by DS Wright never crossed my mind as a way out. There's an old prison saying: 'If you can't do the time, don't do the crime,' which, these days, seems to have been amended to: 'If you can't do the time, grass somebody up.' Since I'm over 21 and fully responsible for getting myself in and out of various situations, grassing never has and never will be a viable option for me.

As it seemed to be a foregone conclusion that a long prison sentence was unavoidable, all I could do was soften the blow and make sure that Laraine and the children were provided for during my incarceration. To this end, I set about getting as much money as possible together in the following months. But, of course, it was something of an uphill battle as I was still in debt to Eugene and Jack. Apart from the monthly millstone around my neck, I would have to make sure I had the original loan to pay back before my case was heard. I had been advised by Ian Oxford that it would more than likely be some time during the summer. This gave me six or seven months at the most.

As soon as Eric arrived back from holiday, I was delivering more paper to him and cajoling him into taking Fridays and Mondays off in order to get in a long weekend's work. As soon as the tenners were produced they were an instant hit, an even better line than the twenties. A major factor in the popularity of the tenners was the 'pass-the-parcel' element.

Due to the fact that a £20 note can only be passed out in change by a barman or shopkeeper if they are given a £50 note, which a great many places won't accept any more for fear that they might be counterfeit, the unlucky recipient is invariably stuck with any dud twenties they might find in their till.

However, with the tenners, anybody finding a dud in their till can quite easily pass it on to the next customer who pays for a drink or whatever with a £20 note. Far be it from me to suggest that any of our law-abiding and upstanding publicans and shopkeepers who scream so loudly about such things as counterfeit money would ever do such a thing, but this is what I have heard. As my old man, Freddie, used to say to me as a small child when I gave him some blatantly ridiculous excuse, it's possible.

Amongst the loudest of the screamers, with regard to what they feel is wrong and what's right when their pockets are affected, are London taxi drivers. If they're not moaning about minicab drivers, they're moaning about the rates they are paid and, heaven forbid, a passenger that actually expects to be taken to a destination which isn't on the cabbie's route home, and so on. And so I found it particularly amusing and ironic that several black cab driver friends of mine employed a rather ingenious little scam to make a few extra pounds. They would always ensure that they had a dud twenty and a tenner on them, so that if a passenger should proffer a £20 note for a relatively short journey costing say £2.50, after taking the note and reaching into the bag of change at the side of his seat, the cabbie would bring his hand back out, but this time holding the counterfeit £20 note.

'Sorry, guv. I haven't got any change. Is this the smallest you've got?'

With the cabbie still holding the counterfeit £20 note, the passenger would either take it back and give the cabbie the correct fare, or if he said the £20 note was all he had, the cabbie, in a display of apparent generosity, would say, 'Don't worry about it then, guv. This one's on me,' and then hand back the fake note.

But surely such a display of generosity from a black cab driver, a notoriously mean, penny-pinching breed of animal, should have alerted the unsuspecting passenger. As everybody knows, there's no such thing as a free lunch — or a free black cab journey.

For a couple of months, business was going well and the tenners most definitely became the more popular of the two lines. Unfortunately, the profit in the tenners wasn't anywhere near as much as the twenties, and it was only by selling much larger quantities that we could make it worthwhile. By the time the profit was split between me, Eric, Dinky Dan and the mystery partner he introduced, it didn't amount to anywhere near as much as I would have liked. Particularly as I was trying to save up for the rainy day that was looming on the horizon in the shape of prison.

Two or three months into the New Year and it must have been apparent to DS Wright that his main hope for a positive lead to the printing works wasn't going to happen. I was aware that my house was under observation and obviously my telephones, home and mobile, must have been tapped, although I felt confident that it was highly unlikely the police knew about my business mobile. I always made a point of changing it every couple of months or so and even Laraine didn't have the number.

Although I was 'under obbo', the police made no attempt actually to follow me at any time. But then, shortly after getting out of bed at about 6.30 one morning, I glanced out of the window and happened to notice a couple of cars pulling up outside. I warned Laraine, who was still asleep, just seconds before the police actually knocked, and I went downstairs to answer the door in my dressing gown. There were several officers, including a policewoman. They came in and informed me that they had a warrant to search the house with regard to counterfeit £50 notes. I was completely baffled by this, as Eric and I hadn't got round to the fifties yet. In fact, I had no intention of printing £50 notes and the only time I had been involved with them in any way was when Bearsie needed a printer in 1985.

Although nothing incriminating was found, I was rather bemused when a large quantity of envelopes that I had in a cupboard under the stairs were put into large plastic bags and taken. Envelopes? What the fuck do they want with them?

By this time, Laraine was distraught as I really thought that this might be no more than a ruse to have my bail revoked. After all, we all knew that a part of the reason I was at large in the first place was to find out for DS Wright and Co that which they were unable to find out by regular detective work.

As we left the house, one of the officers decided to search my car, parked on the drive. Immediately, I remembered that I had an application form for a passport filled out in a different name with a photograph of me attached to it, in a compartment in the centre console.

I knew that, should this be found, then I definitely would have my bail revoked, with absolutely no chance of having it reinstated by a High Court Judge.

I felt like I was in an hypnotic trance as I stared at the movement of his hand touching the compartment lid. His fingers seemed to be operating in slow motion, applying just enough pressure to grip the lid. It began to rise open, and I began to pray, 'Freddie, please do what you can for your little boy. Look down and give us a break,' and, just as I finished my very personal little plea, the lid was fully open. I held my breath and closed my eyes, and then heard the detective say, 'Come on, then, let's go.' I opened my eyes and the console compartment was empty.

I was absolutely dumbfounded. I knew the form was in there, but by some minor miracle it wasn't. I breathed again. I never came across the form or photograph again.

Once at Whetstone Police Station, I was interviewed by two young detective constables, who explained to me that my fingerprints had been found on one of a number of envelopes, containing forgeries of the old-style £50 notes. These were part of a parcel that a man known as Maltese Joe had been arrested with about nine months earlier.

I realised at this stage that this arrest was no more than an attempt to exert pressure on me to co-operate with the funny money squad. Obviously, a fingerprint on an envelope, in itself, didn't constitute enough evidence to warrant any kind of charge. I didn't know Maltese Joe or anything about him, so there was absolutely nothing to link me with him. I told the officer that, amongst other things, I sold envelopes as part of a job lot that I had bought several years previously. Both of us smiled at this explanation, and the DC took it in a light-hearted fashion. I was pleasantly surprised when I was told I was being released an hour later and I was back home at 9.00pm.

In actual fact, I had genuinely given Vindiloo, who apparently knew Maltese Joe, a box of envelopes about a year before, but as far as I can recall they were empty when I gave them to him. But, nevertheless, being hauled into the local nick early in the morning was an experience I could have done without.

# CHAPTER 20

# Too Close for Comfort

Several days after being pulled into Whetstone Police Station, I looked in my rear-view mirror and noticed a car which was definitely following me. Once again, I felt that the police were just letting me know that they hadn't forgotten about me, as there was no real attempt to disguise their presence, no motorbikes or other cars taking it in turns, just the single car. Very strange. I carried on driving in a sedate and orderly fashion, going nowhere in particular. I assumed that it would be no more than a matter of time before my escort tired of following me about on such a pointless journey. Then, as I turned into a small side street, the car drove past and pulled up sharply in front of me. I looked in my mirror and saw that another car had pulled up behind me. Seconds later, the two men in the first car got out and opened my door. One flashed a warrant card and said, 'Stephen Jory, I am arresting you on suspicion of supplying counterfeit money.'

My heart sank and I got out of the car with his hand on my elbow. The three of us walked to the car in front and I got into the back with the man who had arrested me. We pulled away in silence and one of the men in the other vehicle got behind the wheel of my car and we drove off in convoy.

We drove to an area close to Paddington railway station and, at first, I assumed they were taking me to Paddington Green Police Station.

But then I realised that perhaps all wasn't as it should be when we turned into a yard leading to a large warehouse-type building that appeared to be deserted.

'Where we going?' I asked. I turned my head and saw out of the back window, my car and the second police car follow us in. What alarmed me more than anything was the fact that the police car behind stopped and the passenger got out and pulled down a metal roller shutter, which he locked.

Being relatively astute, I sensed that this wasn't like any other police station I had ever been taken to before. In fact, I was beginning to have serious doubts that these men really were policemen. But somehow I didn't think there would be any point in asking to have another look at their warrant cards. In fact, I got the distinct impression that such a request might well be met with a stern look of disapproval, and I certainly didn't want to risk antagonising them in any way.

Since I hadn't been given a reply to my question a few moments before, I decided to keep my mouth shut. The truth of the matter was, I was utterly and completely petrified. I had an ominous feeling of panic.

When reading newspaper reports of people being abducted by the IRA and then never seen again, I have always thought how terrifying such an experience must be, the sudden awareness of how frail and vulnerable we all are when it comes to the final analysis, like a small child totally defenceless and unable to do anything about such a terrible predicament. And now I had some idea of how they must have felt.

'Come on, this way,' one of the men said, and, surrounded by the four of them, I walked up some steps through a door leading into a badly-lit hallway. I could feel my legs shaking uncontrollably as we walked across the hallway to an old goods lift. The door was open, we stepped inside and one of the men pulled the shutters across. A button was pressed and the dirty floor shuddered as the dark container made a whirring noise and slowly started its ascent.

By now my mouth had completely dried up and my heart was pounding at a furious rate. The fact that this abduction had been carried out in such a professional manner and so easily, with access to a deserted warehouse, made me begin to expect the worst. It crossed my mind that if I were murdered now, nobody would even know about it.

I had to fill my lungs with air and breathe slowly and deliberately to stop myself from losing all control. I tried desperately to switch off, somehow to make my mind go blank. I didn't even try to fathom who these people were, and what it could be about. It certainly wasn't a case of mistaken identity, of being in the wrong place at the wrong time. These people most certainly had the person they wanted, and no doubt it wouldn't be very long before I was made aware of what it was all about.

The lift came to a halt on the second floor. The man who had closed the shutters now pulled them open. He then pushed open the gate, and I was beckoned forward as he stepped out of the lift. I hesitated and felt a gentle nudge from behind. I moved forward and walked into a large, empty floor space of about 5,000sq ft. Still nobody said anything and, as much to break the terrifying suspense as anything, I asked, 'What's going to happen to me?'

The man who'd arrested me said, 'Would you come with me please, Stephen?' His manner was suggestive of a policeman's, but somehow different. I have been in the company of heavy villains before and I've also had confrontations with them, and I knew that these were something other than 'heavy boats'. Not policemen and not villains in the normal sense, then I realised just what it was I couldn't pin-point — they had a military persona about them, as though they were all ex-Army. This impression was more of an intuitive thing than anything else, I suppose. I was very, very worried and still struggling to maintain a semblance of self-control.

We walked across the floor and I was directed into a side room. Nothing was said and the door was closed behind me. In the room on my own, I looked around and saw a row of urinals against the wall, and next to them three cubicles with no doors. Behind me were two hand basins with a cracked and stained mirror above them. In a far corner, high up, was a small frosted glass window with a small fan set in it. Clearly, the toilet hadn't been used for a long time; there was dust everywhere and a general state of decayed filth.

I heard the sound of a match being struck and a cigarette lit outside the door. There were low, inaudible sounds of voices coming through. Both voices were English, and most likely London accents. I began to shake nervously and, in an effort to control the movement, I walked past the cubicles. All three were incredibly filthy and had no toilet seats, but the first one had a flat piece of wood over the bowl. For some inexplicable reason, I peered inside the other two and looked down at the filthy, stained porcelain. There was no water at the bottom and, even more inexplicably, I pulled the chain hanging from the ancient overhead cistern. It made a dry, clunking sound and obviously no flush was forthcoming. I repeated this action in the last cubicle. Strange behaviour.

Soon tiring of trying to flush rusted toilets that had no water, I started to pace up and down. I looked at my watch every five minutes or so. I tried to make some kind of sense of the situation, to rationalise just what the fuck was going on. I thought about my assessment of my abductors. They hadn't assaulted me in any way. They hadn't screamed or shouted at me or tried to intimidate me. They had shown no emotions or reactions whatsoever. It was as though they were working to a formula, a set pattern which indicated some kind of formal training. I was more convinced than ever that these men were either military or ex-military men.

Then a somewhat bizarre thought entered my head. There had been a fair amount of publicity in the newspapers about the deployment of MI5 and MI6 personnel in the fight against organised crime, now that their role on the international stage was minimal due to the fall of communism and the peace process in Northern Ireland. Had the police become so resigned to the prospect of not locating the whereabouts of the printing works that they had called in the dirty tricks department? If this was the case, then surely there would be no question of them eliminating me? I had little doubt that, when deemed necessary, such extreme measures are taken when dealing with terrorists and committed enemies of the state. But a counterfeiter? No way. They wouldn't ... would they?

Within a few minutes of thinking about an MI5 connection, I managed to convince myself that that was what this was all about. I wasn't going to be killed, of that I was certain. But what?

I thought about the various programmes I had seen, and articles I had read about the British Secret Service. The empty warehouse scenario fitted their modus operandi perfectly. After all, the MOD must own a great deal of properties and empty buildings, probably through front companies. That way, if a covert operation needed to be carried out, an empty building such as this would provide an ideal cloak of anonymity.

Having decided in my own mind I was in no real danger of being killed, I tried to work out what was likely to happen. In all probability, it would be psychological torture and intimidation of some sort. Bearing in mind the grim surroundings, a gun to the head seemed firm favourite. I completely discounted the possibility of physical torture, and satisfied myself it would be a gun to the head.

In that case, all I had to do was keep calm, pretend to break down in tears and beg for mercy whilst I insisted I didn't know who the printer was.

Would they reveal their identities? More than likely not.

I began to feel a bit more confident about the situation, and started going over in my mind how I would react, what I would say. What if they asked me who I had been working for when I had been arrested? I was working for some guys that I had been introduced to by Vindiloo, in itself quite feasible as he'd been on bail for forged £50 notes when he died. That way, my story couldn't be disproved and all I had to declare was that I only knew these men by their Christian names. I could even give them Vindiloo's old mobile phone number that had been lost several months earlier.

By now I was totally convinced. Eventually they would have to believe me and release me. There would be no danger to them, as who could I tell? And who would believe me anyway?

At this point, I heard the noise of several footsteps outside. The footsteps came closer and stopped by the door. I looked at my watch. I had been there for 20 minutes, but it had seemed much longer. I heard the muffled sounds of voices outside. At length, the handle on the door turned, and I took a deep breath and braced myself for my anticipated ordeal. Although I felt confident that I would come out of it alive, I nevertheless found it difficult to control my nervousness. And then, instantly, my confidence and cautious optimism evaporated.

*Jesus. Dear God in Heaven, please help me. Freddie, this is your baby boy. I need your help now like never before. Now I'm definitely in trouble. All my plans for what I'm going to do when I get out of here, they're worthless. I'm about to die.*

A huge shape loomed in the open doorway. King fucking Kong. Or was it Godzilla? As with Pinky and Perky, I found it hard to tell the difference. He stepped forward followed by a smaller, more average-sized man no taller than myself.

*I don't know what to do, how to react, what to say, I am very close to losing all control.* I fought desperately to hold myself together. I was absolutely petrified. Pure, unadulterated fear.

The Russian colossus displayed no emotion — no peck on the cheek, no friendly hug — and just stared at me. There was no scowling mask of terror, just a penetrating, ice-cold gaze. The other man closed the door behind him. Seconds later, Boris simply said, 'Vilf.'

Scarcely able to speak or make any intelligible sound, I nodded an expression of acknowledgement.

'It has taken some while to find you,' Boris said.

I nodded again. 'Mmm,' I muttered.

'We were all very sorry to know about Mr Tony's dead.'

More nodding. 'Mmm.'

'I think that we have to speak about some things. Yes?'

But this time, instead of nodding, I asked, 'Where's your friend. The other big man?' I have no idea what prompted me to ask such an irrelevant question. Perhaps, subconsciously, I was missing his happy smiling face, and his sharp repartee — *'Ha, ha, Vilf!'*

'I am sorry but he, too, is like Mr Tony. But my friend here, he can speak English.'

The other man merely nodded to me. *'That's handy, perhaps we can have a little sing-song or something.'* Or at least, that's what I would have said had this been a Hollywood blockbuster and I'd been Bruce Willis. But it wasn't, and as I knew more or less what was coming next, it was hard to see just how I could possibly avoid being killed. I was just plain frightened.

'I am sorry about our surroundings, but I am hopeful that this will not take too long,' Boris said.

'I am sure you are aware of our needs. If you can just tell us how we can have our paper back, then we can clear up our outstanding matters,' his friend said.

'Sweets as nuts,' Boris added.

I looked at him and tried to remain calm. I feigned an air of confidence and prayed that my voice wouldn't betray me, then desperately searching for the least incriminating way that I could break the bad news, I simply declared, 'I don't have the paper, I'm afraid.' No other way to say it.

There was no apparent reaction from either man. After a moment's pause, Boris said, 'You remember I told you that I am a man of my word, yes? Well, this is very true. If you, too, are a man who does the correct things, you will tell me where the paper is. You have my word that you will have no harm. I can even say that you will be paid the money for the work that has been done. But you must give us back our paper.'

I thought hard about the overwhelming predicament I was in. Or perhaps 'predicament' is not quite the correct word because, whichever way I looked at it, there were no choices, no decisions to be made. I did not have, nor could I get, the paper.

'I'm very sorry. But you must believe me. I never knew where the paper was when Vindiloo snuffed it,' I said.

Boris and the other man looked bemused. 'What are you saying? — what is, "Vindiloo snuffed it"?'

Under different circumstances, I'm sure I could have seen some humour in Boris's question, but as it was, I couldn't help thinking how long it would be before I was in the same spiritual state as the late Vindiloo. I struggled to answer the question.

'I, er, what I meant was, that Tony put the paper somewhere, but he didn't tell me where before he died.'

Both men stared at me, disbelief written all over their implacable faces. The other man said something in French to Boris. They spoke in whispered tones, and my limited knowledge of French didn't allow me to decipher any of what was said.

'Please go to this room.' Boris motioned with his outstretched hand.

I walked to the first cubicle.

'Sit down,' he said.

I sat on the makeshift seat, touching the piece of wood across the bowl first. Enclosed in the claustrophobic surroundings of the cubicle, I was barely able to think. The whole situation seemed so unreal. *This is not happening.*

Boris's friend leaned against the partitioning panel that divided the cubicles, and Boris stood in the doorframe, eliminating most of the light. 'I cannot say that I believe you. I think that you must have the paper or that you have the printed banknotes.'

'I haven't, I swear to you,' I pleaded.

Boris paused. 'I think that you have,' he said.

Rapidly descending into a blind spiral of panic, I somehow managed to come out with a lucid suggestion. 'Listen, please. I'll do the rest of the printing for you. For nothing. Please, I promise.' I looked hopefully up at the two men.

The other man simply said, 'It has already been printed. The job is now finished. All we want is our paper.'

His reply dashed what little remaining hope I had felt. The real tragedy of the situation from my point of view was that I looked like being killed over the loss of something I had never possessed, and which, although worth a fortune, was a mere pittance compared to the £4.9 billion that had been realised from the main batch of the paper. My head slumped forward and I looked at the floor. I couldn't think, I couldn't speak. My whole body had a strange numb kind of feeling, almost as though I wasn't really there.

'Have you made the paper into banknotes?' Boris asked.

Still staring down at the floor I shook my head. 'No,' I mumbled.

'So why do you not give it to us?' the other man asked.

I paused before speaking. 'I do not know where the paper is. You must believe me. I just don't know.'

Boris remained silent for a moment and then I was aware of him motioning to the other man and they both stepped out of the cubicle. They spoke for about a minute, again in French, and again I was unable to understand what they were talking about. Then Boris remained standing in the doorway whilst the other man left. I looked up at him. His eyes betrayed no emotion and, as before, he maintained a chilling gaze down at where I sat. Minutes later, I heard the sound of his friend returning, the door closing behind him and his footsteps crossing the tiled floor. I looked up to see him passing a dark-coloured towel to Boris. And a gun.

*No*. My thoughts were racing. Boris and the other man had another brief discussion, this time with a more intense feel to it, but still I couldn't understand what they were saying. But by now, even had I been completely fluent in French, I doubt if I could have understood them. My brain and the few intelligible thoughts that were bouncing around inside were concentrated on the gun that Boris was holding.

When their discussions ceased, the stranger shrugged his shoulders and stepped into the cubicle, again leaning just slightly against the partition divide. I now noticed that he, too, had a gun, held down by his side pointing towards the floor.

Boris pulled the chamber on the gun, the towel over his arm. He moved forward and into the cubicle so that he was standing directly in front of me. The gun was now held behind his back and he draped the towel over my head. I noticed the other man holding his gun in both hands — aimed at me.

My breaths were coming at a furious pace, and I had a sensation not dissimilar, I should imagine, to an asthma attack. I felt the end of the gun pressing against the top of my head. Struggling to breathe, and with my heart pounding at an impossible rate against my chest, the thought of swinging my hand against the gun and attempting to grab it raced through my mind. But I knew that, with the other gun pointed directly at me, it would be no more than a futile attempt. Apart from which I still had this strange feeling of numbness, and I wasn't at all sure I could even move. I tried desperately to form some thoughts in my head, but everything just seemed to be a blur. A disorientating kind of haze.

Boris's voice broke into my trance-like state. 'This does not have to happen, you know. You must tell me now where is the paper.' He paused; I couldn't respond. It was as though his voice was coming from far away, from another place. A voice in the distance.

'Even if it has been made into money, you can return it still.' Again he paused; again I couldn't respond. 'If it has been put into bank accounts, it can be put into our accounts. You can still be out of this problem.'

I made a hesitant kind of grunting sound, and just managed to say, 'No.'

I couldn't lift my head. I couldn't move. I was aware of more pressure being exerted on the gun. I could feel it being pushed harder against the towel over my bowed head. And then I groaned uncontrollably as I sensed the trigger being squeezed. More squeezing.

A dull kind of half-clicking sound. And words spoken in Russian. Coming from another place. Still distant. Fading.

Boris moved away. I choked and was nearly sick. Boris ignored me. Preoccupied, he was pulling something on the gun. The other man remained motionless, his eyes fixed on me, his gun still pointed casually at me. I mumbled a feeble, 'Please,' and then again, 'Please.' But my words were ignored, and again the gun was pressed against my head. The jamming of the gun was no more than a brief respite.

Boris spoke again, one last attempt. 'There is still time. Just say, and I will not do this terrible thing. There is not reason for you not to tell me now.' His words were now clear, as were my thoughts. It was as though my ears had suddenly 'popped', after being temporarily blocked. I devised a plan. I thought I could play for time. Just pretend that I could take them to the paper — that I didn't know the address — I would have to take them there. But then my thoughts were so haphazard I said nothing, unable even to speak.

'Well, I am not happy. You do not tell me. This time the gun will work, believe me.'

Silence. An all-embracing lack of sound that seemed somehow to envelope and suffocate my very being.

*Seconds seem like hours. I sense that pressure is slowly being applied to the trigger. I'm chanting a weird kind of prayer, I'm just repeating the word 'please'. The enclosed claustrophobic space is pulsating around my head. 'Please ... please ...' More seconds pass. The pressure increases. More seconds. 'Please ... please ...' More seconds, more pressure. I am barely able to breathe. I feel the gun being removed. Boris steps back, saying something to the other man. They move out of the cubicle and talk again. I'm aware that I'm trembling. I hear Boris say, 'Vilf.'*

Unsure as to what I could expect, I hesitated, then slowly took the towel away and looked up. I saw Boris looking at me and he said, 'Come.' He turned away and walked towards the door leading out of the toilet. The other man turned and looked at me. 'This way,' he said, standing just outside the cubicle entrance. Realising that my ordeal could well be over, I stood up. I felt an overwhelming sense of relief.

*My body feels light. My spiritual being feels light. I — am — alive. I pause before I move forward. I ... AM ... ALIVE!*

Then, in the blink of an eyelid, I felt completely normal. In a bizarre, inexplicable way, it was as if my very close call hadn't happened. I walked out of the toilet feeling perfectly normal. Maybe I was in some kind of state of denial. But I was no longer aware that my heart was pounding against my chest, or that my legs were weak. My mouth was extremely dry, but I had no problem in getting the saliva flowing freely around my teeth and gums. As I entered the area outside the toilet, I even nodded to the two men there. Strange.

Boris and his friend were walking towards the lift. I hurriedly followed them, and the three of us got inside, and the lift descended to the ground floor. We left the lift and Boris opened an office door close to the building entrance. In the sparsely-furnished office, there were four chairs and an old desk. I was told to sit on the other side of the desk and his friend sat next to me. Boris asked me all the details about Vindiloo's death and why I didn't know where the paper was. I pointed out that it was the consortium's idea that Vindiloo should keep one half of the first consignment of paper until the first batch had been printed. I went on to tell him about the drunken episode and the only time I visited the garage, the same day I had delivered the banknotes to him at the Kennedy Hotel in Euston.

I also explained that, after Vindiloo's death, I had asked Bradley, his son, if he knew anything about the two gigantic Russians, or the man with the yacht and the private jet. I also told him about my various efforts to locate the lock-up garage. Without any contact from himself, I said, I felt there was nothing I could do.

I felt slightly relieved when he appeared to believe me. The other man seemed indifferent, and said nothing. Boris informed me that the Marbella Sailor's only means of contact with Vindiloo was via his lost mobile and, consequently, there had been a delay of several weeks before he had been able to find his home number. He had called Vindiloo's home, learned of his death and, after offering his condolences, he asked Bradley if he knew one of his father's friends by the name of 'Wilf'. Bradley didn't and was absolutely certain he didn't have a friend of that name. When asked, he also said, as far as he was aware, his dad didn't know any printers.

I was surprised that Bradley hadn't called me, but then I realised it must have been about the time that I made my regular change of mobile phone, and so he would have had no way of contacting me. Not for the first time, I cursed the unusual chain of events that had turned my world upside down.

I asked Boris how he had eventually located me. He said that, initially, through a contact, he had been given a list of known associates of Vindiloo. I was not on it and nor was anyone named Wilf. His associates who had abducted me had kept an eye on everybody connected to Vindiloo, without any luck. It was only after my arrest that, somehow or another, a connection was made between Vindiloo and me. Boris was informed, and I ended up right where I was sitting now.

After all this, Boris informed me that the original jamming of the gun was planned. He needed to bring me as close to the brink as possible to satisfy himself that I genuinely didn't know where the paper was. He felt absolutely confident that, had I known, I would have told him. Then he would have killed me for not telling him first of all. I asked him what would have happened had I tried to bluff my way out by pretending to know the whereabouts but not the address. He simply said I would certainly have been killed. I thanked God I hadn't been able to speak. As it was, he told me he didn't feel that I should be killed for no real reason, although his friend felt differently. He felt that I should be killed and disposed of with my car, never to be heard of again.

The other man looked at me. 'That is purely good business sense, as far as I am concerned. It is nothing against you, I have no feelings about you one way or the other. But my friend has decided differently, and I must agree with this. It is up to him.' He spoke in a matter-of-fact fashion with neither a smile nor the remotest hint of any expression on his face.

Boris got up from the chair. 'I will open the shutters in the yard for you, and you may go.'

I followed him out into the yard. The two 'police' cars were parked away from the shutters, with two of the 'policemen' sitting in one of them.

'Your keys are in the car,' Boris said. I nodded by way of acknowledgement.

I opened the car door and sat behind the steering wheel. The shutters were pulled up and I edged slowly forward. As I drove through the archway, Boris leaned into the open window and said, 'You will not mention this, or this place, to anybody.'

'No,' I replied.

Then, before I pulled away, he said, 'Many men start to sob very much.'

I looked at him. 'If I had thought for one second that crying would have saved me, then believe me I would have cried like a baby. And then some more.'

For the first time, I saw an expression on Boris's face. It was a thoughtful, quizzical look. I drove away.

The building where I was taken was somewhere other than Paddington, and the name Boris is obviously just my nickname for him. I never heard his name spoken and do not know what it is.

# CHAPTER 21

# Another Lock-up Garage and Kudos for Inspector Morse

After my very close encounter with Boris, I put the affair to the back of my mind and carried on trying to accumulate as much capital as possible before my case was heard. In spite of this, old habits die hard, and I still had a rather cavalier attitude towards money. A prime example of this was an occasion shortly before I was abducted.

I went to visit Hungry Jim to deliver a parcel of twenties. Hungry's main move at this time involved container-loads of duty-free booze. Whilst he made a lot of money this way, at the same time he would lose a lot if a lorry-load should be captured by HM Customs.

At the time of my visit to deliver the parcel, he'd had a particularly bad run, with several containers being seized. So bad was this run, that all of his profits had been swallowed. Combined with his chronic gambling habit which, as chairman of his local Gamblers Anonymous lodge, he kept very firmly under wraps, not only was he back to square one, but also in debt to a number of people. As we sat in his front room, he asked me if I would be able to lend him some money — 'Strictly no more than 48 hours.'

'How much d'you need?' I asked him.

'44 grand,' he said.

Feeling just a little bit sorry that I hadn't been able to accommodate him with regard to the 75 grand that he had asked me for several months previously, I felt almost as though I was obliged to help him out. Apart from this, as old friends who had done a great many trades together, most requiring trust on both sides, I wanted to help out in whatever way I could. I had over £50,000 at home, a stockpile with which I intended to repay Eugene and Jack. But I knew that I could trust Hungry Jim, who had always been a man of his word.

'That should be OK, Jim,' I told him. 'When d'you want it?'

'Soon as possible,' he replied, looking visibly relieved. 'There's a container of women's shoes on its way, due to arrive tomorrow some time. I want to put my name to it. Guaranteed you'll have your cash back within 24 hours after it arrives. I've already got it sold, cash on. Thing is, I've got to pay up first before I can take delivery. There'll be a decent drink in it for you, don't worry.'

I shrugged non-committally. 'Whatever, I'll leave it up to you. I'm just pleased to be able to help out.'

That evening, I took the cash to his house and Hungry promised that it would be returned within two days. 'I'll call you as soon as it's all sorted out,' he said as I left.

After a couple of days, Hungry called to say there had been a slight delay. No major problems. I wasn't concerned and again he said he would get back to me as soon as possible. The next day he called to say that there was still a delay. He apologised and told me that, if I needed the cash back, it was still there at his house for me to collect. If I needed it.

'No problem. There's no urgency,' I said.

The following afternoon, Friday, I received another phone call from Hungry. The deal had fallen through, he was fed up with being messed about, and the money was sitting there waiting for me to collect it.

'I'll come round this evening, then, OK?' I said.

'Well, actually I'm going out to a GA meeting tonight. Can't you come round now?' Hungry replied.

'I don't think so, but if I can get round this afternoon some time, I will do. If not, I'll leave it till the morning.'

And that was how we left it. I called on Hungry Jim to collect the £44,000 on Saturday lunchtime. His wife answered the door and showed me into the front room, where Hungry was sitting, a glum expression on his fat face. He motioned me to sit down.

'There's a bit of a problem,' he said.

'What's that then?' I asked.

'The container turned up this morning. I weighed on for it. The driver took it to the slaughter I had sorted out. Everything's sweet. Then suddenly the Old Bill turned up. Everyone got nicked, lost the load.'

I couldn't disguise my alarm upon hearing this, but before I could speak, Hungry said, 'I've got some of your money here, 20 grand. As luck would have it, one of my punters was waiting at the slaughter and took their load straight off and gave me this. I left John there to take care of things and the Old Bill swooped after I left.'

He pushed the money across the tabletop to me. I cursed my luck in not picking up the £44,000 on Friday afternoon as Hungry had asked me. The loss of £24,000 was something I could ill afford. Combined with this was £5,000 he owed me for the twenties. Just by looking at Hungry's disconsolate expression as he shook his head, I realised there was little chance of getting £29,000 back in the immediate future.

'So what happens now, then?' I said.

'I'll get the 24 grand back to you as soon as possible,' he replied. 'I'll definitely have it in about three months or so. The other 5G I should have next week some time.'

That was fair enough as far as I was concerned, and I said thanks, offered my sympathy and left.

The following week, Hungry had £1,500 for me and told me that he had been knocked for the rest of the money for the twenties. So, once again, apart from the £1,500, all I was paid were promises. From then on, I was well and truly in the waiting room as far as the debts were concerned.

With regard to my forthcoming case, I had various meetings with Ian Oxford, all of which offered little or no hope. As Paul Wright and his colleague had said the last time I had met them, I was looking at going away for a long time.

I can't deny the thought of spending the next four or five years in prison was a depressing prospect. Apart from the worry of the impending prison sentence, I still had the problem of Eugene and Jack. With my funds sorely depleted, it was becoming ever more difficult to get not only the loan money together, but also a respectable amount to leave for Laraine to get by on. And in Laraine's case, an absence of four years would require a great deal of financing.

Then, in April, Ian Oxford informed me that my case was due to be heard some time in July or August. I was now under a great deal of pressure and desperate to get my financial position in order.

I went over to see Jewboy Jack with my monthly payment of £3,000. I gave him the news about my impending trial, and he asked me how long I was expecting. I told him about seven years.

'So what's going to happen about the loan?' he asked.

'I reckon I'll have it back to you in June. That OK?' I replied.

'Yes. That's fine. Good man.' And then, in a magnanimous gesture of rarely seen generosity, he said, 'Under the circumstances, I think we can waive the penalty clause,' and then, after pausing for me to acknowledge his beneficence by way of a nod and a smile, continued, 'So can't anything be done about the bird you're going to get?'

I shook my head. 'Not as far as I can see. I'm bang to rights. I haven't given the Old Bill any help, so the judge won't be too happy about that. So it looks like I'm just going to have to take it on the chin. Seven fucking years minimum.'

'That's a long time, Steve. No way you can get the charge reduced and get, say, 18 months?'

'No, not really. Not unless I stick up a few names, and give them a few bits of work. You know how it is. Unless you're a grass, there's nothing to be done.'

'Won't the Old Bill in charge take a drink?'

'No. I've tried that. Didn't want to know. Just grassing, that's all he's interested in.'

Jewboy Jack remained deep in thought. After some time, he said, 'Well, maybe something can be done. We'll just have to think of something. I'll give you a call.'

'Yeah, sure.'

A couple of days later, I received a call from Jewboy Jack, who told me that he and Eugene wanted to see me. I met them at the pub as usual and, in the ground-floor back room, Eugene told me he had some good news for me. He explained that he had some worthwhile information for me that I could use to get my charges reduced. He went on to tell me that I was to go and see the police, and tell them that I had some information for them that would lead to the recovery of an extremely large quantity of counterfeit money. In fact, the largest quantity ever seized in the UK.

'Really?' I asked.

'Yes. Fifties and US dollars,' Eugene said.

I thought about what he was saying, then said, 'So you're telling me to become a grass?'

'No, not at all.'

'Well, that's what it sounds like.'

'Trust me, Steve, you won't be grassing anybody up, believe me.'

'So who do the fifties belong to then?' I asked.

'Don't worry about that. Just take what's on offer, unless you want to spend the next four or five years in jail,' Eugene said.

After being reassured that I wouldn't be grassing anybody up, I agreed to go and see the police and let them know that I might have some worthwhile information for them.

I met Paul Wright, who this time was with his superior, a real-life Inspector Morse (looking vastly different than he does on TV). I explained the brief details of my possible information and, of course, both men agreed that, if it turned out to be as I said, then no doubt something beneficial could be arranged on my behalf.

But then Paul Wright added a proviso. 'There's just one thing I'd better tell you, Steve,' he said, 'and that's, if we're talking about a lock-up garage filled with funny money, then we're going to need a body to go with it. After all, for all we know, you might just put it there yourself and tell us where it is. So, remember, if you want any help, we need to collar somebody for it.'

'Yeah. OK,' I said, and as I left, his words stayed in my mind. 'Well, that's the end of that idea,' I thought to myself, and I made my way over to Jewboy Jack and Eugene, to give them the bad news. To my surprise, neither man seemed particularly concerned when I told them.

'If that's the case, they'll have to have a body then,' Eugene said, matter of factly.

'Well, that means I'll be grassing somebody up then,' I protested.

'Don't worry about it,' Jewboy Jack said. 'It will all be arranged. You won't be grassing anybody up. Leave it to us.'

I wasn't too happy about the situation, and told them I wasn't going to go through with it, but after being guaranteed that I wouldn't be grassing anybody up, that everything was arranged, I agreed, and a few weeks later Jewboy Jack gave me all the relevant details and instructions as to how I was to approach the police with the necessary information.

I contacted Paul Wright and told him I needed to see him urgently.

I arrived at the police station a couple of hours later and, as I walked into the interview room, both Paul Wright and Inspector Morse looked at me in surprise as I was accompanied by another man. 'Who's this?' Paul Wright asked.

'A solicitor,' I replied and, as I spoke, the young man with me produced his card. He was, in fact, a young employee of a friend of mine who has a thriving practice in Covent Garden. The two police offers looked slightly put out to see him, as I told them that he was to be an independent witness to any agreements that might be made. But, of course, they had to agree to his presence.

'So what have you got to tell us then, Steve?' Paul Wright asked.

'I've come across some information regarding the whereabouts of an extremely large quantity of high-quality counterfeit money,' I said.

Paul Wright leaned forward in his chair. 'So where is it then, Steve? Any bodies?'

'Well, firstly, what's in it for me?' I responded.

'That depends on how good the information is. If it's as good as you say, then we'll go behind the scenes and have a word with the Judge to let him know that you've helped us out.'

'No. That's no good,' I said.

'Well, what do you expect then?' Paul Wright asked.

I decided to chance my arm and said, 'All the charges dropped.'

Both officers looked at me, blinked a couple of times, then Inspector Morse smiled and said, 'Sorry, Steve. You're asking too much. Can't be done. Impossible.' His reply was much as I had expected, but still it was worth a try.

'OK then,' I said. 'How about reducing the charge to Custody of the Goods?' This was my real objective, and one that I was prepared to hold out for, as I knew that the charge carried a maximum sentence of two years, which would work out to an actual sentence of 18 months for a guilty plea.

But still they refused. 'Listen, Steve. If we have a word with the Judge, don't worry, you'll be all right, believe me,' Paul Wright assured me.

'I'm sorry. If you can't reduce the charge, then I'm not interested,' I told him, and got up from my chair, as if to leave.

'Hang on a second. Let's not be hasty,' Paul Wright said. I sat down again, and the two officers had a brief, whispered conversation. Seconds later, Paul Wright said, 'If we agree to your suggestion, how soon could you give us the details?'

'Right now. In fact, if it's not done soon, the stuff might not be there. As far as I know, it's only being stored in transit. I think it's due to be shifted in a day or so.'

'So will there be anybody there to collar?' Inspector Morse asked.

'As far as I know, there's somebody who goes there regularly to check up on it,' I told him.

'But if we keep the place under obbo and this person doesn't turn up, what are we supposed to do? Sit and wait until our men grow long white beards?' Paul Wright asked.

'As far as I know, the guy checks up on it at least once a day, sometimes twice.'

'All right then, you've got a deal,' Inspector Morse said.

'But if nobody turns up,' Paul Wright added, 'the deal's off. Fair enough?'

'Fair enough.'

'Right then, Steve, where's this place?' Paul Wright asked.

'Well, first of all, how do I know you're authorised to reduce the charges for me? The CPS might not agree.'

'We have the authority,' Inspector Morse said.

'Absolutely? Even if the CPS object?'

'Absolutely,' Paul Wright confirmed.

I glanced at the young solicitor busily writing down notes in his pad. 'You got that?' I remarked, and he nodded. 'All right then,' and with that, I gave them the address of a lock-up garage in Bow, in the East End of London.

They immediately made a phonecall, and then Paul Wright said, 'If it's as good as you say it is, Steve, we should be able to get you a suspended sentence.'

'That would be nice.'

That evening, the *Evening Standard* carried the headline: £18 MILLION COUNTERFEIT CURRENCY FOUND IN LOCK-UP GARAGE.

Apart from the newspapers, the item was shown on television and hogged the headlines the following day. The total haul recovered was £10 million in forged £50 notes, and approximately £8 million in $100 bills. A man was helping police with their enquiries.

As soon as the news broke, I called a jubilant Paul Wright on his mobile phone. He told me that he had spoken to the CPS and the charges would be reduced as we had agreed. Furthermore, a note would go into the Judge that should ensure that I would receive a suspended sentence.

The following day, I went to see Eugene and Jewboy Jack, who both greeted me like an old friend. I told them the charges had been reduced and that there was even a chance that I might receive a suspended sentence.

'Terrific,' Eugene said, smiling broadly. 'I think this calls for a little drink.'

'Certainly,' Jewboy Jack said, and he called out to the barmaid, who came into the room a couple of minutes later with a tray of drinks.

'So who's the guy that got nicked?' I asked.

'Don't worry about it,' Eugene said.

'But this means I've grassed somebody up.'

'Trust me, Steve, you haven't grassed anybody up. It's all been sorted, believe me.'

'Well, that's how it seems to me.'

'Listen, you're out of the main charge, and you might not even go to jail, so just be grateful. And stop asking questions,' Eugene said.

'Just one,' I said. 'How much is it going to cost me?'

'We'll sort it out later on,' Jewboy Jack said. So now I was indebted to them.

It wasn't until much later that I found out what had really

happened. The notes belonged to one of Eugene's brothers, who had agreed to go along with Jewboy Jack's idea.

At that time, Eugene was friendly with an ex-bank robber by the name of Danny Alpress, but who for some reason was known as Danny Till. Danny Till had served a long period of time in prison several years earlier, as a result of a series of trials in which the main prosecution witness was a bank robber by the name of Bertie Smalls, the first 'supergrass'. At this particular time, Danny Till was suffering from terminal cancer and had just six months to live. His one concern, he told people, was to try and get hold of some money to leave for his two young children. He was prepared to do anything, he said.

With this in mind, he was approached and asked if he wanted to earn £50,000. Of course he was interested, and he was told that he would have to allow himself to be arrested for something (he wasn't told what) but that obviously, in view of his condition, he would be granted bail and the case would never get to court, as he would be dead by then.

Danny Till was somewhat dubious, and said that for all he knew it might be a murder rap. Even though he was assured it was nothing as serious as that, and that he definitely would get bail, he declined the offer, even though it meant turning down £50,000. So much for being prepared to do anything for his children.

Word of the proposition reached another guy whose name I don't know, and who was in some kind of financial predicament. Perhaps he owed money to Eugene. Well, this person made an approach and said that he was prepared to do whatever the work involved. And he wasn't even dying.

And so it was that, when the police raided the lock-up garage, the chap was arrested but then, incredibly, released on police bail, with instructions to return 28 days later. In the event, the police told him not to bother coming back. So not only did he get bail, but he wasn't even charged.

This was what I was told. How true it is I can't say; perhaps the man in the garage genuinely was looking after the hoard of counterfeit notes. Who knows?

Some time later, whilst in prison, I came across at least two people who claimed that the £18 million worth of counterfeit currency found in the lock-up had belonged to them, and heard of several more who had used it as an excuse to avoid paying various debts. So it would seem that I was not the only one to benefit from what, to this day, is still the largest individual haul of counterfeit money ever found in the UK.

# CHAPTER 22

## Custody of the Goods at Harrow Crown Court

Shortly after this, I heard from Ian Oxford that my case had been listed to be heard at Harrow Crown Court during the first week in July.

I had a conference with Ian and my barrister, Nigel Lambourne, during which very little was resolved, due to the fact that I had no defence. Ian and Nigel knew nothing about the deal I had struck regarding the charges being reduced, and consequently both seemed somewhat bemused by my air of confidence that, maybe, the prosecution would accept a plea to a lesser charge.

Nigel, naturally enough, thought it highly unlikely that any such thing would happen, as the evidence against me to support a charge of conspiracy to manufacture was quite formidable. Nothing was resolved, and Ian and I left a slightly baffled Nigel Lambourne in his chambers wondering just what I was going to do on the day.

As we walked through the grounds of the Inner Temple, Ian emphasised that I had to come up with something pretty soon, or else I would most certainly be 'potted'. But, of course, I already knew exactly what would be happening when we attended court, and so I kept up my air of unconcern.

In the meantime, realising I had no time to lose, I set about getting Eric to print as much as possible for Dinky Dan to go to work with in case I got some 'bird'. It was now approaching the end of May and, by the time of my court appearance at the beginning of July, I had delivered over 300,000 notes to Dinky. Eric was unaware of my forthcoming case, and I decided to leave it until after all the printing had been done. For the time being, I took him his money as it came in.

I knew that I wouldn't be sentenced when I appeared in court, and that sentencing would be postponed until the appropriate reports on me had been prepared. I was expecting a remand until September, as August is a month when the courts work on a skeleton staff basis, and only urgent matters or continuing trials are dealt with. This would give me a considerable breathing space in which to get some more cash together and generally put my affairs in order.

When we attended court in July, it soon became apparent to Nigel that something was in the air, and he told me, in enthusiastic tones, that it appeared that the prosecution might be willing to accept a plea to a lesser charge.

'Really?' I said, trying to look surprised.

Nigel, Ian and I, were sitting in the canteen. Ian seemed as surprised as I apparently was, and then Nigel looked at me. 'I don't know how Ian's managed it, but I think you should thank him, Stephen,' he said.

Ian looked even more surprised and said, 'Well, don't look at me, Nigel, I've got nothing to do with this. I'm as much in the dark as you are about what's going on.'

'Come off it, Ian. You know very well what's going on. How did you manage to swing it?' Nigel asked.

I looked from Ian to Nigel and then back to Ian.

'Yes, Ian, just how did you manage it?' I said.

Ian shook his head and insisted he hadn't done anything. 'Believe me, I haven't spoken to anyone, I'm telling you. I know as much about why the charges are being reduced as you do, Nigel. If you want to believe I've worked some kind of miracle, so be it.'

'Oh very well, Ian, have it your way if you insist, but whatever's going on, it looks as though you'll probably be pleading today, Stephen.'

Later, I appeared in court where the prosecution informed the judge that the charges of Conspiracy to Manufacture Counterfeit Currency, and Possession with Intent to Supply, were not being proceeded with and an alternative charge of Custody of the Goods was being substituted. With this, I duly pleaded guilty, and the case was remanded until 27 July for sentencing and reports.

This was something of a double blow, inasmuch as I was

expecting a much longer remand than three weeks, and 27 July was my daughter Stephanie's seventeenth birthday. With precious little time, I earnestly set about tying up all the loose ends, my chief priority being to ensure that Jewboy Jack and Eugene were paid up.

With just a few days left before my court appearance, I went to see them at the pub in South London, taking £53,000 with me in a case. Jewboy Jack nodded knowingly and took the case. 'So what's in here, then?' he said.

'Fifty-three grand. All double checked and counted.'

'Good. I'll take your word for it, then, no need to check. So I thought you were expecting a suspended sentence?'

'I am, but you never know.'

'I suppose not. So how will we know what's happened to you?'

'I'll get Wedding Bells to go down to the court. He can let you know if I get some.'

'OK. Let's hope you get a bender, then,' said Eugene.

I stayed with them in the pub for a while and then left to go and pay Eric a visit.

Not wishing to alarm him any more than necessary, I told him that I was due in court on a charge of dishonest handling that had come up unexpectedly. I told him that I had made arrangements for him to be paid for however long I was away. I gave him the telephone number of a trusted friend, who would collect the cash for him as and when it came in. Eric offered me his sympathy and wished me luck.

During the next couple of days, I made sure that every last detail was attended to, and my last port of call was Dinky Dan. Although he had over 300,000 notes in stock, they needed to be sorted into individual piles of 1,000, with an approximately equal amount of each serial number in each pile. The easiest and quickest way to do this was to weigh them on a set of electronic scales. These were accurate to within a couple of notes per 1,000.

I explained the relatively simple process of using the machine and had a packet of 1,000 notes with me to demonstrate. I explained that the weight of 1,000 notes was 1,050 grammes, and when the figure showed on the digital screen — *voilà* — we had 1,000 pieces. If it showed less than 1,050g, then just put a few more notes on the pile until it reached the target weight. Simple.

Dinky looked confused, as though I had just tried to explain Einstein's Theory of Relativity. From the way his eyes were darting about, and his lips silently mouthed various words and numbers with his tongue making its way around his lips, I could tell he was making a truly heroic effort to grasp the basics of the mysterious electronic scales. And then, brow furrowed in a quizzical fashion, he said, 'What's that first word you said — volly?'

'*Voilà*?'

'Yeah, that's it.'

I looked at him in amazement. 'Nothing, Dan. It's not really important. So you OK with the scales, then?'

'What? Oh yeah. I think I'll be able to work it out.'

I told him that I had to go, as I still had a couple of things to do and wanted to get home as soon as possible.

'But you'll drop these off on your way?' he said, referring to the small pile of demonstration notes on the scales. He wanted me to take them to an address he used a couple of miles away.

''Course not. I've got to get home. I'm in court tomorrow.'

Dinky looked concerned. 'But what can I do with them? I can't leave them here.'

'Well, take them to your mate's place, then,' I replied.

'I can't do that. I can't drive about with them.'

I found this rather surprising as, when we had first started doing business, I had regularly loaded large quantities into the boot of his car. But since then, other delivery arrangements had been made, and now it appeared that Dinky Dan, the KO Man, had lost his 'bottle' even to drive a couple of miles with such a small package that could easily be hidden in his car.

'Well, that's up to you, Dan, but I've got to go now,' I told him and left.

On the journey home, Paul Wright called me on my mobile and asked to meet me at the pub opposite Whetstone Police Station. I arrived before him and sat outside with a glass of lager. It wasn't long before he arrived with Inspector Morse, who went to the bar and bought a round of drinks. With all three of us sat at the table, Paul Wright explained the purpose of the meeting.

'What we wanted to see you about, Steve,' he said, 'was that we wanted to let you know that we are aware of what went on with the lock-up that you told us about.' He paused to study my reaction, and sipped on the glass of beer in his hand.

I could feel DI Morse looking at me and weighed my words before speaking. 'I'm not with you,' I said.

'You set it up, didn't you, Steve?' DI Morse said.

I tried to look surprised. 'Did I? What makes you say that?'

'Come off it, Steve,' Paul Wright said. 'You know as well as we do, you set it up. We heard it cost you 80 grand, that right?'

I shook my head. 'No. Who told you that?'

The two police officers smiled.

'When we collared that guy in the lock-up, there wasn't a single print anywhere. When we searched his flat, it was as clean as a whistle. There wasn't even an address book in the place. It was as though he was expecting us, you with me?' Paul Wright said.

'Yeah, I understand what you're saying,' I replied.

'Well, as we understand it, all that paperwork was stored there deliberately for us to find, and the guy was paid to go there to take the rap. That's what we heard. Sound about right, Steve?' DI Morse remarked.

'I don't know. As far as I was aware, it was stored there waiting for someone to collect. That's all I know.'

'Pull the other one, Steve. But don't worry, we're not too bothered about it. We just wanted you to know that you haven't had us over, that's all. After all, we still got the credit for a major seizure, the kudos so to speak. So we're not really complaining.' Paul Wright had a wry smile on his face as he spoke.

'Oh, right,' I said.

But after that, I was more or less told that there would be no behind-the-scenes letter to the Judge recommending a suspended sentence, unless ... 'There is something you can do to help yourself,' DI Morse said.

'Oh yeah, what's that then?' I asked.

'Customs have approached us to ask you if you know where Skinny Mick Adams is.'

Skinny Mick Adams was a friend of mine who was wanted by Customs and Excise with regard to a major cannabis importation case. Obviously, they thought I knew his whereabouts which, although I didn't, wouldn't have been too difficult for me to have found out had I been so inclined. Instead, I looked at the two men and said, 'Well, you can tell Customs and Excise, bollocks.'

They both smiled, and Paul Wright said, 'That's what we told them you were likely to say.'

I stayed talking for a short while and then left. 'See you in court tomorrow, then,' I said by way of farewell.

With hindsight, a more sensible reaction to their request about Skinny Mick would have been to think before saying 'Bollocks', and lead them to believe that I could find out his whereabouts, but that it would probably take a week or so. In that way, they would have had to decide whether or not it was worthwhile to keep me on the street. Had they done so, then, of course, I would simply have told them later that I had been unable to find out where Skinny Mick was. But I didn't. Ironically,

Skinny Mick was picked up driving a suspect car a few weeks later.

That evening, Laraine and I had the painful duty of telling James that I would probably be going to prison the following day. As James hadn't been at home when I was originally arrested, he was totally unaware of the fact that I had been on bail since Christmas. At the age of ten, like most young boys, he believed his dad could solve any problem in the world. To have to enlighten him at such a tender age as to his dad's fallibilities was one of the most painful things I have ever had to do.

Laraine and I were able to soften the blow to a degree, by telling him a little white lie. We told him that the counterfeit money I was found with in the lock-up garage was nothing to do with me, but that I didn't feel it was right that I should snitch to the police about who it really belonged to. James's response, apart from bursting into tears, was to urge me to tell the police who the money belonged to, and then I wouldn't have to go to prison.

To see my son so upset and in tears, as a result of my own stupidity, brought home to me how irresponsible it is to risk your liberty when there are young children involved. I can make no excuses for my actions, and the burden of guilt that I bear for the pain and upset that my actions have caused to my family, not just on this occasion, but previously and subsequently, rests fairly and squarely on my shoulders. It is something that I have to live with on my conscience.

Apart from James, there was also, of course, Stephanie who, although older at 17, was still badly affected and very upset at my impending imprisonment. On the morning of 27 July, Laraine and I presented Stephanie with her birthday present, a little Fiat Uno car, together with a set of driving lessons. Naturally enough, she was overjoyed at the surprise present, and this at least helped to detract from my court appearance in the afternoon.

At court, I met Nigel and Ian, with whom I discussed the likely sentence. Having spoken to the prosecuting counsel involved in the case, Nigel was now aware of the lock-up garage information. The only problem was that they, too, seemed to be of the opinion that I had set the whole thing up. 'Not only that, Stephen,' Nigel said, 'it would appear that the judge is also aware of the situation so he's not going to be too pleased with you.'

I shrugged my shoulders. 'So you don't think there's too much chance of a suspended sentence then?'

'I wouldn't have thought so. Probably something nearer the maximum, two years, I'm afraid,' Nigel informed me.

When I stood before the judge, he made a comment to the effect that his powers of sentencing were somewhat limited. Nigel Lambourne, my barrister, made a speech on my behalf, in which he pointed out that I had not wasted the court's time and money, and had pleaded guilty and, as such, was entitled to a reasonable discount on my sentence.

The judge's response to this was to remark that, since I had been caught red-handed, I didn't have much option. Grudgingly, he gave me a lesser sentence for pleading guilty, and I was sent to prison for 21 months, a discount of just three months as opposed to six which would have been the usual amount allowed. Before sentencing me, he passed comment that the amount of £1½ million, albeit in the form of waste sheets, was probably the largest quantity of notes ever to come under the heading of Custody of the Goods. I turned and made my way down to the cells below, the sound of Laraine's sobs still audible as the first door closed behind me. I walked along the corridor, where I was directed to a cell occupied by a young man waiting to be transported to HMP Wormwood Scrubs, the same destination as myself.

After a couple of minutes' conversation, during which he expressed surprise that I was in the same situation as him (he'd assumed from my smart suit that I was a solicitor), Ian and Nigel came down to see me. It was basically a courtesy call, to say farewell and that the outcome was much as they had expected, although they both agreed that an 18-month sentence would have been more appropriate.

Nigel told me he would prepare an appeal against the severity of sentence if I wished him to do so. Before I could reply, Ian assured him that was precisely what I wanted to do. I just smiled and agreed with whatever was said, but then I added, 'Well, I suppose we could point out how helpful I've been to the police.'

Now it was Nigel's turn to smile a somewhat wry smile. 'Yes, we will do, Stephen, but I rather fear the Appeal Court will be fully aware of what actually occurred. And, somehow, I don't think they'll be particularly happy about the situation. Still, we'll have a shot,' and with that they left, Ian telling me he would write soon.

# CHAPTER 23

## Sunset Strip; Long Legs; Goodbye, Dinky Dan

Initially, I was sent to Wormwood Scrubs and, after a few days of the most disgusting and filthy conditions imaginable, I was moved on to the slightly greener pastures of Wayland in Norfolk, where the next ten-and-a-half months passed relatively uneventfully, apart from Laraine informing me that she wanted a divorce.

Upon my release in June 1996, I stayed at my mother's flat in Walthamstow until a house I had arranged to rent became available. The separation from Laraine was totally amicable and it was agreed that Stephanie would, by choice, come to live with me whilst James stayed with his mother.

Shortly before my release from prison, I was granted a home-leave weekend pass and met up with Dinky Dan, who immediately fed me a cock-and-bull story about the delivery of notes before I had gone to prison being 80,000 short. As I had packed them myself I knew this couldn't be so, but he was adamant that the people who had charge of them wouldn't have lied to him. Since there was no common ground on the matter, and I was still owed a considerable amount of money, discretion had to take precedence over valour, and I decided not to push the point. I felt that I would be in a better position to argue such discrepancies when I was out for good in a few weeks' time.

Once released, I went to see Dinky Dan again and we discussed various business matters, the main gist of Dinky's conversation being that the money was coming in very slowly. Furthermore, there was still a great quantity of notes in stock. All in all, according to his figures, which included all manner of expenses (plus the mysterious partner who kept appearing in the figures at regular intervals), the amount I was owed came to £40,000.

This was far less than the £80,000 which I felt was closer to the real figure, but Dinky covered himself on this by declaring that we still had this large amount of stock. I could see at this stage where this road was ultimately going to lead, and so when Dinky asked me if I wanted to accept £30,000 cash right now, instead of waiting for the £40,000 to come in, I readily agreed. I knew it wouldn't be too long before we went our separate ways, and so it would be best to take what was on offer as quickly as possible. Apart from which, I needed the money.

My first month of freedom was spent relaxing, seeing old friends and going out with Laraine and James, and occasionally Stephanie when she wasn't too busy with her friends. Most of our friends found it hard to understand how we were still able to go out as a family. But, since the happiness of Stephanie and James was the most important factor for both of us, and we felt no animosity towards each other, as far as we were concerned, it was perfectly normal.

To my way of thinking, when two people who have lived together for 20 years and have a common interest, namely two children, feel they have to involve lawyers and courts to decide when one of them, usually the husband, can and cannot see those children, then that cannot be normal. I felt, as did Laraine, that in taking Stephanie and James out together as their parents, and not having to make ridiculous appointments to see my own son, then we were behaving in a natural and civilised manner.

At this time, I had no intention of starting up in production immediately and so decided to try and call in a few outstanding monies owed. Most of the people who owed me cash were punters who had promised to drop money round to Laraine whilst I was away. Overall, I had very little success, which didn't come as any great surprise. But more or less everyone said they had quite a few orders, and would be able to pay me as soon as I was back in production. And so I was in the position of having to supply them with more funny money just to have a chance to get my own money back.

The largest single amount owed was £29,000, which I had hoped Hungry Jim would have given Laraine whilst I was away. Instead, all he took round to her was £2,000. I spoke to him on the phone and he told me he wanted to see me about an order for some more tens.

I called on him at his bungalow, and his wife told me to go through to the pool. I went out to the garden and into the wooden construction that housed his small swimming pool. He was floating on his back looking remarkably like a bloated walrus, his huge, obese body protruding from the surface of the water, safe in the knowledge that there was nobody in the immediate vicinity with a harpoon.

Due to the earplugs he was wearing, he failed to hear me enter and, as his eyes were closed, he was unaware of my presence at the side of the pool. I smiled to myself as I surveyed the great landmass. Whoever said no man is an island obviously had never seen Hungry Jim afloat.

'A definite shipping hazard,' I thought out loud.

He opened his eyes and stared at me.

'It's OK, I'm not Captain Ahab,' I said, watching him start to flop about in the water. He paddled to the side and heaved himself out, followed immediately by the rolls of lard that comprised the multitude of layers around his torso. In all probability it was just my imagination, but I could have sworn that he started to flounder at the edge of the pool as though being on dry land was turning him into a beached whale.

I helped him on to his feet before he rocked himself to sleep and, puffing and panting, he made his way to a small table and chairs. It took him a while to regain his breath and, as he did so, his wife brought out a huge plate of food. Hungry's eyes lit up, so much so that I thought he was in danger of suffering an electric shock due to his wet body, but clearly he was well earthed, for within seconds of the food being delivered, he was upon it. Eyes and cheeks bulging from where a whole sandwich had been crammed, he looked his usual fat self as he struggled to get the mechanism of his jaws working. But to a human eating machine like Hungry Jim, a mere half a loaf jammed between both sets of molars presented no real problems.

'I've got quite a few orders for the cockles,' he hurriedly said before shovelling some more food in.

'Well, I'm not in production yet,' I told him. 'I really need to get some money in first.'

Not for the first time I found myself in the firing line as Hungry Jim attempted to devour his food and speak at the same time. Thankfully, I managed to avoid the main salvo of half-chewed lumps of meat, and felt more able to relax as the contractions of his fat neck took on the peculiarities of a python swallowing a live pig. Once the bulk of his mouth's contents was winding its way into the repository known as his stomach, I felt reasonably safe. Hungry pondered my words then said, 'Well, how much do you think I owe you then?'

I can't deny I was taken aback somewhat by his question and, after a pause, said, 'You know how much you owe me — 27 grand.'

He feigned a look of surprise. 'How d'you work that out, then?'

Now it was my turn to look surprised. 'How do I work it out? You know how it comes to that — 24 grand from the parcel of shoes ...'

'Do what? That came on top. You can't expect any money back for that!' he interrupted me.

I looked across at him and, of course, realised what he was playing at. 'Don't start all that, Jim. You know full well you owe me 24 grand from that.'

'But if you're in a swindle like that, you can't expect your money back if it happens to go wrong.'

'I wasn't in the swindle, Jim, and you know it. I lent you the money to help you out. I was never in the swindle as such. You even said you'd get me the 24 grand back as soon as possible.'

'You would have been in for your whack. You was in it with me.'

By now he was blustering, but he was taking a liberty and he knew it. I couldn't believe that, after all the different trades we had been involved in over the years, that he was now trying to pull a stroke like this.

'Jim, I didn't want to be in for my whack. As far as I was concerned, I was just doing you a favour and all I expected was a little drink like you said. Now you know that was the arrangement.'

He continued to back-track on our agreement, still trying to say that I was a partner in the deal. Although at length he conceded the point, I only left with a few hundred pounds and, later on, he again reneged on our agreement. Ultimately, all I managed to get back from him was a couple of thousand pounds, this in spite of the fact that he went on to make a great deal of cash from the booze swindles. In keeping with his avaricious personality, the more cash he made, the greedier he got. Not for nothing was he known as Hungry Jim.

Nothing much was happening with Dinky Dan, but at the beginning of July he wanted to see me. He had some bad news. The 200,000 or so notes that he had in stock had gone missing. Dinky told me that he had stored them all at somebody's house, and the person had disappeared along with the stock. He assured me that he had a search party out for the missing man who had apparently last been heard of in Ramsgate or somewhere similar.

The main story had several different threads to it, but the overall impression I got was that it was a load of crap with just an element of truth to it. He named the culprits as being a guy called George Williams, a name which, though familiar, really meant nothing to me.

The other person was someone I did know — Terry Long Legs.

I hadn't seen Legsie for several years, and the last I heard of him he had been working on one of Hungry Jim's fruit stalls. As they both had a chronic weakness for backing slow horses in fast races, it wasn't exactly a match made in heaven. In between mouthfuls of food, and losing containers of alcohol, Hungry invariably moaned about Legsie for some reason or other.

Dinky Dan explained that, as he didn't want Legsie to know that the parcel of tens and twenties was anything to do with him, there wasn't much he could do, although he did mutter some absurd threat about chopping his hand off. 'And every time he goes to pick his nose, he'll remember the parcel of twenties he nicked,' said Dinky. This was accompanied by suitably terrifying and frightening noises. I was positively shaking with fear just thinking about it, or should that be shaking with laughter?

Dinky decided he should concentrate his efforts on finding George Williams and asked if I could do anything about Legsie. Getting involved in heavy work isn't really my style, so to speak. Having a row, where the dispute is just a matter of having a fight is one thing, but the idea of instigating a more complex situation with genuine heavies involved is something else. However, in this instance, and as there was so much at stake, I decided I would make a few enquiries. I asked Dinky Dan if he knew where Long Legs was living, and he gave me an address. I thought it strange that having an address to start from, that Dinky Dan hadn't got his team on to it earlier. I found it hard to believe his excuse that he didn't want Long Legs to know about his involvement. With the loss of more than 200,000 notes, and his inclination to throw a temper tantrum for no real reason at the drop of a hat, I felt that he should have been pulling out all the stops. Instead of which he was doing little more than acting out a role and saying things like 'Grrrrr'.

I went to see Eugene, who wanted to speak to me about something else, and explained the situation. He said it would be no problem to keep an eye on the address and, if I wanted, to grab Long Legs off the street and then 'persuade' him to reveal all. I had my doubts about this course of action, as I didn't really want to be party to a kidnapping and all the possible complications that might ensue. Apart from which, it's never really prudent to be indebted to someone like Eugene. At least with a straightforward debt, such as the loan that I had, it could be terminated by the repayment of the money.

With these various aspects very much in mind, I told Eugene to hold on for the time being. 'Whatever, Steve, I'll wait till I hear from you, then,' he said. 'Meantime, I need to work out a deal for a parcel of the cockles. What's happening with them?'

'Not a lot at the moment, Eugene. How many were you thinking of?' I replied.

'I'm not sure, I'll let you know. So when are you back at work, then?'

'Well, I want to get this situation with Long Legs sorted out first. Leave it with me and I'll get back to you,' I told him.

We left it at that, and I asked around about Long Legs. From what I was able to find out, it appeared that Long Legs had been flush with twenties and hadn't paid for them, but then that was par for the course with him. I found out more details from a good friend of mine who had access to the inner circle of 'The Hoxton Old Women's Guild', a motley crew of ageing petty criminals such as Mother Greens and Jon Jon Hardy, who spent most of their time gossiping about who they suspected of being a grass and various other world-shattering items of tittle-tattle — 'he said, she said,' etc. I managed to ascertain that Long Legs had stolen or ripped off a parcel of twenties, but it was certainly nothing like 200,000. In fact, from what I was told, it wasn't a particularly large amount at all.

What was certainly true, though, was that Long Legs was potless. Clearly there was nothing to be gained from pursuing him and it looked more and more as though Dinky Dan was using what was probably a small loss as a ruse for what he'd taken himself. With this in mind, I called Eugene and told him to forget the Long Legs affair and that there would be some cockles available in the very near future.

I then received a call from Dinky who told me that he had heard about the failed attempt to kidnap Long Legs in the street outside his home address. Although this news came as something of a surprise, I made no noticeable response other than to say, 'Oh yeah,' or something similar. He went on to say that Legsie had now gone on the missing list and nobody knew where he was. Another 'bag of bollocks', as Shakespeare would say, since Long Legs was to be found at all his usual haunts.

After speaking to Dinky Dan, I immediately rang Eugene who was adamant that, if anybody had tried to grab Long Legs, then it was nothing to do with him. As he pointed out, if it had been his firm then they wouldn't have made such a balls-up. This was true.

With several orders apart from Eugene's enquiry, I went to see Eric to explain the situation. I had to tell him that there was little chance of getting what was owed on the outstanding stock. Since we both needed some money, the solution was as plain as the watermark on a counterfeit £20 note. There was still some stock of paper left, though not a great deal. I told Eric to print it up into tenners, and that somehow or other I would find somebody to supply me with some more paper in order that the wheels of industry might turn more profitably.

After speaking to Eric, I went to see an old friend of mine, Eddie Burns, an independent paper merchant with a small office in Hackney, East London. I had known Eddie for several years during which he had supplied me with paper and card for the counterfeit perfume business. He was a thin little chap in his sixties with a red face and wispy white hair. The skin on his neck was rather taut so that, combined with a permanently confused expression and large glasses, he always reminded me of a fledgling bird pecking its way out of an egg as it hatched.

He was an exceptionally well-meaning and helpful character who knew a great deal about the paper industry. He was, however, the most disorganised and chaotic person imaginable. He had a permanent air of bemusement about him as he drove around in a battered old van making deliveries. On the front seat, invariably, there would be a clipboard with a complete jumble of orders, receipts and written notes attached to it. As well as this, there would be no end of samples and scraps scattered over the seat and on the floor.

Because of his completely inoffensive and eccentrically charming demeanour, I found it ironic that he shared his name with an early Sixties teenage idol who starred in a popular TV series called *77 Sunset Strip*. Ed Cookie Burns spent most of his time in the series cruising along Sunset Strip in an open-top sedan combing his slicked-back wavy hair and surrounded by a bevy of beautiful young girls. The contrast between the two Eddies could hardly have been more pronounced, and so far as I was concerned there was only one nickname for him — Sunset Strip!

The first thing I noticed when I walked into his office was the absence of his son, a young man who, due to the severe effects of spina bifida, was confined to a wheelchair. Although severely disabled, and more than entitled to be dissatisfied with the hand that fate had dealt him, I never knew him to be anything other than cheerful and happy. He managed to keep the bookwork and accounts in some kind of order, which, bearing in mind the general chaos that was an integral part of Eddie's affairs, was something of a miraculous achievement in itself. It was always patently obvious that father and son were devoted to one and another.

But today his son wasn't there, and immediately I sensed that in all likelihood Eddie's beloved son had died. I was saddened to hear that he had indeed died a couple of years or so previously. It was plain to see that Eddie missed him a great deal and, not surprisingly, his desktop was in an even more extreme state of disarray than ever.

I told him the type of paper I required, that it was 85gsm and UV resistant and made by Tallis Russell.

'Oh, you want the same paper that you used for the counterfeit money before. Am I right?' Eddie's delicate, articulate tones hit me like a sledgehammer.

'How did you know about that?' I asked.

'Well, the police called me in the first place. Apparently, they got the name of Tallis Russell from some waste sheets of counterfeit money that were packed in their wrapping paper. From the numbers on the paper, Tallis Russell were able to tell them that it was me who had ordered it in 1994,' he explained.

'Did they mention me?' I asked.

'Oh no. They merely asked for whom I had ordered it. I told them the truth, that a stranger calling himself Mr Davis had come in and paid cash for it. I hadn't seen him before and haven't seen him since.'

'So how did you know it was anything to do with me, then?'

'Your old friend Walter Mitty dropped by one day to tell me that you had been sent to prison for counterfeit money. He seemed quite pleased about it, which I must say I found rather odd. He also asked me to inform him if I saw anything of you and not to sell you any paper.'

I shook my head in disbelief at how petty and malicious Walter had become. 'When was that?' I asked.

'A short while ago. He bought some card from me.'

'Well, do yourself a favour, Ed, I'm not interested in what Walter's up to, but take a tip from me; if he ever buys any paper off you, make sure he pays first. He's got a bad habit of not paying for anything he gets on credit. And next time you see him, please don't mention that you've seen me at all,' I said.

'Oh, jolly good. Actually I don't expect I'll be seeing him too soon, he still owes me £1,200 for the last consignment of card that he took. I've tried to contact him, but he gave me a false telephone number.'

Eddie didn't look at all happy, as £1,200 was a considerable amount of money for him to lose, but giving people he regarded as good friends whatever credit they needed was typical of his trusting nature. I told him that any paper I ordered from him would be paid for strictly COD, so he would have no worries. When he asked if I needed it to print more counterfeit money, I told him, 'No. Actually I'm printing Magic Eye posters. You know, those strange patterns that have a peculiar 3D effect when you look at them in a particular way.'

'Oh, that's OK, then. Because the Tallis Russell paper isn't UV resistant any more,' he replied.

'What?' I exclaimed. 'How d'you know that?'

'Because not too long ago somebody else asked me for some ...'

'The mysterious Mr Davis?'

'Oh no. Another person I didn't know. I believe he said his name was Mr Clarke.'

'Mmm.' It seemed to me that half the scallywags in East London were somehow finding their way to Sunset Strip's nondescript little premises tucked away in the corner of a yard at the end of a dead-end back-turning in Hackney. To a rather naïve and unsuspecting Eddie Burns, there was nothing out of the ordinary in strangers walking in off the street offering to pay cash for UV-resistant security paper.

'He also said it needed to be UV resistant,' Eddie continued.

'Did Mr Clarke say why he needed it to be UV resistant?'

'Oh yes. He said it was for Christmas wrapping paper.'

'Why would anyone want Christmas wrapping paper to be UV resistant?' I asked.

As always, Eddie had a slightly confused look on his face and then, after a moment or so pondering my question, he replied, 'D'you know, that's just what I thought at the time. Apart from which, it was nowhere near Christmas.'

I laughed at the very thought — Christmas wrapping paper! At least my prepared reason, paper for Magic Eye posters, was feasible. But wrapping paper? Just no imagination some crooks!

Eddie went on to tell me that when he ordered just one packet of Tallis Russell paper for 'Mr Clarke', after checking it out, it turned out to be no longer made in UV resistant material, although ostensibly it was the same paper with the same name. Obviously, after finding the Tallis Russell wrappers at the time of my arrest, the police or the Bank of England must have asked Tallis Russell not to provide any UV resistant paper to anyone other than bona fide security printers. A shame, but that's how it goes.

As much by luck as judgement I found an alternative manufacturer. This was supplied by my old friend Bernie on the Isle of Wight. He was trying to produce his own brand of perfume, and so he came to me for advice. During the course of conversation, the subject of the UV problem came up, although I told him that I was enquiring on behalf of somebody else. He told me about his friend who gave him some advice at the time of the postage stamp scam, and who happened to work at Harrison's, the security printers in High Wycombe. As we both knew, they printed foreign banknotes and stamps. On the promise of a few pound notes, Bernie said he'd find out from him whatever he could.

Within days, he had the name of a manufacturer for me, together with all the specifications and details. I gave Bernie a couple of hundred pounds and immediately went to see Sunset Strip. I gave him the details and specified the paper should be UV resistant.

'Are you going to use it for Christmas wrapping paper as well?' he asked.

I smiled and said, 'No, of course not. Don't you remember? I told you, I'm printing Magic Eye posters. And if they're not printed on UV resistant paper, the 3D effect doesn't work.'

'Oh, I see. What did you say they're called again?'

'Magic Eye posters.'

'Yes. Right. I'll have to try to remember that. Magic ... what was it again?'

'Magic ... I'll write it down for you so that you can't forget, Eddie. And remember, enter it all in your books, and don't forget to charge me the VAT. And if anybody should ask you, you can say that you supplied the paper to me, and that as far as you know, it's for Magic Eye posters. Got that?'

'Yes. Magic Eye posters.'

With that I gave him my order, and told him to page me as soon as the paper came in.

'What message should I leave?' he asked.

'Just say Sunset Strip and I'll know it's from you.'

Shortly after this, the first batch of £10 notes was ready. I contacted a couple of my regular punters, such as Don the little Irishman, and left them each with a worthwhile amount to go to work with. Then I visited Jewboy Jack and Eugene in South London. Naturally enough, they were pleased to hear that the tens were ready. As far as I was aware, they had a customer coming over from Spain to collect them, but, of course, I didn't make myself too busy in that quarter. We came to an agreement that would allow me to work off my indebtedness to them by means of a series of deals with the funny money. Being a part-payment, part-debt deal, it was of mutual benefit, but until it was cleared, I obviously wasn't earning a great deal of money. Not that I was complaining.

A week later, Sunset Strip paged me and I collected the first consignment of paper. I took along the small UV testing machine I had and, before I took the paper, tested it just to make sure it was UV resistant. Eddie and I leaned over the desk and placed the machine on a small corner of the sheet, and then switched it on.

'There you are,' Eddie declared, 'that's what you need for your Magical Eyes, isn't it?'

'Yes. That's just perfect.

We loaded it on to my van and I paid Eddie the £1,500 or so that it came to. He gave me a receipt marked 'Paid Cash' and 'filed' his copy amongst the mass of sheets and endless bits and pieces on his desk.

I asked him to order another batch for me and to page me in the same way as soon as it was ready to be collected. He looked pleasantly surprised at this further order and said, 'Oh, jolly good. So the Magical Eyes must be going well, then?'

'Very well, Eddie. I think it's going to be a very good line.'

I met up with Dinky Dan several days later, ostensibly to talk about his hunt for George Williams. Of course, he was no closer to finding him and nobody knew where Long Legs had disappeared to (apart from half the criminal fraternity in Hoxton and Essex, that is). And still Dinky Dan, the KO Man, was taking it remarkably philosophically. No huffing and puffing, no foot stamping, no temper tantrums. It was as though he really wasn't that concerned about the loss of 200,000 notes.

Dinky went on to mention the fact that there was a load of £10 notes in circulation. 'You don't know anything about them, do you?' he asked.

I looked across the table in the Little Chef restaurant and, staring him in the eye, said, 'Why should I know anything about them?'

'I don't know, I thought maybe your printer might have done some for himself,' he replied.

'I doubt it. But if you like, I'll ask him, eh?' I was still staring at him, which always seemed to unnerve him somewhat. He was one of those types completely unable to maintain eye contact. Instead, he had a strange manner of staring at the side of my head when he spoke to me. I began to think that maybe he found my ear sexually attractive. We left it at that and I departed. Soon afterwards, I rang him to say that not only had my printer not done any notes, but also he wasn't going to do any more. He was fed up with being fucked about and he'd had enough.

As I expected, this little wind-up started Dinky Dan off huffing and puffing.

'Well, I'm telling you there's a load of tens floating about. How do I know they haven't come from your printer?'

'Because I just told you, he said he hasn't done any, and that's all there is to it. Besides, how d'you know these tens haven't come from the parcel that Long Legs and this fella George Williams nicked?' I replied, speaking calmly and without any trace of anger.

Dinky Dan seemed just a bit flustered by this and screamed down the phone line, 'Tell you what, just tear my phone number up!' and the line went dead.

I called him back but his mobile phone was switched off. I went back into the pub where I had been having a drink with Gersh. Since it was Gersh who had brought me and Dinky Dan together, I told him about the phone conversation and we had a good laugh about it and carried on drinking. That was the last time I spoke to Dinky Dan.

It wasn't too difficult to work out his strategy. Obviously, through somebody else, he had been buying the security paper from Tallis Russell. After my arrest, the Tallis Russell paper was no longer being supplied as UV resistant, and so he must have decided that, if it was no longer possible to get the correct paper necessary for the success of the forgeries, then he would keep as many of those we had in stock for himself.

My being inside, combined with Long Legs stealing a few, gave him the perfect opportunity and cover to say that they had *all* been stolen. The idea that over 200,000 notes would be stored in one person's house, a person who as a ducker and diver was quite likely to get a spin from the police over totally unrelated matters, beggars belief.

As Shakespeare said in *Romeo and Juliet*, 'Bring up another, bigger, bag of bollocks.'

# CHAPTER 24

## A Cuckoo in the Nest and Colonel Pervert

After the split from Dinky Dan, the business was running smoothly and my life was on a relatively even keel. The money was coming in at a healthy rate and I made sure that my family saw the benefits. Amongst other things, I took James to Las Vegas to see his hero, Iron Mike Tyson, get himself knocked out by Evander Holyfield and Stephanie started a Fine Arts degree course at Middlesex University.

For James's twelfth birthday, I laid on a special treat and, together with several of his friends, Laraine and I took him out for the day in a chauffeur-driven stretch limousine. I spent Christmas with Laraine and the children and it's fair to say that Laraine and I were genuinely the best of friends.

For the first month or two of the New Year, the shutters were down on the business, and I took a couple of holidays abroad whilst I decided what I was going to do business-wise. I had no intention of remaining in the funny money business ad infinitum, and my plan was to get enough cash together to buy a large house and a wine bar. As soon as possible, I intended paying off the mortgage on the house for Laraine, and some time in the future buying a flat for Stephanie which I knew she would like sooner or later. She was now 18, and the idea of me buying her something which would be an investment for her future as a twenty-first birthday present appealed to me immensely.

This, of course, would all cost a considerable amount of cash, and taking girlfriends on holidays abroad, and generally spending money as though it was going out of fashion, wasn't really the best way of going about it. But it was certainly fun.

Barry was released from prison in January, and had plans to go into property. All well and good, but in the event he proved about as good as me at applying himself to the self-discipline required to be successful in business. It wasn't too long after his release, and the collapse of all his good intentions, that he separated from his long-term girlfriend, Madeline. This gave him the incentive and drive to dedicate himself to full-time drinking and part-time women. This was highly commendable, but it proved rather expensive for me as I was paying for his ticket on the gravy train. But, as I said, it was fun.

The sales of the tens and twenties were going well and, overall, the business was running smoothly. By now, in spite of my spending, and in spite of the 6ft 9in cuckoo in the nest, I was accumulating a fair amount of money.

Some time around March, Barry mentioned that he had come across a couple of good deals regarding some property. He assured me they were too good an opportunity to miss and, taking his word and judgement for it, I pulled up the money.

The only hesitation I had in respect of the deals concerned the possible involvement of one of his associates, by the name of Dean O'Connell, since I had lost about £60,000 a few years earlier in a couple of property deals involving him and Dave Hawkins. The truth of the matter was, it was my own fault for being too trusting and leaving it to them to run the show whilst I got on with other matters.

At the time, I believed Dean and Dave knew what they were doing, and that the cash was wisely invested. The problem came about because just the opposite was true. This time, I stipulated that under no circumstances did I want anything to do with it if Dean was involved.

Barry swore to me he wasn't involved and also assured me that the deal was being done through a solicitor, signed and sealed, so to speak. On this basis, I gave him £20,000 for a vacant plot of land in Birmingham with planning permission for two houses. Not long afterwards, I gave him another £22,000 as part-payment on some property in Kennington in South London. For the time being, I was quite happy about my 'investment' and left it in Barry's hands.

All this time, the funny money business was going well and, apart from the little property investment with Barry, I was looking out for a suitable premises to be opened up as a wine bar. The idea of being the boss of an upmarket watering hole, staffed entirely with terminally beautiful young barmaids, certainly appealed to me. I knew from my experiences as the boss of a number of perfume factories with a selection of women working for me, that being the man who pays the wages is a powerful aphrodisiac.

As Barry was in the property business, and his godfather was the chairman of the second largest property corporation in the UK, the pair of us went out scouting in the City of London for suitable-looking properties. This we made sure involved a great deal of practical groundwork, involving the necessary study of the dozens of different wine bars in the area. Enjoyable work.

As his godfather's company owned a great deal of property in the City, it was natural for Barry to ask him if he had any suitable sites. Although he was quite helpful, and came up with one or two premises that were likely to be vacant in the near future, I soon realised that the cost of fitting them out would be prohibitive.

In the meantime, however, I came across vacant premises in Old Street, more or less next to Moorgate. A friend of mine, Johnny Gadget, had some influence with the landlords, and it looked likely that a highly beneficial rent, and a rent-free period, could be negotiated, thus helping to offset the cost of fitting the place out. I told Gadget to do his best and that I would come in as soon as I was in a position to proceed. At this stage, I was certainly thinking in terms of winding up the funny money scam and going into legitimate business. I truly believed I was on the verge of going straight. At long last.

I had another couple of deals with Eugene and my indebtedness to him was now cleared up. From now on, any deals would be in a normal, straightforward way, although he did negotiate a better price than anybody else was getting. I didn't particularly fancy arguing about it and made the concession.

One of the most obvious problems that presents itself when a person such as myself acquires large amounts of cash on a regular basis, without being involved in some kind of legitimate business requiring application and self-discipline, is the question of free time. As Shakespeare said, 'The Devil finds work for idle hands.' In my case it wasn't so much the Devil finding me work — I think he had already put enough my way — but rather me wasting a great deal of time drinking in a variety of different pubs. With hindsight, I can see what a useless way this was for any intelligent person to waste his life, although in fairness to myself, I always found time to visit my ageing mother and regularly take her for day trips to the seaside or into the country. As well as this, I never neglected to spend time with James and Laraine, and Stephanie when she wasn't too busy with her student chums.

During the course of my daily pub crawls, generally with Barry, I often came across my friend Paul Sabbato. He and Colonel Blimp were now heavily involved in the invoice-factoring fraud. But whenever I spoke to Paul, he seemed concerned and invariably had a worried look about him. Without my asking, as I always try to keep to a policy of not concerning myself in other people's illegal activities, Paul informed me that the Colonel was becoming something of a liability. The problem, as Paul explained to me, stemmed from Blimp's liking for 'charlie' — cocaine.

As money had started to trickle back into the coffers, he started to indulge his insatiable appetite. Every penny that came his way was spent on the Devil's snuff and Colonel Blimp would spend days at a time indulging in his favourite pastime of shovelling as much of it as possible up his nose, while surfing the internet for pornographic websites.

The nickname Colonel Blimp had been bestowed upon him by me, not for any organisational abilities, but rather because, on more than one occasion, he had been caught spying on people engaged in sex and invariably masturbating. I can't deny I found this rather strange behaviour, but that was his problem. I suppose it's fair to say that he was something of a pervert. On one or two occasions Paul and I met him in a particular pub in Shoreditch called Brown's, where strippers performed every lunchtime. When we walked in, Colonel Blimp would be standing at the edge of the stage along with several elderly gentlemen, peering upwards as he strained his eyes to get a more intimate and detailed view of the female genitalia on display. Bearing in mind the Colonel's physical appearance — short and fat with a bald head — he made a very odd and humorous sight, drawn like a magnet to the edge of the stage.

When Paul originally voiced his concerns regarding Blimp, who, as the front man, played a crucial role in the operation, I expressed my opinion that with Colonel Blimp out of the game as much as he was, then it was only a matter of time before the 'wheel came off'.

With this in mind, both Paul and I, on several occasions, tried to tell him he was doing too much coke, and that he was starting to lose the plot. But he became oblivious to any outside warnings and carried on his own sweet way. Invariably, he would say as he left us that he was going down the 'Yellow Brick Road'.

So worried was Paul about the Colonel's behaviour, that he once asked me to go with him to the Colonel's house in Harlow, after he had been unable to get any sense out of him on the telephone. It was a journey I wish that I had never made, as both Paul and I discovered that, far from being a humorous reference, the term 'Yellow Brick Road' had very real, evil connotations.

After knocking at his front door for some time and receiving no reply, we went round the back. Paul turned the kitchen door handle and found it to be unlocked. We walked in and looked in the downstairs rooms, which were empty. Paul led the way upstairs where, in a small study room, the Colonel was sitting naked at his computer screen. There was a pile of cocaine on the desk next to him and the Colonel was totally oblivious to anything that was going on around him.

This bizarre situation, as perverted as it seemed, wasn't really anything to do with us and, not wishing to embarrass the Colonel in his porno paradise — after all, it was in his own home — I nudged Paul to indicate that we should go downstairs from where we could call up to him and wait till he came down.

But then we both caught sight of what the Colonel was watching — the most disgusting and sickening child pornography imaginable. The images were far worse than anything I could have imagined and, spontaneously, we charged into the room and I shoved his head hard into the screen.

The fat little pervert fell on to the floor, not understanding what had just happened. With the vile images still on the screen, I picked up a heavy ashtray and slammed it against the glass surface, shattering it into a thousand pieces.

I could see that Paul was on the verge of laying into him and giving him a good kicking, which he thoroughly deserved. But even though I felt like joining in, I didn't and stood, still in a state of shock, as Paul delivered several kicks into his fat, disgusting little body. I think I was worried that if we both beat him up then there was a very real danger of him ending up dead. As it was, I pulled Paul off him, and we dragged him out of the study and into his bedroom. He sat on the floor, whimpering and crying.

'I'm so sorry,' he mumbled, 'I'm so sorry.'

I couldn't feel sorry for him, but I wondered just what had driven him this far. Had it been the excess of cocaine? Or was it just an extension of his already perverted personality? We listened as he babbled on with some kind of ridiculous excuse, none of which made any sense. It wasn't long before the sight of his disgusting, perverted fat body made us both feel sick, and I told him we would wait downstairs while he pulled himself together.

Downstairs, we sat at the kitchen table with a couple of beers, and discussed what to do. For my part, I felt he should be reported to the police. This to me was one of the very few situations that I would feel fine about reporting to the authorities. As far as I'm concerned, anybody involved in anything to do with paedophilia deserves to be locked away for ever. Colonel Blimp's other sexual peccadilloes were entirely his own concern, but this was totally unacceptable.

Paul agreed whole-heartedly, but pointed out that this wasn't an option, due to the factoring fraud. I took his point, and we both decided that, as obnoxious as it was, the only possible choice was to try and talk some sense into him.

About 15 minutes later, he came downstairs in a tracksuit, looking exactly what he was, a sad and pathetic excuse of a man. He tried to tell us that he had only come across the paedophilia by accident while he was surfing the Net. He further went on to say that, when he went on those cocaine binges, he lost all control and didn't know what he was doing.

For Paul's sake I went along with the impromptu counselling session and, after an hour or so, I decided I had to leave. Colonel Blimp begged me to take him along with us, as he couldn't bear the thought of being in the house on his own. But the idea of being in his company a minute longer than necessary was too much. Even worse, it meant the pervert sitting in my car. Paul felt much the same and we told him firmly 'No'.

As we left the house, he asked if we were going to tell anybody. Paul assured him that, if he straightened himself out, then we would keep it to ourselves.

On the way back to London, I think both of us were in something of a state of shock. We discussed the situation, but I pointed out it really wasn't my problem and he would have to deal with it as he saw fit. But, of course, because of the sensitive and advanced stage of Paul's factoring scam, we had to keep the vile secret that Colonel Blimp was a paedophile.

After this, I had nothing more to do with Colonel Blimp, and Paul decided that just as soon as their swindle was over and done with, he, too, would have nothing more to do with him.

# CHAPTER 25

## Wedding Bells Loses a Parcel

In May 1997, I witnessed at first-hand the violent, psychopathic side of Eugene's personality. It concerned a deal I had with him for a large quantity of twenties — 100,000, to be exact. Without knowing the exact details, I believe it involved paying for a large parcel of cannabis in Spain with the funny money. I found out, later on, that the intended victims were a group of French smugglers, who had something of a reputation themselves. But Eugene and his brothers really didn't worry themselves too much about other people's reputations. In fact, I often got the impression that he relished the prospect of a potential conflict, particularly if it involved a 'garlicky Frog' as he referred to the French. For some obscure reason, he had a venomous hatred for all French men.

On this occasion, I had arranged to meet Wedding Bells with the parcel of twenties. The agreed meeting place was a regular rendezvous that featured daytime strippers. We often met at this particular pub for two reasons. It was a little bit out of the way and we were therefore unlikely to bump into anybody we knew and, second, it was part-owned by Eugene's brother, Sammy.

Sammy was totally different both in looks and personality to Eugene. Older by five or six years, he was about 5ft 8in tall with a powerful, stocky build and thinning ginger hair. He was always laughing and joking and he and Wedding Bells were the very best of friends.

As different as they were, it was difficult to see how Eugene and Sammy could be brothers, but they had one very particular trait in common — Sammy was most definitely not a man to cross. It was said that he was absolutely fearless in every respect. He would fight anybody, regardless, and was never known to back down from a confrontation, and he had a reputation as a man who would take whatever measures were necessary to come out on top.

He had done a great deal of villainy out in Spain, on the 'Costa del Crime', and had made a great deal of money in the drugs business. Along the way, as seems to be unavoidable when drugs are involved, he also made a few dangerous enemies. Apparently, two or three of them disappeared without trace shortly after he was stabbed several times in a bar in Fuengirola. It wasn't long after this that he returned to England and invested in several pubs, specialising in strippers and lap-dancers.

Fortunately, he and I got on famously, which I always found a source of great comfort. Unlike Eugene, I never felt on edge in his company, and he was always in a good mood and ready for a joke and a laugh.

At midday, I was at my self-storage unit in Hackney loading the twenties into the boot of the car I had picked up from Wedding Bells that morning. Although 100,000 sounds like a great deal, in terms of space, it's just ten compact little boxes that fit comfortably into the boot of a car, with ample room for a number of dummy boxes on top.

My little chum who worked the fork-lift was there as usual to bring the pallet with the ten boxes on it down from the first-floor loading area. On previous occasions, when bringing down a pallet-load of boxes using the fork-lift, I could never help feeling just a tiny bit anxious in case one of the boxes should fall off. I was always alert and ready to run around to the other side should one start to wobble. If necessary, I was prepared to dive full-length and make a catch. I'm sure I would have put any England fielder to shame. But my little chum was a most diligent and conscientious fork-lift operator and, of course, it never happened.

I drove over to the pub and left the car in the car park. As Eugene assured me he would have the cash in full in just a few days' time, I felt very happy about the deal. As far as I was concerned, it meant I was that much closer to going straight. I arrived at 1.30pm and Wedding Bells was at the bar talking to one of the girls who was sitting on a stool with a glass of wine in her hand. And, yes, she was stark naked.

I can't deny I found the view most enjoyable as I reached across to the bar for the Budweiser Wedding Bells had just bought for me. Sammy wasn't in the pub and, apart from the two of us, the only other customers in the place were a couple of groups of office workers.

I told Wedding Bells where the car was parked and gave him the keys. He in turn gave me the keys to my car which he had taken that morning. I stayed and had a few drinks with Wedding Bells and was sorely tempted to remain, but I had a few people to meet and, more importantly, money to collect. Displaying an absolutely phenomenal resolve and strength of character, I refused to allow the naked women strolling around to distract me from what I had to do and after a week (or was it an hour?) I left!

The following day, I received a call from Jewboy Jack asking me to meet him and Eugene at the pub in South London where I normally met him. I asked him what it was about, but he merely said that Eugene needed to speak to me about something and could I be there by 2.30pm.

I wasn't particularly busy and so at 2.00pm I was on my way to South London. Twenty minutes later, I was walking into the saloon bar and, as usual, it was empty apart from an old chap who was always in the corner nursing a pint of brown ale. Apart from selling a few sandwiches, it was hard to see how this place took any money at all. Jewboy Jack was standing at the bar talking to the middle-aged woman who served behind the bar. As always, he extended his hand upon seeing me, which I shook as I nodded 'hello' to the barmaid. He bought me half a lager and we stood talking for a while. He told me he was just waiting for Eugene who had phoned to say that he would be arriving shortly. I asked him what the meet was about, but he remained vague and just said there was a bit of a problem with Wedding Bells. Although I failed to see what this could possibly have to do with me, I said nothing. I knew I had nothing to fear, as there was nothing that Eugene could be annoyed with me about. But even so, I didn't really like mysteries, especially where Eugene was involved.

Ten minutes later, Eugene came through the door accompanied by Wedding Bells and two other men, one of whom, named Wally, I knew vaguely from several years before when I had been in HMP Wandsworth serving a sentence for manufacturing counterfeit perfume. I had never particularly liked him, as he always came across as too flash and too loud. I think the feeling was mutual, although on his part I'm sure he was jealous of my devilishly handsome good looks!

Wedding Bells didn't look too happy and gave me a half-hearted kind of smile as he came in. Eugene had a serious look on his face but, nevertheless, gave me what was, for him, a friendly greeting as he shook my hand.

'Shall we go upstairs, Jack?' he said, not so much a request as a direct order.

'Sure,' Jewboy Jack replied and we all followed him through the door to the back and up the stairs. The room on the first floor was the 'office', somewhat spartan, containing a desk, a few chairs and an old television. Jewboy Jack disappeared into a small kitchen across the landing, and came back with a few cans of lager. After passing them around, Eugene sat behind the desk and instructed Wedding Bells and me to sit down.

'I'm afraid there's been a bit of a development,' Eugene said. 'Hasn't there, Tony?'

It didn't take the brains of Lloyd George to tell that Eugene wasn't in a particularly pleasant frame of mind, and that Wedding Bells was a worried man.

'I suppose you could put it that way,' he replied.

'Well, I do put it that way. Unless, of course, you can think of a better fucking way to put it!'

I winced as Eugene swore. Not because the sound of bad language upsets me — I've been known to cuss myself on occasion — but rather because whenever Eugene swore, it was generally a prelude for worse to come. And this 'fucking' coming so soon from Eugene struck me as very ominous. Very ominous indeed.

Wedding Bells was obviously lost for words, because he made no comment. Clearly, he couldn't think of a better way for Eugene to put it.

'Tell Steve just what the fuck has happened,' Eugene said, then turned to me. 'You'll like this, Steve.'

*'Mmmm, I'm sure I'm going to love it.'* These are the words I would have liked to say, but in all honesty I didn't have the 'bottle'. Instead, I merely responded with, 'Well, er, whatever.' It didn't have quite the same panache, but at least it had the more endearing quality of being 'safe'.

Wedding Bells gave a nervous cough as he turned slightly in his chair to look at me before speaking. This I found somewhat disconcerting, as I had never known Wedding Bells to be at all nervous when talking to me.

'You know when I saw you in the pub yesterday, and you, er, left the gear in the car. In the, er, car park?' Wedding Bells paused and stared at me.

I really didn't like the way this was going. I had a feeling I knew just what it was leading up to. 'Yeah, that's right. So what?' I said.

'Well I, er, I got a bit pissed. Like, you remember that bird I was with ...'

'I'm not likely to forget her, she was stark-bollock-naked for fuck's sake. Well, perhaps not *bollock* naked.'

Wedding Bells laughed nervously at this and continued, 'Yeah, that's the one, well, you see, I got a bit carried away with her.'

Now I was beginning to feel a bit bemused, even though I could see how easy it would be to get a 'bit carried away' with her.

Becoming a trifle impatient, Eugene spoke. 'What this cunt's trying to say, Steve, is that instead of doing what he was supposed to do, which was to take the parcel to the slaughter, he stayed in the fucking pub all afternoon, got blind fucking drunk, took the fucking tart home, fucked the arse off it and when he goes back this morning, the fucking car's gone. It's been fucking nicked, for fuck's sake.'

Now unless I had misheard, that added up to rather a lot of 'fuckings' and one 'cunt'. I don't know if 'fucked the arse off it' could be counted as gratuitous swearing, but nevertheless I sensed that Eugene was more than a little annoyed. And that last bit, about the car with the 100,000 twenties in it being stolen, made me realise that my first suspicion was correct. I *did* know just where this was leading to. I was going to have to stand the loss. But before we reached that stage, I would have to witness a chilling display of violence that left me feeling physically sick.

Wedding Bells said nothing. He sat, mortified, as Eugene seemed to be working himself up into an uncontrollable rage. And then, without warning, Wally whacked Wedding Bells over the head from behind with a full magnum of champagne he had picked up unnoticed.

In spite of the force of the blow, the magnum remained intact, and Wedding Bells slumped forward, barely conscious. He fell from the chair on to the floor, and seemed to be propelled forward in a strange reflex action on his knees. This sudden, unexpected act of violence made me move back in my chair, and I gasped out loud as blood from Wedding Bells's head seemed to spurt out like a fire hydrant on the streets of New York.

Eugene jumped up from behind the desk and Wally once again smashed the bottle on to Wedding Bells's bloodied skull. Incredibly, he didn't pitch face-down, but instead reacted with an anguished bellow and lurched forward by virtue of what was clearly no more than a reflex, not dissimilar to a headless chicken running around the coup. At this instant, the second man ran towards him and slammed his fist, which had the adornment of a set of knuckledusters, hard into the side of his jaw. Wedding Bells swayed over, but somehow remained conscious and, by reaching out for the edge of the desk, managed to stop himself from hitting the deck. In a desperate and impressive display of durable strength, he somehow staggered to his feet just as Eugene came round the desk.

Wedding Bells groaned chillingly and reached out for Eugene's throat, but a sickening punch to his ribs from the knuckleduster made him scream out loud. He screwed up his eyes in agony and Eugene, deflecting his arm, stepped forward with a bone-cracking head butt to the nose. At 6ft 2in, Wedding Bells was exactly the right height for a 'Gorbals handshake' from the 6ft Eugene.

Wedding Bells swayed backwards and Eugene lunged forward, swinging his hand in an overhead motion. It was only at the last second that I saw the knife gripped tightly in his fist. I couldn't help calling out as the blade was plunged into Wedding Bells's neck. At the same time, the other two were attacking him mercilessly from the side and behind. The brass knuckleduster was being slammed into his ribs and the side of his head, whilst Wally, thankfully, had put the champagne bottle down (I think he must have realised it was Dom Perignon) and was punching and kicking from behind. A truly nauseating onslaught executed with a staggering degree of ferocity.

Eugene really looked as though he was completely out of control and, to my absolute horror, again plunged the blade into Wedding Bells's neck, who now seemed to be fading away in a haze of blood and unbridled savagery. I couldn't help recalling different accounts that I'd read over the years about the murder of Jack the Hat by the Kray twins. And, to be honest, as sickened as I was by this murderous attack on a fellow human being, my prime concern was about becoming a witness to what the newspapers would undoubtedly refer to as 'a gangland slaying'.

I didn't fancy being victim number two due to the fact that I was the only eye-witness. But then I realised I wasn't, as I heard Jewboy Jack's voice from behind me — 'For God's sake. No more. No more.'

By now, Wedding Bells seemed to be no more than a blood-soaked corpse collapsed on the floor, which his three assailants continued to kick. I felt sick as I caught sight of the knife sticking out of his neck. Again, I heard Jewboy Jack cry out, 'Eugene. No more, Eugene,' and then became aware of him moving towards them. I got up from the chair, and walked over just behind Jewboy Jack. The furore subsided as Eugene was somehow snapped out of his raging frenzy by the sound of Jewboy Jack's voice.

Wedding Bells was lying in a pool of blood, slumped on the floor with his back to me. All three men moved away from him, almost as though only now aware of the enormity of their actions. Eugene was swearing to himself, and making a determined effort to calm down by breathing in as deeply as he could. The other two stepped back, with concerned looks on their faces. Jewboy Jack knelt down to examine his former friend more closely. As I leaned forward and peered down at Wedding Bells's misshapen and bruised head, I felt a sense of relief upon seeing that the knife was actually embedded in the front of his shoulder. I was even more relieved and amazed as Wedding Bells made a low moaning sound when Jewboy Jack touched his neck, presumably to feel for a pulse, although, such was the amount of blood everywhere, it was impossible to tell exactly what part of his neck he was touching. But the groan told me exactly what I wanted to hear — at least he was still alive.

Again, I was amazed to see what I had earlier thought was a lifeless body coming back to life, as Wedding Bells started to move. With some help from me and Jewboy Jack and the other two, he got back to his feet and we manoeuvred him on to the chair where he slowly came round, even though he had little idea of where or who he was. His head and face were a misshapen mass of cuts and bruises covered in blood. His jaw hung listlessly at an impossible angle, and the right side of his head was completely swollen like a small cushion stuck to the side of his face. The top of his head was still bleeding, as were the stab wounds in his shoulder. His nose was spread over the left-hand side of his face and, with both eye sockets just a mass of congealed purple bruising, it's fair to say he looked proper poorly. But at least he was alive. Somehow.

I've never seen such a violent and brutal attack on anybody, and I'm sure that if it were not for the fact that Wedding Bells was such a powerful and strong man, he wouldn't have survived it. As concerned as I was for him at the time, I reconciled the fact that I was more concerned for my own well-being with the certain knowledge that he had himself taken part in a great many beatings, and was by any standards an extremely violent man. As Shakespeare once said, 'Those who live by the sword ...'

Now that Wedding Bells was definitely alive, I was anxious to be on my way. If he was going to die, I really preferred not to be there. I looked down at my watch — *My, my, is that the time already. Doesn't time fly when you're enjoying yourself?* — but this was one situation where I most certainly curbed my desire to come out with any humorous remarks.

'Eugene, Jack, I'm gonna shoot away. All right?'

By now Eugene looked as though he was back on the same planet as the rest of us.

'What? Oh, yeah. Sure,' he said. 'Listen, mate, I'm sorry about this. I really am. But you can see what I have to put up with. Slags like this taking liberties. I just wish there was something else I could do for you, but at least you know he didn't get away with it.'

I paused at Eugene the psychopath's banal justification for what he had done, and the inference that he had done it just to appease me. Before the brutal attack, I had momentarily toyed with the idea of pointing out to Eugene that I had kept my part of the deal, and had actually delivered the goods to his man, Wedding Bells. Surely it wouldn't be unreasonable to expect him at least to meet me half way on the cost? But for some reason I thought better of it and instead remarked, 'I know what you mean. Developments happen,' a mildly sarcastic reference to his opening statement prior to the floor show — 'There's been a bit of a development.'

As I anticipated, it went straight over his head and he merely said, 'Yeah. Right.'

The unexpected loss of 100,000 twenties was something of a body blow to my finances, as I still had to pay Eric. But like the failed Vindiloo affair, there was nothing for it other than to put it behind me and look forward to the next deal. I was just grateful Eugene didn't ask me for another 100,000 pieces to replace the ones that had been stolen. At first I thought this was rather strange, but then assumed the cannabis deal involving '*les Frogs*' had fallen through.

I had a few more deals and started to build up my tank. I also received another offer of a legitimate business venture. This came from an old friend of mine, Peter Fryett, who had a small retail furniture business in Hackney. I visited his shop to buy some bits and pieces for the house and, as we hadn't seen each other for some time, he naturally enough asked how I was doing. Without telling him my actual line of business, I let him know that I was doing OK, and was looking for sound legitimate business ventures. It wasn't too long before he approached me with a view to opening a large furniture warehouse. My initial reaction was one of enthusiasm, but after giving the matter some thought, I realised that I might be overstretching myself. It looked as though the premises at Old Street that I had in mind for the wine bar would soon be sorted out and, of course, if that went ahead as I hoped, then I would need every penny to furbish the place exactly as I had in mind. My recent setback only added to my expenses. So, unfortunately, I had to inform a disappointed Peter that at the moment I wasn't in a position to invest any money with him. Maybe some time in the future.

Amongst my regular customers was Pat, the man who had made the intro to Wedding Bells and subsequently Eugene and Jewboy Jack. He was strictly small-time, a couple of thousand here and there, every month or so. Like Vindiloo, he spent a great deal of time in Amsterdam and, similarly I believe, had something going on there with the twenties. But as with everyone, I wasn't at all interested in whatever moves he had. With regard to the merchandise, as Shakespeare once said, 'Out of sight, out of mind.'

Shortly after I refused Peter's retail furniture offer, Pat also put a business proposition to me. This proposition, however, was most certainly illegal. In fact, it was very illegal.

Sitting in a small café close to my home, he explained to me just what he had in mind.

'The thing is, Steve, I've got some blinding transport on offer. It's sweet as a nut.'

By 'transport' I knew that he was referring to the smuggling of drugs into the UK.

'To be honest, Pat,' I replied, 'I'm not really interested.' I told him this, not because of any moral objection to drugs (in fact, I am firmly of the view that all drugs should be legalised and so controlled in the same way as tobacco and alcohol), but rather because, from what I've seen of it, the faces involved in the drugs game are not the kind of people I would care to do business with. But that's another story. Apart from this, far from getting involved in further criminal activities, I was looking forward to the time in the not-too-distant future when I would be a walking crime-free zone.

But Pat was adamant and simply refused to desist. The basics of his scheme were that he had a good contact in the West Indies who could supply cocaine for £4,000 per kilo. Pat, in turn, had 'blinding' transport to Holland. From there, it could be moved to the UK and sold for top money, £30,000 per kilo, or sold in Amsterdam for £18,000 per kilo.

'If you fancy it, we could have eight kilos over within three weeks. All I need is 40 grand. That's 32 for the charlie and 8 grand to cover all the exes. Well, what do you reckon?' he said, an enthusiastic look on his face. In spite of my categoric refusal earlier on, he seemed to be willing me to say 'Yes'.

I looked down at my watch, giving him the obvious impression that I would soon be leaving. 'Pat, you're wasting your breath. I've had a couple of offers to pull up for puff and I'm not even interested in that, so I'm hardly likely to get involved in charlie. No way, Pat. I'm just not interested. You'll have to go elsewhere for it.'

He looked disappointed, as though he had genuinely expected me to agree to it. I left him soon afterwards, but not before he had tapped me for £1,000, after he had given me a heart-wrenching sob-story about how badly in debt he was, and that the council were threatening to evict him and his wife and kids over rent arrears. He took the cash, and swore that he would pay me back just as soon as he could.

'It might take a few weeks, is that all right, Steve?'

'Yeah. OK, I'll wait to hear from you, then.'

After this, I didn't hear from Pat and thought little about it, reasoning that he would be back in touch just as soon as he needed some more tens or twenties, and hopefully then he would be in a position to repay me the money I had lent him.

A couple of weeks later, I heard from Wedding Bells, who said that he needed to speak to me about something quite important. It had now been nearly two months since the beating that he had received from Eugene and friends. I had heard that he was now back on the firm with Eugene, which didn't surprise me as much as perhaps it might have done. Knowing Wedding Bells as I did, I could see that he would regard Eugene's petulant fit of pique philosophically. And then, when violence, even extreme violence, is a part of everyday life, such an attitude, for a man in his position, isn't perhaps so surprising.

When I met up with him he looked remarkably well recovered. He told me that he had only just had the pins removed from his jaw, which had been wired up until the previous day. He was finding it difficult to talk but managed to tell me that, as well as the broken jaw, his skull had been fractured, his cheek cracked, a couple of his ribs broken and permanent damage done to his vision. And, oh yes, there was some damage to his eardrum.

The stab wounds to his shoulder, although lacerating some tendons, had caused no permanent damage. I could see without being told that his nose had been badly broken. But all things considered, the fact that he was standing in front of me on his own two feet was nothing short of miraculous.

The reason he wanted to see me was because he had a buyer for some funny money. I had no qualms about supplying him or the fact that he didn't want Eugene to know anything about it.

'So how are you and Eugene getting on these days?' I asked.

'Me and Eugene?' Wedding Bells said, as though he couldn't see why there should be any question of how they were with each other. 'Yeah, we're fine. No problem.' He noted the look of surprise on my face and added, 'I know he took a bit of a liberty, but you know Eugene. He's a bit excitable.'

'What, like boyish high spirits you mean?' I commented.

He held on to his jaw and said, 'Don't make me laugh, for fuck's sake.' He paused to try and control his chuckles. 'No, it's just how he is, I don't suppose he can help it really. But we're best of friends again now.'

'I'm glad to hear it. So how many notes d'you need?'

'Ten to fifteen thousand, first up. I've got a good punter for them cash on. I think it'll lead to a few good deals.'

'When?

'Next week, Monday.'

I arranged to meet him with 10,000 twenties and, after agreeing all the details, I left him to go about my business.

The following week we met as arranged, Wedding Bells took the parcel, and this time managed to deliver it without mishap. A few days later, he paid me half the money, and informed me that he would have the other half by the weekend, together with another order. I told him I was off on holiday the following week, so if any further orders were in the pipeline, it would be as well to let me know as soon as possible.

I had rented a luxury apartment in Marbella for Laraine and James to stay at for the month of August. I intended to drive to the resort in Laraine's sports car with Barry, whilst she was flying out with James and her friend, Gina, and her two children. Gina was going to stay for a couple of weeks and then fly back. We had promised her the holiday as a Christmas present.

Although not really able to afford a holiday due to her constant struggle to keep her head above water, she was reluctant to accept what she regarded as an extravagant present. But we managed to persuade her that it wouldn't be fair to the children if she refused. Finally she agreed, with the compromise that she paid her way in restaurants and all the other bits and pieces that are involved in a holiday abroad.

My plans involved staying in the apartment for ten days and then leaving the car with Laraine and flying back with Barry. After that, I would return for the last week of August to drive the car back.

Wedding Bells called me just a couple of days before I was due to leave, and wanted another 20,000 notes. After being assured that the remainder owing for the last delivery was in hand, I agreed.

I met up with him in a quiet little pub in North London and put the two boxes in the boot of his car before going into the bar. Wedding Bells was sitting there talking to the barman whilst sipping a glass of lemonade. Due to the medication he was taking, he was strictly forbidden from drinking alcohol. I greeted him in a friendly manner and told him the two boxes were already in the boot of his car. Not surprisingly, he was pleased to hear this and immediately bought me a drink.

'There's been a slight hold-up,' he said. 'Only a couple of days.'

'What?' I said.

'The money. My punter couldn't make it this morning. But there's no problem, I'm meeting him the day after tomorrow.'

I wasn't sure whether he remembered that I was leaving the

following day and this was a deliberate ploy to get some more notes from me before the last consignment had been paid for but, as I had already delivered the 20,000 pieces, I decided to give him the benefit of the doubt. Having some last minute running about to do, I didn't really have the time to take them back to the slaughter anyway.

'So long as it's definite for when I get back, Tony,' I said, to which he replied, 'Absolutely no problem, sound as a pound, mate. Just give me a call when you're back and I'll have it sorted out.'

I stayed in the pub for a while, discussing various different people and local happenings when, after a short time, Wedding Bells said, 'What do you think about that dirty bastard Eugene?'

Knowing that he had not long been back on the firm with Eugene, I found this a somewhat surprising question-cum-statement. 'What's he done now, then?' I said.

'That big parcel you delivered to Sammy's pub, what got nicked?'

'Yeah?'

'I just found out. It didn't get nicked. Eugene and Sammy fucking set me up.'

I looked at him barely able to believe what I had just heard.

'Set you up? What you talking about? How d'you know?'

'That bird.'

'What, the one you were with, Lady Godiva?'

'Lindie Godiva? No, that's not her name. The bird with the big bristols, remember?'

I didn't bother explaining my feeble attempt at humour and said, 'Yeah, I remember. What about her?'

'I copped 'old of 'er again the other night. She had a few drinks and a few lines of gear, and started going on about what happened to me.'

I listened intently, and made no comment as Wedding Bells paused to take a sip on his lemonade.

'"They took a right liberty," she says, after I give her a good servicing. An' then she says, "I didn't know they was gonna do anything like that. I felt terrible when I 'eard about it." So, of course, I says, "What you talking about? Like, what do you mean you didn't know they was gonna do nuffin like that?"'

He paused for another sip and, again, I remained silent, not wishing to interrupt the flow of words.

'So anyhow, I fink she suddenly realises she's said somefin' she shouldn't 'ave, and she starts saying fings like, "Aw nuffin'. I didn't mean it like that." And I starts to get the 'ump a bit. You can imagine, can't yer? Like 'ere I am, I've nearly been done in, I've 'ad me fucking jaw wired up for weeks, and all of a sudden this prat says somefin' like that!'

Another pause, this time to slowly shake his head and stare at the floor. Concerned that he might lose his train of thought, I prompted him. 'So what did you do then?'

Wedding Bells looked up. 'What? Oh, yeah. Right, so now I'm getting wound up and I fancy giving 'er a slap. Y'know, not too much, just enough to tell me what she's on about. But then I fink of somefing a bit more subtle like. I decide to use me brain.'

He sipped again on his drink. The suspense was killing me as I wanted him to continue. The very thought of hearing about how Wedding Bells decided to use his brain had me on the edge of my seat. *'There's a first for everything,'* I thought.

'So instead of just using brute force like, I laid out a nice couple of lines of charlie. Right big 'uns. Then I say, "Fancy a toot?" So, of course, she goes to pick up the old straw, I 'ad one of them big fat ones you get in McDonald's, and I puts me hand just over the gear. An' I tells her, "Now, what's all this about, sweet'eart, all this about you not knowing nuffin', an' feeling bad about me getting done," so at first she still tries to 'old up. So I takes the straw off 'er and does one of the lines. Gorgeous bit of gear, absolutely blinding. Any'ow, I can see she's mad for it an' then, slow like, I goes to do the other line. "'Ere," she says, "I thought they was supposed to be mine, you greedy bastard." So I tells 'er, "Tell me what you was on about, then." So she says, "Give us a line, then, but promise me you won't let anyone know." So I says OK and gives her the straw. Well, anyway, she reckons that Sammy gave her a long 'un, to fire into me, make sure I got drunk, plenty of charlie, y'know. And make sure we got a cab back to 'er place and let me fuck the arse off it. She reckons she didn't know what it was all about and just thought it was a bit of a laugh.'

'Did she know anything about the parcel in the boot of your car?' I asked.

'No. Definitely. Anyway, there's no way Sammy would've said anyfing. But I just can't believe that slag Sammy. Like I've known him since I was a kid. When I fink about it, I just can't believe it. Eugene, yeah, OK, everyone knows he's a fucking lunatic. But Sammy? Like we're best friends.'

'Just as well you're not enemies. Then you really would be in trouble.' In spite of Wedding Bells's very real and very sad loss of faith in human nature, I couldn't resist a little humorous quip.

'Fuck me. I'd probably be sitting here with no arms or legs or somefing!' he said.

I laughed out loud as Wedding Bells's statement conjured up an actual image for me of him sitting there, just a torso perched on top of a bar stool. Within seconds, I was convulsed in a chronic fit of giggling. Wedding Bells, revealing the opposite side of his personality, joined in with the laughter, simultaneously holding his jaw with both hands, imploring me to stop giggling — 'It only hurts when I larf.'

After a couple of minutes, the pair of us regained our composure, and the reality of the situation came home to us, Wedding Bells coming very close to being beaten to death and me being cornered for a rather large sum of money.

'So it looks like we've both been fucked.'

'The three of us,' Wedding Bells said.

'Three of us?'

'Yeah. Don't forget the bird. Take it from me, she got well and truly fucked.'

Again the pair of us started giggling like a pair of schoolboys.

# CHAPTER 26

## Marbella, a Rock and a Hard Place

The next day, Barry and I drove down to Portsmouth to catch the ferry to Bilbao. By now, my feelings towards Eugene had altered dramatically. Although I always knew and regarded him for exactly what he was, a homicidal psychopath, I still felt that in matters of business he was someone who would pay his debts. But now I had received a very expensive lesson that a pound note was most definitely his *Guv'nor*.

I suppose his brother Sammy's involvement was more of an eye-opener. Most certainly his open and friendly personality belied a ruthless characteristic that was clearly ruled by money, too. For this reason, it made him an inherently more dangerous man than Eugene. At least everybody knew Eugene for what he was. But with Sammy, the general consensus of opinion was that, if you played the game with him, then you had nothing to worry about. But now I knew different and, to rub salt into the wound, there was absolutely nothing I could do about it.

Trying, but not succeeding, to put all thoughts of Eugene out of my mind, I was interrupted by the sound of my mobile phone.

'Steve, you all right, friend?'

Immediately, I recognised Eugene's voice.

I was tempted — 'Eugene? *You no-good fucking slag. So you thought you'd get away with it, you and that scumbag of a brother, you pair of mugs. Well, do yourself a favour — when I get back from Spain, you just have my fucking money. D'you hear me? Just get my cash, or you've got serious problems. You're not dealing with Wedding Bells now, this is me, BIG STEVE!'*

Meanwhile, back on planet earth, the simple fact of the matter was, I had to swallow it. But even so, my pride, tempered by common sense, compelled me to make a stand of sorts.

'Eugene. Yeah, how's things?' I said.

'Yeah, fine. Listen, I need some of those football tickets. When can I see you?'

Football tickets being his coded term for the twenties, I knew exactly what he meant.

'As it happens, I'm just on my way to catch a ferry. I'm off to Marbella for a couple of weeks,' I replied.

'Ah, fuck it. Can't you put it off for a day or two, it's important and it would mean a lot to me.'

By phrasing his words in such a manner, I realised I was being put in something of an awkward situation. I had already decided, since being told the truth of the situation, that I wouldn't supply Eugene any more. But to say that outright would cause me several problems. As '*it would mean a lot to me*', any refusal to supply him would amount to a personal insult.

I would have been in a far better position had Eugene blatantly told me that he just wasn't going to pay me for the 100,000 twenties, and then it would have caused animosity between us and I would have been perfectly justified in having no more to do with him.

But as it was, Eugene was my 'friend'. Eugene and Jewboy Jack had loaned me the cash to buy the press in the first place, albeit at an extortionate rate of interest. From his warped viewpoint, he had done me nothing but favours. Eugene had even taken it upon himself to beat Wedding Bells close to death, just for being stupid enough to 'lose' my parcel of twenties.

And so, rather like a reluctant guest at the Mad Hatter's tea party, where the normal values of everyday life are turned on their head, I was beholden to my benefactor.

Without a doubt, I was most certainly stuck between a rock and a hard place. For the moment, I decided to stall for time.

'To be honest with you, Eugene, I can't do that, and anyway there's only a handful left in stock. Since that parcel got *stolen* ...' (the word nearly stuck in my throat) '... I've been having a few problems with my printer, I've fallen behind with him, and he won't do any more till I straighten him up.'

'The cheeky bastard. And I bet he's earned a right nice few quid out of you, eh?' Eugene said indignantly.

'Well, what can I do?' I replied.

'All right, then. But try and sort it out as soon as possible. When you back from Spain then?'

'Ten days.'

'OK. Have a nice time, and I'll see you when you get back, friend.'

I pressed the disconnect button, and leaned my head back against the headrest, with both eyes closed. 'Friend' — Eugene's verbal trait made the word a chilling paradox. As Shakespeare once said, 'With friends like that, who needs enemies?'

The ferry trip took 30 hours, during which time Barry and I were drunk for about 29. After leaving the boat, Barry proved to be an even worse driver on the right-hand side of the road than he normally is on the left. After about ten minutes with the top down, touching speeds of 130mph, I really couldn't see us making it to Marbella alive. For some curiously insane reason, he kept swerving dangerously close to the sides of articulated lorries as he overtook them. So much so, that I begged him to pull into the first service station we came to and from there on I took the wheel. We made it in good time, foot down all the way, and only applying the brakes just in time to stop us carrying on into the Mediterranean.

The apartment was every bit as luxurious as I had imagined it would be. I spent the next ten days with Laraine, James, Gina and her two children, and Barry, just relaxing and having a good time going to restaurants and lazing by the pool. All thoughts of Jewboy Jack and Eugene were consigned to the tray marked 'pending'.

During this time away, Laraine mentioned that she was getting bored back home in England and fancied the idea of going into some kind of business, using the money her mother had left her when she died. Being a fairly cautious type of person where her own money is concerned, she was interested in something relatively safe and certainly not anything which was at all risky. At the same time, something too safe, like a newsagent's, just wasn't for her.

It was while we were by the pool, a couple of days into the holiday, that I mentioned Peter Fryett's proposition. As Laraine had known Peter almost as long as I have, the idea instantly appealed to her. We both knew that Peter was completely trustworthy and honest, and felt that we could rely upon his judgement in a business venture. It wasn't too long before Laraine decided that the idea grew on her and I called Peter from Spain to let him know that Laraine was interested in going into partnership with him, if he fancied the idea.

Virtually there and then, Laraine and Peter shook hands on the deal down the telephone line. As is always the case, the time flew past and Barry and I were soon back in England. My first undertaking was to contact Wedding Bells and collect my money. Unfortunately, I had overlooked my address book when packing and, being unable to remember his mobile number, hadn't called him from Spain as I would have liked to do. Being out of contact for over ten days, I was more than anxious to establish that everything was as it should be. In other words, I wanted to pick up my cash as soon as possible.

But Wedding Bells's mobile was switched off. I called him at least four times every day, but every time I heard the same woman repeating the same message: 'The mobile phone number you are calling may be switched off, please call again later …' and always in the same smug, self-satisfied tone of voice.

'Yes, I know it's fucking switched off, all the fucking time it's switched off.' But all she did was repeat the same message over and over again in exactly the same tone of voice, word for word. And, of course, screaming abuse at a recorded message didn't do me any good, and I began to fear the worst.

In between futile phone calls to Wedding Bells, I visited Peter at his shop in Hackney. He was delighted to be reassured that Laraine was basically committed to going ahead, and that it would be OK for him to put the wheels in motion for whatever he had in mind.

'All things being equal, Laraine should be in a position to release the funds upon her return at the end of August,' I told him.

Meanwhile, I continued trying to contact Wedding Bells, and continued to be told that the phone was switched off. Had I known where he lived, I could have knocked on his front door, but I didn't so I couldn't. And if I made myself too busy with other friends of his, there was always the chance that Eugene would get to hear about it, and that could lead to all kinds of awkward questions.

Then after a few days, Eugene called me. Naturally, I knew exactly what he wanted, and once again I informed him that I was having problems with production, telling him, amongst other things, that there was a problem obtaining the paper. It wasn't too difficult to detect from the tone of his voice that he was becoming agitated by the delay.

'To be honest, Steve, I really thought you'd be able to deliver the parcel by now, or at worst before you go back to Spain,' he said.

'I'm sorry, Eugene, there's nothing I can do about it,' I said.

The line remained silent for a few seconds, until Eugene said, 'Y'know, if it wasn't for that dopey cunt Wedding Bells, we wouldn't have this fucking problem. I would have done that last parcel, you would have copped a nice big wedge and your printer man would be happy as a pig in shit. I can't believe what he fucking did to us. I really can't.'

I listened, incredulous at the apparent authenticity of Eugene's words. It was as though he had genuinely convinced himself that Wedding Bells was to blame for the lack of funny money. I really didn't know how to respond or what to say, and merely remarked, 'Yeah.'

'OK then, I suppose there's nothing we can do for the moment. But, come on, Steve, you've got to get it sorted out for when you come back. OK?'

'Yeah.'

'OK, then, have a nice time and I'll see you as soon as you get back, friend.'

At this point, it dawned on me just what a predicament I was in. Getting away from Eugene wasn't going to be easy. But, then again, what was the alternative? I simply couldn't afford to lose another 100,000 notes. Even more so, now that it looked increasingly as though I might not get paid for the 20,000-plus notes I'd given to Wedding Bells. On top of this, another couple of my regular punters were having problems as a couple of their people had been arrested. I felt as though my world had been hit by a couple of earth tremors that could develop into a full-scale earthquake.

I was due to fly back to Marbella on 21 August, and it was now the nineteenth. As of yet, I still hadn't managed to get through to Wedding Bells, and I was beginning to despair. And then, to make matters worse, another punter who owed me for 15,000 notes was arrested and remanded in custody. Each day, my situation somehow went from bad to worse. And then more bad news, although it didn't affect me directly. Paul Sabbato, together with Colonel Blimp, had been arrested in connection with the invoice-factoring swindle. Not really that much of a surprise but, nevertheless, bad news for Paul. Blimp, as far as I was concerned, didn't exist, so his demise was of absolutely no consequence to me whatsoever.

I flew back to Marbella, this time with Stephanie, who decided that she fancied a week in the sun. The last couple of weeks at the apartment were shared with Laraine's aunt Eileen who had flown out there and another friend, Joan, who was a teacher at a local school where Laraine used to work as a voluntary classroom assistant.

As before, I enjoyed myself in the sun, even more so this time as both Stephanie and James were there. Stephanie travelled back in the car with me and we stopped en route to spend a couple of nights in Madrid.

Although we visited some fine art galleries and museums, my overall impression was that it was possibly the most boring capital city I have ever visited. In fact, when we first arrived, I thought it was closed. But our brief stay was memorable for an event totally unconnected to Spain or Madrid.

It's often said that everyone over a certain age remembers exactly what they were doing when they first heard the news that President Kennedy had been shot. I know that I do. I was in the changing rooms of a boy's club in Hackney, called Eton Manor, where I used to box. I was 14 years of age and, like most young kids, I had a small transistor radio. Transistors had not long been invented and were all the rage. I heard the news of the shooting on it and, like all the other boys and young men there, I was shocked beyond belief and hoped and prayed that the US President wasn't dead.

Sunday morning on 31 August, I had got out of my bed before Stephanie was awake and was getting ready in the bathroom. After showering, I called out to Stephanie, still asleep, that I was nearly finished and that the bathroom would be free for her to use. Upon waking, she sat up in her bed and, waiting for me to come out of the bathroom, she switched on the remote control for the TV set. Within seconds, she called out to me to come into the room.

'Now, Dad, now!'

I rushed out, concerned by the urgency of her voice.

'What is it?' I asked.

At first, the enormity of the constant news bulletin was almost beyond belief. In fact, for the whole of the rest of the day, it just didn't seem possible that Princess Diana was dead. Another Kennedy memory for another generation.

# CHAPTER 27

## Members Only in This Nightclub, Sir!

Back home from Spain, and it was back to business. Wedding Bells's mobile phone was still switched off, and the people I asked about him all said the same thing. It was as though he had vanished from the face of the earth.

Top of my list of priorities was to chase up some of the money owed to me. I wasn't having too much luck, and then, after I'd been back for two or three days, I received a call from somebody I didn't know. I was in the passenger seat of Barry's car. The call came through on the business line and, as I didn't recognise the voice, I was alarmed when the stranger at the other end said, 'Is that Steve?'

'Who's that?' I replied.

'Is that Steve?'

'No. Who's that?'

'It's a friend of Pat's. He asked me to call you.'

'Pat?' I was very wary and the sound of a stranger's voice on the 'hot-line' disconcerted me.

'Yeah, Pat. He asked me to ring about the money. Is that Steve?'

I was about to say 'No' and switch the phone off, but then asked, 'Why didn't he phone me himself?'

'He can't. He's away. But we've got some money for Steve to pick up.'

Realising he was referring to the £1,000 I had lent to Pat, I dropped my guard and said, 'Oh right. Yeah. This is Steve.'

I wasn't too happy about my business number being given to strangers but, as I was on the point of changing it, I wasn't that concerned. I decided I would pull Pat about it when I next saw him.

'Can you meet me, then?' the stranger asked.

I wasn't doing anything particularly important and said, 'Sure, where?'

'Well, I'm at Dalston right now. Can you make your way down here? It's a bit awkward for me, I haven't got a car.'

'OK, whereabouts?'

'There's a caff opposite the train station. How about there?'

I knew the area well, having been born in Dalston, and told the stranger I would be there in about 30 minutes. I gave Barry, who was driving, the directions and it wasn't long before we were sitting in the café drinking coffee. As we sat there, I had an uneasy feeling that this might be a set-up by the police, an attempt to draw me into something. With this in mind, I told Barry to wait outside and gave him my address book, together with several counterfeit £20 notes in a sealed envelope that I had as samples for somebody.

Moments after this, a young, light-skinned guy with a Puerto Rican appearance came into the café.

'Steve?'

'Yes, that's me. You Pat's friend?' I asked.

'No, he's over the road.' He indicated towards an ex-cinema which was now a nightclub called the 4 Aces. (The name 4 Aces Night Club was more of a euphemism for a piss-hole.)

'He asked me to come over and get you, if that's all right,' he added.

'So why didn't he come over here?' I asked.

'He's a bit busy at the moment. That's why he asked if you can go over there.'

I thought about it and, although the 4 Aces isn't the kind of establishment I would normally walk into, even during daylight hours, I couldn't sense any danger. It wasn't as though I owed Pat any money, just the opposite. We crossed the road and, after a couple of knocks, the door was opened.

I stepped through into a dark and dingy entrance area. The young Puerto Rican closed the door behind me and, with its closure, I instinctively realised I had made a mistake. A stupid, dangerous mistake. What the fuck was I thinking of stepping into a dive like this?

Without a doubt, it was time to leave. Turning to go, I said, 'I've changed my mind, mate.'

'Hold on, man. This way,' said the Puerto Rican.

But, by now, there was no doubt in my mind that I had been set up. I raised my hand, shook my head and moved towards the door, and then stared in horror at the blade he now held in his hand.

Knives have always held a particular fear for me. As a young man, I was never really worried about having a fight, if unavoidable, but the fear of being stabbed was something else. Equally, I could never see myself being able to stab another person except, maybe, in extreme circumstances of self-defence. And now here I was facing a stranger with a knife.

'GET DOWN THE FUCKING STAIRS, YOU CUNT,' he screamed, and pressed the knife under my chin. I made a desperate move to one side, but then I was grabbed from behind by someone else. Before I had a chance to react, my head was wrenched backwards as the tip of the knife was pushed under my chin by the Puerto Rican. Then a third man appeared from the shadows.

The three of them laid into me, kicking, punching and screaming. In a split-second they were all over me. All I could see was the handle of the door moving further away. Desperate to remain on my feet, I attempted to fight back and at the same time struggled frantically to reach out. Attempting the impossible, I tried to disregard the blows pummelling my body and force myself towards my only means of escape.

*My hand feels tantalisingly close. No more than inches. My fingers spread out, but like a rushing tide in the sea, I'm being swept back. I'm struggling, resisting in vain. I'm going under. A constant hail of kicks and punches. I'm drowning, tumbling down a wooden staircase. I'm on the floor of a pitch-black, filthy basement area. I'm trying to get up. I'm stumbling backwards ... Kicks to my ribs ... My head's being punched ... Darkness ... The whole world is spinning. All I can hear are screams and shouts.*

'WHERE'S THAT SLAG? WHERE IS HE, YOU CUNT? WHERE'S THE FUCKING MONEY, YOU FUCKING CUNT? THE MONEY — CUNT!'

Then it stopped. I lay there, my chest pounding, my thoughts racing. What next? I felt something warm and sticky at the side of my thigh, my left leg felt stiff and I became aware that I had been stabbed.

How badly I had no way of knowing, but I guessed it wasn't too bad. Breathing heavily, panting, I looked up in the darkness. My eyes took a while to adjust to the lack of light but then I managed to distinguish the outlines of three men, three dark shapes looming over me, mumbling to each other, breathing heavily and glaring down at me. I felt a trickle of blood from my nose, I raised my hand to wipe it away, but only succeeded in smearing my face with dirt.

I now realised just how much danger I was in, but just why, I had no idea. But I knew I had to attempt the impossible and get out of the basement where I was trapped. Slowly, I tried to get to my feet. I felt that if I hobbled slowly forward and made out I couldn't stand up properly, I might be able to take them by surprise and rush through them. But then reality set in again as my foot touched the floor and an unbearable pain shook my body. If not broken, then it was most certainly badly twisted. And I knew beyond any doubt that I wasn't going anywhere. And not for the first time in my life I was all too aware of my own mortality.

'What the fuck's this all about?' I said.

'Just shut your fucking mouth. Understand?'

'Just tell me what the fuck's going on,' I said, ignoring the last command.

A kick in the ribs was my answer. The pain shot through my body and again I felt the rush of panic. Why didn't I wait in the café? What was I thinking of? I must have been mad.

One of the men flipped a light switch, illuminating the basement with a single bare bulb hanging from the ceiling. It had the effect of casting as much shadow as light. Even so, I was able to see the three men more clearly. Apart from the Puerto Rican, there was another black man, more African in appearance, thick-set, about 5ft 9in and older than the other two, probably early thirties.

The third member of the trio was white, stockily built, about 5ft 8in and about 25. He was wearing a Tommy Hilfiger top and jeans.

'Get up, cunt.' The African looked down at me, an expression of contempt on his face. 'Where's Pat? Where's the money?'

'What? I don't know where Pat is,' I said. 'I thought I was supposed to be picking up the money he owes me.'

'Just get up and stop fucking about.'

I struggled up and fell on to an old chair by a desk against the wall. 'What d'you want?' I said. I could feel my jaw aching and closed my eyes.

'You know. We want that cunt Pat.'

'I told you. I don't know where he is.'

A million confused thoughts ran through my brain. *Jesus — am I going to get out of here? This can't be happening.*

I struggled to breathe, each breath telling me how bruised my ribs were. I tried to flex my leg muscles, but all I could feel was a dull ache. Looking down, I saw the blood at the top of my leg, a crimson stain spreading its way down to my knee.

The African and the Puerto Rican started whispering and the Puerto Rican went upstairs. The African and Tommy Hilfiger remained, staring hard at me. I tried to keep calm but couldn't help wondering just what might happen next. Then Tommy Hilfiger mumbled something. He looked at me and laughed. I stared back at him and he went upstairs.

The African leaned against the wall and lit a cigarette. He paid me no attention and blew smoke up towards the ceiling, flicking ash on to the floor.

'What happens now?' I asked.

He ignored me and continued studying his cigarette and the grey curls of smoke winding their way upwards. I didn't bother asking again. Shortly afterwards, the other two came back. I stared at them and, as I looked, my heart began to pound even harder. I struggled to take in what I saw. Tommy Hilfiger was carrying two baseball bats. The Puerto Rican was holding a scimitar-shaped weapon, the biggest scimitar I had ever seen.

The African took the scimitar and grinned. The other two each held a bat at their sides. I knew what was coming and there was nothing I could do about it. I tried to stand up, but again my ankle gave way.

*There's absolutely nothing I can do. Nothing at all. They're moving towards me. They're holding the weapons as though they're about to start swinging them at me. I'm breathing hard. And I'm panicking.*

'No, don't.' My voice was barely a whisper. And all of a sudden, in one swift movement Tommy Hilfiger swung the bat at me. It was an instinctive reflex that made me raise my arm and the bat slammed into my forearm. The impact drove me off the chair and the floor spun towards me. More frantic swings and blows smashed into me.

The three of them were now swinging the bats and the scimitar madly. I struggled to move away across the floor, but there was no escape. I just tried to curl up into a ball. All I could feel was the constant pain. The speed of the onslaught made their shapes in the dimly-lit shadows no more than a blur. I was now barely conscious but an overwhelming fear somehow numbed the pain.

*I must stay alive. I can't die. Not now. Not here. But now it's stopped.*

I moved just a fraction and felt my body aching from the effort. I was somehow weighed down by sheer agony. I opened my eyes and looked up to see the African holding the scimitar over his shoulder. I was transfixed as he raised the weapon. Like a rabbit in the glare of a car's headlights, I knew what was coming. And, like the rabbit, I was powerless to avoid it. I gasped out loud as he brought the scimitar down towards my leg.

For a split-second, I believed my leg was about to be severed. But the blunt edge connected with my shinbone and I screamed out in agony, a paralysing agony that gripped my entire body like a vice, but even as I screamed I was aware of a perverse relief — my leg wasn't being hacked off.

The heavy weapon came down again, and again the agonising, vice-like pain gripped me. I was on the verge of throwing up when he stopped.

'Next time you get the sharp edge, man. *Real* agony, real fucking pain!'

Then it was the turn of the Puerto Rican. With a maniacal expression of contorted rage, he swung the baseball bat down towards my leg. The same leg that the African had taken a dislike to. He swung it again and again until finally the bat snapped in two. He threw it down in disgust and hawked up a large piece of phlegm, which he spat at me.

I moved my head in a reflex action, but still some of the foul, disgusting mess caught the side of my face. 'You fucking slag,' I mumbled as I raised my hand to wipe it away. But then Tommy Hilfiger swung his bat at my crooked elbow. I felt an immediate crunching sensation as the wood connected with bone and then the bat came down again. My arm was shielding my head but then fell listlessly across my chest.

'That's enough.'

The African's voice stopped the bat in mid-swing before it crashed down on my skull. My arm was swollen and throbbing, with very little feeling left. The only sounds were my moans and Tommy Hilfiger complaining about my blood on his jeans.

And then, lying there staring up at the ceiling, I became aware of the silence. I was alone with just the sound of my breathing.

After a few minutes or so, I tried to move. Somehow, I managed to get to my knees and pulled myself up into the chair. It exhausted me and I closed my eyes in an attempt to get my thoughts together. The sound of the three slags coming back down the stairs made me open my eyes. I could feel the stiffness of my neck as I raised my head to look up. I noticed the African had a plastic carrier bag in his hand.

The Puerto Rican came over to me and again pushed the knife under my chin. 'Now you gonna tell us where the slag is, or d'you want some more?'

Wearily I replied, 'I told you, I don't know where he is. I barely know the little rat.'

'So what was that about him owing you money, then?' Tommy Hilfiger asked.

'I told you, I lent him some money. He was in trouble,' I said.

'How much money?'

'A grand.'

'And you reckon you hardly know him? How come you lent him a grand, then?' the Puerto Rican demanded.

'I told you he was in trouble, I just helped him out.'

'BOLLOCKS. WHAT D'YOU TAKE ME FOR? A CUNT? IS THAT IT? YOU THINK I'M SOME SORT OF MUG CUNT.' By now he was screaming at my face.

'No, I don't,' I said, trying desperately to stay calm.

'That's a load of shit about you lending him money. When I said to you I had some money for you from Pat, you thought I was talking about the money he's had, didn't you?' Tommy Hilfiger said, not quite as hysterically as the Puerto Rican.

By now I was totally confused. Just what was the slag talking about? I said, 'What are you on about?' What money?'

Again the Puerto Rican started shouting, 'DON'T GIVE US THAT. DON'T TAKE THE FUCKING PISS, PAL, YOU FUCKING MUG CUNT. I'LL FUCKING RIP YOU TO PIECES, YOU UNDERSTAND THAT?'

I couldn't speak. It was all I could do to keep my thoughts together.

'Do yourself a favour, pal. Tell us where that fucking, no-good slag is. Give us his fucking number, or I'm telling you, pal, you're fucking dead,' Tommy Hilfiger said

Looking at each of the men, I tried desperately to convince them I didn't know anything. 'I'm telling you,' I said, 'I really don't know where he is. That's the truth, you've got to believe me.'

Then the Puerto Rican was in my face again. 'THAT'S IT, YOU FUCKING MUG,' he screamed. 'I'M GONNA OPEN YOU UP, YOU CUNT.' He exerted more pressure on the knife, forcing my head back. 'D'you fancy that? Being opened up like a can of beans?'

*Swallowing hard, I can smell his rancid breath. He's in my face. Get out of my face, you no-good, fucking, low-life piece of shit. I wish, I just wish, I had a gun. I could blow your fucking brains all over the floor. I'd watch your scumbag friends beg for mercy before I do the same to them. Blow all your fucking brains all over this dirty, stinking basement. But it's not going to happen. I'm dreaming a beautiful dream. My dream's being interrupted by the African's voice.*

'Mind out the way, I'm going to put the bag over his head,' he said in a matter-of-fact way. The Puerto Rican pulled the knife away and

I saw the African's grim, dead-pan face. And then, as he moved towards me, I became aware of a nauseating smell and my head began to spin. Petrol! The bag had been dripped in petrol.

The fumes began to overwhelm me and I stared, petrified, at the bag held open by the African. I moved my head away and raised my hand. I tried to grab the bag, but then started to panic as the Puerto Rican wrenched my arm backwards

Tommy Hilfiger gripped my neck in a stranglehold, and then the bag was put over my head. Instantly, I felt as though I was about to pass out. I started to choke and fought desperately not to breathe in. I knew my efforts were in vain and my eyes began to sting unbearably, no matter how hard I kept them closed. I heard a voice — 'Give us a lighter' — and then, in spite of the nausea overwhelming me, I was jolted back to reality. All at once, I knew why they had put the bag over my head. My thoughts were suddenly out of control and spiralling into a free-fall of panic as I visualised the plastic bag fusing its way into my peeling skin.

*I can't shout. I can't even whisper. This can't be happening. Please God, don't let this happen. I'm praying. Prayers for my life. Prayers that I won't die. I can hear the sound of a lighter clicking. My head's spinning. I'm confined within this claustrophobic, fume-filled space. This pounding inside my head. A mad, hysterical crescendo. Please stop. That clicking noise again. The crashing, deafening noise of the lighter is shattering my senses. That fucking noise. Silence. No more sound. No noise.*

*'Hi, Dad.'*

*'Stephanie? Is that you, my darling?'*

*Stephanie is standing before me. Smiling, surrounded by whiteness. She is a ballerina again. 'Are you going to take me to Trafalgar Square, Daddy,' she asks. I can feel a tear rolling down my cheek. Why am I so sad? Stephanie's voice fades away. She dances off into the distance.*

My head jolted as the slap brought me back to the basement. Was this reality? Another hard slap. Tommy Hilfiger was standing over me but the bag was no longer over my head. I could see. My vision was blurred but I could see.

But then I became aware of a whirring noise. I started to panic, then realised the noise was in my head. A loud, whirring, buzzing noise. I closed my eyes in a futile attempt to close out the drone and the pain that wracked me. But I was alive, I was still breathing.

How long had I been unconscious? Not long. It couldn't have been. I was still on the chair staring down at the floor trying hard not to fall forwards. But the floor kept spinning madly.

'You OK, mate?' I looked up, still not sure what was happening. Tommy Hilfiger leaned towards me, his hand on my shoulder. 'You OK?' he repeated.

'Mmmm.'

My head still felt as though a thousand tiny hammers were pounding away inside my skull and my eyes felt as though they had been rubbed across a sheet of sandpaper.

Tommy Hilfiger lowered his voice and said, 'Listen, mate, you've got to give us that slag's number. I'm telling you he's had the wrong people over. They're not just gonna let him get away with it. If you don't want to get one in the nut, just give us his number. You'll be OK then. I want to help you here. I don't want to see you get done in. But you gotta believe me, if you don't give us his number, or an address, it's serious.'

I stared at him, listening to him speaking in earnest. I was confused, unable to think straight. I asked myself if he was my friend. *'He's trying to help me. He wants me to get out of this alive. I've got to give him Pat's number. He's my friend. Pat's number ...? Who's Pat? Where am I?'* My thoughts were confused and then I mumbled, 'I don't know his number.' And then I heard a mobile phone. And then I heard someone talking. I tried to lift my head and saw the African slowly, very slowly, walking towards me. Slow, slow, motion.

I felt more nauseous, more sick than ever, as though I was dying. It seemed like I didn't have time to process all the thoughts in my head. But uppermost there was one recurring thought: Would I ever see my family again? Probably not. And with that I felt a deep, forlorn sadness. The African leaned forward and whispered in my ear, 'You know who's coming down here, don't you?'

I made no reply and just sat, my head slumped forward on my chest. I felt as though my whole body was on fire, a thousand red-hot needles pressing into my brain.

The African whispered again, 'You know what's going to happen, don't you?'

I tried to lift my head, but the pain from the effort was just too much. The room started spinning and I felt my stomach churning over. Breathing in deeply, I tried to control the heavy contractions ripping my insides apart. But to no avail. The emetic side-effects of the bag were not to be denied, and an avalanche of vomit cascaded on to the floor.

The African jumped back. 'You fucking pig,' he screamed, grabbing the baseball bat on the table beside him. Totally out of control, he swung at my head. My damaged arm shot up in a reflex action and I screamed out yet again as the bat slammed into my swollen and shattered elbow.

Back on the floor and staring up in terror at the slag standing over me, I heard myself gasp, 'Please, no more.' My plea was no more than a half-hearted whisper and the African stared coldly down at me.

'I'll tell you what's gonna happen, mug. You're gonna get one in the nut. Understand what I'm saying? One in the fucking nut.'

I lay there, eyes closed, thinking about his words, 'one in the nut', and then my thoughts took hold. *'Is he talking about me? Is this really how it's all going to end? It can't be me he's talking about. Talking to.'*

A few minutes passed. Still on the floor, it was as though I no longer existed. The three slags just stood around talking and smoking. For one bizarre moment, I thought they must have forgotten me. Totally ignored, I was no longer there. For some obscure reason, I felt as though I had to get up. I felt more vulnerable than ever. I had to get up. Struggling to move, I reached out for the chair.

But then the Puerto Rican strolled over to where I was struggling and, in an equally nonchalant movement, slammed the baseball bat down on my knuckles and kicked the chair away.

I fell back on the floor, too numb to feel any real pain in my hand, only a bruised, throbbing sensation. Once again, I found myself lying motionless on my back, my eyes closed. Just how long I had been in the basement I couldn't tell. I suppose I must have lost track of time as I felt myself lapsing in and out of consciousness.

Once again, I heard my 'friend' Tommy Hilfiger talking to me, begging me almost, 'Why don't you just tell us? Just let us know where that slag is. You don't owe him anything.'

Unable to reply coherently, I felt myself lapsing again, my eyelids refusing to open. I heard Tommy Hilfiger say, 'For fuck's sake, tell us. I think you're gonna be done in. We're just waiting for someone to turn up. I think it might be someone you know. Listen, if you don't know nothing, you gotta convince the other face when he gets down here, otherwise you're dead. Understand?'

I understood and nodded obediently. I felt him putting his hands on my shoulder, helping me to sit up. And all the while I could feel a pain in my head like I've never felt before.

'Listen, there's a sink over there in the corner,' he said. 'If I help you over there, you can wash that blood and dirt from your hands.'

He helped me to my feet and, somehow, with his help, I hobbled over to the filthy, stinking sink. Using my right arm, I tried to turn the tap, but nothing happened. From the dry, dusty state of the sink it was obvious it hadn't been used for a very long time.

'There's no water,' I croaked.

'I think there's another sink in the back room,' Tommy Hilfiger said.

But by now I was past caring and I said to all three slags, 'I don't think I'll bother. If I'm gonna be done in anyway, it's not going to make any difference if I've got bloody hands.'

At this point, my mobile phone rang. It was in my inside jacket pocket and, incredibly, was undamaged. The three slags looked alarmed as I somehow managed to take it out. The Puerto Rican started screaming hysterically as I said 'Hello' upon hearing Barry's voice. Barry! I had completely forgotten about him waiting patiently outside. I tried to give him some kind of warning, and assumed that he would be able to hear the screaming and shouting in the background and so realise what was happening. But then he was cut off.

'Who the fuck was that?' one of the slags demanded.

Sensing that I had a lifeline, I said, 'It's a pal of mine. He's waiting outside for me. He knows I'm down here.'

I felt certain that they wouldn't be so mad as to kill me knowing I had a friend outside. Suddenly, there was a new dimension to the situation which threw the three slags into a state of confused panic.

The Puerto Rican rushed upstairs, and I staggered over to the sofa by the wall. Feeling a sense of relief, I leaned back and closed my eyes.

*Barry — he's still outside. He's heard the screaming, he'll know something's wrong. Somebody outside who knows I'm down here. My lifeline. I begin to feel excited. Maybe he'll be able to get me out of here. Footsteps on the wooden stairs. I struggle to open my eyes. I look up to see who this person is. I see Barry. He's followed by the Puerto Rican. No. I can't believe it. My lifeline. Barry, no, I don't want you down here. But now it's too late.*

I saw the look of horror on Barry's face as he set eyes on me, confused by the scene before him. 'Steve? What's going on?' he said.

Before I could reply, the three slags screamed at him to sit next to me on the couch. I could see the confused look, and then the realisation that, like me, he was trapped. He sat down and looked at me. 'You all right?' he asked, and I managed to nod my head and murmer, 'Yeah.' The three slags started to scream and shout at Barry. Now they believed that he knew Pat as well. But as they demanded to know where he was, Barry just stared at them.

'I don't know what you're talking about,' he declared.

The Puerto Rican raised the bat he had in his hand, and moved towards Barry, and then made a movement as though he was going to swing it at his head. Barry seemed to have a disorientated, disbelieving state of calm about him and looked as though he was preparing to try to deflect the blow.

Although I don't recall it, Barry told me afterwards that, as the slag moved forward, I pushed my arm in front of his head and assured them that he definitely did not know anything about Pat. And if they were going to start swinging the bats again, they might as well swing them at me, as I was completely fucked and didn't give a shit any more.

All I can say is, I must definitely have been delirious. I mean to say, I've heard that a friend in need is a friend indeed, but that's ridiculous!

But one thing I do recall is becoming aware of a new sound, a strange, alien noise, a wheezing, whistling noise. I was able to make out the slow, heavy thud of footsteps coming down the stairs. The wheezing got louder. Although my eyes were closed, I knew there was somebody standing over me. The wheezing noises became the sound of deep, laboured breathing, as though the exertion of coming down the stairs had been too much.

'Get up!'

I opened my eyes to the sight of a large, fat slob of a man staring down at me, dressed in a dark-blue shell-suit. An obese gut hung over the waistband. He stood hoisting up the bottoms of the shell-suit with one hand, and holding the scimitar in the other.

Wheezing some more, he repeated his demand.

'Get up.'

Obviously shouting down at me required some considerable effort, as he needed to wipe his sweating brow with the back of his hand.

'I can't move,' I said.

By now, my arm was completely numb and hanging limply on my lap. I sat with my leg stretched out and felt it throbbing. The fat slob stood in front of me. Reaching down, he grabbed hold of my hair and, in a quick, violent movement, pulled my body forward. He jerked my head upward and let go of my hair.

'Look at me,' he demanded, and I could see the scimitar held now with both hands. 'This is coming right down on your fucking nut. I'm gonna slice it open like a fucking coconut.'

I stared up at him, transfixed by the bizarre sight of this obese piece of stinking scum in front of me, the scimitar held high above him.

*With no strength left in my body, I close my eyes and allow my head to fall forward. I open my eyes and stare down at my shoes. I'm too tired, too weak to move or resist. I'm just so fucking tired.*

*A gruesome, inexplicable thought runs through my mind. What will it feel like as the heavy metal slices into my head? I'm breathing faster.*

'Now, you gonna tell me where that slag is? Because I'm telling you now, pal, if you don't fucking tell me, you're not leaving this fucking place. Do you fucking hear me?'

'Yeah. But I can't tell you what I don't know. Please believe me.'

'Well, I'm sorry for you, pal. Because I just don't believe you. It's your choice.'

My head slumped forward on to my chest. I was just so tired.

*I pray silently. 'Please God, please let me live.' But I can't help feeling as though I'm about to die. And all I can think of is where I am. I'm going to die right here in a dirty, filth-ridden, poxy little basement in the East End of London. A sad, pathetic, death after 47 years. Is this all it comes down to? Is this what it's all about, being murdered by someone I don't even know in a dingy little basement? There's no glory in this, not here.*

*Why am I thinking these thoughts? I don't know. I'm thinking about the last time I was in this building. Nearly 40 years ago when it was a cinema, The Plaza; Norman Wisdom during the school summer holidays. I'm thinking about the German Hospital where I was born, just half-a-mile or so away. In 47 years, I've only travelled half-a-mile. Not far. I'm staring death in the face and all I can think about is Norman Wisdom and the hospital where I was born and the piss-hole where I'm about to die. My life isn't flashing before me. All I can think of is where I am.*

*Seconds become minutes become hours. I'm going to die. A voice, a sound.*

*What's happening? I'm so fucking confused.*

*'Fuck off.' The voice of the slob.*

*I hear sounds. I'm aware. I'm aware that something's different. I look up, the fat slob's walking away, talking to the African. Tommy Hilfiger says, 'Go. But don't you say nothing to no one. Remember, you even think about the Old Bill — we got your address. Your family, your kids. Think about it.'*

*Barry helps me up and, as he half-carries me up the stairs, I think about Tommy Hilfiger's words — 'Old Bill. We've got your address.'*

*Old Bill? If I ever see you slags again, it won't be the Old Bill involved. Slags.*

At the top of the stairs, the Puerto Rican opened a side exit, which led out into a small yard with a gate to the side street.

Bright sunlight. Fresh air. I filled my lungs. Normality.

'I think I need to get to hospital,' I said as Barry helped me to the gate.

'No problem. My car's parked up in this street.'

At that moment, my phone rang. Barry took it out of my pocket.

'It's Mickey Blewit,' he said and passed the phone to me.

'Hello, Mick.'

'You OK? You sound out of breath.'

'I am sort of ... I've had a little *accident*. I'll have to call you back, Mick.'

# CHAPTER 28

## If the Bad Boys Don't Get Ya ...

We made it safely to Barry's car. Carefully, he managed to get me into the passenger seat. I leaned back and closed my eyes, savouring the pleasure of being alive. Feeling as though I was still in a state of shock, I began to calm down, in spite of the pain of my body.

Barry eased the car away from the kerb, and then, from nowhere, a police squad car came alongside and swerved to a halt in front of us. The officers jumped out and suddenly I found myself at the wrong end of a gun.

'Get out of the car. Armed police,' one of them commanded.

Barry froze in his seat and the police officer pulled open the door. He stepped back and aimed his gun at Barry, who immediately raised his hands and got out of the car. Similarly, on my side, the door was pulled open and another police officer stepped back and aimed his gun at me. 'Get out of the car. Now!' he demanded.

*No doubt about it, this is not my lucky day.*

'I can't,' I stammered.

'Get out of the car. Now!' he repeated.

I turned my head slowly and painfully to one side. I could see the man out of the corner of my eye, standing legs apart with the gun held in both hands at arm's length in front of him. 'I can't move, ' I repeated.

'Get out of the car.' His voice now had a more urgent tone to it, as though he was thinking that I was deliberately refusing to move.

*Now I'm starting to panic. Does he think that I'm armed? If so, this won't be the first time that an unarmed man gets shot by the police. Is he expecting me to make the proverbial 'false move'?*

'Get out of the car now!'

I remained frozen. Time to start praying again?

'I'm telling you, I can't move, for fuck's sake. I'm badly injured.'

I sat waiting for his next reaction, my fate quite literally held in his hands. If I hadn't been so absolutely drained, so numb, I could have laughed at the irony of the situation. After escaping by the skin of my teeth from the bad boys, I looked like getting shot by the good guys. Fortunately for me, the officer must have had steady nerves and thought carefully before deciding his next move.

'Put your hands on the dashboard. Slowly,' he shouted.

This I was able to do, in fact slowly was the only way I could make any kind of movement at all. I did as he said. Immediately, another officer rushed over and manhandled me out of the car, whilst I screamed in agony. I fell against the side of the vehicle as I was pulled on to the pavement. I then screamed out some more as my arms were pulled, none too gently, behind my back and my hands were cuffed together.

Leaning face forward on the car, standing on one leg, I looked over to the other side of the road, where Barry was leaning against the wall, hands and legs wide apart, being frisked by a police officer. There were police and cars everywhere, and crowds were beginning to gather at the end of the road which had been sealed off. All the guns had now been safely put away, and I began to feel that at long last I was out of danger.

At this moment my mobile phone rang. One of the plain-clothes men answered it and said, 'I'm sorry, he can't speak to you, this is the police. Yes, I'll tell him.' He switched off the phone and then said, 'That was your wife.'

I was informed that I was being arrested on suspicion of attempted murder, to which I replied that I was the one who had nearly been murdered. After several minutes, when everyone had calmed down, I asked the police officer if he could remove the handcuffs, due to the fact that I thought I might have a broken arm, and that, having my arms in an unnatural position behind my back, might cause me to faint from the pain. The policeman looked at me somewhat dubiously for, although I had blood all over me and my jacket was ripped in several places, my injuries weren't immediately apparent.

'I'm telling you, please, I feel like I'm going to collapse,' I said.

An older officer, a sergeant, seeing my obvious discomfort, told the younger man rubbing me down to handcuff me with my hands in front of me.

'Carefully, please,' I pleaded.

After that, I was placed in the back of one of the squad cars, where I was allowed to moan away to my heart's content. I saw Barry being taken away and put into another car and driven off. A minute or two later, the car I was in was driven off and I asked the driver where we were going.

'Stoke Newington Police Station,' he replied.

I groaned at the thought and said, 'I'm not being funny, mate, but I really think I need to get to hospital as soon as possible.'

'What's the problem?'

'I think I might have a broken arm and a broken leg. But apart from that I don't feel too bad.'

The other officer laughed, and then, looking at the general dishevelled, bloodied state of me, radioed through to Stoke Newington Police Station. It was soon agreed that perhaps it would be best if I were taken straight to hospital. The drive to Homerton Hospital was almost as frightening as everything I had experienced so far. The flashing blue light and siren went on, and the driver put his foot down to the floor.

I suppose for him, used to driving at such breakneck speed in the heavy London traffic, the journey was nothing unusual. But for me, huddled up in pain in the back, and seeing red lights looming in the distance as we approached at hair-raising speeds, the experience was quite nerve-shattering.

Barely slowing down, both police officers quickly scanned the traffic coming from left and right at the crossroads and continued across. Cars and buses were overtaken and oncoming traffic swerved to one side as 'Sterling Moss' cut through the traffic like a bat out of hell. I heaved a sigh of relief when we pulled up outside the casualty unit of Homerton Hospital.

*If the baseball bats, scimitars and guns don't get you, the driving surely will!*

One of the policemen went into the hospital and came back out with a porter. I was helped into a wheelchair and pushed into the reception area, where my details were taken down and written on to a card. After asking me about my injuries, a young nurse cut along the seam and gently eased my arm out of the sleeve of my jacket. I was wearing a short-sleeved shirt and what I saw, had I been faint-hearted, would have caused me to keel over. The immediate area around my elbow and forearm had swollen up into a grotesque-looking mauve and purple balloon. The two policemen winced at the sight, as did the nurse. I must admit I couldn't have imagined how bad it looked. By now the joint had stiffened up, and I was totally unable to straighten out my arm.

I was taken up to a ward, where a couple of nurses helped to undress me. The whole of my body was a complete mass of deep purple bruises, with a few ugly-looking cuts where the skin had split open. Fortunately, the stab wound to my thigh was little more than superficial, with no real damage. My right shinbone looked like a swollen, mangled mess, although it was perhaps not quite as bad as my left elbow. At this stage, I truly thought I was going to end up with a crippled leg and spend the rest of my life with a permanent limp. As for my arm, I certainly didn't expect to get full use of that back. Miraculously, apart from a couple of minor bruises and grazes, my face was unmarked.

Initially, I wasn't allowed any visitors or to make any phone calls, as officially I was still under arrest. A police constable was assigned to stand, or rather sit, on guard by my bed. I was attended to by several different doctors who asked me various questions about the nature of the 'accident', and several diagnoses of the seriousness of my injuries were made. I was asked if I had been hit about the head, and told the doctor that the only serious blow I could recall was being kicked in the back of my skull. He examined my eyes, and determined that they were slightly out of focus. To my surprise, when he asked me a few simple questions, such as 6 times 7, I was totally unable to answer him. The conclusion was that I was suffering from mild concussion. After examining the back of my neck and top of my spine, which was also severely bruised, I was fitted with a cumbersome, uncomfortable collar to prevent me from moving my head any more than necessary.

By this time, I was anxious to let Laraine know where I was and to reassure her that I was all right. I knew that, strictly speaking, I wasn't allowed to use the telephone, but at one stage the police officer at my bedside received a message on his receiver and left the ward for a while. At the first opportunity, I called a nurse over and asked her to bring a phone over to my bed. She told me she would be back as soon as possible, and I lay there hoping the constable wouldn't be back too soon.

Unfortunately, he returned at the same time as the nurse came back with a portable phone. In spite of my pleas that I needed to speak to my wife, he was adamant that, as I was still under arrest, I therefore couldn't be allowed to talk to anyone. I asked him if the offence of attempting to murder yourself carried a long term of imprisonment. He laughed at my little joke, and apologised for not being able to let me use the phone.

Shortly afterwards, Paul Wright, the officer who had arrested me on the counterfeiting charge, came to visit me. 'How are you, Steve?' he asked.

'I've been better,' I replied.

'What on earth were you doing in a piss-hole like the 4 Aces?'

'Nearly getting killed.'

He shook his head in disbelief. 'I'd have thought you'd have a bit more sense than to walk into a dive like that.'

There wasn't much I could say to that and just shrugged my shoulders. 'Tell me about it,' I said.

'So what was it all about?' he asked.

Suspecting he already knew, I just said that someone owed me money.

'But if you were owed money, how come you got beaten up?' he asked.

'Well, the guy that owed me had this little firm over for quite a lot of cash.'

'Pat the Rat?'

I couldn't help but be surprised at the mention of Pat's name, but said nothing.

'You look surprised, Steve. Well, you'd also be surprised what I know about Pat and this little firm. Pat's a very petty crook and drugs dealer. I wouldn't have thought you'd be mixing with the likes of him. Well, he's obviously upset the wrong people this time. They've already broken into his house, trying to find out where he's gone. If you know where he is, Steve, let me know — for his own protection.

'Believe me, if I knew where that little scumbag was, I wouldn't be lying here now. I owe him nothing. The slag told them more or less that I was his partner and gave them my mobile phone number. When I went down there I thought I was going to pick up the money that was owed to me. Instead, they thought I knew where he was, and tried to beat the information out of me.'

Paul Wright looked dubious, then said, 'So what are you going to do now?'

'What do you mean?'

'Are you going to press charges against these guys?'

'I don't think so. All those blows to the head, I think I've lost my memory.'

He smiled at my reply. 'They're all in custody, you know,' he said.

'Really?'

'Yes. They were all captured as they came out of the club. Stoke Newington have got them banged up now.'

'All of them?'

'Yes I think so. Four or five of them, I think.'

'What about Barry, where's he?'

'He's banged up as well.'

'He had nothing to do with it,' I said. 'He was trying to help me.'

'Well, I shouldn't think he's got any problems, then. But at the moment, they're just trying to sort out who's who.'

We carried on talking for a while and finally he asked me if I was sure I didn't want to make a statement.

'No. Not really,' I told him. 'I'm just glad to be alive.'

'OK, then, it's up to you,' he said. 'Anything I can do for you?'

'Actually, there is. Can you let Laraine know what's happened, and where I am?'

'Sure, no problem.'

An hour after he left, Laraine came to see me. Looking distressed and tearful, she said, 'The children are outside. I wanted to see how you were before I brought them in. Do you want to see them?'

'Of course. Bring them in,' I said.

With that she leaned over and gave me a kiss. 'I'm so glad you're not too badly hurt. When Paul Wright called to say what had happened, I started to panic. If anything had happened to you, I don't think I could have gone through anything like that again.'

I knew what she meant by 'anything like that'. In 1972, a year or so before I had met her, her father, Harry Barham, had been set up for a large amount of money. He was a wealthy bookmaker, who was in trouble with Customs and Excise for taking large bets without paying the tax. Unfortunately, he had also lost a large amount of money in the scam, and in an attempt to raise money to pay the tax owed plus a fine, he had borrowed heavily in order to finance a proposition that had been put to him.

The proposition involved buying some precious metals and, had it been successful, would have earned him enough to pay the Customs, plus the money he had borrowed. Unfortunately, the precious metals deal was a set-up. After meeting the people involved, they had gone for a drive, Harry with the money in a briefcase, and in a side street in Stratford, he was brutally murdered. Whoever had set him up shot him in the head and stole the money. His body was found in the car the following morning. The murderers were never arrested.

The effect upon her family was obviously traumatic, particularly upon her younger brother, who was just 11 years of age at the time. When I thought about her father, I realised just how lucky I had been.

Laraine came back to my bedside with James and Stephanie, who naturally were pleased to see that I wasn't at death's door. I tried to make light of the incident, and told them what I had told Paul Wright. They stayed for an hour, during which time the police officer on guard received a message to say that I was no longer under arrest. Before he left, he informed me that I could have an armed guard if I so desired. I thanked him and declined the offer.

I was operated on that evening, and woke up with both my right leg and my left arm in plaster. My shinbone had been fractured in two places just below the knee. I was fortunate that my kneecap hadn't been shattered. Had it been, I'm sure I would have been left with a permanent limp. My left elbow joint, however, was completely shattered, and had to be reassembled using a metal loop and a couple of pins inserted into my forearm, which was also fractured. Fortunately, I eventually regained virtually full use of my arm.

The following day, I was visited by two detectives from Stoke Newington CID. They pressed me for a statement against the basement boys, but I declined. Then they suggested I made a statement without specifically identifying anybody. Again, I declined. Finally, they suggested that if I gave permission for a blood sample to be taken, then a case could be made against the men, on the basic facts of what occurred. Combined with the fact that the weapons, including the broken baseball bat, had their fingerprints and enough of my blood on them, and the men had my blood on their clothes and hands, there would be enough evidence for a conviction even without a statement from me. Again I declined.

'You realise we'll have to let them go, then?' one of the officers informed me. 'We've got nothing to hold them on.'

'I'm sorry, but that's how it will have to be, then,' I replied.

Regardless of any other factors, I just couldn't bring myself to help the police to put someone in prison, even scum of the earth like the basement boys.

A day or two later, I was transferred to a private hospital, King's Oak, close to where I lived, courtesy of my Bupa subscriptions. Laraine came in to see me and help me to shower every day. Apart from the obvious discomfort of not being able to move about, and being confined to bed, my stay in the comfortable conditions of a private room with my own television wasn't too bad.

Obviously, lying in bed all day meant that I had plenty of time to think about everything that had happened. I realised that Pat the Rat, living up to his name, had cornered somebody for a considerable amount of money, in all probability using the ploy of having connections in the West Indies to buy cocaine at a reasonable price. Just how and why I fitted into his scheme wasn't altogether clear. I knew that he must have given them my mobile number, but just why, I couldn't really understand. It wasn't as though I knew these people, so just what was the point of telling them about me? But for the time being I put all thoughts of my narrow escape to the back of my mind with a promise that, if I ever came across Pat again, he would have more to worry about than the £1,000 I'd lent him.

Two days after being transferred from Homerton Hospital to King's Oak, Barry came to see me. He still looked visibly shaken by his ordeal in the basement. It was Sunday morning and I was watching the sombre images of Princess Diana's funeral procession and the masses of people lining the route. It soon became apparent that Barry wasn't his usual talkative self. After a period of small-talk whilst we watched the TV, Barry suddenly thanked me.

'For what? Getting you into a situation where you could have been murdered? Think nothing of it, old boy.'

Barry smiled half-heartedly. 'No, what you did.'

By now, trying to keep up with the TV commentary, I became very slightly agitated.

'I don't know what you're going on about. Spit it out, Pike, you stupid boy.'

'You know. When that cunt went to swing the bat at me.'

'What?

I was still none the wiser as to what he was talking about. And then he went on to tell me that I had put my arm up (the good one), and told the three slags they might as well carry on bashing me, something I had absolutely no recollection of.

'I did what?' I exclaimed.

'Yeah. Thanks anyway.'

'Oh, well, if I did, it was only because I was delirious or something. I didn't know what I was doing. It must have been a reflex action.'

We talked about the circumstances surrounding the attack but, like me, he couldn't fathom out exactly why Pat had given them my mobile number in the first place. He then told me he had seen quite a few men lurking about outside the 4 Aces before he came down. He recognised some of them later as plain-clothes police officers. It seems as though the building was surrounded before everyone was arrested.

'If that's the case, I just wish they'd made themselves busy sooner,' I said.

'Well, you're still alive, that's the main thing,' he replied.

'Where did they take you?' I asked.

'Stoke Newington Police Station.'

'How many? Just you and the slags in the basement?'

'Not the fat one. I heard they took him to Hackney Police Station.'

'I don't suppose you managed to catch any of their names, did you?'

'No 'fraid not. But I'll tell you one thing. Those two younger guys were absolutely shitting themselves,' Barry informed me with a smile.

'What about the other one, the real black one?'

'He didn't seem particularly bothered. Just sat there staring at the wall. Didn't say a word.'

I thought about what Barry had said, then asked him, 'Tell me, Barry, why did you come down into the basement? I mean, didn't you hear all the screaming and shouting, and me trying to tell you I was in trouble?'

Barry looked slightly confused then said, 'I couldn't hear anything except a load of static after you answered the phone. Bad reception. Then when that guy came out and asked if I was waiting for Steve, I just said, "Yeah", and he said you wanted to see me.'

I couldn't help feeling guilty at having inadvertently involved him in a potentially lethal situation that was nothing to do with him. Perhaps that explained my 'heroic' action in volunteering to take his place in the batting queue in the basement.

After Diana's funeral, and after eating most of my fruit, Barry left, and I lay in bed still trying to make some sense of the situation.

The bedside phone rang soon after he had gone. It was Ruth, a girl I had been seeing. I was amazed that she knew where I was because, as far as the world knew, I was in Homerton Hospital.

Ruth explained that she had heard about my absolute misfortune from one or two of my friends, who had told her I was in the Homerton Hospital. After learning from the hospital that I had been transferred to a private hospital, but not which one, she proceeded to phone around every hospital in North London and, eventually, tracked me down. She came to visit me the next day which was very thoughtful of her.

My other visitors during the time that I was in hospital were mainly family and Barry and one or two concerned punters. Concerned, that is, that there might not be any more funny money. Upon being told that there would be just a temporary hold-up, they didn't seem quite so concerned about my welfare.

After I had been in hospital for five or six days, I received an unexpected visit from Wally, Eugene's friend whom I'd known in HMP Wandsworth. I can't say that I was particularly pleased to see him and, apart from relishing the state I was in, I think the feeling was mutual.

Apart from this, his appearance came as something of a surprise. Obviously, he hadn't paid me a visit out of the goodness of his heart — he hadn't brought me a bunch of grapes.

'How are you feeling?' he asked.

I shrugged indifferently. 'Yeah. As well as can be expected.'

'D'you mind if I have a grape?'

'Yes I do. Go get yourself beaten up and put in hospital, then you'll have your own,' I retorted.

Wally smiled a sarcastic grin, as though enjoying my discomfort. 'So what do the doctors reckon, then?'

'About what?'

'Y'know. When you'll be up and about again.'

'Is that what Eugene sent you here for? To find out when he can have some more apples?'

'Partly. Well?'

'I don't know yet. All depends, I suppose.'

'On what?'

'How long it takes for the bones to knit back together again.'

'And what about your arm?'

'I don't know. I probably won't get back full use. I just don't know. My leg should be OK though.'

'Right.' Wally sat next to the bed looking thoughtful.

'So what else does your Lord and Master want, then?' I asked before telling him to leave.

Wally looked at me, a slight smirk covering a serious expression. 'Eugene mainly wants to know when he's going to be getting his money. All of it.'

Hearing this made me even more confused than I had been before. 'Money? What money? What the fuck you talking about?' I said.

'The 'undred grand that Pat the Rat and Wedding Bells nicked. That money,' he replied.

I stared in amazement at the flash bastard. So that was what the beating in the basement was all about. But I was still baffled as to how this had anything to do with me.

'I'm still not with you, Wally. If Wedding Bells and Pat the Rat had Eugene over for a lump of dough, what's that got to do with me?' I asked him.

Wally grinned even more. 'Yeah, all right, Stevie boy, whatever you say. But all I know is what I've been told. When Pat the Rat went to Eugene for the money, he told him that he had a blinding move for bringing back charlie from the West Indies. What's more, he reckoned that you knew all about it, and that you were standing guarantee for the 'undred grand ...'

'Do fucking what?' I interrupted.

'You heard. What's more, Wedding Bells vouched for what he was saying. Wedding Bells and Pat the Rat, both your mates. So I don't think Eugene wants no silly stories about how you weren't involved,' Wally said.

I paused to let his words sink in, then said, 'So who was that fat slob down the basement, then? I thought Eugene enjoyed carrying out the physical side to his business personally?'

'That was the geezer who actually pulled the money up. He's a pal of Eugene's. Now Eugene's promised to get it sorted out for him.'

Wally paused and sat back in the chair, more than honoured to be the bearer of Eugene's bad news.

I felt an intense hatred for the flash, skinny git coursing its way through my body. 'So what about Wedding Bells, then? What's happening to him?' I said.

'Don't worry about Wedding Bells, mate. You just concentrate on getting Eugene's little problem sorted out.' He picked up a couple of grapes from the bunch beside my bed. And then he couldn't resist adding a little snippet. 'Eugene knows all about you going behind his back and serving Wedding Bells with a parcel of twenties. I thought you told Eugene you didn't have none?'

I couldn't be bothered to respond to this last piece of information but it was certainly food for thought. After Wally had shoved a few more grapes into his smirking face, and spat the pips out on to the floor, I said, 'So is that it, then?'

Wally swallowed the last of the grapes in his mouth and replied, 'Er, let me see now, was there anything else?' He paused, pretending to be pondering my last question. 'Oh yeah, he gave me this for you,' he said and pulled an envelope out of his pocket.

I opened it up. Inside was a 'Get Well Soon' card, signed, 'With love and kisses from all the boys south of the water', and inside the card was a forged £20 note.

I looked up at Wally's grinning face. 'Fuck off, errand boy,' I said, unable to contain the anger and contempt I felt for him. The smile disappeared and a scowl quickly replaced it.

'It's as well you're laid up in bed,' he snarled.

'Well, don't worry. I won't be like this for ever. Any problems, the two of us can sort them out then. Errand boy!'

I had obviously hit a sensitive nerve and, still growling and pulling all kinds of frightening faces, he turned and stormed out.

'Fucking toss-pot. Mug,' I said out loud and turned back towards the TV.

Lying in hospital for several days, I was constantly puzzled as to how an armed response unit had just happened to be waiting outside when Barry and I had made our exit. It wasn't until some time later I discovered that the drugs squad had been listening in to the fat slob's phone conversations, and were also following him around. In this way, it was purely by chance that they heard him talking to the three slags from the basement when he was making his way to the 4 Aces.

Apparently, after realising from the conversations that there was a possible murder in progress, the nearest police station was alerted and, consequently, an armed response unit was sent along.

'All part of life's ever-changing pageant,' as Shakespeare once said, just after being run over by a double-decker bus.

# CHAPTER 29

## Signs Furniture and No Property

I was discharged from hospital ten days later and, due to the fact that I was able to do very little for myself, I stayed at Laraine's. I spent the days propped up on the couch in the front room watching TV and reading. Although still in a great deal of discomfort and suffering quite a bit of pain, I was nevertheless on the mend.

Laraine involved herself with the opening of the new furniture business with Peter, a large warehouse in Edmonton. He had managed to locate an empty building on the Lea Valley Trading Estate, and secured a good deal on it. The building, 20,000sq ft on two floors, had previously been a sign manufacturing factory, and outside had a large neon display reading: 'SIGNS'.

The sign actually looked very impressive and so, rather than dismantle it, Laraine and Peter decided to utilise it in the best way possible. The new venture was christened Signs Furniture.

Signs Furniture warehouse was opened in October and, although in a wheelchair, I managed to attend the opening party. In spite of all that was going on in her life, Laraine still found the time to attend to my needs as an invalid. But my main problems were not my temporary physical disabilities, but rather my lack of finance and, of course, the spectre of Eugene, which haunted my every waking moment and, more often than not, my sleeping ones as well.

I had no immediate way of paying Eugene the kind of cash that he was demanding and, apart from this, as dangerous and violent as I knew him to be, I still found the idea of paying off a bully-boy a very bitter pill to swallow. So much so that I knew I couldn't do it.

Soon after the opening of the furniture warehouse, I received a call from Jewboy Jack telling me that Eugene wanted to see me the next day. Even though I explained my difficulties in getting about, he was most insistent that I had to meet Eugene. He sounded genuinely apologetic, but at the same time quite definite that I couldn't put off seeing my favourite psychopath.

At length I agreed. 'OK, Jack, what time tomorrow?'

'2.30 at the pub, OK?' he replied.

'No way. If you think I'm going over to the pub to meet that fucking lunatic, you're mad. I've nearly been beaten to death once this year, I'd at least like to make a recovery before I take the chance of something similar happening again.'

'Y'know what he's like, Steve. Once he's off his own manor he thinks everyone's out to kill him. He'll only meet you in the pub. I promise you faithfully nothing's going to happen. You have my word.'

'Well, this might shock you a little bit, Jack,' I said, 'but your words of reassurance mean nothing to me. And if Eugene can't overcome his paranoia, that's too bad. There is absolutely no way I'm going anywhere near that poxy little pub ever again.'

Jewboy Jack eventually realised that I wouldn't be dissuaded, and compromised on a neutral location, a busy pub with a restaurant that we both knew.

The next day, Barry drove me to the agreed meeting place and waited outside whilst I made my way in, supported on crutches. Jewboy Jack and Eugene were sitting in the restaurant area and spotted me the moment I hobbled through the door. I made it over to them, and Jewboy Jack rose from his seat and took the crutches as I sat down. Eugene remained seated and stared across at me. There was no pretence of civility on his part, and he remained silent, just fixing me with his steely gaze. His mood of intimidation didn't have its intended effect and I merely glanced at him before saying 'Thank you' as Jack poured me a glass of wine.

'So what's happening, *friend*?' Eugene said.

'What d'you mean?' I replied. 'Jack told me you wanted to see me.'

'You know what I'm talking about, the fucking money.' Already one 'fucking'. Not a very good start to the meeting. But I wasn't feeling in the mood to be bullied by Eugene, or anyone else for that matter. Having had time to reflect upon what had happened in the basement, the intense hatred I felt for the man just got worse. Nevertheless, I chose my words with some caution.

'Well, for a start I haven't got any cash to give you or anyone else for that matter. I'm skint,' I said.

'Well, you'll just have to get hold of it, won't you?'

'Listen, your pal didn't give the 100 grand to me, he gave it to that slag Pat the Rat. I didn't even know anything about it.'

I could see the anger building up in Eugene, as could Jewboy Jack, who pre-empted him, saying, 'We know Pat took the cash, but only on your say-so. He said you were guaranteeing the loan ...'

'And Wedding Bells,' Eugene added.

I knew it was going to be pointless to dispute Eugene's logic, but I had decided there was no way I was going to bow down to him or his brother without some kind of resistance.

'I can't be responsible for what they might have said. Anyway, why didn't you call me to make sure?'

'Because you were away in Spain, Steve,' Jewboy Jack said.

I took a sip of the wine, all the time keeping my eyes on Eugene's hands. I was extremely wary and on edge, ever mindful of his psychopathic and volatile nature, a precarious coalition to say the least.

'Well, that's hardly my fault, is it?' I said.

'Listen, I don't give a fuck whose fault it is. All I know is, my pal's laid out 100G and Pat the fucking Rat's disappeared with it. Someone's gonna pay, friend. And it looks like it's you. Understand?' Eugene's tone was harsh and uncompromising.

'So that's how it is, then ... you can't get hold of Pat and so you decide to put it down to me, is that it? Even though you know it's got fuck all to do with me? Yeah?'

Eugene was making a very real, even commendable, attempt to contain his rising anger and, through teeth very nearly clenched, said, 'Don't give me that shit, *friend*. You knew full well what was going on. Did you fancy getting some of your money back over the parcel that got nicked, was that it?'

'I don't know what you're talking about,' I said in all honesty.

Eugene paused, his eyes glaring rage at me. Jewboy Jack spared him the inconvenience of talking and continued on his behalf. 'We know that you think Eugene and Sammy stole the twenties that were in Wedding Bells's car.' He looked for some kind of reaction, but I remained impassive to his words, and said nothing.

Then Eugene spoke. 'Well, fucking say something, then. Or can't you speak? You too shocked to realise we knew what you thought, eh?'

I must admit I was more than a little surprised to hear that they were aware of what I knew, but certainly not so shocked I couldn't speak.

'What d'you want me to say?' I replied.

'Nothing really, because it doesn't make any fucking difference what you say,' Eugene said. 'You thought you was being clever, getting those other two slags to come into me for a lump of cash, because you thought I'd nicked your poxy fucking twenties. Well, I'm telling you now, what happened down that basement, that's fuck all to what's gonna happen if you don't get that fucking money back. Believe me, you're gonna end up one fucking way!'

Now I genuinely was having a hard time thinking just what to say. But his low-key tirade certainly had the effect of chilling my blood. Several 'fucks' or 'fuckings' in one sentence — now that's bad. I was in dire straits here, that much I knew. But even so, I just couldn't bring myself to say, 'All right, then, I'll get your money for you.' I had done nothing other than lose a large parcel of twenties to him and nearly got beaten to death. I just couldn't do it.

'Well, I'm sorry, Eugene, I just haven't got it and that's all there is to it.'

Jewboy Jack spoke. 'You'll have to get some more funny money printed up, then. We'll take the debt in notes.'

'There's not going to be any more. The printer's pulled out,' I lied. 'It's finished.'

'Well, you'd better just get him to pull himself back in, and do some more,' said Eugene. 'Or else you're in a lot of fucking trouble, friend. And, believe me, I'm not joking.'

Somehow, I rather sensed he wasn't joking and, with that, the two men got up from the table.

'Believe me, I'm not fucking about. It's up to you, friend, your choice completely.' Eugene poked his finger as he threatened me, and then walked away.

'Don't leave it too long, Steve,' Jewboy Jack quietly remarked, placing his hand on my shoulder in an avuncular fashion as he passed.

I sat there feeling very worried. Seconds later, a young waitress came over. 'Have the two gentlemen left, sir?' she asked.

'Pardon? Oh, yes, they've gone,' I told her.

'Oh, well, will you be paying the food and bar bill, then?' And she placed a bill on the plate on the table and walked away. I turned it up. £30. I left the money and hobbled out on my crutches. Outside in the car, Barry couldn't help but notice the worried look on my face.

'Everything all right?' he asked.

'Not really. But I'll just have to try and get it sorted out, I suppose.'

On the drive back, I tried to think of some way out of my predicament, other than submitting to Eugene's extortionate demands and threats. Over the next few days, I knew I had to sort the problem out one way or the other. It wasn't going to go away on its own, and I couldn't just bury my head in the sand. Not if I didn't want my body to follow it, that is!

Being totally dependent on others to drive me about, and being confined to the house most of the day, I had a great deal of time on my hands to worry about the situation. I have to admit, it did cross my mind more than once to take the easy way out and comply with their wishes. After all, it wouldn't take too long to get the funny money printed up, and maybe I could give it to them in dribs and drabs whilst I served my more agreeable punters. But then again, I just couldn't bring myself to capitulate so easily. Although having no pretensions to being a gangster or heavy boat, I can truthfully say I've never allowed myself to be bullied, whatever the circumstances, and so, a couple of days later, I got Barry to drive me to a pub in Essex. I knew that I would find a friend of mine in there and, sure enough, as we walked into the saloon bar, he was standing with a regular group of friends, most of whom I knew. He bought Barry and me a drink and asked how I was. I told him I was healing up very well and that soon I would be more or less back to normal.

He sympathised with my plight, and made the usual remarks about what a liberty it was and so on.

'As it happens,' I said, 'I wanted to have a little word with you about it. If you're not too busy, that is.'

The man I was talking to was one of the most feared and respected men in the criminal fraternity, a genuine, bona fide heavy. Although no longer a young man, and these days a successful businessman, his name still carried a lot of weight and, if it came to the crunch, the vast majority of heavy boats in London would back down rather than get involved in a dispute with him.

We moved away from the small crowd and sat down at a table by the window. 'You know what this is about?' I said, referring to my visible injuries.

'Yeah. I did hear,' he replied.

'Well, I've got a serious problem.' I explained the pressure I was under from Eugene, and how it had come about. He seemed to be well informed of the overall situation.

In the past, I had done him one or two favours and, no doubt, with this in mind, he said, 'So what d'you wanna do about it, then?'

'Well, to be honest, I want to go back at them. Let them know they can't have it all their own way. I want to tell them to fuck off,' I replied.

He thought for a moment and, after taking a sip of his drink, looked at me and said, 'You being serious?'

'Yeah. Absolutely.'

'You do realise what you'd be up against with that little firm?'

'Yeah. I think I know what we're talking about.'

My friend paused for a couple of seconds, and then said, 'I'm gonna tell you something I found out about the other day. If I tell you, you gotta keep your mouth shut. Don't tell no one, not a soul, right?'

''Course not, I wouldn't say anything anyway,' I replied.

My friend leaned forward, and spoke in a slightly hushed tone of voice. 'They done that geezer in, y'know, that big fella.'

'Who's that?'

'Y'know. He was on their firm, but he had a bit of trouble with them a little while ago. He got bashed quite bad. 'Ad a funny nickname.'

'Wedding Bells?'

'That's it.'

At first, I felt a sense of disbelief. Then said simply, 'You sure?'

'Yeah. I'm sure. Apparently, he had Eugene and Sammy for a lump of wonga. Him and some other geezer. Pat someone or other.

'Pat the Rat.'

'Is that his name? Anyhow, they've done that Wedding Bells geezer in.'

'What about the other guy, Pat?'

'No. He's fucked off. Apparently he's in Ireland.'

'So what happened to Wedding Bells?'

'Well, from what I heard, they got hold of him but he didn't have the dough. He reckoned the other geezer had it. Apparently, they strung him up and tortured him until he told them everything he knew about that Pat geezer. Then they gave him one in the nut. End of story.'

As annoyed as I had been at being cornered by Wedding Bells, I couldn't help feeling sorry for him. It was bad enough that he'd been murdered, but to have been tortured beforehand made it ten times worse. But at the same time, he must have been mad or had a death-wish to pull a stroke like that on Eugene. I could only surmise that, after the savage beating he received, his show of being friendly with Eugene and Sammy must have just been an act.

In all probability, he must have intended going abroad with the cash, and decided to withhold my payment for the 20,000 twenties, plus the balance that he owed for the earlier batch, to top up his tank. And now he was dead. It was most certainly food for thought.

'I just thought I should let you know, Steve,' my friend said. 'Just so you're exactly sure you want to go against them.' He could see the look of apprehension clearly visible on my face. 'If it's what you want, I'll back you up. They know me, especially Sammy, and they won't wanna fuck around with me. But just remember, you've got to be prepared to go all the way. They don't fuck about, that little firm. So you gotta think double-hard about it. It's your choice.'

I pondered his words. I thought about Laraine and the children. I thought about the late Tony Wedding Bells, and Danny Goodman, and others too numerous to mention. I thought about how close to death I had come, not just recently, but in 1995 with the aftermath of the Vindiloo affair. Even a cat's only got so many lives. At the moment I was paddling, but very soon I could well and truly be out of my depth.

'Yeah, I know what you mean,' I replied.

'Listen, Steve, think about it. And if you still fancy it, I'll back you up. Wait until you can get about properly, and let me know, OK?' But as my friend was speaking, we both knew his words were no more than common courtesy. He knew I had already made my decision.

The safety and happiness of Laraine, Stephanie and James were more important to me than anything else in the world. After the trauma they had endured as a result of my beating not long ago, I knew I couldn't even consider taking the risk of putting them through any more.

The only option now was to come to some agreement with Eugene. An odious choice, but given all the circumstances, and the fact that I was no gangster, it had to be the wisest one.

With this in mind, I decided it was time to chase Barry up about the property investments. Up until this time, nothing of any note had occurred, and I decided to find out just what was going on. If necessary, the piece of land up in Birmingham would have to be sold. As for the other deal in Kennington, my understanding from Barry was that we had as long as we required to complete on the purchase. That being the case, it would surely be no problem to sell the option.

After a considerable amount of pressure from me, Barry ultimately came clean. The deals had been done through my anathema, Dean O'Connell. I simply couldn't believe what I was being told. After everything that I had said to Barry, after all his reassurances and promises, he had blatantly disregarded everything I had said and had quite simply passed the cash to Dean. As if this wasn't bad enough, he had lied to me about the contracts being drawn up through a legitimate firm of solicitors. He had further lied to me that the deeds to the property in Birmingham were in the name of the property company he had formed upon his release from prison.

The truth of the matter was, everything was actually in Dean's name. Soon after finding this out, it came to light that the property deal in Kennington had virtually fallen through with the loss of the deposit. Far from there being an unlimited amount of time allowed before the completion balance of £200,000 had to be paid, it had already run out.

The only suggestion that Barry could come up with was that, if I pulled up another £10,000, the freeholders would allow an extension of a further two months before completion. I declined this generous offer. But there was worse to come. When I pushed him to obtain the deeds for the property in Birmingham, in order for me to transfer them into my name, it transpired that Dean had borrowed £21,000 against them. In short, Barry had lost, or rather thrown away, £42,000 of my money.

This body-blow couldn't have come at a worse time. As much as he apologised about the affair, I still felt that Barry had completely let me down and betrayed my trust by telling me so many bare-faced lies. I had several meetings with Dean about the situation, and he was in no doubt about my feelings on the matter.

The truth was, I felt like punching his lights out and breaking his jaw. But, of course, this wouldn't have got me my money back, and so I listened to his promises and just hoped they would come to something. Looking back, I wish had followed my initial reactions and broken his jaw.

I made a fairly miraculous recovery, and my leg healed up perfectly. My shattered elbow also healed up exceptionally well and, apart from the scar of the surgeon's knife and a minor lack of flexibility, it was virtually back as it should be.

The agreement I came to with Eugene involved me supplying him a large quantity of twenties and tens at marginally more than cost price. This was the best compromise I was able to negotiate and at least it allowed me to earn a small profit and provided for a great deal of saving face on both sides.

Although the incident in the basement had no long-term effects, and I was completely able to put it to the back of my mind, even to the extent that if it was mentioned in conversation I usually made a joke of it, Barry, unbeknown to me, took the affair more to heart. It would seem that this, and the guilt that he felt over the property fiasco, combined to have a profound effect upon him. Of course, the irony of all this is that I was the one who had been severely beaten and had lost a large amount of money. Then, to further compound the irony, Barry went missing. After trying to contact him without success for a couple of days, I called his parents who lived out in the country. They, too, had heard nothing from him, in spite of the fact that he had made arrangements to visit them and stay for a couple of days.

Barry's mobile phone was switched off, in itself a cause for concern, as he was very much a mobile phone junkie. He was rarely to be seen without one seemingly glued to his ear. In the car, he always had the phone plugged into the cigarette lighter, and he always had a spare battery with him. But for the last couple of days his phone had been switched off.

Without doubt an ominous sign.

His parents, naturally, were most concerned and I did my best to try to reassure his mother that I felt sure he would turn up like the proverbial bad penny. I gave her my mobile phone number and we agreed to call each other, depending on who heard from him first. After speaking to her, I called around to everybody I could think of who might have been in contact with him. All to no avail.

In spite of my confident optimism when talking to his mother, I was becoming more and more concerned as each day passed. After a week, during which time no sighting of his lumbering 6ft 9in frame was made, I began to become seriously worried, and even feared the worst. I knew that, in the normal way of things, it would be inconceivable that he would have gone walkabout without informing, if not me, then his parents, neither of whom were in the best of health.

In spite of his outward display of supreme confidence in himself, the truth of the matter was that he was an extremely insecure person, who constantly needed the reassurance and support of those close to him. He was also prone to bouts of depression. Although I have never suffered from a depression-prone disposition, I have had times in my life when, as a result of circumstances, such as losing all my money combined with the prospect of a long prison sentence, I have known just how debilitating true depression can be. For this reason, I have a great deal of empathy for people unfortunate enough to suffer from the illness of depression on a regular basis.

Whilst Barry didn't seem to be as badly affected as many people I have known, he did, at times, become very low and pessimistic about his future. And now nobody had seen hide nor hair of him for more than seven days. I had several conversations with Laraine, and expressed my concern that his body might be found in a hotel room somewhere. I just prayed that my fears were exaggerated and totally unfounded.

Thankfully, Barry surfaced after nine days. But although he was quite safe, my fears hadn't been totally without foundation. After visiting his parents to put their minds at rest, he came to see me and I took him to a local pub restaurant for a drink and something to eat. He told me that the basement incident had affected him most profoundly. He was unable to dismiss it and found himself going over it time and time again and dwelling upon the possible outcome — what might have been. He was then consumed with guilt over his blatant disregard for my trust and money. Although I tried to make light of the matter, saying that I didn't bear him any grudge, which was true, I do, in fact, feel extremely annoyed and let down by him, to this day.

The final straw for him was the premature death of his godfather shortly before his retirement as chairman of the property corporation. The culmination of all this angst was the descent of a huge cloud of depression that totally engulfed him. He then got into his car and drove to a friend's country cottage, which was empty, and to which he had the keys. It was a classic example of wanting to get away from everything and trying to get his head together. This, in itself, was perfectly understandable, but what wasn't acceptable was his decision not to let anybody know. As I pointed out to him, all he had to do was inform his parents, or his sister, that he was going away for a week or so. It wouldn't have even been necessary to give a reason. He had no choice but to agree with me, but also revealed that, during his absence, he had indeed had some very dark thoughts and even contemplated suicide. Even now, as I spoke to him, he was still clearly extremely depressed. I did what I could by giving him something of a pep talk.

'Listen, Barry, I know I've got one or two problems,' I said, (something of an understatement). 'But one way or another, I'll soon get them sorted out. Next year, I'll get a few quid together and, as soon as I can, I'm definitely going to go into the pub business, or a wine bar. I might even try to get a decent pub, a restaurant around the Ascot area.' This was a favourite part of the country for him, somewhere that he knew many people and had many friends (and a few enemies). 'If I can get hold of the kind of cash I'm hoping to, I should be able to get a pub as well as a wine bar. Maybe you could run it for me, and eventually we'd get some kind of partnership deal going, if we decided to expand. How's that sound?'

Barry still looked very dispirited, but at least he managed a half-hearted smile and said, 'Yes. It sounds like a good idea. Mind you, how d'you know I wouldn't let you down again?' He made this remark in a self-deprecatory fashion, an obvious result of his continuing depression. Realising this, I maintained an optimistic and upbeat attitude in the conversation. Although it was clear that Barry was still in a sad and sorry way, it did seem as though he wasn't quite as depressed as he had been an hour or two previously.

Before leaving the pub, Barry had a contrite confession to make. With a shame-faced expression on his face, he said, 'Er, you know that couple of grand of yours that you left in my car?'

I had a feeling I knew what was coming next.

'Yeah?' I said.

'Well, I, er, I'm sorry but I've, er, I've spent it.'

# CHAPTER 30

## Visits to the Ville, New York and the Isle of Wight

Approaching Christmas, a degree of normality had found its way back into my life. Barry, although not as depressed about his life as he had been, was still very much lacking any kind of motivation. Apart from trying to get him to adopt a more optimistic outlook, there was little that I could do on a practical level.

Paul and Colonel Blimp were held on remand in Pentonville Prison. Although the police were anxious to make more arrests, ultimately it was just the pair of them who were present and correct.

Barry and I made a point of visiting Paul on a regular basis, but I could never bring myself to visit Blimp. However, I kept my word and never told a soul about the terrible truth of his paedophile secret. Paul did likewise. If such a thing had been known about him, he might well have been killed in prison. As it was, Paul informed me that Blimp had barely stopped apologising and swearing blind that it had never happened before and that it was the excessive amount of cocaine he had been taking that had messed his head up. Even though both Paul and I gave him the benefit of the doubt, the fact remains — once a paedophile, always a paedophile, and for my part, I wanted no more to do with him.

It was just a matter of days before Christmas that Barry received an offer he couldn't refuse. Through a friend of his named Paul, he was offered a job in the US as an assistant manager in a huge table-dancing club. Like me, he was concerned about Barry's general welfare and, being a decent type of person, put himself out to see what could be done for him. For the previous few months, Paul had been working in the States as a financial consultant, and it was through his contacts that he came across the potential opening. Obviously, the idea of having a well-spoken, 6ft 9in Englishman as a manager must have appealed to the company that owned the club. A touch of class, so to speak, much like the prestige of having an English butler.

Being something of a table-dancing club junkie, this was definitely Barry's dream job come true. In fact, only a few months previously he had fallen in love — a fairly regular occurrence for him — with a young dancer-cum-stripper named Fay, whom he met at a club when she danced for him and stripped off at his table. As I had been with him on this particular occasion, I was quite familiar with all her hidden charms. Wary about telling his mother about Fay's job, he nevertheless enlightened his father with a truly classic comment. Totally oblivious to the obvious innuendo in his words, he told him, 'What you see is what you get.' 'Nuff said!

With encouragement from me, he packed his case and milked his last workable credit card for as much as he could — a couple of hundred pounds. I gave him what I could, which wasn't a great deal, and like the Pilgrim Fathers a few hundred years before him, he bravely ventured into the New World.

After Christmas, I decided I'd had enough of the funny money business or, for that matter, anything illegal. But as I still had to give Eugene a couple of batches of cut-price twenties, I was in no position to pull out immediately. Apart from this, I had nowhere near enough cash behind me to open the type of up-market wine bar I had set my heart on. As I had to carry on with the business anyway, it made sense to print as many as possible before I retired from the game.

In view of the fact that the police appeared to have no interest in me at this particular time, a call I had from a punter of mine had me more than a little baffled. My friend had some important news for me that came from a friend of his who had been arrested in Amsterdam in connection with drugs offences. It's difficult to remember the exact details but, for some reason or other, the man had been visited in prison by a couple of English police officers from the counterfeit currency squad. Just why they chose to visit him, I'm not sure; perhaps he had some counterfeit money on him when he was arrested. Or maybe he was connected in some way with Vindiloo, or Caroline, the girl who sold the twenties for him.

Anyhow, whatever the precise details, the gist of the important message was that the English police had some massive operation under way in which the star of the show was a man named 'Jury' or 'Drury'. My friend thought it as well to let me know, as he thought it might be something to do with me. As far as I was concerned, there was no doubt about it. My surname is very often mistakenly referred to as Jury and even Drury.

Of course, I found this disconcerting, to say the least, but I couldn't take any more precautions than I had been doing and I knew, absolutely, that nobody had even tried to follow me anywhere. I had even thrown in a few red herrings by making thinly-disguised arrangements on my business line mobile phone to meet one or two associates with several thousand twenties or tens. I knew that, if the police had somehow found out my number and were listening in, they would surely ambush me at the point of passing over the boxes. The boxes, of course, would contain something completely legitimate. But nothing ever happened, and whoever I had chosen to help me in this charade was never followed away from the dummy handover.

In my own mind, I felt absolutely confident that if the police did suspect that I was behind the funny money, they weren't doing anything other than tapping whatever phones of mine that they knew about, and hoping for a lucky break in the most likely form of a grass. As unlikely as I thought this possibility to be, the most that any of my punters could tell the police was my mobile phone number. Nobody, apart from myself, knew the location of Eric the printer, which was what the police wanted above all else.

Even so, this unexpected snippet of information was something of a jolt, and I became even more careful than ever, almost to the point of paranoia. There were times when I would pop out to the off-licence to buy a few cans of Budweiser, and by the time I had taken a ten-mile detour around every back turning and side street in the area, the shop would be closed! A slight exaggeration perhaps, but at times it felt like that. At one stage, I was changing cars at least three times a day, and had seven cars at my disposal which were never seen anywhere near either Laraine's house or the house where I lived.

I had made up my mind that I would go straight, and much like Britain's entry into the single currency system, the Euro, it would be when all the political and economic criteria were met. In other words, just as soon as I had enough dosh.

Sales were going well and, by Easter, I had Eugene off my back. I had delivered the last consignment of twenties I had agreed to give him to clear my 'debt'. Although Wedding Bells was no more, as far as Pat the Rat was concerned I made myself a promise that, if ever I found out his whereabouts, I would personally break every bone in his scumbag body.

After paying off Eugene, I decided on a break and flew to Megéve, in France, to see Ruth. She had been working abroad as a chef in a hotel since Christmas as she had a habit of getting into trouble in England and inevitably got sacked from whatever job she had, usually after about six weeks. Presumably, in France there were fewer distractions and bad influences (me being the main one, according to her) to make her stray from the straight and narrow. In spite of her idiosyncrasies, she was good fun and I had an enjoyable time there away from the day-to-day stress of the funny money business. The truth of the matter, however, is that I have always found criminal activity rather enjoyable rather than stressful. I suppose this can be fairly described as a personality trait, and without doubt the cause of 99 per cent of all the trouble I have had in life.

Upon my return to England, it was back to business and, generally speaking, the wheels of industry were turning without mishap. I even had a few more trades with Eugene and, although I was living somewhat dangerously, I made him pay in advance. At first, he was vehemently against this, and clearly regarded it as an affront to his integrity. At one stage, his brother Sammy had to restrain him when he flew into an uncontrollable rage. Knowing that he always carried a tool in the form of an old-fashioned flick-knife and, more often than not, a gun, it was just as well that Sammy was there. After that, I only ever dealt with Jewboy Jack, as I honestly and truly believed that Eugene was mentally unstable. Paranoid schizophrenic is the correct term, I believe. Fling in a few more long words such as psychopathic and homicidal, and that would just about sum up the dear boy.

Barry by now had left the table-dancing club, something I found incredible, and was involved business-wise with an Internet website company. Although completely devoid of any common sense, causing me to refer to him as Pike, the stupid boy from *Dad's Army*, there was no doubt he had an excellent brain as far as computers were concerned. Hopefully, the Internet was suited to his particular talents, because I really don't feel, somehow, that his original choice, property, is what the good Lord put him on this Earth for.

I spoke to him regularly on the telephone, and he always gave me glowing accounts of how well he was doing. This pleased me no end, as I thought maybe, one day, if he was doing as well as he said, he would be able to repay me the £42,000 he had given to Dean O'Connell, and also the £25,000 that I had lent him in bits and pieces since his release from prison in January 1997.

On a day-to-day basis, everything was running smoothly. Smoothly, that is, apart from a slight hiccup which, in one of life's cruel ironies, was to have a completely ruinous effect upon Ken's life.

Eric had a mild heart-attack, and it looked ominously as though his days as a prolific counterfeiter were over. With the main linchpin laid up and advised by his doctor not to do anything physically or mentally exerting, it looked as though the business had ground to a halt at a most inopportune moment.

Still without the kind of finances I needed to realise my plans for a wine bar, and knowing that Ken had a number of financial problems, I made a tentative approach to him as to whether he would be interested in doing some 'soft pornography' on the press, his euphemistic term for what he knew full well Eric and I had been printing for the previous three-and-a-half years.

Much to my surprise, Ken agreed and, more surprisingly, took to the work like a duck to water. The money he earned seemed to be the godsend he needed to sort out his financial problems. Ken's involvement in counterfeiting amounted to no more than a couple of months' work as Eric made a full recovery, allowing Ken to bow out gracefully.

With the return of the completely fit and fully committed Eric, I was feeling optimistic about the future and estimated that I would be able to pull out of the funny money business by Christmas. I even had a couple of chaps who were interested in buying the set-up from me. With the money I would get from the business as a going concern and the cash from the sales, I would be able to turn my back on crime for ever and go straight.

With some kind of positive financial plan for the future, I decided it was time to buy somewhere of my own for Stephanie and me to live. It didn't take us too long to find a flat in Muswell Hill that we both really liked. With four bedrooms and two bathrooms, there was ample space for us both, and no problem if Stephanie's boyfriend or her friends should stay for the weekend, or sleep over during the week.

Because of the various problems during the previous months, most of my cash was spent in bringing Eric's money up to date. But I calculated that, from July to Christmas, all I needed was a clear run without mishaps and I would be home and dry.

Meanwhile, I was still visiting Paul Sabbato on a regular basis in Pentonville. It was on one such visit that he told me he was considering throwing in the towel and pleading guilty on the basis that he was just the 'gofer' on the firm and so receive a fairly light sentence. He went on to tell me that Colonel Blimp was in something of a panic as his solicitor had told him to expect seven years, on the basis that he was one of the main perpetrators. (Apparently, the police had wrongly assessed him as being one of the organisers due to the fact that some paperwork had been found which referred to him as 'The Colonel'!)

Personally, I found this high estimation hard to believe. But then solicitors are notorious for telling their no-hope cases to expect higher sentences than normal, and so, when somebody such as the Colonel receives two or three years less, they can receive the credit.

But in the Colonel's case, according to Paul, he was an absolute nervous wreck, petrified at the prospect of receiving a substantial prison sentence. As he had no defence, he was now rambling on about a spurious legal argument to get his charge thrown out of court. But it was plain to see that the Colonel had no chance whatsoever, and was just deluding himself.

At the next hearing, Paul pleaded guilty, but the Colonel adamantly refused to concede defeat. And so his legal team prepared an argument to have his charges dropped.

In July, even though we were divorced, I took Laraine to New York for four days on a shopping trip as a wedding anniversary treat. Upon our return, we decided to take my mother, along with James and a friend, to the Isle of Wight for a short break.

It was now the beginning of August and the four days we spent at a small hotel there were probably the hottest of the year. Laraine drove us down there in the Land Rover Discovery I had bought her for the furniture business. We spent most of the time seeing the sights of the island, and the boys and my mother had a good time. Both Laraine and I felt pleased that we had managed, by chance, to select such a good time to take my mother away. Little did we know that it was a holiday that was to ruin both our lives.

Whilst there, I decided to look up my old friend Bernie. Although no longer working for me, I still owed him some money for the work that he had done. Aware that the police could be following me at any time, I took the precaution of driving around the island on a couple of occasions on my own, maintaining a vigilant eye in the rear-view mirror, to ensure that there was nothing suspicious following me. With plenty of quiet country roads on the island, it wasn't too difficult to ascertain that there was nobody on my tail. I knew that if anybody had followed us from London on the drive down to the island, then, of course, Laraine couldn't be expected to spot them. With the use of motorbikes and several different cars, a police surveillance team can only be spotted if the person being followed goes out of their way to drive along quiet side roads, and then, notices a repetition of the same cars behind him.

During one of my precautionary tours of the island, I passed the grim citadel more commonly known as Parkhurst and instinctively felt a certain empathy with the residents detained within the perimeter walls. And with that empathy a somewhat prescient thought ran fleetingly through my mind — there, but for the grace of God, go I ...

Feeling satisfied that I wasn't under surveillance on the Isle of Wight, I called Bernie and made arrangements to meet him in the lobby of the hotel. This, in itself, was a basic mistake. Had I been thinking more clearly, and not been in a relaxed holiday frame of mind, I would have arranged to drive to him, thus ensuring absolutely that we weren't under observation. As it was, not being too familiar with the different areas of the island, when Bernie told me on the phone that he was in East Cowes, I felt it would be easier if he came to me. As I have said, this was a basic and stupid mistake. But then again, Bernie had assured me on several occasions that he had absolutely nothing incriminating left, either at his workshop or at his house.

At first, Bernie was unable to find the hotel, and was waiting at the wrong venue. After an hour or so, I called him back, to find out what had happened to him. After giving him further instructions as to the exact location, I decided to wait outside the hotel for him. Several minutes later, he came strolling along, looking fit and well. We stood and talked for some time, during which we discussed how he was doing with his plastics moulding business and various other bits and pieces, such as how he and his son were coping since the recent death of Bernie's wife.

As we stood and talked, Bernie produced a small sheet of paper with some details of how much money I owed him. I studied the list and, as I did so, I happened to notice a young woman walking past who turned her head slightly, as though interested in Bernie and me. This in itself alarmed me, but as the woman carried on walking, and the turning of her head was so slight as to be almost imperceptible, I told myself I was merely being paranoid.

Bernie and I carried on talking for several minutes, during which I gave him £1,000 as part-payment of the money I still owed him. All the time I was with him, I felt on edge, a strange, inexplicable feeling of being watched. But once again, I dismissed my feelings as nothing more than paranoia. Bernie left shortly afterwards, and I told him I would be in touch soon with the balance of what I owed him.

The next couple of days were spent in a completely relaxed and happy way, all of us enjoying the sunniest spell of the year. When we returned from the Isle of Wight, Laraine and I had another holiday to look forward to in Portugal. We had booked a luxury villa for two weeks on 19 August. We were taking James and another of his young friends, and Stephanie had intended flying out there for the second week with her boyfriend.

At this time of my life, I was beginning to feel more relaxed and comfortable with the way things were going than I had done for a long time. For the first time in years, I was feeling genuinely optimistic and happy about the future.

# CHAPTER 31

## Return to the Island

After returning from the Isle of Wight, I arranged a few more deals prior to my departure for Portugal. I left sufficient quantities with my regular punters to tide them over until I returned at the beginning of September. From then on, with the cash that I would collect upon my return, I had decided, most definitely, that every penny I earned up until Christmas would be put into my piggy bank.

My dealings with Eugene were conducted exclusively through Jewboy Jack and we actually got on fine without any heavy presence involved.

I also had a business meeting with the two guys, Micky and Bob, who wanted to buy the business from me. I explained how it operated and all the ins and outs of the various supplies that were needed on a regular basis. And, of course, I would introduce them to Sunset Strip, Ed Burns.

I had already spoken to Eric about my plans and asked him if he wanted to carry on with the new proprietors. After being assured by me that they were good people, he was more than happy to extend the contract. The final price, £250,000 for the machinery and equipment, together with the sheets of film for the plates and a number of introductions to reliable punters including Jewboy Jack, whom they knew anyway, was agreed on a handshake. This would all be completed shortly after Christmas and, as these people were always holding plenty of cash, I felt confident there would be no problem.

The only real change to the set-up, apart from me leaving, would be the operational base. Everything would be moved, lock, stock and barrel, to their own premises. And I didn't want to know where that was. In the meantime, I arranged a deal with Micky for as many of the twenties as I could spare. After telling him I would get back to him as soon as possible, we went our separate ways, all three of us more than happy with the agreement we had reached.

Paul called me from Pentonville on a regular basis for, as a convicted man awaiting sentence, his visits were now restricted to just two every twenty-eight days, and so I saw nothing of him. And then Colonel Blimp was released. This was incredible, as the legal arguments his barrister put forward really were lightweight, to say the least. Understandably, he was overjoyed and went to visit everybody he knew, spending most of his time celebrating with his old friend, *Charlie Cocaine*.

For my part, I deliberately avoided him, but as far as everybody else was concerned, he was just good old Colonel Blimp — *lucky* old Colonel Blimp. I was tempted to let it be known about his paedophile activities on the Internet, but as he had sworn his life away that it was a one-off incident caused by too much cocaine, I gave him the benefit of the doubt, and kept my word. And nobody, apart from Paul and me, knew.

Since the person regarded as one of the main perpetrators had walked out scot-free, it was reasonable to expect that Paul, viewed as the mug on the firm, would receive a reflected light sentence, say 18 months, which would enable him to be released, having already served time on remand. But, instead, he was sentenced to three-and-a-half years. This was later reduced to two-and-a-half on appeal, but still quite lengthy under the circumstances. Life, however, goes on and, while Colonel Blimp was out partying, Paul got on with doing his 'bird'.

On Monday, 17 August, I received a call from Micky. He told me he had to see me urgently. As he wasn't the type of man prone to over-reaction in any situation, when he said, 'Can you meet me straight away? It's absolutely urgent. I'll tell you what it's about when I see you,' I readily agreed, and made my way to a little pub where he regularly drank.

I arrived at the pub barely half an hour after his call, and found him already there with his partner, Bob. Micky bought me a Budweiser and we carried our drinks over to a far corner table.

As I sat down, Micky said, 'Take a look at that,' and pushed a copy of the early edition of the *Evening Standard* towards me on the table. I picked it up and stared down in horror at the headline that jumped right off the front page and poked me in the eye.

'Massive counterfeit currency ring smashed on the Isle of Wight.'

I sat staring at the words in a state of shock and disbelief. 'Is that anything to do with us?' Bob asked.

I shook my head. 'No, it can't be.'

'Just seems like a big coincidence. I mean, didn't that guy who used to put the silver lines on the notes and burn the waste live on the Isle of Wight?'

'Yeah. That's right. But there's no way it could be him.'

'Why not? You went down to the Isle of Wight a couple of weeks ago.'

'Yeah, I know. But my man on the Isle of Wight hasn't got anything to do with the money. Remember, it was four years ago that he did anything for me. I collected every last note that he did. Apart from that, all he had were a few packets of waste sheets he burned for me.'

'You sure he burned them?'

'Certain. He even told me what a big bonfire he needed to get rid of it all. I mean to say, no one in their right mind would have stuff like that hanging about for four years.'

They both looked doubtful. 'Just seems like one fucking big coincidence to me, that's all,' Bob said.

'Well, that's what it must be. A coincidence,' I said, not altogether convinced myself. I picked up the newspaper and read the report. It related how several homes had been raided by police and £10 million worth of counterfeit currency had been seized. Several men from the Isle of Wight were '*helping the police with their enquiries*'. As I read the report, as much as I told myself it couldn't have anything to do with Bernie, I had to agree with them that it was a very big coincidence.

Bob's words interrupted my thoughts as he said, 'This guy on the Isle of Wight, he doesn't know where the printer is, does he?'

'No.'

'You sure about that?'

'Absolutely. I'm the only one who knows who the printer is.'

'Good. Well, let's just hope that your friend on the Isle of Wight isn't anything to do with this little lot. But even if he is, so long as he doesn't know where the printer is, it shouldn't affect us. D'you think he'll stick your name up if it is him?'

'There's just no way it can be him. He told me absolutely that he'd burned everything. There's just no way he'd have £10 million worth of notes around him. No way.'

Bob seemed less than convinced, and said, 'Yes, but just supposing it *is* him, d'you think he'll stick your name up?'

I thought for a few seconds. 'I don't know. He's never been nicked before. He might do, I suppose. Mind you, if he does, I'll just say I don't know what he's talking about. It will only be his word against mine.'

'OK, I'll leave it up to you, then. Just be careful,' Bob said shortly before I left him.

During the day, I tried several times to contact Bernie on his mobile phone and his pager. His phone was switched off, and there was no response to the messages I left on his pager. I tried his phone at the factory, and also his home number. No reply. By late afternoon, I was beginning to fear the worst. But still I was completely baffled as to how he could have been caught with several million pounds' worth of counterfeit currency. The whole situation made no sense at all.

That evening I took James to watch Arsenal play at Highbury. Before the game we had a pizza, but before that I decided to try Bernie's home phone number again, still hoping against hope that it wasn't him who had been arrested. I stopped at a phone box outside the Pizza Express at the Angel, Islington. The phone was immediately answered by Bernie's son, Robert. As he spoke, I knew it was going to be bad news. Robert told me his dad wasn't available, and when I asked if he was in any trouble, he told me he was.

'Is it anything to do with the police?' I asked.

'Yes.'

'Has he been arrested?'

'Yes.'

'Is it to do with the counterfeit money that's in the papers?'

'Yes.'

'Where's your dad now?'

'The police have kept him.'

'Will he be getting out on bail?'

'I don't know.'

Robert sounded as though he was in a state of shock and, after trying to reassure him that I was sure everything would be all right, I hung up. Of course, I knew everything wouldn't be all right, but for some reason or other, which I'm at a loss to explain or understand, it was as though I was unaffected by it all. James and I enjoyed our pizzas and then had a good time at the Arsenal.

Apart from feeling extremely sorry for Bernie's plight, I felt completely unconcerned about the situation. I suppose this lack of concern stemmed from the fact that I felt that the worse that could happen, as I had told Mick and Bob, was that Bernie might stick my name up. Without the printer, there was little that could be done to me. If Bernie had been so stupid as to store the waste sheets, instead of burning them, as he had been paid to do, then that was nothing to do with me. Apart from which, as the sheets dated back four years, then I had already been arrested and served a prison sentence in relation to them.

I took James home and stayed at Laraine's house that evening. After a couple of bottles of wine, and lounging in front of the television, I felt completely relaxed, as though I didn't have a care in the world. Never mind that Bernie had been arrested, and was by now probably singing like a canary, it was as though none of it was anything to do with me. All I seemed to be thinking of was the relaxing time I'd be enjoying in Portugal in a few days' time. Looking back now, I must have been having some kind of brainstorm, and brainstorms are not the kind of luxury you can afford if you're involved in serious skulduggery such as printing counterfeit money. That night I slept like a log. Not a care in the world.

The following morning, I went about my business in the normal way, still totally unconcerned about the previous day's bad news. It wasn't long before I noticed a motorbike on my tail. But, incredibly, I still wasn't too bothered. After all, I had nothing in the car to interest the police, apart from which, I knew I wouldn't be stopped unless they saw me visiting somewhere that might be of interest to them.

After a while, without really trying, I lost the police tail. But since I didn't have anything important to do, it didn't make too much difference. I spent most of the day shopping for clothes to take away with me on holiday. I took the clothes back to my flat in Muswell Hill, and did some packing. That evening, I went to Laraine's and enjoyed a delicious home-cooked dinner, after which I relaxed in front of the television and got through another couple of bottles of wine. As I had some important things to do the following day, I decided not to stay the night at Laraine's and instead got a cab back to the flat in the early hours of the morning.

By leaving the car that I had been using, a Ford Granada, parked outside Laraine's house I reasoned that the police would assume that I had stayed there, and that I was still inside the following morning. With the police watching Laraine's house, and the Ford Granada, that should leave me free to use an XJ6 that I had parked up outside the flat, without any hassle. Initially, it seemed as though my scheme had worked.

When I left the flat, on Wednesday morning, 19 August, there was nobody following me. After making certain I didn't have a tail, I stopped at a phone box and made a couple of calls. I then got back into the Jag and did a U-turn, heading back in the direction of the flat, where I had forgotten something I needed. As I drove along, I noticed a motorbike pass me from the opposite direction.

I looked into my rear-view mirror and saw the motorbike do a U-turn some considerable distance along the road. So now the bike appeared to be following me, albeit from a distance. I cursed my stupidity at not driving straight out of the area when I had left the flat earlier. I drove back to the flat and parked up. As I walked along the road, I saw what I knew were undoubtedly two plain-clothes detectives drive past. One of them couldn't resist turning his head slightly to look at me as they passed.

I collected what I needed from the flat and hurried back out to the car. I swiftly pulled away, checking my rear-view mirror as I did so. By the time I got to the end of the turning, I was surprised to see nobody behind me. I can only assume the police hadn't expected me to leave the flat so soon after arriving. Seizing my opportunity, I accelerated away at speed into the main road and quickly turned off into a small side street. After travelling through several back turnings at something more than 30mph, I joined another main road, and from there turned on to the busy North Circular Road unaccompanied.

My first destination was an ink company in Reading. Eric was running low on supplies, and I had decided to stock up before I went on holiday the next morning. I made it all the way to Reading completely safe in the knowledge that nobody was following me. I picked up the inks, and made my way over to the workshop. On the way I stopped to call Mick. I gave him the news about Bernie, but, of course, his main concern was that I was all right.

I explained to him the situation, but that there was absolutely nobody following me now. I told him I was going to see the printer, and suggested that since I was leaving for Portugal the following morning, perhaps it would be an idea if I delivered whatever stock was ready.

After being reassured that I definitely wasn't being followed, Mick agreed, telling me he had £15,000 he owed me, which he would give to a mutual friend who would pick up the parcel. For some reason, he also informed me that the most he could take at that time was 36,000 notes.

I told him I would call him later to fix up a time and place for his driver to meet me. I arrived at the workshop an hour or so later and delivered the specialised inks that Eric required. I packed Mick's parcel into a couple of holdalls. Since Eric wasn't aware of Bernie's existence and vice versa, I didn't see any need to alarm him unnecessarily. I knew that, in the event of the very worst happening, there was no possibility of Eric's existence coming to light.

In total, he had 90,000 £20 notes ready, which was considerably more than I had anticipated. Not wishing to leave any behind, I called a punter I knew as 'Beef Curry', who was more than happy to take the remaining 54,000 notes. My only reservation was that he had a considerable overdraft which I was loath to increase. However, when he promised to pull up all that he immediately had available, £17,000, I agreed on condition that he made another substantial payment upon my return from Portugal.

After leaving Eric, I met up with Beef Curry's driver and delivered the three holdalls containing the notes without mishap, and just as smoothly I relieved him of the £17,000.

During the day, I had various other people to see, and felt quite confident about the situation; to the extent that I even met up with Eddie 'Sunset Strip' Burns and paid him £1,700 for another paper order. Not dissimilar, I suppose, to Nero fiddling whilst Rome burned. But, for whatever reason, mainly, I suppose, the knowledge that I couldn't conclusively be tied in with Bernie's predicament, I drove around as though I didn't have a care in the world. No matter that half the police force in the South of England was probably looking out for me.

I called Mick, and told him I had his consignment on board. After reassuring him yet again that I definitely wasn't being followed, I made arrangements to meet our mutual friend in the car park of TGI Friday's in Enfield. With hindsight, this was a stupid choice of location as Enfield isn't that far from Barnet, a matter of just three or four miles. As the police had missed me in the morning, it was a fairly obvious conclusion that they would be out in force in Barnet and surrounding areas. A more prudent choice of location would have been one 20 miles or so away from Barnet. Shortly after 6.00pm, I pulled off the A10 and into the restaurant car park.

Once there, I spotted Mick's driver and quickly handed over the two holdalls. After placing them in the boot, he told me he would be back in a couple of minutes with the money and to wait in the restaurant for him. I parked the Jag up in one of the bays, and got out of the car. As I turned the key in the door lock, I heard the dreaded words that froze me to the spot.

'Police. Don't move. Stay where you are.'

Barely able to believe what I had heard, or what was happening, I turned my head to see a young plain-clothes police officer approaching me with his warrant card held out at arm's length in front of him. I was holding a bottle of Budweiser that Mick's driver had given to me before he'd left, and I was told to put it on the ground. This I did, and the officer came up to me and told me to put my hands on the car. At that moment, another couple of police officers approached from different directions, and I was searched, cautioned and arrested. Obviously, the police had caught sight of me en route and then spotted me turning off the A10 but hadn't arrived soon enough at the car park to see me offloading the two holdalls of funny money.

As I was standing against the car, Mick's driver returned in a different car, and looked on in amazement at the scene that confronted him. Obviously, I paid him no attention and the police assumed he was just another customer pulling up to go into TGI Friday's. After a minute or so, he'd seen enough and pulled away. Had the police arrived in the car park a minute sooner, no doubt he would have been arrested with the holdalls on board. As it was, I thought all would be OK, as obviously the holdalls containing the counterfeit money had been spirited away, driven off by somebody else in the car that Mick's driver had originally been in.

In a move typical of most of my so-called friends, rather than taking the £15,000 to Laraine, the scumbag kept the cash for himself.

After searching my car, and finding £15,000 or so of the £17,000 that Beef Curry had paid me, the police officers radioed for a patrol car to attend the scene, and I was taken to Enfield Police Station.

By now, I was aware that the driver in the car containing the holdalls had been stopped and arrested by another patrol car. At this stage, I felt as though my world had collapsed. With the discovery of the holdalls containing the 36,000 counterfeit notes I was in serious trouble. Very serious trouble.

Apart from my own predicament, my main concern was for Laraine and the children. I knew the police would go straight round to Laraine's house with a search warrant, and also round to the flat. The thought of Laraine being given the news that I had been arrested the day before we were due to go on holiday completely devastated me, as did the thought of Stephanie being alone in the flat when the police went there and gave her the bad news.

All at once, my plans for a happy future were shattered. My life, once again, was in pieces. Even worse, of course, was the heartache and pain that my actions would inevitably cause to my family. I pictured Laraine almost on the point of breaking down in tears, but trying to be strong for James. How would she explain to him that his dad had been arrested? And, in all probability, wouldn't be home again for a very long time.

The guilt and shame I was feeling overwhelmed me to such an extent that I was in a complete state of shock. I was to learn later that Stephanie had actually been arrested on suspicion of being involved in the manufacture of counterfeit money. The police made an extensive search of the flat lasting several hours, after which they proceeded to drive her to Bishopsgate Police Station. Fortunately, before they arrived, a call came through that she should be released as, clearly, she wasn't involved in any of my business activities. It's difficult to see any justification in the arrest of Stephanie as I was already in custody, and as far as I can see, was no more than petty-minded maliciousness on the part of the police.

I was taken first to Enfield Police Station and from there to Bishopsgate station in the City of London. Upon my arrival, I was greeted by DS Paul Wright, who said, 'Don't you read the newspapers, Steve?'

Still in a state of shock I replied, 'Pardon ...?'

'The Isle of Wight, Steve. Didn't you read about it?' His question just served to emphasise how stupid I had been in paying such scant regard to the importance of Bernie's arrest.

I was placed in a holding cell. As the door shut behind me, I sat down on the thin, plastic-covered mattress. I held my head in my hands and a thousand different thoughts raced through my mind.

Thoughts about Laraine, thoughts about Stephanie and thoughts about James. Thoughts about how they would be feeling. About the floods of tears. About the pain they would be suffering. I thought about the times I had put them through this kind of ordeal before. The times over the years when I had been involved in the pirate perfume business, the times when I had lost everything and had been sent to prison. And here I was, yet again, languishing in a prison cell, but this time facing the prospect of being inside for a far longer time than ever before. I tried desperately to reconcile myself to the enormity of my situation, but without success.

Paul Wright came in to see how I was, and said, 'You know, Steve, yours is the only set-up where I haven't managed to locate the printing press.'

I made no reply, and he didn't push me for an answer. Clearly, when the police had raided Bernie's house and workshop premises, they had expected to find the printing press, only to be disappointed. This, at least, gave me a small feeling of satisfaction. Eric was safe and, as I was the only person who knew the whereabouts of the press, so was Ken.

Paul Wright stayed in the cell for a short while discussing various matters, and asked me if I had made a full recovery from the beating I had received in the 4 Aces. I told him I was more or less fully recovered, and after a while he left me alone with my thoughts.

For the next hour or so, I couldn't stop thinking about the waste sheets of printed paper that Bernie had kept stored for four years. I thought about the bonfire that Bernie had described to me, how long it had taken him to burn it, and all the while he had kept it all stored in his garage, *for four fucking years*!

In an attempt to switch off the avalanche of regrets and thoughts that were driving me mad, I asked to see a doctor. In my briefcase, I had some prescription tranquillisers that I occasionally took to help me sleep. A doctor was called and, after I explained to her that I felt as though I needed a couple of the tablets to help me calm down and think straight, she allowed me to take two, and wrote out a note that I was to be allowed one in the morning and one in the evening whilst I was in custody.

The immediate effect of the tranquillisers was to make me feel drowsy, and consequently the next few days were something of a blur. I can recall Laraine visiting me in the police station and bringing me some clean clothes and me telling her to try not to worry. A pointless suggestion under the circumstances. After Laraine left, I was visited by a young duty solicitor named Daniel Berman. My usual solicitor, Ian Oxford, had retired and, as the young lawyer seemed intelligent and enthusiastic, I agreed to him representing me.

Daniel Berman proved to be an extremely efficient solicitor, good at his job and more than capable of doing a good job for me. However, under the circumstances, it would have taken Harry Houdini to help me out of the mess I was in.

Shortly after Daniel arrived and spoke to me about the circumstances of my arrest, I was interviewed by two police officers who had been investigating the funny money for some time.

Most of the interview was, and still is, a blurred haze due to the medication I had taken. In spite of Daniel's advice to answer 'No comment' at this stage, I started answering the officers' questions. One of the side-effects of the medication I had taken is to make you more talkative, due to the feeling of relaxation they induce. Otherwise, I would most certainly have given a completely 'No comment' interview.

As it was, I made up a totally implausible story about not knowing what was in the holdalls. I answered several more questions in an equally ludicrous fashion until an exasperated Daniel Berman asked for the interview to be halted whilst he had a consultation with me. This annoyed the two policemen, who objected to him interrupting the interview. For my part, I was now in cloud cuckoo-land, albeit an extremely disturbed and worrying cloud cuckoo-land. The medication was taking its effect and all I really wanted to do now was go to sleep.

Reluctantly, the police officers allowed Daniel his consultation with me, and they left the room. Daniel emphasised to me the importance at this stage of the proceedings of answering 'No comment' to all questions. Eventually, in my dozy state, his advice sank in.

Not surprisingly, the rest of the interview was a bit of a non-event, with each question being answered — 'No comment', much to the annoyance of the two policemen. Unfortunately for me, the plain truth of the matter was, no matter how their questions were answered, I was well and truly in the shit, and all the 'no comments' in the world couldn't get me out of it. That night, I was allowed eight hours' rest in the cell before I was questioned again the following morning.

After this, I was driven, along with the courier, Martin Watmough, down to the Isle of Wight. We were taken in separate cars under armed escort. Presumably, the Hampshire Constabulary regarded us as a pair of extremely dangerous criminals, liable to be sprung by a gang of desperadoes on the journey south. We arrived at the ferry in double-quick time, in spite of the car that Martin was travelling in breaking down on the motorway.

Obviously, ever-conscious of the imminent danger of a highly-organised hijack on the police convoy, a replacement squad car was rushed to the scene, and Martin and his police escorts were quickly transferred over. Once at the docks, we were driven straight to the head of the queue, and were the first on. After appearing at the Isle of Wight Magistrates' Court, we were remanded in custody to HMP Camphill on the island.

There I met Bernie, who didn't look too good. Not surprisingly really, as at the age of 65 it was the first time he had ever seen the inside of a prison. This, combined with the fact that he was a chronic chain-smoker and had no cigarettes, made him look as though he had the worries of the world on his shoulders, which, to all intents and purposes, he did. (I can't deny that I felt much the same.) After giving him a packet of cigarettes, I asked Bernie why on earth he hadn't burned the waste sheets as he had been paid to do.

He had no logical answer, but now that the damage had been done, there was no point in going on about it. Even so, I would have thought that four years was sufficient time to have got rid of it all. When I asked him whether he had said anything about me, he swore to me that my name had never been mentioned. I knew immediately that he was lying but, under the circumstances, it was of little consequence.

I was as friendly as I could be to Bernie and genuinely felt sorry for him, despite the fact that he had lied to me about burning the waste. Had he done so, then none of us would have been in prison in the first place.

Laraine and the children came to see me the next day. Laraine managed to put on a brave face, but Stephanie was totally unable to contain her tears. James tried his best not to cry, and looked sad and confused by the whole situation. There was nothing I could do or say to make them feel any better, other than to say that I would be all right, and that they weren't to worry about me. Looking at the teardrops rolling down Stephanie's cheeks, I was painfully aware of the futility of my words.

When the visit was over, I went back to my cell, feeling more guilty and ashamed than ever, as though I had abandoned the very people who genuinely mean more to me than life itself.

After being on the low-security wing of Camphill Prison for a couple of days, a warder came to my cell and told me to pack all my stuff and belongings. I was being moved. I was placed in the block. When I asked why, I was informed that I had been categorised as a high-security prisoner and was being transferred to Parkhurst.

I found this hard to understand, and found out later that Bernie had made a complaint to the effect that I had been threatening him, and that he was in fear for his life. After being as nice as I could to him, and having known him for several years, during which time I had often lent him money in times of need, I found it hard to believe that he would make up stupid stories about me. The reason for his behaviour, although I wasn't aware of it at this time, was that he had told the police when he had first been arrested that I had been threatening him and had virtually forced him to do the work for me. Apart from this, he also made up a bizarre story about me meeting him in a yellow Mercedes, and having a load of drugs on the back seat of the car.

This and many other incriminating fantasies came out later on in the proceedings. I suppose, knowing that I would find all this out sooner or later, Bernie was in something of a panic and desperate to make sure that I wasn't in the same building as him. As annoyed as I was when I found out, I can't say I wished him any physical harm and, in fact, I honestly felt sorry for him. In many ways, his life, at the age of 65, was in an even worse mess than mine.

I remained in the block for a couple of days, after which Martin and I were transferred to Parkhurst. As we walked into the reception area, we were left under no illusions as to what kind of regime held sway. Immediately, we were warned not to ask for anything because we'd get nothing. So much for the room service and a full mini-bar!

The whole atmosphere was totally oppressive. After being strip-searched, we were placed in bare, individual cubicles. At this time, my mind and thoughts were still very hazy, and I was still very much in a state of shock. After remaining in the reception area for a couple of hours or so, it was decided to transfer us from Parkhurst to Winchester Prison on the mainland.

# CHAPTER 32

## HMP Winchester

Although I had only experienced the conviviality of Parkhurst on a transient basis, I nevertheless felt it was enough to form a considered opinion. My first and subsequent impression of HMP Winchester was that it was a vast improvement.

Martin and I were placed in a double cell together, where at first we spent most of the time listening to the radio. As we were locked up for 22 hours a day, inevitably we got on each other's nerves. A prime factor making our incarceration even more difficult was that Martin, who before this time was unknown to me, blamed me for his being there in the first place. But, obviously, there was nothing I could do to change the situation. Apart from arranging for his wife to be sent some money to pay off various bills, all I could do was feel overwhelmed with guilt about the whole sorry mess.

Within days, the sheer tedium of prison life had set in. Each morning at 7.00am a loud foghorn-type blast wakes the inmates. At 8.00am the cells are opened up and it's down to the servery for a bowl of cereal and toast. Back to the cell. Open up again an hour later to empty the rubbish buckets. Back to the cells. Open up again a couple of hours later to walk round the exercise yard for an hour. Back to the cell and then down to the servery to collect lunch. Back to the cell for a couple of hours. Open up to empty the rubbish bucket. Then there's 'association' for a couple of hours, during which phone calls can be made. Then it's back to the cell for half-an-hour or so. Then at 5.00pm the evening meal. Back to the cell. Open up at 6.00pm to empty the rubbish bucket and get a flask of hot water. Then lock up till the following morning. Then the next day at 7.00am, the foghorn sounds again.

The only variation in the routine is the timing of the association period. This alternates from day to day, between the morning, afternoon and evening. Apart from this, the only other break is the afternoon visits from friends and family. As a remand prisoner, these are allowed each day and last for approximately 45 minutes. But, of course, life goes on outside and, consequently, it's too much to expect people to visit a depressing place such as prison too often. I suppose I was fortunate in that I had regular contact with my family, and one or two friends kind enough to visit on a regular basis.

My main problem initially, like many people in prison, was concern for my family, and trying to cope with the overwhelming sense of guilt at what my incarceration was doing to them. But once again, it was a situation I had no way of influencing to any degree. All the guilt and remorse in the world couldn't ease or change the pain and suffering that they were enduring.

Several days after arriving at Winchester, I was lying on my bed talking to Martin, and listening to the radio. Some time during the evening, the regular news bulletin came on. Upon hearing the first item, I was left once again in a state of shock. The item concerned a police raid on a lock-up premises in Essex and the seizure of several million pounds' worth of counterfeit currency. The newscaster went on to say that a man and a woman had been arrested, and a printing press had been discovered. I lay on the bed desperately trying to convince myself that it wasn't Eric.

'That's not your printer, is it?' Martin asked.

'No. It can't be,' I replied.

'Is he in Essex?'

'Yes.'

'Well it's got to be him, then, hasn't it?'

'It can't be. There's no way they could have found him.'

'Well, how many printers d'you think there are in Essex printing up millions of pounds' worth of currency?'

Although I realised the truth of what Martin was saying, I still hoped against hope that it was just a coincidence. 'I don't know,' I said. 'But Essex is a big place.'

Martin chuckled. 'Not that big.'

I lay there, my head spinning, waiting for the next bulletin in an hour's time. Once again, the news of the counterfeit money operation in Essex was the first item to be broadcast. But this time, the details were more explicit. The lock-up had been discovered in Rainham.

'Rainham,' I exclaimed, convinced now that it wasn't the workshop at Ken's house.

'So your printer's not in Rainham?' Martin said.

'No,' I replied.

'Anywhere near there?'

'About a mile or two away.'

Once again, Martin chuckled. 'And you still reckon it's not him?'

'He hasn't got a lock-up, anyway,' I said. 'No, it can't be him.'

'Well, let's just hope you're right, then,' Martin said before going to sleep.

I lay there for about an hour, during which time I told myself over and over that it couldn't be Eric. It couldn't be him. The following day, I listened attentively to the radio for any further news items relating to the arrests in Rainham, but there were none. Still, I told myself, it wasn't Eric. It *couldn't* be *Eric*.

The next day, on association, I made my way along the landing to the stairs leading down to the telephones. Upon reaching the top of the stairs, I looked down and saw not Eric, but Ken. I immediately went down to him. He was confused and disorientated.

'Ken, what the fuck are you doing here?' I asked, under the circumstances a very stupid question.

Ken just shook his head, as though he was in a different world.

'You OK, Ken?' I asked, not knowing what else to say.

'Er, yeah. I'm all right. I've got to go up to the threes. Where's that?' he asked.

'That's the same landing as me. What cell number?'

Ken looked down at a card he had been given, and read out the number. I helped him carry his bed pack up to his cell, and sat down with him to find out what had gone wrong.

At first, Ken just sat there shaking his head, as though totally unable to believe that, at the age of 61, he was in prison. At length he spoke.

'They came round the other morning. Loads of them. A few cars, dogs, there was even a helicopter hovering above the house.'

'I can imagine. Did they tell you how they found out about you? Because I swear to you I never said a word. I didn't have your phone number written down, and definitely nobody knew anything about your place, apart from me and Eric,' I said.

'Yes. I know. They found some pamphlets I'd printed.'

'Pamphlets? What pamphlets?'

'On the Isle of Wight. When they went through all those sheets that they found on the Isle of Wight, they found a sheet of advertising pamphlets that I'd printed years ago for a company called Cranham Caravans. After that, it was no problem for them. They asked the people at Cranham Caravans who did their printing for them and, of course, they told them. When the police went to the firm, they told them they'd only just bought the business, and gave them my home address. And that was that, simple for them, really.'

It didn't take the brains of Einstein to work out what had happened. When Eric and I had first started to proof the £20 notes, I had asked Ken if he had any plain white sheets of paper at his firm that he could let Eric use. Amongst the sheets there must have been a printed sheet with the name of Cranham Caravans on it. And so it slipped through unnoticed, and ended up amongst the waste sheets I had taken to Bernie to destroy.

As we sat in the cell that was to be Ken's new accommodation for the foreseeable future, he went on to tell me that Eric had phoned him and told him about the events on the Isle of Wight and that I had been arrested and was in prison.

In a panic, Ken attempted to get rid of the evidence and took the sheets of paper with the watermarks on them to a self-storage premises in Rainham. Unfortunately, he took the receipt home with him and the police found it. Being the curious little sods that they are, they couldn't resist visiting the premises, just to see what was stored there.

Both Ken and I sat there trying to take in the absolute misfortune that had overtaken our lives. I thought back to the four days on the Isle of Wight that had led to such a catastrophic chain of events, with such devastating effects on not just our lives, but also on Bernie's and Martin's, to say nothing of our families.

Ken gave me all the details of how the police had searched his house and workshop and found the printing press. The money they found was, in fact, plain sheets with just the watermarks printed on them, but nevertheless there would have been enough to print about £10 million worth. And so, even though his involvement in the long-running scam had been minimal, the fact of the matter remained, the two of us were equally in DDS, and there was nothing that I could do or say to change the harsh reality of the situation for Ken.

Seeing Ken in prison was the first of two similar shocks that confronted me at this particular period of time. A couple of days later, I found myself walking along the landing, and looked up to see Eddie

Burns, the paper merchant.

This gave me an even greater shock than seeing Ken, whom I had at least had some kind of warning about via the radio news bulletin. But Eddie? The man hadn't done anything more than his job, which was supplying paper.

Eddie, too, was an elderly man, 66 years of age. At best, he was absent-minded, and always seemed somewhat confused. Looking at him now wearing prison clothes, he looked even more absent-minded and confused than ever. At first, he didn't seem to recognise me as I went over to him and started speaking.

'Eddie, it's me, Steve,' I said.

Looking startled, as he always did, he replied, 'Oh, hello. How are you?'

'Well, I'm so-so. But more to the point, how are you, and what on earth are you doing here?'

'Well, you see, the police came to my office and asked me about the paper I'd supplied to you.'

'How did they know it was you who had supplied it?'

'From the serial numbers on the packets they discovered.'

'So, how come they nicked you, then? You put it all through the books and paid the VAT, didn't you?'

'Oh yes. Of course.'

'Well, if it was all straightforward and above board, how can they charge you with anything? After all, it's only plain paper.'

'Well, actually, they weren't going to at first.'

'What made them change their mind?'

'They asked me if I knew that you had been to prison for counterfeiting.'

'And what did you say?'

'Well, I told them, yes, I did.'

I stood in front of him, amazed at what he had just told me. But then Eddie had never had any dealings with the police in his life before, and saw no reason to tell them anything but the truth.

'You shouldn't have said that, Eddie. You should have said you knew nothing about me going to prison,' I told him.

'Well, I did tell them that you told me you were no longer involved in anything to do with counterfeiting, and that you wanted the paper for something else,' Eddie replied.

'Didn't you tell them about the Magic Eye posters?' I asked.

'The what?' Eddie replied.

'It doesn't matter. So what happened then?'

'They merely said that if I knew that you had been in prison for counterfeiting, then I must have known that you were going to use the paper for printing counterfeit money again. Then they charged me with conspiracy to manufacture counterfeit currency.'

'Why didn't you get bail?'

'The police objected strongly, and the magistrates remanded me in custody.'

I was incredulous that a 66-year-old man who had never been in trouble with the police in his life, and with such a tenuous connection to the operation, had been refused bail. To my way of thinking, it smacked of more petty-minded maliciousness, which seemed to be the hallmark of Hampshire CID. Ultimately, the injustice of Eddie's situation was recognised when, a couple of weeks later, he made a bail application to a higher court, and the Crown Court judge granted him bail.

Meanwhile, it was clear there was no chance of bail for me whatsoever. Martin made a couple of applications to the Crown Court and then to the High Court, but all to no avail. Ken was eventually granted bail shortly before Christmas, much to the annoyance of the police, who put forward the strongest objections possible.

Outside, Laraine and Peter opened another furniture warehouse at Romford. All in all, she seemed to be managing OK, and the extra work involved with the expansion of the business seemed to help to take her mind off my situation.

At the beginning of September, I received a visit from Laraine and the children during which she informed me a man had visited the furniture shop and given her £500. She told me that the man had asked her to give me Jack and Eugene's regards and they hoped that everything would turn out OK for me. Although they had sent over some money to Laraine, I recognised it for what it was, a subtle warning not to say anything to the police about their existence, which I wouldn't have done anyway. Still, it was handy to receive the £500.

# CHAPTER 33

## A Guilty Plea and a Trial

The period between August and Christmas 1998 was, not surprisingly, a time of great concern and worry for me. The initial few weeks are, even now, very much a blur. But through the haze of depression and worry, I can recall my worst fear being the penalties that I would have to face and the attendant prolonged trauma that would inevitably be inflicted upon my family; several years of visiting me in a succession of different prisons.

I knew that the maximum term of imprisonment for counterfeiting was ten years. This, in itself, was a daunting enough prospect, but apart from this I faced the prospect of a large fine, a fine which, in all probability, I wouldn't be able to pay.

During the course of various consultations with Daniel Berman at court appearances on the Isle of Wight, it's no exaggeration to say that I drove myself mad trying to ascertain just what exactly the situation was with regard to the financial penalties. Accompanied by Simon Myers, the barrister whom he'd instructed, he was hard pressed to give me any encouraging news. Simon Myers, a most affable man with a commanding courtroom presence, had taken the time to refer to the appropriate section in his reference book and had photocopied it for me. To my horror, I read that the maximum fine was £1 million or ten years' imprisonment in default. As the case was now being presented as a £50 million crime (and rising), I felt sure I was facing the prospect of a maximum fine being imposed.

'And as you may or may not know, Stephen,' Simon said, as I read the relevant details, 'a term of imprisonment imposed in default of payment of a fine is not subject to parole or remission.' In other words, ten years meant ten years. A quick mental calculation told me that, should I receive the maximum penalty of ten years, I would have to serve 6 years 8 months at least, *followed* by ten years in default of a large fine.

'At that rate, I'll be banged up for the next 16 or 17 years,' I declared. Nobody said anything, and Simon, Daniel and I exchanged glances for a few seconds.

'I'm sure it won't come to that,' Simon said. 'The courts never impose a longer term in lieu of a fine than for the actual offence. Leave it with me and I'll find out the exact legal position.'

His words were of little comfort to me, and didn't really sound too convincing. For a moment, I knew I was in a great deal of trouble. As far as I could see, my life was in ruins. Although I knew I didn't have a leg to stand on, I had no choice other than to fight the charge. It really seemed to be a case of having nothing to lose.

During this period, Martin and I made several court appearances on the Isle of Wight. We were transported from Winchester in the sweat box vans that are used for prisoners, remaining in the tiny cubicles in the van while on the ferry, and then on to the courthouse. It was something of an endurance test. Generally speaking, a day out at court was several hours of purgatory. I often wondered whether it was legal to keep us in such a confined situation on the ferry, as clearly, if the boat sank, our confinement would render escape an impossibility. Needless to say, the ferry never sank.

Each time we appeared at court, Bernie was conspicuous by his absence. After questioning Daniel and Simon about this, I was told he had really got carried away with his concocted tale about being terrified of me. So much so, that he refused to sit in the dock whilst I was there. He managed to convince the police and authorities that he was genuinely in fear for his life.

The situation became so ludicrous that, on one occasion when Bernie was required to be in the dock with me, both Martin and I remained handcuffed to the guards and there was a cordon of armed police around the dock! After the brief hearing, I complained to Daniel that if ever I had to remain handcuffed whilst in the dock again, then I would simply refuse to enter the court. I think the crass stupidity of the incident typifies the attitude of the Hampshire CID who had taken the case over from the squad based at Bishopsgate Police Station in London.

The officer who had originally been in charge of the investigation at ground level, DS Paul Wright, had completely rubbished the suggestion from Bernie that he was terrified of me, pointing out, amongst other things, that there was nothing in my antecedence which supported such a stupid claim. However, the Hampshire Police seemed to take everything that was said on board without question. And so, of course, when Bernie maintained his ridiculous pretence, the squad, led by DS Merrit, carried on the charade and supplied an armed guard in the courtroom.

Another prime example of their crass stupidity was an occasion when both Ken and I were taken to Winchester Police Station. Our attendance was requested to answer further questions, primarily with regard to the manufacture of postage stamps. This hardly seemed particularly relevant compared to the money counterfeiting. Consequently, I wasn't unduly concerned when I was charged with conspiracy to manufacture postage stamps. At the end of the session, during which I had given the standard reply of 'No comment' to every question, I was asked if I would be prepared to give a sample of my handwriting. Although I had the option of refusing, I complied with the request, as I knew that the police had nothing incriminating in their possession that was handwritten by me. I was asked to write various names, such as Biggles, Mo, Pee-Wee and others. After a few minutes of writing out what appeared to me to be continuous nonsense, I became bored and put the pen down.

'I'm fed up with this silly game. That's your lot,' I said.

The other officer in charge of this little exercise looked crestfallen. 'There's only a few more items to write out,' he implored me.

'So? I've had enough. That's it.'

'Why not? You said you would.'

'Listen, I've just told you. No more. Finish. Understand?'

At this point, the officer started to behave in such a way that, if I hadn't seen it for myself, I wouldn't have believed it. The officer (a grown man, remember) adopted a little-boy-type attitude and said, 'Oh, go on. Tell you what, I'll be your best friend, yeah?'

I looked at him, gesturing like someone retarded, and said, 'What? Are you being serious? Listen, or if that's a problem, read my lips. I'm not giving you any more handwriting samples.'

To further compound the stupidity of his manner, he continued, 'I'll never slag you off in the pub if anybody says you never buy a drink, yeah?'

Presumably, this was some pathetic attempt to lure me into thinking, by way of a humorous, jokey attitude, that he was my pal. But as I've said, this was a grown man, who as far as I could see was making a complete fool of himself. So much so that I could no longer be bothered even to respond. Thankfully, he stopped playing the part of the Hampshire village idiot, and didn't ask again.

After this, I had my fingerprints taken (again) and during this process the village idiot remarked upon the fact that I looked very worried. With the probability of spending several years in prison, this was undeniably true and I admitted as much.

'Well, in that case, haven't you thought about a letter to the judge?' he said.

'Letter to the judge? What kind? A love letter? What you talking about?' I replied.

'You know how it works. You give us a bit of information. Doesn't have to be about this. Anything. So long as it's useful to us. Then we'll make sure the judge knows how helpful you've been, it will all be written out and placed in a sealed envelope. Nobody need know, not even the prosecuting counsel.'

I looked at him and replied, 'Well, that's where you're wrong. Somebody will know.'

'They won't, I promise you. We've got people doing it all the time. Nobody ever knows.'

I had no reason to disbelieve him, but I said, 'Well, I'm afraid I'm not interested, because I know absolutely, somebody will know.'

'No they won't, you've got my word.'

'What about me? I'll know. And I'm the person who's got to look in the mirror every morning. So, thanks, but no thanks.'

After this, I had some good news when Simon Myers had managed to ascertain the exact position with regard to the matter of further imprisonment in default of payment of a fine. Any financial penalty would involve an amount equivalent to the confiscation of the guilty person's assets.

In my case this involved £15,000 that I had in my car when arrested, the car itself and the flat that I had just bought. So now I knew I was facing a maximum term of imprisonment of ten years. This, at least, was a slight improvement in my prospects for the future. In fact, I suppose not having to serve an extra ten years was a great improvement.

A few days before Christmas, I was visited by a police officer who had come to Winchester Prison to serve a restraint order on me appertaining to the flat. As well as the property, I also had a building society account containing £15,000 through which the mortgage repayments were paid.

I asked the officer if a special dispensation could be granted with regard to the money in the account being available to continue paying the mortgage for the next few months. As Stephanie was still living in the flat, this was of some importance to me.

The officer seemed to be relishing the situation when he said, 'It's not really anything to do with me, but if I was you I wouldn't worry about it. You're going to lose the flat anyway.' With that he put his papers back into his case and, as he left, he said, 'Merry Christmas.' If this was intended to upset me, it was a wasted effort. Christmas, as far as I'm concerned, just doesn't occur in prison. But I didn't make him aware of this; after all, it might have spoilt his Christmas for him.

My main problem now was in trying to cobble together something that might resemble a defence. Obviously, I spoke to Daniel and Simon about this and told them, as it was obvious from the evidence that I had done what I did, my only excuse was that I was under pressure to carry on with the counterfeiting. But could this be anything more than mitigation?

It was explained to me that a defence of duress is acceptable in a British court of law, but that it would be extremely difficult to establish. The standard required would be that I would have to show to a jury that, over a period of four years, I was under so much pressure from persons not arrested, that I had no choice other than to do the counterfeit printing. I would have to show that I was in genuine fear for my safety and that of my family.

This, of course, would take quite a bit of proving. Although I was able to point to the beating in the basement as an example of what I'd had to endure, my lifestyle was hardly that of a man distraught with worry and fear. Spending two or three hundred pounds fairly regularly at London's leading restaurants and flitting off to New York and France and various other foreign destinations whenever the fancy took me, wasn't really consistent with a man desperate to pay back money to heavies such as Eugene. But, for a while, I managed to convince myself that duress was a viable defence. Not surprisingly, both Daniel and Simon were less than enthusiastic, but in the short period of time that they had known me, they had come to realise that I would reach my own decision, one way or the other. And so, upon my instructions, they started to prepare my defence.

I had the right to a QC to act in my defence due to the very serious nature of the charge, and there was no doubt in my mind as to who I wanted to represent me in this coveted role — Geoffrey Robertson.

In my opinion, Geoffrey is arguably the finest criminal barrister in the country. The only problem would be whether or not he would be available. Geoffrey had represented me on a few occasions in the past with regard to my perfume cases, and so I knew from first-hand experience just how brilliant a barrister he was. But even so, I knew, deep down, that even Geoffrey Robertson, QC *nonpareil*, wouldn't be able to get me out of this one. It wasn't a QC I needed, it was Perry Mason! But he agreed to act on my behalf, with Simon as his junior, primarily because he had quite enjoyed the cases he had been involved in with me, and we had built up a certain rapport.

So now I knew I had the best team possible for my defence, and it was just a matter of looking at the defence itself. And the harder I looked, the more hopeless it seemed. Apart from this, there was something else that concerned me, the 'inconsequential' matter of the postage stamps.

I knew that the majority of judges in England would regard the ten years maximum sentence as wholly inadequate in this case. With this in mind, I had the uneasy feeling that I was in very real danger of risking not just a ten-year term of imprisonment by running a trial, but also incurring a consecutive sentence of three or four years for the postage stamps. And so, at the back of my mind, I knew that, ultimately, I would be pleading guilty. For the time being, however, it was important to create the impression to all concerned, in particular the prosecution, that I would be running a long, drawn-out trial. In this way, when the possibility of a guilty plea was canvassed on my behalf, the prosecution team might be more amenable to making some concessions.

A few months into 1999, we attended court and a trial date was set for 4 October. In the dock, apart from Martin and me, were Ken Mainstone and Eddie Burns, and also a man whom none of us knew, Tony Wilkie. Bernie had already pleaded guilty and had been taken back to Camphill Prison on the Isle of Wight.

Tony was a friend of Bernie's who, prior to his arrest, had a tool-making business in High Wycombe. His involvement with our case came about because he had made the perforating tool for the postage stamps and was in the process of making a press-tool for pound coins for Bernie. Unfortunately for him, Bernie chose to tell the police about Tony's existence and so he was arrested and bailed. Although not involved in any way in the counterfeit £20 notes, he was roped in with us because of Bernie's scheme for manufacturing pound coins.

Now we had an actual date for the trial, Martin's barrister indicated that he would be pleading guilty to the charge of possession with intent to supply in due course. This was agreed with the prosecution and so, for now, it looked as though there would be no further court appearances until the actual start of the trial at Winchester Crown Court.

Daniel and Simon came to the prison for regular visits, and we talked about the pros and cons of the defence, and they made a concerted effort to assemble something worthwhile based on the defence of duress. It was always pleasant to see and talk to them but, generally speaking, all three of us knew we were flogging a dead horse. The truth of the matter was, short of the jury comprising 12 deaf, dumb and blind counterfeiters, I had no chance at all.

During one of Daniel's legal visits, Simon broached an interesting aspect of the charge concerning my earlier sentence of 21 months for possession of counterfeit currency. It was a point of law that had actually occurred to me, but which I had dismissed as being too absurd to be viable. As we spoke about the possible benefits of a guilty plea, Simon said, 'Well, looked at from a purely logical point of view, as the offence for possession falls within the conspiracy period for the manufacture of the notes, it therefore follows that, as the maximum penalty allowed in law is ten years, that twenty-one months must be deducted from the ten.'

'And so, therefore, it also follows, by a simple set of sums, done without the aid of a calculator, that that makes the maximum sentence for me eight years and three months,' I replied.

'Yes. In fact, we could argue a case of "*autre fois*". In other words, you can't be tried for the same offence twice.'

'Oh, that's handy. I'll pack my bags and leave with you chaps now then, shall I?' I said, very much tongue-in-cheek.

Both Daniel and Simon smiled.

'I'm afraid it's not quite that simple. I'm afraid if we were to argue *autre fois*, in all likelihood the prosecution would simply change the dates on the indictment to exclude the date of your original arrest. Even so, it's still very much an interesting legal argument on the charge as it stands. We shall see.'

What tended to support the premise that I had effectively served a portion of any sentence that might subsequently be imposed on me was a ruling by the judge hearing the case, that my earlier conviction was a part of this offence and could therefore be revealed to the jury in the event of my running a trial.

It wasn't too long after this meeting, and knowing I stood no chance of being acquitted, that I finally made up my mind that I had no choice other than to plead guilty. I told Daniel about my decision and, in due course, Geoffrey Robertson made an approach to the Crown Prosecution Service as to what, if anything, in the way of concessions would be made in return for a guilty plea.

Geoffrey had suggested to them that I was not the main perpetrator in the conspiracy and that, in fact, there were others above me who hadn't been caught. He also suggested that I had no hidden finances stashed away and that the beating in the basement was as a result of my efforts to discontinue the funny money business.

The prosecution wouldn't accept any of this, aside from the fact that there was no actual evidence to show that I had any large sums of money. But this, in itself, didn't necessarily mean that I didn't have any hidden away. As far as they were concerned, I was *Mr Big* and the beating in the basement had nothing whatsoever to do with the counterfeiting.

So, all in all, the prosecution weren't really prepared to make any concessions. But there again, they did say they would accept a plea on just the counterfeit currency charge and not proceed with the stamps. And, as inconsequential as this may have seemed, I felt it could, in fact, make a great deal of difference to my eventual sentence. The prosecution were notified that I would not be contesting the charge and that was that. And so now there was little to do except sit and wait, a depressing prospect while being locked up for 22 hours a day but then, fortunately, the education department put up a notice asking for artists to take part in a project involving paintings to be hung in Winchester General Hospital. And so, within a week of the poster being placed on the notice board, I was on the art class spending weekdays doing something I genuinely enjoy, regardless of my surroundings and circumstances.

Shortly after joining the art class, I was notified that, together with the other defendants, I would be required to attend Winchester Crown Court. This was, in a way, bad timing for me as I was waiting to have my ears syringed, and was barely able to hear anything that was said to me. As a result, sitting in the dock, the proceedings were very much a mystery, not having managed to master the art of lip-reading. But the main purpose of the hearing was to take all the pleas. Why this had to be done then, and not on 4 October as planned, I wasn't told. But in the event, by mutual consent, the prosecuting counsel accepted that the various minor points had to be finalised and so my plea of guilty to Count 1 on the indictment could wait until 4 October, with no loss of credit for my plea of guilty at the earliest appropriate moment. This was also agreed by His Honour Judge Brodrick.

Martin also tried to defer pleading until the trial date, but was informed that his position was different to mine and consequently, if he wanted full credit for a guilty plea, he would have to make it there and then, which he did.

His wish not to plead guilty until the last possible moment was simply because there were a number of minor advantages to being on remand as an unconvicted prisoner. These amounted to more association time during the day and being allowed to spend £30 per week of personal cash. But in the event, Martin's circumstances barely changed as he got himself a cushy number working in the library.

Apart from this, the boredom of the proceedings was interrupted for me when I thought I heard a muffled reference to somebody dying and the police viewing the corpse. Being almost totally deaf, I strained my ears to hear what was being said in court, but to no avail. After the hearing, I asked Daniel and Simon what had occurred, and was told that Bernie was too ill to attend court. He had been diagnosed as having terminal cancer and wasn't expected to be alive for the trial. The mention of a corpse and a death certificate referred to a ruling that, in the event of his death, a formal identification of the corpse by one of the detectives in the case would be required. A mere death certificate would not be accepted as evidence of Bernie's death. A quite incredible ruling, bearing in mind that his illness must have been diagnosed by an expert in the treatment of cancer.

Six weeks later, on 4 October, I was back at Winchester Crown Court in front of Judge Brodrick, and I made my plea of guilty. Ken, Eddie Burns and Bernie's friend, Tony Wilkie, all pleaded not guilty. The trial was expected to last four to six weeks and, in the meantime, I was interviewed by a probation officer who made out a pre-sentence report. Soon afterwards, Daniel showed me a copy of the report which, to my amusement, came to the conclusion that 'due to the serious nature of the offence', she was unable to recommend a community service order. Something of an understatement considering that the charge against me involved £50 million of counterfeit currency. Another observation I found rather ironic was her belief that I would commit further offences upon my eventual release. The reason I found this ironic was because it was probably the first such occasion that I hadn't put on an act, and it was the first time that I had genuinely meant it when I declared that I had no intention of returning to a life of crime upon my release. And yet every other time I had always been believed, and had been given reports that expressed the view that I wouldn't commit further offences.

Four or five weeks after the start of the trial, Martin and I began speculating as to when it would all be over. Our longest estimate was no more than six weeks. But then six weeks became seven weeks, which became eight. The trial finally ended after 11 weeks, and on Monday, 20 December 1999, the jury was sent out to consider its verdict.

By Tuesday, there was still no news. Similarly on Wednesday, no news, until at 6.00pm I watched the news on TV and learned that Eddie Burns had been acquitted and that Ken had been found guilty on both counts of conspiracy to manufacture counterfeit currency and postage stamps. Tony Wilkie had been found guilty of conspiracy to manufacture postage stamps and pound coins. Both were remanded in custody until 19 January 2000 when, together with Martin and me, they would be sentenced.

The following day, the newspapers gave our case full coverage, some of which was fairly accurate, most of which wasn't. Upon reading the report in the *Daily Mail*, which was among the most accurate, I was amused to see the caption refer to us as the Lavender Hill Mob, and me an underworld gangster. Something else that immediately caught my eye was how much, judging from the published photograph, I require a savage face-lift!

As was to be expected, it wasn't the merriest of Christmases for the two new boys in HMP Winchester. But for Martin and me, it was just another day. After more than 16 months, we had become acclimatised to our surroundings.

During our daily strolls around the exercise yard, the main topic of conversation inevitably revolved around our expected sentences. My prediction was seven or eight years each for Ken and me. For Martin, I predicted three years, which would mean release during February. For Tony, whom I had never met before, I told him I was prepared to be generous due to his previous good character, and his age, 60. Combined with the fact that Bernie only paid him a few hundred pounds, and neither of his conspiracy charges amounted to more than a bowl of rice, I sentenced him to 12 months, 18 months maximum.

For a month, we discussed the possible sentences every day. As well as speculating about the ultimate outcome, I told Ken that I had expected him to plead guilty at the first opportunity.

I expressed the opinion that he would have been much better off to have pleaded guilty to the currency charge and had the postage stamps dropped, even more so in view of the fact that he was genuinely innocent of it. That way, he could have detailed his very minor involvement in the counterfeit currency, and I would have been quite happy to have corroborated his version of events. But because he was out on bail I had no chance to convince him of the sheer folly of fighting the case. A condition of his bail was that he made no contact with me.

Another topic of conversation was Bernie's stupidity in not burning all the waste as he told me he had done. And then Tony informed me that Bernie regularly had several counterfeit notes on him and often passed them on the mainland. I just couldn't believe that anybody could be so stupid and greedy as to hold on to so much waste, merely to look through them for the very few that could be cut out of the sheets and passed off. For the sake of a few hundred pounds at the most, Bernie's lies, greed and stupidity had landed us all in prison.

Bernie himself had been totally discharged from the case due to his ill health and, on 30 December 1999, he died.

# CHAPTER 34

# Sentences and Conclusions

*Wednesday, 19 January 2000*

The big day has finally arrived, after 17 months. My legal team consisting of Daniel Berman, Geoffrey Robertson QC and Simon Myers are here. Geoffrey will be mitigating first on my behalf as his presence is required in New York this afternoon to give a lecture. In court, the prosecuting counsel has summarised our various roles as seen through the eyes of the Crown Prosecution Service and the police. And surprisingly, he concedes that the 21-month sentence already received by me does form part of the overall conspiracy. Armed with this concession, Geoffrey states his reasons, point by point, why he feels that my sentence should be nearer the midway mark of a ten-year sentence rather than the top end of the scale. His main points revolve around the fact that I deserve full credit for pleading guilty and that the 21-month sentence should be taken off. And, of course, I agree wholeheartedly, although, somehow, I rather think that the judge might be of a diametrically opposite opinion. One thing's for sure — he's not going to recommend me for the Queen's Award to Industry.

Geoffrey finishes his piece, and there's no doubt about it, he's convinced me. During the course of the day, the other barristers try to paint as rosy a picture as possible of their clients. Having resigned myself to the fact that I will be extremely fortunate if my sentence is anything less than seven years and a trifle unlucky if it's any longer, I don't expect any surprises.

At the end of the day, sentence upon all of us is postponed until tomorrow, as Tony Wilkie's barrister is unable to attend court until the morning, when he will put forward Tony's mitigation.

Back at Winchester Prison, all four of us again debate the likely sentences. I still say that I believe Ken and I will get seven years apiece. Although, in reality, I fear that Ken is facing eight to nine years, his penalty for running a trial that was unwinnable in the face of such damning evidence against him in the form of fingerprints in the workshop, on the press and on the paper and handwriting samples. Tomorrow, all four of us will know our fate. I have a headache.

*Thursday, 20 January 2000*

For the last time, I have to go through the boring routine of passing through the prison reception, changing into my own clothes and suffering the body searches as I pass from one area to another, until eventually I'm in the tiny cubicle in the prison sweat box van.

The journey to Winchester Crown Court, which is within walking distance, takes a few minutes. I alight from the van, handcuffed to one of the civilian guards. All four of us are taken to a large holding cell beneath the court. And, yet again, we discuss our possible sentences. Martin is the most excitable of all of us. He believes he might be very close to being released. For some strange reason, he takes to walking along the seating that runs around the interior wall.

Now we are back in court, sitting in the dock. Tony's barrister mitigates on his behalf, and emphasises his very minimal involvement in the conspiracy and that he had nothing to do with the funny money. His barrister concludes his speech and sits down. All four of us stand up. And now it's the turn of His Honour Judge Brodrick. He soon makes it clear what he thinks of our mitigation and, more importantly, our offence. And now, listening to him, I'm aware of just how right I was in my assessment of the judge's attitude to a maximum sentence of ten years. He more or less tells the court it hardly seems adequate for a crime of this stature. A crime that dwarfs any comparable enterprise to come before the courts.

I can't argue with that, Judge, old boy. £50 million. Two thirds of all the counterfeit money passed in the UK from 1994 to 1998. And, what's more, it's still trickling back to the Bank of England now. Although, thankfully, it seems to be coming to an eventual halt.

The judge's words interrupt my thoughts and he continues speaking. And now ominously, he mentions consecutive sentences. At least I know that can't apply to me, and at least I know I have to receive a discount on the ten years maximum. But let's forget about five or six years, eh, Stevie boy? Brodrick appears to apply an illogical kind of logic when dealing with the question of the 21-month sentence already served. From my understanding, he is merely stating that he cannot accept the legal argument of double jeopardy, because upon my release I continued counterfeiting.

But, Brodrick, old chap, surely you're not applying your huge legal intellect to the argument — same offence, then the sentence must be part of the overall maximum, otherwise the sum of the parts adds up to more than the whole, doesn't it? But the judge is in charge and what he says goes, so keep your thoughts to yourself, Stevie boy, and just pay attention to how long you get!

Now, after the judicial foreplay, we finally come to the legal orgasm.

'Stephen Jory, you have an atrocious record ...' at this comment, I feel like taking umbrage but restrain myself from expressing the view too vociferously that the manufacture of bogus Chanel No 5, as was the case in most of my previous convictions, hardly makes me Public Enemy Number 1, but then that's another story — '... and as to whether or not you were the main instigator behind this crime makes little difference. You were high enough up the ladder for your offences to attract the maximum penalty. I am unable to give you full credit for your plea of guilty for, unlike Watmough, you did not plead guilty until the first day of the trial. I therefore sentence you to eight years' imprisonment.'

I turn to leave the dock and now I can hear him addressing Ken. I hear him again mentioning consecutive sentences and, as his words blend into the background, I just hear him say nine years. And now I'm back in the small room behind the court. I'm standing here waiting for Ken to enter. How long has he got in total? 11 years? No, it can't be that long. It can't be.

Ken's looking straight through me, as though there's nobody else near him. He's sitting down now.

'Ken?'

'Twelve years.'

I can't respond. Tony enters the room, followed by Martin. Ken's just staring at the floor. He still seems unaware, or perhaps too aware of what's hit him. All three of us look at one and another.

'Nine-and-a-half, and two-and-a-half years consecutive for the postage stamps.'

Martin's pleasure at receiving three years is overshadowed by the enormity of Ken's situation. Martin can't express how happy he is, and feels almost a sense of guilt that in four weeks he'll be free.

Tony doesn't look happy, not just for Ken's sake, but also for himself. A sentence of two years for making the perforating tool for the stamps, and 21 months for the tool for the coins. Consecutive. This, too, seems rather harsh.

So now there's no more speculating. Now we know. At least I've been prepared for a possible eight-year sentence. And at least I've got 17 months under my belt. But Ken? I can't say anything. Now the security guards come in. I'm handcuffed to one, and we descend the narrow, winding staircase and eventually arrive at the bottom, from where we go back to our communal holding cells.

Eight years for me. Twelve for Ken. All over. I've still got a headache.

Shortly afterwards, Daniel and Simon came downstairs to see me, and we discussed the courtroom's very recent events. Like me, it seems that everyone in the court was taken aback by the length of Ken's sentence. Although I reasoned correctly that the judge would use the stamps charge as a means of 'topping up' the sentence, I never really thought that such a measure would be used against Ken on his own. After our initial talk about Ken, we discussed what I already knew would be two points for an appeal against the sentence.

Both Simon and Daniel agreed that the judge was wrong to penalise me with regard to his decision not to allow me full credit for my plea of guilty, as he basically sanctioned the decision to allow me to plead guilty on the first day of the trial.

Point two concerned his view with regard to the 21-month sentence. Like me, they felt that he had simply chosen to disregard the apparent maximum sentence anomaly. My instructions to Daniel were to lodge an appeal the moment Geoffrey returned from New York. *Come back, Geoffrey, the lovable rogue needs your brilliant legal expertise!*

So now the worst is over. I know the worst possible scenario. I will be in prison for anything up to a further three years and ten months, assuming I don't lose any remission. If I'm granted full parole, I'll be released in August 2002. And, then again, there's always the possibility of a reduction in sentence on appeal. But I know better than anybody that the Appeal Court will only take that course if some Honourable Lord Justice, together with two Mr Justices, can find no legal option. If my sentence is reduced by even the smallest amount, it won't be as a result of any sympathy for me, or because the Appeal Court feels the sentence of eight years is even a day too long. So I won't hold my breath.

My initial reaction to my arrest in August 1998 was that it was a combination of bad luck and carelessness on my part. This was, in fact, true up to a point, but it didn't really explain everything. In itself it didn't clarify just why the police interest in me had been reawakened. But, sometimes, these things just happen. 'Life's a bitch,' as Shakespeare used to say.

In fact, I might well have left it at that had I not been told something that I found very curious, to say the least. A week or two after being arrested and remanded in custody, I received a visit from a friend who told me that the police had been searching houses and flats all over the place. This, in itself, didn't surprise me, as I was aware that the police had a fairly extensive list of suspects they had compiled over the years from their own resources, primarily grasses. Most of these suspects were people whom I knew or knew of, but didn't actually deal with. Although a couple of my punters were turned over, the main men who were not known to the police remained untouched.

A few of the less intelligent amongst those whose homes were searched, such as Mother Greens, immediately jumped to the conclusion that this was as a result of me co-operating with the police. As these were people with whom I had no dealings, I'm at a loss to understand what they believed I had to gain from grassing any of them up.

Amongst the chosen many was a friend of mine, Eddie Urgent, so called because of his habit of paging me with the message, 'Phone Eddie. Urgent!' Unfortunately for him, he had some illicit substances indoors. The fact that he had been spun was something of a surprise to me, as he wasn't one of my punters. As far as I'm aware, he has never had any connection with the funny money, and I didn't have his name or number in my address book. Nevertheless, the police warrant specifically referred to counterfeit money. Although difficult to comprehend at the time, it became perfectly clear later on.

The search of Eddie Urgent's place bore a certain similarity to an incident that occurred a month or two before my arrest, when the houses of two of my friends were spun. Like Eddie Urgent, both Johnny Gadget and Big Johnny L never dealt in the funny money and both had legitimate businesses. I knew both of them on a purely social basis, and so, as with Eddie, the search of their houses for counterfeit money was something of a mystery.

But, like most situations when a grass is involved, it generally tends to come out in the wash. This particular set of mysteries began to unravel when Ruth, the delinquent chef, visited me in Winchester Prison a couple of weeks after my arrest. She informed me that the latest raid had been on the house of a guy named Simon, who, although a friend of several people I knew in the Loughton area, wasn't known to me. Apart from hearing his name mentioned once or twice in conversation, I had never met him and didn't even know his surname. But one thing I did know, he wasn't involved in the funny money. So when Ruth told me about the search of his house, I listened in amazement as she related the details.

Apparently the police knocked on his door armed not only with a search warrant, but also a JCB digger. They informed him they were acting on information received that he was involved in the manufacture of counterfeit money, and that he had the various plates, film and the necessary computerised optical disc buried beneath his swimming pool. In spite of his protests, they proceeded to dig up the pool. Needless to say, nothing was found either in the house or underneath his swimming pool.

Knowing about my arrest, Simon's immediate reaction was to conclude that I had stuck his name up and was ranting and raving to anyone who would listen that I had sent the police round to him. Obviously, Simon's no rocket scientist for, if he had stopped to think for just a split-second, he would have been able to work out that it couldn't have been me, as apart from not knowing him or his surname, I didn't know where he lived, or that he had a swimming pool. And then there's the very simple question — what would be the point? As I said, Simon's no rocket scientist, but even he managed eventually to work out who the culprit was.

Initially, I failed to make any connection between the searches of Gadget's, Big John's, Eddie Urgent's and Simple Simon's homes. But back in my cell, as I sat and thought long and hard, the common link soon became apparent. And if it hadn't have been for the swimming pool incident, quite possibly I might never have been any the wiser as to who, if anybody, had grassed me up.

The give-away lay in the fact that Simon's wife was none other than Colonel Blimp's girlfriend, Vicki. The very same Vicki who had been arrested in France with the Colonel, and whom I bailed out. I knew for a fact that the Colonel was completely paranoid about Simon, and early on in his relationship with Vicki he was convinced that Simon knew his name and address (which he probably did) and that he had tried to burn down his house (which he probably hadn't). But all this, of course, was between the Colonel, Vicki and Simon and had absolutely nothing to do with me or anybody else.

But the Colonel was so obsessed with Vicki that he developed an equally obsessive hatred for Simon, and at one time even expressed the view that he would like to have him killed. It soon became obvious to me just what had happened. The Colonel had grassed me up in order to get his own charges on the invoice-factoring fraud dropped. But he couldn't resist the urge to kill two birds with one stone, so to speak. The more I thought about the overall situation, the more convinced I became that the Colonel had grassed me up.

Johnny Gadget and Big Johnny L were also friends of the Colonel, and clearly he had assumed, wrongly, that they must have been punters of mine. When this little bit of grassing didn't produce any results, the police must have put pressure on him to come up with something positive if he wanted his own charges to be dropped.

His main problem in this respect lay in the fact that he wasn't able to give them any detailed information, such as who the printer was. It was perhaps significant that Big Johnny L had a print business and Colonel Blimp probably jumped to the conclusion that he must have been the supplier of film and plates. Apart from this, all he would have been able to tell them was that it was me who was behind the long-running scam. This probably came as something of a surprise to the police, who I know were undecided as to whether or not I was still involved in the funny money business. This was for a variety of reasons. Knowing that, upon my release from prison, the police would undoubtedly be tapping my telephone conversations, I arranged for one or two of my friends to call me and ask in thinly-disguised terms if I was still involved in the funny money business and, if so, could I get them any, to which of course I replied that I was completely straight and no longer did anything illegal.

Apart from this, I had two mobile phones. One I knew the police would be aware of, as Laraine called me on it from her house, and Stephanie called me on it from our rented house. This I termed my domestic line. If the police ever listened in on it, they would never hear anything more incriminating than conversations between me and my family, and a handful of friends, as opposed to 'business' contacts. The other mobile was a pre-paid phone, not registered in any name, and was strictly for business.

By using two phones, I reasoned the police listening in on one of them would expect to hear, at the very least, one or two people occasionally calling me and asking me to ring them back from a call box — if I was engaged in any illegal activities, that is. By not hearing anything remotely suspicious on the phone, and by not acting at all suspiciously on the odd occasion when the police were following me about, it would be a fairly logical conclusion that I was no longer up to anything.

In a nutshell, Colonel Blimp pointed the police back in the right direction, and gave them various details as to how I operated together with details of my various friends and one or two girlfriends. Obviously, the Colonel knew nothing about Eugene and his associates and so wasn't in a position to mention them, although I doubt very much that he would have done so, even if he had been aware of their involvement

Everything fitted into place, but even though there really was no doubt in my mind as to what had occurred, I felt that I had to be certain. Unlike most people, the label 'grass' is not one I would attach to my worst enemy without being absolutely certain. Conclusions, no matter how compelling, can often be arrived at wrongly, and so I set out to confirm my suspicions, one way or another.

Through a mutual friend I managed to convey a message to a bent copper that I wanted as much information as possible with regard to the Colonel and his miraculous escape from justice, and what, if anything, it had to do with me. For a reasonable fee, I soon found out what I needed to know. Colonel Blimp, sexual pervert and paedophile, had grassed me up. Confirmed, along with various relevant details.

I immediately informed Ruth in order for her to let people know who might be having anything to do with him, just what he was all about. Somehow or other, Simon had already come to know that I had nothing to do with the demolition of his swimming pool. For some bizarre reason, he felt motivated to have an extremely childish pamphlet printed up stating that Colonel Blimp was a police informant. His intention was to post these up around the Loughton and Chigwell area. Just what this was meant to have accomplished, I've no idea. Personally, I found it akin to school playground behaviour. I could almost imagine the Colonel poking out his tongue and declaring, 'Sticks and stones may break my bones, but words will never hurt me.'

Even more amazingly, after I had let Ruth know the truth about the Colonel, and most of Essex was enlightened about the fat, bald-headed little scumbag, Gersh, my old friend, who had actually first introduced the Colonel into our social circle a few years previously, went out for a drink with him. To make matters even worse, he took him around to Johnny Gadget's house, who promptly told him he wasn't welcome. Eventually, the full horror of the Colonel came to light when Eddie Urgent had to appear in court on charges relating to the illegal substances found at his place. Knowing that the Colonel was behind it, his barrister made some kind of request for the police informant to be identified in court. This apparently caused a variety of problems and, by way of compromise, Eddie was allowed to plead to a lesser charge and was given a non-custodial sentence.

I was told later that the judge in Eddie's case was the same judge who had dismissed the charges against the Colonel, and so he knew full well the Colonel's involvement. What's more, it transpired that the Colonel had been giving information to the police as and when it suited his purposes for the previous ten years.

In more ways than one, the last 17 months have been something of a revelation. Apart from the stupidity and petty-minded greed of the late Bernie Farrier on the Isle of Wight, I also had to suffer the pathetic lies he told about me in order to try and squirm his way into a lighter sentence; and Bernie was an 'old friend' whom I had always helped out in whatever way I could.

Then there's Colonel Blimp, the paedophile, another 'old friend' whom I'd helped out on several occasions. Words fail me. And as I sit here in prison, I can't help thinking about all my other so-called friends who owe me large amounts of money and earned well out of me when I was out and about. Somehow, it's as though I no longer exist. None of them has had the decency to even get in touch with Laraine to check whether she was OK or how I am. Where are you Gersh? Little Don? Barry? And many others?

There have been a couple of exceptions, namely the loyal Ruth, who has proved herself to be a good friend, and likewise Micky Blewitt and Jenny, as well as Pee-Wee, Bonzo, Paul Sabbato and Danny. Many heartfelt thanks.

And, of course, there is my priceless family, who I know will always be there for me, even though at this present time I can't be there for them. My sister and her two sons, Robert and Spencer, who I know still appreciate the time Laraine and I gave them when they were little more than babies when their absent father invariably had more important appointments to keep.

And my dear mother, who I'm sure still regards me as her little soldier. And even though we are now divorced, it's good to know that I can always rely upon Laraine in whatever way necessary.

And finally Stephanie and James, for making sense of the madness, and giving me a reason.

* * *

Ironically, it's as much to do with the way that the vast majority of my 'friends' have let me down, as well as the way that my family never have, that has decided me to call it a day as far as the skulduggery business is concerned.

As the guy in the TV series *Alias Smith and Jones* used to say, 'If there's one thing I gotta get, it's out of this business.' Or was that Shakespeare?

# Epilogue

At the end of August 2000, my appeal was heard at the Royal Courts of Justice in The Strand.

The first argument concerning the amount of 'credit' for my plea of guilty was dismissed on the grounds that, to obtain full credit, I should have effectively pleaded guilty right there and then in the car park of TGI Friday's — 'OK, guv, it's a fair cop. The swag's in the bag.'

In spite of various favourable High Court rulings concerning the policy of discount for guilty pleas, and my rights under the Human Rights Act to legal advice before entering a plea, the learned judges thought differently.

The second argument, that my previous sentence of 21 months was imposed for an offence that constituted a part of the present conspiracy, was upheld. However, in a perverse decision, instead of reducing the sentence of eight years by the 21 months of my earlier sentence, just 12 months were taken off (perhaps the learned m'luds confused the figure of 12 for 21). And so the final sentence stands at seven years — par for the course.

Ken, proportionately, fared even less well, having no actual legal points to fall back on. With just the slender hope that the Appeal Court would exercise compassion for a man in his sixties with a previously unblemished record, he was very much in the lottery that constitutes the

British judicial system. Whereas one panel of judges might well have been sympathetic to his plight, this was not such a panel (in fact, there were only two instead of the usual three).

His previous good character was of no consequence, due to the 'sheer criminality' of the offence. However, it was conceded that the totality of the two consecutive sentences was excessive and, consequently, the two-and-a-half years for the postage stamps was reduced by 12 months, leaving Ken with an 11-year sentence. Ken will be eligible for parole after serving five-and-a-half years. Taking into account the three months he spent on remand, his earliest date for release will be April 2005.

My earliest possible date for release on parole is 17 February 2002. However, given the magnitude of the crime, and the trial judge's comments, effectively that ten years' maximum was hardly adequate, not to mention the Appeal Court's observation as to the 'sheer criminality' of the caper. I won't hold my breath. Failing that, it's April 2003.